SPEER

'Fest's analysis is both convincing and rounded – he is understanding about Speer without being sympathetic.'

Hew Strachan, *Daily Telegraph*

'His latest biographer is one of the most eminent writers on the Third Reich...He knows the subject backwards, and he writes with authority.'

Geoffrey Wheatcroft, *New Statesman*

'A cool, persuasive account of the most interesting of Hitler's acolytes, by the master historian of the Nazis.'

Evening Standard Books of the Year

'Joachim Fest's biography is the most rounded and satisfactory of the various studies to date. Fest, a writer of immense experience and stature, wastes no words.'

Norman Stone, *Spectator*

'Joachim Fest, Germany's most insightful historian of Nazism, has given us the most convincing and stylish account of the Speer phenomenon to date. If there is one biography of Speer people should read, then this is surely it.'

Michael Burleigh, *Mail on Sunday*

Joachim Fest was born in Berlin in 1926. After the war, in which he served and was taken prisoner, he joined the radio station RIAS-Berlin where he became the head of the Department of Contemporary History. In 1961 he became Editor-in-Chief of TV for Norddeutscher Rundfunk. Following Albert Speer's release from Spandau Prison in 1966, Joachim Fest worked closely with Speer as the general editor of *Inside the Third Reich* (1970) and *Spandau: The Secret Diaries* (1976). Fest's own books include *The Face of the Third Reich* (1963), *Hitler* (1973), the first comprehensive German life of Hitler since 1945, and *Plotting Hitler's Death* (1994). One of the world's leading authorities on the Nazi period, Joachim Fest lives in central Germany, near Frankfurt.

ALSO BY JOACHIM FEST

The Face of the Third Reich
Hitler
Plotting Hitler's Death

SPEER

The Final Verdict

Joachim Fest

Translated by Ewald Osers
and Alexandra Dring

**PHOENIX
PRESS**

5 UPPER SAINT MARTIN'S LANE
LONDON
WC2H 9EA

A PHOENIX PRESS PAPERBACK

First published in Germany
by Alexander Fest Verlag, Berlin in 1999
First published in Great Britain
by Weidenfeld & Nicolson in 2001
This paperback edition published in 2002
by Phoenix Press,
a division of The Orion Publishing Group Ltd,
Orion House, 5 Upper St Martin's Lane,
London WC2H 9EA

A CIP catalogue record for this book
is available from the British Library.

Printed and bound in Great Britain by
Butler & Tanner Ltd, Frome and London

ISBN 1 84212 475 7

CONTENTS

ILLUSTRATIONS

The author and publishers would like to thank the following for permission to repro-
duce photographs: Archiv Hewel, and the Tete Böttger Collection, Göttingen: 96, 100
(both); Bayerische Staatsbibliothek: 218, 345; Bildarchiv Preussischer Kulturbesitz,
Berlin: 20, 53, 61, 70 (bottom), 114, 130, 135, 145, 149, 163, 169, 186, 215, 237, 240, 251,
335; Bilderdienst Süddeutscher Verlag: 41, 48, 139, 155, 173, 182, 208, 225, 248, 254, 275,
278, 279, 280, 287, 290, 294; Bundesarchiv: 326 (picture 146/68/36/22); Landesbildstelle
Berlin: 34, 80, 107, 119; Privatarchiv Speer: 13, 15, 23, 50, 60, 70 (top), 72, 74 (both), 87,
92, 102, 105, 313, 319; Ullstein Bilderdienst: 26, 31, 58, 63, 104, 109, 158, 166, 178, 197,
202, 228, 244, 278, 301, 322; the drawing on page 304 comes from Matthias Schmidt,
Albert Speer: The End of a Myth (London 1985).

PREFACE

At one point in this book there is mention of the fact that I was the adviser whom Speer had asked his publisher Wolf Jobst Siedler to provide when working on his *Inside the Third Reich* and *Spandau: The Secret Diaries*. Speer was hoping for help with editorial and general historical questions. But above all he wanted to have his attention drawn to omissions or to passages he might have dealt with too superficially and where a reader might wish for greater biographical detail. Towards the end of 1966 I was therefore approached by Siedler. He asked me whether I could take on the task of an 'interrogating editor'. As I had just started the preparatory work for my Hitler biography (published in 1973), the proposal struck me as being both interesting and useful for my own work. In the evenings after our conversations, which always took place over several days and were usually conducted together with Siedler, I would make notes, first only occasionally, then, as time went by, more and more regularly. Since Speer was a unique witness to the era these notes soon contained everything worth recording, whether it was useful for my own project or not. I therefore continued this practice even after the publication of my Hitler biography and occasionally extended it to incorporate Speer's reactions to the feedback from his books. Wherever, in the following pages, it says 'author's note', I am referring to these notes.

They require two explanatory observations. Firstly, they are not verbatim quotations, but summaries made from memory, although wherever possible they try to capture Speer's diction. Secondly, there is a natural preponderance of notes connected with the dramatic events in Speer's life. That is why they deal less frequently with the thirties, the years of Speer's extravagant architectural designs, or with his early years. Had I known then that I would be writing his biography one day, I would have asked Speer more detailed and more persistent questions about his conflicting values and motives, questions in which he got hopelessly entangled at the end. Nonetheless, the information obtained adds significantly to the overall picture.

I am indebted to the Munich Institute for Contemporary History, and especially to its director, Professor Horst Möller, as well as to the Federal Archive in Koblenz, especially Herr Gregor Pickro, for their generous help. I am also grateful to Herr Friedrich Wolters for his kindness in allowing me to see the papers of his father, Rudolf Wolters; also to Albert Speer junior for various pieces of information, and to Herr Tete Böttger, mainly for a number of unpublished photographs from the estate of Walter Hewel. Professor Hagen Schulze (Berlin/London) kindly agreed to read the manuscript; he has given me valuable advice.

I am particularly indebted to Hugh Trevor-Roper, who had planned to write Speer's biography himself, but he never got round to it and he suggested that I should do so. I also owe thanks, in some cases heartfelt thanks, to many others. Those concerned will know who they are.

Joachim Fest

Introduction

QUESTIONS, CONTRADICTIONS
AND MORE QUESTIONS

Albert Speer undoubtedly deserves a central place in any portrait gallery of the Hitler regime. He belonged to Hitler's personal entourage for most of the period and was scarcely known to the broader public. But his three years as Armaments Minister propelled him to the forefront. Indeed he himself had reason to assume that he had become the 'second man in the state'. He did not have the macabre personality traits which, for all their histrionic joviality, marked most of the leading figures, beginning with Hitler himself, and which gave the regime its sinister aura. Even his appearance set him apart from the burly, thick-necked political leaders who rose to the top after the Nazis seized power and pursued their own interests while promoting national renewal. Tall and intelligent, clearly intent on maintaining his reserve, Speer always stood out from the mass of noisy and pushy courtiers, as if he had accidentally strayed into their midst.

Nevertheless he was one of them, and this ambivalence is an indication of the contradictions that make up the enigma of Speer's life. Many who had followed the regime unconditionally also claimed to have felt the same mixture of distance and belonging, at least in retrospect. They liked to think they recognized themselves in Speer, in his idealism, efficiency and dedication and in his silent reserve. After his release from prison there was a further development. When Speer's memoirs were published in the late 1960s, he became for many a symbol of exoneration. He seemed to prove that it was possible to have served Hitler wholeheartedly, even in a leading position, and yet to have been ignorant of the horrors which had been committed. In those years, whenever conversation turned to the 'good side' of National Socialism, to the job-creation programme of the autobahns (which soon became a cliché), or the welfare schemes, Albert Speer's name often cropped up.

His exceptional position before and after the Hitler years makes it all the more astonishing that there is not even a remotely adequate biography of Speer. Matthias Schmidt published a polemical study in 1982, which admittedly makes a significant contribution to a brief phase of his life. Then there are two lives published in England about a decade and a half later. One of these, which enjoyed remarkable publicity, was by the well-known author Gitta Sereny. Based on the testimony of many contemporary witnesses *Albert Speer: His Battle with Truth* is not so much a biography in the traditional sense as an extensive report on Speer's personality as well as on the issues of personal guilt, recognition and transformation. The other book is written by Dan van der Vat, a respected journalist of Dutch extraction, who was for many years the correspondent of the London *Times* in Germany. Equipped with the quick grasp and forceful expression of his trade, he at least provides an outsider's view of such an oddly German character as Speer.[1]

Once the attention he received as an author and, for a period following the publication of his books, also as a kind of media star, had waned, Speer's life aroused little interest in Germany. There are many individual studies about his architecture and his work as armaments minister. But in biographical terms Esther Vilar's stage play is an exception. Constructed around a witty punch-line, it received its premiere in 1998 in the very rooms of the Berlin Academy of Arts where Speer and Hitler had designed and built a vast model of Berlin as the 'World Capital Germania'. Two years later David Edgar's stage adaptation of Gitta Sereny's book was performed at the National Theatre in London.[2]

The reluctance to devote a proper biography to Speer may partly be due to the fact that his life does not lend itself to the immediate answers which the world increasingly demands. An ambiguous character such as his runs, as it were, against the spirit of the age and resists the banal mind which seeks information from black-and-white stereotypes.

The historical profession is also responsible for this lack of interest. Since the end of Hitler's rule, historians have unearthed mountains of material and investigated the prehistory, the power structures and the aftermath of those events in an increasingly complex manner. The Nazi period has now been researched and explored more than any other. Yet the tendency of professional historians to look down on biography as a genre continues, even though 'the lives' of the protagonists would tie up many loose ends and provide a clearer picture of the process of progressive involvement and self-persuasion. It has been suggested that this neglect has led to attempts to stage *Hamlet* without the Prince of Denmark.[3]

This disregard for personal drama has robbed history of an entire dimension. The conflict cannot be resolved. Scholarship invariably tries to arrange a confusing flood of images into regular patterns. But the protagonists are made up of the very contradictions which the profession finds intolerable. That may be why the question as to how Hitler came to power, secured it, consolidated it, and ultimately gambled it away has been so exhaustively researched. And yet the riddles still remain. For human beings are more inconsistent than scholars like to acknowledge. The story of Albert Speer's life provides countless, often scarcely comprehensible, examples of this mutability.

One of the main reasons which make it more difficult to understand the events of 1933 is the deep moral collapse which many observers today detect at the time of Hitler's rise to power, precisely because they know about the subsequent horrors. Contemporaries, on the other hand, were not, or only rarely, aware of the breakdown. The events of that stormy spring tended to raise expectations, however vague. 'We only wanted things to get better,' Speer remarked on various occasions, 'that was all.' As a young, unemployed architect, he had been a member of Hitler's Party for about two years, and was not therefore without some hopes for the future. But even those who were worried anticipated, at worst, an authoritarian, temporarily perhaps even draconian, regime similar to those that had been established in many European countries. Without any experience of a totalitarian system, no one could or wanted to imagine how far the regime would go in depriving people of their rights, persecuting them and committing mass crimes.

Speer personified a type in which many recognized themselves, not only because of the great expectations Hitler's seizure of power evoked in him, encompassing a range of emotions. The initial sense of a new dawn and the jubilant naivety eventually gave way to disappointment and the (often suppressed) feeling of having followed a criminal regime. Although he too had been carried along by the political tumult, he prided himself on his abstinence from any kind of politics. Like many people, Speer had a public world and a private world, and the two were kept strictly apart. One was governed by decency, civilized forms and a strict set of rules, distinguishing what was permissible from what was not; the other was a realm where no norms applied and where crude interest possessed a basic right which overrode all objections. It is true that the persecution of opponents of the regime, which started early on, the harassment of minorities, and the establishment of the first

3

concentration camps, reported by the press and even illustrated with photographs, produced feelings of malaise and even fear. But that was 'just' politics, people said, usually with a trace of contempt. 'What did all that have to do with me?' was Speer's response to the description of a repulsive scene from the spring of 1938, and that was more or less his reaction whenever there was talk of violence and arbitrary use of power. It is significant that, having been part of Hitler's closest entourage for some time, he felt his first doubts when he saw Hitler slip his mistress Eva Braun an envelope at a banquet in a Munich hotel. Speer soon discovered that it contained money. This procedure struck him as both shameful and abhorrent; certainly it shocked him more than the injustice all around, which did not escape him. But he suppressed it to such an extent that towards the end of the war he was still talking of the 'ideal world' in which he had moved for so many years.

This division of the public and the private has deep roots in Germany's national culture. It had another directly political consequence, which is also relevant to Speer. For Hitler's chancellorship had given the new men some executive power. The system provided them with a reliable and efficient civil service. This was all the more important as the men who were now sweeping into key positions were mostly retired officers, failed academics or otherwise unemployed. Having been derailed from their bourgeois tracks, they were now taking advantage of the general confusion and making politics their new profession. They often came equipped with little more than a crude mixture of activism, thirst for power and faith. Of the state, of its machinery and complex structures, they knew virtually nothing.

The regime was helped out of this predicament on all levels by a huge corps of experts. Without the slightest sense of disquiet or hesitation they lent the new men their skills and experience. It was these bureaucrats, local administrators, police chiefs, ministerial mandarins and other officials who enabled Hitler's men to assume power. In spite of what was soon recognized as an 'overthrow', as the transformation was commonly called, they discharged what they saw as their duty conscientiously and with customary dedication, although it often reversed what until yesterday had been the law.

The traditionally anti-parliamentary mood, especially among the executive class, paved the way for this acquiescence. Many also believed that they would be able to control the 'young' movement and direct its crude impetuosity, while they had in effect already become accomplices to its strategy for seizing power. Among them were the Reichsbank

President Hjalmar Schacht, who was for a time Minister of Economic Affairs; Franz Gürtner, who was appointed Minister of Justice in the Weimar period and stayed in his post without interruption until his death in 1941; and Rudolf Diels, who had been a senior assistant of the Social Democratic Prussian Minister of Justice since 1930, and who from 1933 onwards devoted his professional abilities to the creation of the political secret police that soon acquired a proverbial reputation for terror as the 'Gestapo'. There were countless others. Every one of these experts more or less unanimously asserted their lack of interest in ideology, thus confirming precisely what they were seeking to conceal: the enormous contribution they made in the overall context of the 'hidden revolution'. For they enabled the regime to present itself as the champion of a higher interest, independent of any party bias.

One would be missing an essential aspect of National Socialism if one did not see it as a collective movement of the supposedly a-political against the progressive politicization of society. The new rulers responded with a promise of 'non-political' achievement to the sense of unease produced by the growing weight of the political parties, their quarrels and perpetual squabbles, and the general cacophony of voices that is part and parcel of a democratic system. After the politicizing tendencies of the unloved Weimar Republic, a rapidly growing majority was decidedly grateful to the Nazis for being released into the seeming objectivity of pure efficiency. Many recollections, at least of the prewar years, are coloured by the idealistic but fallacious misunderstanding that only the National Socialist regime had made possible a return to resolute decision-making processes and that it had accomplished what was necessary without endless discussion. Speer's later surprise that Hitler had never invited him to join the Party reveals how little he saw through that strategy, even at the end.[4]

In a broader sense Speer also belonged to that a-political 'other type' which paved the way for the regime and which made many critical observers at home and abroad question their own reservations. The successes the regime achieved and the prestige it gained were largely due to the vast number of reputable experts whom the new leadership managed to recruit. In that respect the question as to whether and to what extent Speer was, contrary to his own assertions, 'political' is somewhat irrelevant.[5] Over the years he certainly stood apart from political events in the narrow sense, from the intrigues and power struggles at Hitler's court, looking down with undisguised contempt at the gold-braided officials all around him. His self-assured, unsubservient manner indicated his distance from the false camaraderie of men such as Ley, Streicher, Ribbentrop or Bormann. At times his coolness seemed positively demonstrative. Speer's reputation for being haughty was not unfounded and he never quite shed it. Perhaps the sense of detachment which he made everyone feel was not just a problem of those years or that environment. 'I have never fully belonged anywhere,' he once observed.[6]

Speer did nothing to avoid accusations of arrogance. It was as if he tried to make up for the concessions to his superior background, his taste and his lifestyle, which his constant contact with the crude and primitive *camarilla* around Hitler forced him to make. But he never got far enough away from 'those people'. He was one of them and as he became more involved in the workings of the court, he reached numerous agreements with members of the entourage, he made tactical alliances and took his seat beside them on the VIP stands. Rather than being the exception that he believed himself to be, or even a contradictory figure, Speer, like others of his kind, in fact complemented them.

The price that Speer had to pay from the moment when, as a young man less than thirty years old, he had ended up in Hitler's circle almost by accident soon after the seizure of power, was a position that was always under threat and dependent on the Führer's goodwill. Unlike nearly all the other party satraps he lacked a power base and the cohorts that went with it. In the interest of maintaining the balance of power between his officials, Hitler continued to respect these power bases for some time. As his architect, Speer initially had no need of such trappings. But after his appointment as minister of armaments at the beginning of 1942, this lack of support weakened him. However, he soon learned to cope and to win Hitler over time and again with his charm, skill and play-acting.

Speer, in turn, received far more than the favour accorded to a courtier. There is much to suggest that he engaged Hitler's feelings from the outset and became, more than anyone else, including Eva Braun, the object of a deep affection, tinged with eroticism – 'Hitler's unhappy love', as one of Speer's staff remarked. This account will furnish ample evidence of this. While this emotion lasted, Speer was almost invulnerable, no matter how many jealous rivals operated against him. Only Hitler's mood swings made him feel that he could never be entirely sure of his position, both in professional and in personal terms.

This became particularly clear towards the end of the war, when a dark shadow already hung over the strange brotherhood. The estrange-ment may even have induced Speer to put the trust that Hitler had placed in him to the test over and over again and to play for high stakes in a risky game with the dictator. Throughout the preceding years his faculty of perception had not impaired his devotion to Hitler, leading him to adopt the radical positions expected of him. However, he evi-dently preserved some degree of his inner independence amidst all the yes-men and courtiers. One of the more astonishing features of his life is that he remembered his own autonomy at the penultimate moment. Then, in another about-turn, he confessed to the Nuremberg Tribunal that he had been a friend of Hitler's – as far as Hitler was capable of any feelings of friendship. At that point he evidently still regarded himself as a 'friend' of the dictator, at least as far as the shared and unforgotten architectural dreams were concerned.[7]

This strange and unique relationship provides the principal key to Speer's life. The unlimited opportunities Hitler offered him, the prefer-ential position within his entourage combined with the ambition of the wooed vassal blinded him to anything outside his own sphere. Human consideration was not one of them. Speer's indifference was reinforced by his admiration for the 'mover of the world', as he called Hitler in one of his extravagant moods.

Speer later complained that Hitler had corrupted both his emotions and his values. But how intact were they when, as a result of an exceed-ingly rare act of personal distinction by Hitler, Speer moved in at the Obersalzberg, where however much he liked to keep his distance, he associated with old Party warriors and rough-house heroes, or when he rode in the Führer's car, showered with flowers by cheering crowds? It remains a mystery how such a rational character could develop the naive faith that was a prerequisite for belonging to Hitler's inner circle. How did he cope with the folly of the so-called *Weltanschauung*, the world-view, which, to his own alarm, he once described as 'humbug' during a tea party at the Berghof, in Hitler's presence?[8] And it remains hard to understand how he could reconcile his yearning for a primitive life and the curious pleasure in prehistoric tribal rituals, where men stood up in a body, raised their arms, intoned battle songs or swore oaths of loyalty, with the technological futurism of rockets and jet aircraft whose cham-pion he was as minister of armaments? How did he square the parasitic greed of the Party bosses, which he recognized early on, with the 'dignity' of the common cause which he also spoke of, or Hitler's 'crim-inality' with the pain and the relapses which he suffered years later when he tried, perhaps unsuccessfully even then, to free himself from him?

One could go on and on asking these questions and reveal new contradictions. They certainly throw light on the society from which Speer came. The formative experience of his early years, he claimed, had been a general sense of a decline in values and a feeling that the ground was shifting wherever one stepped. Everything was doubtful, nothing was secure. Of course it had been clear that the National Socialism he was introduced to in the early thirties was a confused jumble of longings, anxieties and resentments. But perhaps the very arbitrariness of the diffuse recipes with which it responded to the crisis suited these muddled emotions, giving political strength to something that was singularly embarrassing in intellectual terms. At any rate, Speer explained, he had learned then to live with contradictions. In one of his prison reflections he wondered whether a man like Hitler, who knew how to appease, or at least distract, people with confused and radical theories, really had helped him attain those certainties which he had been looking for.[9] In this respect Speer has a wider significance as the embodiment of problems which still remain as relevant now as they were then. If approached with an open mind, the story of his life, despite all its particularities, may be read as a piece of German social biography.

A case such as Speer's with its many contradictions almost inevitably leads to the most contradictory judgements. The phase of self-examination that he later made public in several books began at the Nuremberg Tribunal, if not before. He was stunned when he was indicted as one of the principal war criminals. Appalled by the countless, documented, mass crimes of the regime, he broke ranks with the collective defence organized by Göring. By adopting a tactic which has been described as his 'master stroke', he avoided the death sentence, not least because he accepted the prospect in a kind of fatalistic spirit of self-sacrifice. There were those who then accused him of treason, dishonourable behaviour and even masochism. Others accused him of hypocrisy, which, they claimed, he had learned in Hitler's proximity and developed into the 'most cunning apologia of any leading figure of the Third Reich';[10] while a third group interpreted his restless preoccupation with the past as a kind of pride in sin. They simply saw the preoccupation with responsibility as another attempt to manoeuvre himself into the limelight to which he had become accustomed. In this way, they maintain, he had fooled first the Allied Tribunal and then the whole world.

In the face of these accusations those who believed Speer, and particularly his assurance that he had known nothing about the mass crimes, gradually found themselves in a minority. John Kenneth Galbraith was one of the American investigating officers who were given the task immediately after the war of gathering information about the effects of the bombing campaign. He soon gained the impression that Speer had been so willing to answer his questions because he wanted material for the erection of the edifice of lies in whose subterranean vaults and escape passages he then successfully barricaded himself. And the British major Airey Neave, who belonged to the Nuremberg prison administration, noted coolly and dispassionately: 'He was an impressive figure among the broken-down street politicians of the Nazi Party. His appearance was striking, even in his prison clothes. He was tall and dark, with a strong, intelligent face. His manner was persuasive ... But', he added with a vague doubt, stemming perhaps from the dichotomy between the highly cultured manner of the defendant and the incomprehensible entanglements which had determined his life until then, 'I felt uneasy in his presence.' And, as though he wished to warn himself and anyone who would ever have to judge Speer, he wrote after a visit to his cell: 'We must not come under his spell.'"

Many of the questions raised by Speer's life are unresolved to this day; some will never be cleared up. At some point they will confront anyone who does not believe that he already knows the answers to the events of those years. During one of the interrogations in May 1945, when Speer had spent hour after hour speaking in the dispassionate and sober manner that was characteristic of him about his years with Hitler, about the power structure, about his colleagues, his adversaries and his own part, one of the officers, Captain Burt Klein, suddenly interrupted him: 'Mr Speer, I don't understand you. You are telling us you knew years ago that the war was lost for Germany. For years, you say, you have been watching the horrible in-play among these gangsters who surrounded Hitler – and surrounded you. Their personal ambitions were those of hyenas, their methods those of murderers, their morals those of the gutter. You knew all this. And yet you stayed, not only stayed, but worked, planned with and supported them to the hilt. How can you explain it? How can you justify it? How can you stand living with yourself?'

After a moment of embarrassed silence Speer began to answer. He said the captain did not understand him. He did not understand anything about life in a dictatorship, nothing of the ever-present fear and nothing of the game of danger that also went with it; above all he understood nothing about the charisma of a man such as Hitler.

When Speer had finished, Captain Klein got up and left the room.[12]

Chapter One
AWAKENING

Any survey of a life inevitably starts at the end. Only when the actor has left the stage do the lines emerge from the tangle of existence to form a picture. Historians are easily tempted to describe as inevitabilities what are no more than those strange accidents that are part of every life. This applies particularly to figures who rose to the top in the Hitler period. It has been common practice to ferret out particular circumstances in their parental home that appear to explain their career. A lack of attention, for instance, prevented self-esteem from developing, an authoritarian upbringing engendered submissive attitudes, parental severity led to emotional impoverishment, while excessive parental love produced egotists, and so on. The arbitrary rules of this kind of psychology allowed diametrically opposite conclusions to be drawn from identical states of affairs. A child who was beaten would develop into an aggressive type, and so would one who was never beaten. Ultimately any misdeeds were attributed to the damage done in the parental home. In truth, however, all such statements merely raise the questions to which they purport to be the answers.[1]

Albert Speer, born in Mannheim on 19 March 1905, is a perfect illustration of how unpredictable life is. He came from what in his day was a 'normal' family, though privileged by belonging to the haute bourgeoisie. His early years followed the pattern of a regulated and uneventful youth in the provinces. There is hardly anything striking to report about it. His days passed in agreeable lassitude. Nothing upset the pleasant harmony between home and school, adventure games by the water, sports club and first love. Biographers have dissected many characteristics from the few incidental discoveries made about those years: the unapproachability of Speer's father, the apparent haughtiness of his mother and the distant relationship between the three brothers were said, more or less, to have led to the lack of emotion and the shyness of the second son that were apparent at an early age. But these simple conclusions tell us virtually nothing about how Albert Speer got into Hitler's entourage and then rose to his unique position at the dictator's court.[2]

Like his paternal grandfather, Speer's father was an architect who had made a name for himself with administrative buildings, luxury residences and villas in the Mannheim area. He had in addition acquired some affluence when, in 1900, he married the daughter of a Mainz merchant, who was descended from Wallenstein's field marshal, von Pappenheim, and who although a forester's son had become a successful entrepreneur. With typical circumspection Speer's father had invested his new wealth mainly in houses and building plots well beyond Mannheim's city limits, all the way to Heidelberg.

Speer grew up in an upper-middle-class world with the constraints typical of his day. His socially ambitious mother never quite got over having had to leave 'golden Mainz' and being marooned in the sooty industrial town of Mannheim. She tried to compensate for this misfortune by an extravagant lifestyle. In the fourteen rooms of her house she commanded a large staff with the cooks all in white, the maids in black dresses trimmed with white, and the male servants in purple livery with a made-up coat of arms. Everything was exaggerated and staged with a somewhat ostentatious penchant for the grand manner. There was also a chauffeur who looked after the family's two cars, a limousine for the winter and an open vehicle for the summer, as well as a French governess, Mademoiselle Blum, who was of Jewish descent. She used to march the three sons down the street in strict formation. In the entrance hall, heavy Dutch furniture was grouped around a sham fireplace with old Delft tiles; the reception rooms, on the other hand, were in the French style with lighter furniture, crystal and Lyonnais silk furnishings. Even in the affluent town of Mannheim few families could have afforded anything like it, Speer later observed.[3]

For all its spaciousness the house seemed strangely crowded and despite the large staff it was somewhat lifeless. It never really appealed to Speer and he felt almost liberated when the family moved to Heidelberg in the summer of 1918. Among the plots purchased by his father there was one on the hillside behind the castle, originally intended for the family's summer residence. On the edge of a park-like forest of ancient beeches and oaks he built a villa in the heavy, fortress style of the day. Far below lay the town and beyond its silhouette a panorama of the Rhine plain opened.

When Speer looked back on his youth it was mainly images from his

Speer's mother came from a wealthy merchant family. Never reconciled to exchanging Mainz for industrial Mannheim when she married, she attempted to make up for this misfortune by indulging her social ambition.

Heidelberg years that he remembered. The state school he attended after private tuition in Mannheim, the friends he made, and playing games of cowboys and Indians in the nearby wood opened the door to new worlds. Once outside the parental home, he was offered the leading place as a matter of course wherever he went. In the rowing club he was made cox of the four and, shortly afterwards, stroke of the eight. Decades later he tried to note down impressions from those years, as they came to him. The first was of his nursemaid teaching him simple songs, then of his mother in grand attire and behind her the dark, dignified outline of his father. Another recollection was of a visit to Heidelberg Castle, with a Zeppelin silently gliding above its venerable ruins. In between there were memories of poems, a performance of Weber's *Freischütz* and his first visit to the theatre to see Schiller's *Maid of Orleans*, of which he only remembered that it had been 'a tremendous experience'.[4] On further reflection he realized that technological and romantic matters had stayed with him more than anything else – aircraft on the one hand, and poetical and musical experiences on the other.

Relations continued to be difficult with his parents, who were virtually strangers to him. Nor did his relations improve with his brothers. They were noisy and robust, while Albert was physically delicate and of unstable health. He admired his father, but found him too reserved to feel able to confide in him. The inhibitions that all observers later remarked on, were already conspicuous in those early years. Speer's mother, who had sought refuge from various disappointments in a restless social life filled with receptions and house parties, remained aloof. All the possessions she accumulated failed to fill the void that surrounded her. By cultivating an ostentatious style she tried to perpetuate the circumstances and standards which had once made the middle class great. But now these trappings seemed like imitations, an empty spectacle on an overloaded stage set, revealing the very vacuum it sought to conceal.

Unlike his mother, Speer's father had strong principles. He was practical, always correctly dressed, with a gold watch chain, a twirled moustache and his hair cut short. For all his sobriety, his background and his new found family pride equipped him with a sure sense of middle-class values. On a visit to Berlin in the mid-thirties, he attended a theatre première with his unexpectedly high-powered son and Hitler invited him to his box in the interval. No sooner had he been presented than he was overcome by a violent trembling. He turned pale and as if paralysed he let the torrent of words beat down on him. Speer later suspected that his father had sensed the frightening aura of otherness that Hitler radiated. It was, as the conservative historian Otto Hintze described the dictator, like suddenly finding oneself in the presence of a person with something 'utterly alien' about them, 'something of an otherwise extinct primordial race, which was completely amoral'. Speer's father took his leave as soon as Hitler had ended, bowing stiffly without a word of response.[5]

Politically Speer's father regarded himself as belonging to that liberal tradition that had always championed the interests and libertarian views of the bourgeoisie. He particularly identified with Friedrich Naumann's social reformist views, although in the twenties he had abandoned Naumann's nationalist ideas for the pan-European ideals of Count Coudenhove-Kalergi. He always realized that no democratic order could survive on its own: the individual had to have and, if necessary, defend intellectual and political independence, and be determined to take responsibility at a professional level. No doubt he felt more upset than Speer's account suggests, when, after passing his school-leaving

Speer's father was a successful architect in the Mannheim/Heidelberg neighbourhood. Always correctly dressed, he combined family pride with solid middle-class instincts. Politically he regarded himself as a liberal and maintained his views even after 1933.

examination with flying colours, his son expressed the wish to study his favourite subject, mathematics. With that, his father pointed out, he might possibly become a university professor or a teacher, but he would not attain that self-determined existence which would meet his personal expectations and social requirements. In the end he persuaded his son to follow the family tradition and study architecture.

Despite his independent judgement, however, Speer's father was also afflicted by the prejudices that revealed the defensive attitudes so widespread among the middle class since the turn of the century. In his Mannheim years Albert Speer had already displayed a disturbing preference for the children of caretakers and for impecunious school-mates outside his own social circle. At first his parents were dismayed when in 1922 he fell in love with the daughter of a joiner, only slightly younger than himself. Then they became increasingly indignant, although their social superiority over the master joiner Weber was far from great. After all, within a few years he had built up a prosperous enterprise employing some fifty workers. As a Heidelberg town councillor, he belonged to the town's leading citizens. The Webers' social rise basically matched that of the Speers only a generation earlier. But in keeping with the prejudices of the day, the Speers looked down on the Webers and were never able to forget the gulf between them.

The following year, when the young people announced their decision to get married as soon as possible, not only Speer's parents but, significantly, the Webers also did everything possible to foil this intention. While Speer went to Karlsruhe to take up his studies, Margarete Weber was packed off to a boarding school in distant Freiburg. It is quite possible that parental opposition merely strengthened the two teenagers' affection which, from the outset, seemed sensible and curiously lacking in passion. Certainly the letters they exchanged during the years of separation deal more with their mutual love of the theatre, of classical music and literature than with their love for each other. Much as Speer may have been attracted by his girlfriend's simple, unspoiled and modest nature, there are no expressions of passionate emotion in those letters. The strongest motive of his attachment may well have been the natural warmth he had first experienced at the Webers' house. It must have seemed very different from the chill in his own home. Right to the end, and without his usual emotional reserve, Speer gratefully recalled the kindness he had encountered in the house of the respected master craftsman. When after the completion of his studies he finally married his teenage sweetheart it was seven years before the young bride was invited to his parents' house.

It was a world where, in one way or another, the cracks were beginning to show. The bourgeoisie was still governed by the strict rules, the seriousness and the ethos of achievement to which it was so deeply indebted. But no one was really sure what higher purposes they served, what values guided them, and whether the brilliant social gatherings at which those who belonged congregated reflected anything more than self-satisfaction and a sense of an impending end. The famous 'front' which everybody had to maintain was indicative of a world that had, along with other signposts, lost the self-assurance that had made its rise possible.

People have often wondered why the bourgeoisie in Germany submitted to National Socialism so passively when elsewhere it managed to offer weak but ultimately successful resistance to the politically organized radicalism of the centre. A comprehensive answer would have to include a multitude of historical, social, political and other reasons which obstructed the emergence of an organic and self-assured middle class. Since the middle of the nineteenth century, when Germany was on the verge of unification, it had tried to make up for its economic backwardness. Despite its successes or perhaps because of them this turbulent process was too precipitate, too diffuse and hence too unstable to nurture the solid traditions essential to bourgeois self-assertion. The short answer is that by the end of the 1920s a middle class that was politically even halfway united or capable of offering effective counter-measures no longer existed.[6]

Step by step, the First World War, the Revolution and the troubles that followed it, had displaced the bourgeoisie from the key positions it had only recently gained, revealing not only its weaknesses but also the deep divisions which were not bridged by any common interests. The disastrous experience of inflation shortly afterwards destroyed the economic basis of the so-called middle classes in particular. Along with their often modest savings it also undermined their trust in their own strength and their social self-esteem.

The liberalism under whose broad cloak the frequently divergent bourgeois streams had united politically was by then just a memory of better days, particularly as the Weimar Republic never managed to establish the tranquility which the bourgeois parties, unlike the others, required. In the 1919 elections to the National Assembly the liberal parties still managed to obtain nearly a quarter of the vote. But the onset of crisis after crisis and the unrest caused by the changes in the social structure drove the voters either to the extremists or to new splinter groups. The depth of the destruction was reflected not only in the rapid decline of support for the bourgeois parties but also in the progressive political disintegration of the bourgeois camp. In the 1919 elections the bourgeois splinter groups accounted for a mere 1.5 per cent of the vote; barely ten years later, in 1928, some 14 per cent were condemning themselves to a total loss of political influence by voting for parties which were often minute.

To make matters worse the bourgeoisie was depriving itself of its power just at the time when it was under attack as never before. A feverish desire to expose its weaknesses, long established in literature and science, increasingly spread to politics. The two great mass movements of the day, political Marxism and National Socialism, were both anti-bourgeois and anti-liberal. More importantly, they had the young on their side, whereas all the other parties, from their leaders down to the programmes they offered, seemed more or less 'exhausted', as if they were uttering epilogues to an age that was heading for the abyss. Different slogans now drew a following. The bourgeois concept of liberty and self-determination was being replaced by new movements proclaiming the principle of leadership and of unconditional submission. It is one of the curious features of that time that such slavish maxims suddenly seemed to signify grandeur, dignity and the future. Both movements, moreover, promised to bridge social divisions and establish the egalitarian order that the bourgeoisie, with its exclusiveness and pride in status, had always abhorred, the Marxists with the catch-phrase of the 'classless society' and the National Socialists with the promise of the 'community of the people'.

This was the great shadow that hung over the epoch, pointing to the demise of the liberal order in which, despite all the contradictions, the bourgeoisie had seen itself and its ideal most accurately reflected. To an increasing number of people, nothing seemed more out of keeping with the time than the democratic 'system'. The derision it received from all sides was intensified by the fact that it could muster little more to oppose the approaching crises than the admission of its own impotence, so vividly reflected in trivial parliamentary squabbles and the wheelings and dealings of the political parties. What the defenders of the democratic order described as a sacred cause was very soon seen by many as a parody of the state as they knew it. A growing mood of weariness, of contempt and at times of resignation fed doubts about the effectiveness of the democratic order in the face of the approaching era of the masses. Arthur Moeller van den Bruck, the writer and political philosopher, thought that nations would be stifled by liberalism. Such reservations were by no means confined to Germany, even though they were most evident there. Mussolini wrote at that time that all the political experiences of the period were 'illiberal'. He referred to the 'goddess of liberty' who was about to 'close the doors of her temple which the nations have abandoned'.[7]

Despite all the bad omens Albert Speer's father remained attached to the political principles of liberalism, out of affection for what they stood for and from a loathing of Hitler, whom he despised as a 'criminal upstart'.[8] He may also have been motivated by a patriarchal belief that one should not surrender even a lost cause. How unusual such steadfastness was even within his most immediate circle later emerged when Speer's mother confessed that she had joined the Nazi Party as early as 1931, after an SA march through the streets of Heidelberg. She had simply been impressed by the orderly columns and by the confidence with which they had confronted the general sense of gloom. For years she kept this secret from her husband and her sons. She regarded it, with good reason, as a breach of the family tradition.

As for Speer himself, even after he had begun his studies in nearby Karlsruhe, politics remained outside his own world and anything to which he attached importance. Like many bourgeois families, his parents had upheld the principle that money, erotic escapades and politics were taboo subjects within one's own four walls. Nevertheless it seems odd that Speer should have kept to this strict rule in such turbulent times. For months and even years dramatic events had followed in rapid succession, beginning with the unexpected turn of the war and the Revolution, leading to the abdication and escape of the Kaiser. Speer remembered hearing about Versailles and that Germany had, in a popular phrase of the day, been sent home 'with a dunce's cap on its head'.[9] But he failed to take note of the move of the Constituent National Assembly from the unstable atmosphere in Berlin to Weimar. The sinister doings of the Free Corps, the coup and the rebellions in central Germany all seem to have passed him by. Only news from their relations in Mainz about the arrogant behaviour of the French occupation troops, the ban on newspapers from the rest of Germany, enforced billeting, house searches, expulsions, the employment of coloured troops that was seen as a deliberate humiliation, and other outrageous matters was occasionally discussed. It had, Speer said, only made the already gloomy atmosphere at home even more depressed. But any topics of wider significance continued to be barred from conversation: 'It did not occur to anyone to challenge this.'[10] One is tempted to view this silence as a reflection of the traditional separation of the public from the private sphere, where politics was regarded as an awkward or even vulgar subject.

Speer conceded that, as far as politics was concerned, a few emotions and slogans may at the most have made a superficial impression on him in those years, and what we know about him then confirms this statement. Like everyone else he was affected by Versailles and the overwhelming sense of national affront, coupled with growing misgivings about the inadequacies of parliamentary government. Yet not even his move to the university, where the rigid family ban on political discussion did not apply, brought him any closer to politics. In shutting themselves off from the outside world the majority of the universities were no different from the bourgeois homes from which most of their students came.

Speer with his young wife at the time of their wedding in 1928. Acknowledging cultural tradition, they were married on 28 August, Goethe's birthday.

It was obvious, however, that this attitude was beginning to shift. New revelations of the hardships endured by the country, the collapse of its institutions, the bankruptcy of values and other indicators of change seemed to turn the past upside down. At the same time the men who had been too young to fight in the war, the so-called war youth generation, were no longer able to keep politics at bay. Much was written at the time about their emerging attitudes, their values and their 'style'. One of those studies claimed, not without a degree of 'frosty admiration', that 'simplicity' and 'seriousness', the ability to 'place the cause above personal interests', but also 'laconic reserve, and…at times brusque coldness' were among the foremost characteristics of that generation. In a perspicacious essay, published in 1932, about the generation of thirty-year-olds, which included Speer, the writer and future publisher Peter Suhrkamp noted: 'Their most significant feature is their lack of humanity, their disrespect for anything human.'[11]

One of the peculiarities of Speer's life almost to the end was that he walked a tightrope. He never joined any trend or particular grouping and yet he shared many of the tendencies that haunted that unquiet period. He was indeterminate, and for that reason alone he kept aloof from politics. Neither the occupation of the Ruhr in early 1923, at the time he began his studies, nor Hitler's coup in November of the same year made a mark on him in any way. Even the shattering experience of inflation, which led to the tragic collapse of his own social class, evidently had no impact on him. He was fortunate in that his father had sold his parents-in-law's properties in Mainz for dollar treasury bonds shortly before the total collapse of the currency. That enabled him to give his son a monthly allowance of sixteen dollars, an exorbitant sum under the circumstances. The only 'political' insight Speer admitted to was that he began to realize then that the world, such as it was and would be, had shaky foundations.[12]

In keeping with the traditions of the cultured bourgeoise he found refuge in literature and the arts generally, as well as in a deep attachment to nature. His literary tastes were predominantly for the classics, especially Goethe, to whom he was drawn by his warmth and by his civic values, but also Schiller and Kleist, whose humane rigour deeply impressed him, and Ibsen and Georg Kaiser. However much the works of these poets and of the romantic composers and artists in particular, fascinated him, these formative experiences lay buried beneath the pressures of professional and social advancement. Not until the end of his life were circumstances such that Speer could re-evoke that experience.

His love of nature was even more formative, and probably also more typical. The mountain tours that he made with his future wife in those years and paddling in a kayak or canoe were, he later said, a form of 'bliss'. This euphoria was inspired by the simple life in mountain huts and boat houses, the hours of silent harmony and being deeply moved by nature. The world was far away. Up on those heights there were unforgettable moments when he experienced pity for the 'wretched people' below the cloud banks who were subjected to the narrowness, the noise and the bustle of the city.[13]

This was the side of the 'war youth generation' that shunned reality. Speer called their predilections an escape 'from the demands of an increasingly complicated world'; with one of the ideological pace setters of the period he might have said that 'books and dreams' had been the element of their lives.[14] This rejection of reality was not an individual impulse but a widespread mood of the day. It stemmed from a growing distaste for the radical changes wrought by the industrial age and the fears of the losses that were felt all round. A number of influential figures such as Richard Wagner, Julius Langbehn or Paul de Lagarde, and a host of lesser prophets in their wake, had given this malaise a response that was stronger and more radical in Germany than anywhere else. It gave rise to a specifically German tradition of despairing of modernity. Filled with terror they identified the dictates of the hour from the crisis into which their familiar world had plunged, combining their reaction with the 'world role' they assigned to their country, although it had only just been united and attained power. That role consisted of the specifically German mission to preserve 'culture' against the destructive assault of detestable 'civilization'. The country's defeat and the 'disgrace' inflicted upon it merely intensified the pain of what was happening, lending it universal significance.

At the turn of the century, these moods had already produced a vanguard of associations and circles, the most notable of which were the life-reforming groups which sprang up everywhere, the *Wandervogel* and the *Bündische Jugend* scout movements. They rebelled against the bourgeois world and all that went with it: the neuroses and the high-flown banality, the hypocrisy and the sham, the operatic Germanic myths and the indoor palm. They wanted to replace them with simplicity, love of nature, dedication and the values they engendered. These categories in themselves reveal how far removed from reality those who subscribed to these new beginnings were. None of the rebellious demands they made of their world contained a feasible model of society. It often seemed that they did not so much intend to change the state of affairs they all deplored as just to vent their anger at it. Certainly the new world which they sought as they wandered or debated was far removed from the world in which they lived. 'Swayed by youthful passion and mindless,' is how Speer characterized himself, looking back at those years. But the description applied to his generation as a whole, and any 'bliss', no matter how deeply felt, merely amounted to empty self-satisfaction. 'We were always dreaming of solitude, of drives through quiet river valleys, of hiking to some high mountain pasture, we never felt the lure of Paris, London or Vienna, even ancient Rome failed to tempt us.'[15]

The romanticism of that generation is worth mentioning for another reason. The rejection of reality, the horror of industrialization, of the city and of the unstable social scene inevitably included an aversion to politics, which was simply an exaggerated response to the threats posed by the modern world. Although Speer never belonged to any of the

In the early 1920s Speer fell in love with Margarete Weber, the daughter of a respected Heidelberg craftsman. The young couple were swept along by the boy-scout spirit of the period; this included music and literature, but above all a love of nature. The two of them spent all their free time on long mountain hikes or canoeing.

associations into which the protest against the age was channelled, he was certainly part of the environment from which they sprang. Indeed it provides the missing explanation for his lack of interest in politics. When in the spring of 1924 he left Karlsruhe in order to continue his studies in Munich, he had, as far as he remembered, not even heard of the 'Nazis' who had terrorized that city for so long. Only a few weeks previously they had been temporarily faced with ruin after their unsuccessful coup in front of the Feldherrnhalle.

In appearance and behaviour Speer also personified the 'youth movement'. Many of his fellow students remarked on his free and easy manner, his disinterest in appearances and, generally, his demonstratively 'unpolished' nature. At the same time he was generous in financial matters, always ready to help, and with a remarkable knack of making friends and winning collaborators who would relieve him of unpleasant duties for 'piece wages'. On the other hand, he discharged the academic duties that mattered to him with almost playful ease. In Munich he first met Rudolf Wolters who, like him, was the son of an architect and came from Coesfeld in Westphalia. Unlike Speer he was open and impulsive. But whenever there was a clash of opinions between them, their literary predilections and their love of nature brought them together again. Later Wolters characterized his friend as 'decidedly unconventional', 'totally indifferent to religion and national issues' and a 'brilliant idler'. Never had he seen in him 'the glutton for work he was to become'.[6] Their relationship endured almost to the end of their lives.

Summing up this phase we are faced with an immature but gifted young man, caught up in the prejudices and moods of his day. Nothing in him suggests any disorder caused by parental neglect, or any complexes or deformations. He had even remained untouched by the political and artistic extremes of the 'wild twenties', which captured almost everybody, at least for a time. That pattern was set to continue, and it is the very 'normality' of his life that has made Albert Speer so typical. At any rate the break he made shortly afterwards with the world from which he came was due far more to the total absence of any political values, to his inclination to escape from life, his indifference to people and reality, and to his innocent and joyful days of hiking which he was so fond of remembering, than to those formative experiences of which so much has been made.

In the autumn of 1925 Speer and a few fellow students transferred from Munich to the Technical University in Berlin in order to continue their studies with Hans Poelzig, one of the leading architects of the day. Poelzig, however, made a strict selection among the applicants and, as Speer's gift for drawing was not up to requirements, he, like Wolters, was rejected. A solution was found when Heinrich Tessenow came to Berlin shortly afterwards; his architectural vision was simple and almost sparse, defined by a few, clear lines. His designs were conceived in deliberate opposition to the bold and often exaggerated modernity then fashionable. Tessenow believed that man should look on the buildings he erects as home, not as an aesthetic Utopia. As a result he was often accused of lacking imagination, but in his hatred of bombast he was intent on replacing the overpowering contemporary style with a simple architecture based on traditional craftsmanship. 'A minimum of display is crucial,' was the message he taught; one of his books was prefaced by the motto 'The simplest is not always the best, but the best is always simple.'[7]

From the very first Speer felt an earnest, schoolboyish attachment to Tessenow and his strict principles. It drove him to make a special effort. The solitary professor of architecture with his watery eyes behind gold-rimmed spectacles, his thinning hair and his reddish-blond beard had barely been in Berlin for eighteen months when Speer passed his exam with him. Shortly afterwards Tessenow appointed him as his assistant.

He was twenty-three years old. The unusual distinction led Speer to assume that his teacher must have noticed the admiration and veneration he felt for him. But it is more likely that Tessenow had developed a liking for the young man who captivated the world with his charm, his background and his youthful directness, qualities which so often worked to his advantage before they led to his undoing.

Although the hapless Weimar Republic had a brief breathing space in the late twenties, Berlin was seething with political excitement. On closer inspection it was obvious that the hostile camps in the capital were preparing for a final battle. In November 1926 Joseph Goebbels had been placed at the head of the shattered Berlin Party organization as Gauleiter. Impudent and unscrupulous as he was, he immediately began to recruit an army of thugs who provoked brawls, disturbances and shootings, and subjected the far larger and tightly organized Communists to constant attack. Goebbels was willing to accept defeats so long as they brought him and the Nazi Party publicity. Fatal casualties on his own side were even more welcome because they evoked conspiratorial feelings sealed with blood. Within a few months he had made substantial inroads into the powerful front of so-called 'Red Berlin'.

Even these events seemed to pass Speer by. In his memoirs, *Inside the Third Reich*, the endless series of clashes, which a police report stated 'outclassed anything experienced so far',[18] do not appear at all. Instead there is frequent mention of concerts and theatre visits, of Max Reinhardt, Elisabeth Bergner or the sumptuous revues of Charell. More importantly, the well-paid post as Tessenow's assistant finally enabled Speer to get married in 1928. Making a bow to the traditional values of educated Germans he set the wedding for 28 August, Goethe's birthday. For a while he considered spending the honeymoon in Italy, the classic country not only of honeymoon couples but also of lovers of art and architecture. But his escapist tendencies proved stronger. With two folding canoes and a tent the newlyweds spent three weeks crossing the deserted chain of Mecklenburg lakes, starting at Spandau. 'It was a wonderful time,' he later recalled.[19]

Inevitably the world to which he turned a blind eye caught up with him in the end. In 1929 the National Socialists called for an 'assault on the universities'. Needless to say, this was not achieved by force of ideological conviction, but, as nearly always, by that power of persuasion that relies on brute force. This was applied so ruthlessly that in the summer of 1931 the University of Berlin had to be closed for some time.

After studying in Karlsruhe and Munich, Speer moved to Berlin, where he soon
developed a profound admiration for the architect Heinrich Tessenow, who taught an
unadorned, ascetic style, far removed from his pupil's designs in later years. After a
mere eighteen months, Tessenow appointed Speer his assistant at the exceptionally
early age of twenty-three. Later their paths parted.

Significantly, Speer's Technical University registered the strongest
growth of the National Socialist Students' League. Within a single year
its share in the elections to ASTA, the Students' Union, rose from
barely forty per cent to two-thirds of the votes cast.[20]

Again Speer appears to have taken hardly any notice of this development. His statement that he 'did not even dream' of following the students' swing towards Hitler's cause certainly sounds credible. However,
this political indifference was not as unpolitical as it seemed. By retiring
into a kind of contemptuous offside, he may not have helped either of
the radical opposing parties, but his attitude deprived the democratic
institutions of their legitimacy and made increasingly broad circles
receptive to any promise of change. Ultimately this indifference contributed as much to the demise of the republic as the subversive
activities of its most determined opponents.

The misconceptions are clearly revealed in Tessenow's case. Despite
being a firm opponent of the Hitlerites, he kept aloof from politics.

Widely dubbed a 'philosopher among architects', he based his views on deep, though often somewhat far-fetched, reflections. Tessenow sought to instil his students with sufficiently firm values to make them invulnerable to all the radical movements of the day, politically, artistically and generally. He was all the more bewildered to see them joining the Nazi Party in droves, just as Poelzig's students were rallying to the parties of the left. The process not only reflected the increasing politicization of the universities. What attracted Tessenow's students to National Socialism also had something to do with the connection between his architectural ideas and the ideology of the rising mass movements, notwithstanding his own opposition. Both Tessenow and the Nazis were motivated by a powerful anti-civilizatory feeling, by a hatred of modernism, and a horror of the Moloch-like industrial age, preferring a rosy vision of the simple life, investing in people, the soil, roots and innocence. The dividing line between Tessenow and the other side was all too finely spun, however stubbornly he defended it.

Speer listened attentively to these disputes, which also involved the students. According to the testimony of his friends he would occasionally make a comment. But what he said always seemed to come from a great distance, as if the arguments so passionately conducted by the others did not really concern him. The political tensions simmering behind these differences of opinion stopped him from taking sides, and it was probably at that time that he began to see himself as an artist who stood above such ephemeral quarrels. For the same reason he looked down on the famous architects of his day, whose concepts were often linked to political visions of the future; Speer ignored the avant-gardism of his time. 'I saw myself as a later-comer,' he said once, but he did not regard his aloofness from the present and its mad excrescences as a weakness. Tessenow had taught him that architecture was determined by enduring laws, whereas the Mies van der Rohes, Tauts or Gropiuses of this world were merely witty or 'topical'. Perhaps, he remarked in one of his later self-examinations, he had 'simply been waiting for Hitler'.[21]

But all this proud exclusivity was shattered in one fell swoop. At the beginning of December 1930 Speer was urged by a few participants of his seminar to attend a political meeting at the Neue Welt, an assembly room in Berlin's Neuköllner Hasenheide. When the small group arrived they found more than five thousand professors and students waiting for Hitler to make an appearance. The heated atmosphere in the

hopelessly overcrowded room made a deep impression on the unsus-
pecting Speer. He had occasionally heard Hitler described as a hysterically uninhibited circus orator prone to raving fits, who presented
himself to the masses with a riding crop, brown shirt and wild mane, as
a kind of backyard messiah.

Speer was all the more astonished by the man who stepped up to the
lectern, wearing a dark-blue suit that indicated his concern for bourgeois correctness. Furthermore he did not treat the audience to one of
his theatrical turns. Instead he gave a carefully reasoned lecture, only
occasionally slipping into demagogy. Speer's memory of that evening
was dominated by his surprise at the hesitant, almost timid, voice that
began to speak. He put it down to Hitler's nerves. In reality, however,
this probing opening was one of his well-tested tricks of oratory, which
enabled him to gauge the mood and establish the rapport with which he
captivated his audience. Hitler spoke of the weakening nations and their
decline, of the 'politics of the inferior', but also about unity, honour and
resurgence. Everything he said was underpinned by historical excursions
and spurious political evidence which Speer had little objection to.
Hitler did not dwell on the countless problems of everyday life. Instead
he mapped out a huge historical panorama into which he set the
present crisis as part of the never-ending struggle of the forces of good
against evil. It was the vagueness of his programme, delivered with all
the authority of the charismatic leader, promising nothing and commanding everything, that left the strongest impression on Speer and
those present. This speech, like all of Hitler's speeches, owed its effectiveness to the orator himself and the almost tragic gravity with which
he invoked the many troubles which beset the country: communism,
unemployment, impotence. In spite of the apocalyptic visions he
painted, he remained full of aggressive confidence. That above all was
what drew the frightened masses to him and elicited rapturous applause
from his audience at the Neue Welt.

After the event the group of students went on to a beer cellar, but
Speer did not join them. He later wrote that he left 'a changed person',
walking past the same advertisements, the same dirty poster columns,
under the same leafless trees of the Hasenheide as on his way to the
assembly hall. But nothing was as it had been.[22] Overcome and confused, he wanted to be alone. He drove out to the Havel woods in his
car, not returning home until hours later.

Much though it moved Speer, taking part in a political meeting was
not what made that evening stand out to such an extent. Nor can the

impact be fully explained by his sudden awareness of the seriousness of the situation. The writing had long been on the wall but it had taken Hitler to interpret it for him. Speer felt admiration for the apparently cool yet passionate man in the dark blue suit, who, as he hoped, might save Germany, but he also reproached himself, made excuses and new resolutions. He was brimming over with confused, exhilarating feelings.

However, these factors are not the whole answer. Speer's strange need to be alone after a political meeting and to engage in a spiritual exercise in the Havel woods is better explained if one looks on that evening as an awakening, with all the pseudo-religious, magical, alarming and sudden insight associated with that concept. In a striking turn of phrase Speer remarked of that speech that Hitler had taken hold of him then and had not released him since.[23] There can be little doubt that an unexpected experience of that nature was bound to lead a serious young man, who was in love with his dream of the world, politically astray.

For a time he continued to hesitate. A few weeks later, when his students invited him to attend a rally staged by Goebbels in the Berlin Sportpalast, he was utterly repelled by the cutting diatribes of the speaker and by his cold-blooded rhetoric. But afterwards, when mounted police came galloping out from the side-streets, scattering the crowd with rubber truncheons, Speer's mood changed again. On 1 March 1931 he went to a Party office and, as he put it, joined not the NSDAP but Hitler's Party. He was given the membership number 474,481.

There followed nearly eighteen months of idleness, emptiness and a feeling of wasting time. Now and then Speer took part in competitions, but he never got more than a third prize. Because he owned a car he was appointed leader of the NSKK, the Nazi Motor Corps, for Berlin-Wannsee and was occasionally employed as a courier. At the beginning of 1932 he gave up his post with Tessenow when academic salaries were cut, as part of the increasingly stringent economies. He returned to Heidelberg to look for commissions using his father's connections. But these efforts remained fruitless in the face of the economic slump then approaching its climax. His father eventually entrusted him with the management of his properties, but this did not stop the discouragement he felt from living off his parents' money. In his youth, he once remarked, he had, like everyone, dreamed of something great and sensational. Unlike everyone else he had always been sure he would achieve it, even during those paralysing months of unemployment.[24]

A few months earlier, in one of the Berlin Party offices, he had come across Karl Hanke, an unemployed technical school teacher about his own age, then in charge of the Kreisleitung West. One day Hanke had invited him to do up a dilapidated Grunewald villa recently rented by the Party. This was just one of those occasional jobs with which the young architect tided himself over. Some of Speer's biographers have seen his readiness to accept Hanke's commission as a sign of his heightened political interest. But his behaviour during the Reichstag elections of July 1932 gives little indication of this. Admittedly he had come from Heidelberg to Berlin towards the end of the campaign in order to help the Party, and on one of those occasions he had seen Hitler again. This time he was imperious, brusque, constantly waving his riding crop which he smacked against his boots as he waited impatiently. But the indifference Speer felt for the campaign that had been waged with such bitterness that it left hundreds dead or wounded can be deduced from the fact that he had planned to continue his journey on the Thursday before the election on Sunday. He was planning to spend a few weeks sailing the lonely East Prussian lakes with his wife. Their folding canoes and camping gear were already stored at the railway station.

A few hours before his departure news reached him that Karl Hanke, who had become the organizational head of the Gau Berlin, urgently wished to speak to him. When Speer called on him, Hanke asked if he would be interested in fitting out the new Gau headquarters in Voss-strasse, as he had the Grunewald villa. Demoralized after months of searching unsuccessfully for commissions, Speer accepted without much reflection and cancelled his trip to the Mazurian lakes. Years later he reflected on the strange accidents which had repeatedly diverted his life in totally unexpected directions. A few hours later and Hanke's call would have come too late. Speer would have been untraceable for weeks in the remoteness of the East Prussian forests.

The house in Voss-strasse was much larger and more extravagant than the Party could afford in its disastrous financial situation. But the final stage in the struggle for power was clearly approaching and the organization had acquired the building in the government quarter in order to stake its claim from a suitably impressive location. Time was pressing, and for the first time Speer proved his ability to meet exceedingly tight schedules by careful organization and constant urging. He was not invited to the inauguration of the premises, but he was told that Hitler had expressed his approval. With the job done Speer returned to Heidelberg, to the hopeless, empty life of draining inactivity.

Karl Hanke in 1933. After attending a mass meeting addressed by Hitler, Speer joined the National Socialist Party on 1 March 1931. Soon afterwards he made the acquaintance of Hanke, an unemployed teacher of about his own age, who was then heading a Party organization in the west of Berlin. It proved a decisive meeting. Hanke procured a number of commissions from the Party for Speer, which enabled him to make a name for himself.

He barely took notice of 30 January 1933 when Hitler was appointed Reich Chancellor, even though it was 'his' Party and 'his' Führer who had achieved that long-hoped-for success. The desolate circumstances in which he found himself made the event seem remote. He could hardly remember the day and merely assumed that, along with so many others, the news had led him to hope for some vague improvement in the state of affairs. Now and again he would attend some local Party meetings, horrified at the pettiness and the bloated talk that went on there.

A few weeks later, however, he heard from Hanke again. He asked Speer to come to Berlin. Hitler had concluded from the disappointing outcome of the Reichstag elections of 5 March 1933 that the public was still behaving obstreperously and that he needed what today would be called a skilful 'spin doctor' with ministerial powers. In a flagrant breach of the agreement with his German-National coalition partners he had therefore appointed Goebbels to be Reich Minister for Public Enlightenment and Propaganda only a week after the elections. When

Speer arrived in Berlin, Goebbels took him to the future site of his ministry, the Leopold palace in Wilhelmsplatz. The building dated from the first half of the eighteenth century but it had later been remodelled by Schinkel in the Prussian neoclassical style. Even before his official appointment the new minister had employed a team of SA building workers. In the dead of night they ripped stucco decorations and wood panelling from the walls and tore the 'stuffy moth-eaten drapes' from the windows. This drastic action was, as Goebbels noted in his diary, not only meant to bring light and air into the rooms but also to symbolize the new style. 'Just as a clean sweep has to be made in the rooms, so it has to be made among the people', he wrote.[25]

Speer's reconstruction of the ministry was widely applauded. Almost imperceptibly he found himself being swept into a new world. From one moment to the next he had commissions, duties and recognition. In no time at all, events took their own course. Shortly thereafter in the anteroom of Hanke's office he discovered plans for a mass night-time rally at the Tempelhofer Feld. Hanke was by then head of the secretariat in Goebbels' ministry. The rally was to be the concluding event of 1 May, which had been declared a public holiday for the first time. When Speer remarked that the intended backdrop looked 'like the stage set for a Schützenfest, a riflemen's gathering', he was told that no one was stopping him from coming up with something better. During the following night he prepared a series of sketches which revealed both his gift for improvisation and his sense of theatrical splendour. At the front of the parade ground he placed a wooden platform. Behind it two vertical swastika banners were hung on either side of a Reich flag in the imperial Black-White-Red. And at the magical centre in front of these huge flags he placed Hitler, picked out of the darkness by spotlights, which had been quickly procured from a filmset. He stood high up and far removed from the waiting throng, his figure bathed in glowing brightness, invoking the awakening of the nation, unity at home and strength towards the outside world, two thousand years of history, and at the end God's blessing: 'Lord, we will not abandon You.'[26]

The evening of that 1 May marked the hour when the nation began finding itself again: the National Socialist mass celebration had found the style which Speer developed into an increasingly perfect liturgy designed to overwhelm the audience. Hitler was so impressed by the backdrop that Goebbels thought it wise to present it as his own invention. But when Speer asked Tessenow for his opinion he received the chilling answer: 'Do you think you have created something? It's showy, that's all.'[27]

By then Speer had moved too far away from his teacher. Success and praise from all sides widened the gap. A short while later Goebbels asked him to renovate his official residence which he had high-handedly taken away from Alfred Hugenberg, the leader of the German National Party, for his own use. He wanted to enlarge the house by adding a spacious hall-like living-room, thus giving Speer his first building job. In his eagerness Speer agreed to have the house, including the new hall, ready for occupation within two months.

Reckless though this promise was, it brought him to Hitler's attention for the first time. At any rate, Goebbels told Speer that Hitler did not believe the deadline could be met. The surprise was all the greater when Speer handed the house over on the due date. He got a little closer still to Hitler when he was invited shortly thereafter to design a dignified backdrop for the first Nuremberg Party Rally after the seizure of power. Since none of the Party bigwigs dared judge Speer's proposals, he was sent to Munich to get Hitler's personal decision. But contrary to his expectation that meeting was utterly impersonal. As Speer entered the apartment on Prinzregentenstrasse, Hitler was cleaning a pistol. The parts were scattered over the table. All he heard after a brief interested examination of the plans was a curt 'Agreed!' Not a word, not even a glance at the visitor. As Hitler turned back to his pistol Speer left the room, disappointed.

However, Hitler remembered him when, soon afterwards, he instructed his architect Paul Ludwig Troost to restore and refurnish the partially dilapidated chancellor's residence in Berlin. Troost was really an interior designer who had made a name for himself by equipping the luxury liners of Norddeutscher Lloyd. Years before, Hitler had entrusted him with the construction of the Brown House in Munich's Königsplatz and later commissioned him to build the two temple-style mausoleums at the entrance to the square, where the dead of 9 November were buried. As Troost lived in Munich and was unfamiliar with the Berlin building business and the local craft enterprises, Hitler summoned the young architect who had finished Goebbels' apartment in such record time and appointed him Troost's liaison man in the capital.

As soon as the rebuilding work began, Hitler came on site almost every day from his temporary accommodation on the next floor up. When he arrived Speer would give him a progress report, after which Hitler would turn to the workmen. He moved among them with impressive ease, handing out praise, asking questions and urging haste.

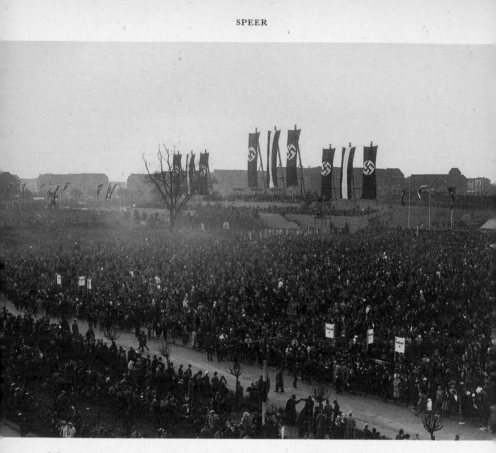

When in April 1933 Speer saw the first designs for a May Day rally at the Tempelhofer Feld in Berlin, he quipped that they reminded him of a village rifle club event. Asked by Hanke if he could do better, he sketched a simple setting lined with flags. It met with Hitler's and Goebbels' approval.

He hardly seemed to notice Speer. However, one day Hitler asked him out of the blue if he would like to have lunch with him. Speer hesitated for a moment because a trowelful of wet mortar had fallen on his jacket during his inspection. But Hitler said he would put that right.

He sent for one of his jackets to be fetched from his apartment upstairs. Having made sure it fitted, he entered the dining-room accompanied by his guest; ten of his closer courtiers were assembled there already. Goebbels was the first to voice his surprise at finding Speer in their midst and he noticed before the others that the new arrival wore on his jacket the badge with the golden Party eagle which was reserved for the Führer alone. Angrily he asked the meaning of this, but Hitler pacified him by saying that it was quite all right. As if to add a hidden reproof to his answer he invited Speer to sit next to him.

At table he drew him into lengthy conversation, noted by those present with some surprise. For the first time Speer had a foretaste of those conflicting sensations that would perhaps be his fate henceforth. Euphoria alternated with nervousness, amazement and happiness. But at the same time he sensed the envy and malevolence around him, he felt the suspicion that he aroused by the rare distinction accorded to him by Hitler. As he left the room he thought that the door to the innermost circle was now open and that everything else was now up to him alone.

What was to hold him back? Of course, the temptation was irresistible. True, the grand style, into which he was to slip at Hitler's court, did not mean much to him, and power and splendour held little attraction for him as yet. Contrary to the assertions of most of his critics, Speer was no opportunist always out for his own advantage. Certainly the wasted years that lay behind him had been extremely discouraging, and the letters and advertisements to which he never received a reply had undermined his self-confidence. Yet Hitler's show of favour had not made him feel that he had reached a turning point or been faced with a political, let alone a moral, decision. 'After years of frustrated efforts' he was simply 'thirsting for action', ambitious and impatient, he confessed. 'For a commission to build a great building I would have sold my soul like Faust.'[28]

That was the point of breach. For years to come Speer saw himself merely as an architect who stood outside politics. This self-deception was what made him and his career typical. Along with millions of 'non-political' Germans he had insisted on the separation of professional and political tasks in the face of occasional unrest. On the way to the NSDAP office two years earlier he had, significantly, made himself believe that he was not joining a party but that he was following the call of a charismatic leader who stood above all ephemeral squabbles and bound the nation together by holding its higher interests in trust.

This error was compounded by the general impression that Hitler's slogans sounded strangely 'non-political' or at least removed from reality. It was largely that tone which made them irresistible to Speer and to many others. The contradictory mixture of nationalism and the grandiloquent call for fraternization, rigorous order, anti-modernism and technological ambition encompassed so many diverse feelings that most contemporaries saw Hitler and National Socialism as the force that would preserve Germany in its familiar shape and, simultaneously, lead it towards a better future.

Added to this were the opportunities which were soon open to all. Ever since his visit to Hitler's apartment Speer felt they had come more within his reach than anyone else's. He was twenty-eight, and all of a sudden he was being offered jobs, he was earning a reputation and even fame. Speer was enough of an artist to succumb to the temptation of the opportunities which unexpectedly presented themselves to him.

The only thing that might possibly have countered this were the weakened values of that middle-class world to which he still felt he belonged years later during his detention at Spandau prison. But they only affected the values he upheld in his personal life, so that nothing that had happened since the Nazis had seized power had alarmed him. Despite some arbitrary measures, the country was clearly overcoming its crisis. Order was gradually returning and the hardships which could not be overlooked were no longer the same hardships since confidence had been restored. What, then, should have aroused his mistrust when Hitler invited him to lunch?

Later Speer repeatedly observed that he had been well aware of a questionable and at times even unsettling atmosphere surrounding the dictator. But these misgivings, in so far as he ever experienced them in those early days, were swept aside by his romantic inclinations and by Hitler's aura of strangeness and unpredictability which, if anything, enhanced his allure. Not until much later, towards the end of his imprisonment at Spandau, did he realize what dangerous territory he had strayed into. On rereading Thomas Mann's *Buddenbrooks* his thoughts had gone back to his own family, to the standards which had made them all feel so secure, and to their unwavering instincts: 'They had no doubts whatsoever', he wrote, 'about right and wrong, good and evil. It is inconceivable to think of my father or grandfather in the circle of Hitler and his cronies.'[29]

He then realized for the first time that they had drawn their security from the middle-class world. Although he had only known that world in its decline and, as he believed, had sometimes suffered from it, he had never hated it, let alone fought against it. He had never been infected by the anti-bourgeois fever, which was one of the opiates of the age. The only outward expression of his rebellion against his parental world was in his careless style of dressing and his informal manner. No stronger judgement about it survives than his remark that he found that world not to 'his liking'.[30]

This oddly feeble protest explains, at least to some degree, his most striking characteristic: a lack of resolution, of knowing where he stood, and of passion. In a character such as his there was no room for principles. From one day to the next, he jettisoned all the rules that Tessenow had taught him, from the pathos of sobriety and mistrust of mere effect to the false grandiloquence which he now adopted. At the heart of it all lay the faintness of his convictions. Just as he had failed to notice that he had slid into politics, so he was evidently unaware of the bridge he had crossed as an architect.

Of course, Speer was not alone in his contempt for principles or for the arbitrary way in which beliefs were expounded and retracted. Soapbox prophets proclaiming the dawn of a new age, noisily calling for strong convictions because convictions had ceased to mean much, were two a penny in those years. People were changing allegiances as they did shirts and nearly every biography of that time contains some conversion or other. One need only look at the mass desertion in 1933 from the Communist battle groups to yesterday's enemy, the Brown camp, and it became apparent again in 1945 when the Hitler regime fell apart. Suddenly everyone sought to distance themselves, all those former protestations of beliefs and all those oaths of loyalty were drowned in silence as if they had never existed.

In the end the bourgeoisie fell victim to its profound doubts in the justice and truth of its own cause. The vehemence with which, only one generation earlier, all the world had railed against that way of life was proof of how its ideas, its values and its *raison d'être* were as deeply rooted as the resentment it caused. Admittedly, the often eccentric way in which literature, the theatre and the arts dealt with the crisis of the bourgeoisie was a product of its own intellect. Albert Bassermann, one of the greatest actors of the day, who came from the same Mannheim haute bourgeoisie as Speer, scored some of his greatest successes on the stage with characters from the anti-bourgeois repertoire: that string of secretly moribund strong men who had been broken by their extravagance, colossal greed and the yawning emptiness behind it all. Yet Bassermann openly rejected the unreasonable demand of the new rulers that, at the end of a performance, he should step up to the apron of the stage and salute Hitler in the former imperial box with a raised arm. Despite the efforts of the regime to keep him, he chose exile.[31]

But that was the world of yesterday. Those now in the ascendant were often not aware of the conflict which troubled their elders or of facing a crucial decision. They were, in a sense, beyond such subtle distinctions. The new generation, like Speer, no longer attacked the bourgeois world because they had quite simply forgotten it, because it and everything it stood for no longer meant anything to them.

When he moved into Hitler's circle Speer had felt that 'something swooped me up off the ground at the time [and] wrenched me from all my roots.'[32]

Chapter Two
WITHIN THE
INNER CIRCLE

As in any relationship it is hard to tell what brought Hitler and Speer together towards the end of 1933. There is no doubt that Speer was elated when his inkling became a certainty that the almighty dictator not only favoured him but positively courted him. Invitations to his table became more and more frequent and soon he was also being asked to accompany Hitler on his walks. To begin with the tone was noncommittal, but gradually these meetings turned into discussions and then developed into more of a personal exchange of ideas: on architecture and its confused state ever since it had been affected by the subjectivism of the visual arts, on the suitability of glass for industrial but not for official buildings, on the eccentricities of the Bauhaus, on townplanning in general and, more specifically, on individual projects such as a new Reichstag building.

Although Hitler was easily agitated when the subject turned to 'factory art' or 'vulgar architecture', the hours Speer spent with him were harmonious and good-humoured. Occasionally the telephone would ring around midnight. An adjutant would enquire if Speer had any new plans to submit; the Führer needed diversion. Something of his initial rapture was apparent whenever Speer recollected those meetings and the increasing attention which Hitler showed towards him. It went far beyond the conscientious displays of affection in his relationships with his friends and even with his wife.

Various critics have detected 'traces of an erotic motif' in the relationship between Hitler and Speer,[1] with architecture providing the common ground for discussion and agreement. Indeed the strange friendship very soon transcended professional amity. It developed into an attachment of a kind unfamiliar to both men, and beset with many inhibitions. In later years, when the untroubled days of architectural dreaming and planning were over, the friendship was occasionally placed under considerable strain. But it endured right up to the very last hours, when Speer returned to a Berlin engulfed by flames to say goodbye to the man who, he believed, had put the world at his feet and then destroyed it.

Hitler's role in this relationship was easily the stranger of the two. This was the only time he overcame the emotional disorder which left his life so conspicuously devoid of human beings, in spite of the constant mass rallies. The attachments Hitler managed to form never surmounted that wall of coldness and unapproachability which he believed to be a necessary part of his historic mission. Whatever emotions he was capable of, were always crippled in some way. Throughout his life he never had a single selfless relationship and those who were closest to him were only the least distant, with the possible exception of his niece Geli Raubal, who shot herself in Hitler's Munich flat on Prinzregentenstrasse in the early thirties. It is significant that of the six women who figured – marginally – in his life, five died by suicide or at least attempted to do so.[2]

Hitler tried to find a kind of substitute in his encounters with the masses. The idea that his rhetorical performances not only roused them but also satisfied some deeper urge in him is confirmed not least by the number of speaking appearances he made during the so-called period of struggle. In those years he would address crowds, which he was fond of equating with 'the female', up to fifteen times a day. It is also significant that towards the end, when the desperate war situation forbade public appearances, he progressively deteriorated and seemed to all eye-witnesses a 'spectral ruin'. Not surprisingly the most apposite descriptions of Hitler as an orator have used terms with sexual connotations.

The ardour with which he entered the tightly packed ranks, the shrill shrieks of expectation which accompanied his progress through the crowds and heightened the charged atmosphere in the hall, revealed the copulative character of these occasions before Hitler had even started to speak. Then, after the probing ritual of his hesitant opening sentences, he triggered the first storms of applause which roused him from his trance, lifting him higher and higher, up to passages which seemed to flow as though he felt liberated; he then accelerated, urged and drew things out, clenched his fists in front of his face, bringing them down with his eyes closed, and pointed his index finger as he named the culprits and traitors as if in a frenzy, until finally, shaking and his voice breaking, he reached the spasms of his concluding phrases. All this led

Nuremberg Party Rally, 1934. One of the highlights of the event was the moment when Hitler, followed at a respectful distance by SA and SS leaders and accompanied by the sounds of a funeral march specially composed by Ernst 'Putzi' Hanfstaengl, solemnly strode over to the Heroes' Memorial in the Luitpoldhain. The liturgy of the ceremony was devised by Hitler and Speer.

many a contemporary who tried to describe the obscene magic which emanated from Hitler himself, to make comparisons with the sexual antics of witches on *Walpurgis Night*. The images we have of him after his exit, crouching in some artist's dressing room, bathed in perspiration, weary and with a vacant gaze are part of the whole picture. *Post coitum triste.*[3]

The intoxication he sought on the rostrum compensated for many things, above all his need for contact and arousal which he could not imagine without an element of lustful violence. In that respect Speer really was an exception, unlike Hitler's intimate friend Ernst Röhm, or Eva Braun and many others. When asked what had brought him together with the novice architect Hitler always gave an ambiguous answer. But he could not have overlooked how far removed the imma-ture Tessenow disciple was from the 'official style' of Troost, especially since Speer had been unsuccessful in the summer of 1933 with his entry for a competition to build a 'Reich Leader School of the NSDAP'. To

Speer he merely remarked, with striking matter-of-factness: 'You attracted my attention during our rounds. I was looking for an architect to whom I could entrust my building plans. He had to be young; for as you know these plans extend far into the future. I need someone who will be able to continue after my death with the authority I have conferred on him. I saw that man in you.'[4]

Perhaps Hitler thought he recognized himself in the attractive young man who seemed, for all his reticence, to be very confident about his own talent and who was as carefree as he was adroit and full of imagination: his alter ego, but a more effortless version, with the assurance of a good background and untainted by the malevolent hand of fate, which Hitler blamed more than anything else for shattering his dream of being an artist. Once when Speer voiced doubts about his own ability as an architect, Hitler retorted with a hint of jealousy: 'Oh, you, you would have made your way in any case!' In an article of 1939 he paid an unusual tribute, even calling him a 'genius'. Elsewhere he spoke of him as a 'kindred spirit' for whom he had always had 'the warmest human feelings'.[5] We shall see that Hitler saw in Speer not just an outstanding architect, his favourite minister and a possible successor, but also a 'friend' and conceivably his only passion, however surprising the term may seem. At any rate, Speer aroused his feelings more than anyone else and he may even have had a palliative effect on him.

What drew Speer to Hitler is much easier to determine. Those who knew him well all pointed to the burning ambition beneath his restrained exterior; they thought that his matter-of-factness was just a mask concealing his almost boundless and rarely challenged egotism.[6] Feelings of reverence for the statesman were mixed up in a tangle of emotions. Hitler's enthusiasm for architecture and his increasing power meant that Speer was not only entrusted with exceptional duties, but he soon realized that his whole *raison d'être* had received a great boost. In a revealing note Speer described the force which gripped him at that time. From the moment he met Hitler, he wrote, 'everything changed; my whole life was as if under constant high voltage'.[7]

He was undoubtedly aware that something alien was taking possession of him, something that became even more persuasive in the emotionally charged atmosphere surrounding Hitler. But, as he occasionally admitted to himself, it was not seduction. Hitler did not need to 'convert' him. Like the majority of his contemporaries, he began to find himself more and more in agreement with the new rulers as time progressed, or at least with the national and social programmes they loudly proclaimed. He continued to regard anything beyond that as 'politics', which were not his business and which, he believed, were in the best of hands with Hitler.

Speer was not so naive as to overlook some of the repulsive traits of the regime, despite the idealized image presented by the propaganda machine: the extreme pressure it exercised to subject people to submission, the way everything was enforced in the daily exercise of power, the crude and levelling determination to fuse a variegated society into a colourless mass. But such reservations were swept aside by the sense of a new beginning, which engulfed the country and soon engulfed him too. If any objections remained they disappeared with his personal advancement through Hitler which, in his own words, he came to 'need like an addict his drug'.[8] He therefore endorsed the dictatorship, the pervasive ruthlessness and the principle that Hitler's word was law. Even when 'war' or 'world dominion' were mentioned, and even when doubts and fears later surfaced about 'victory' or, failing that, 'doom', he displayed not so much alarm as a romantic vision of destiny elevated by the grandeur of the hour.[9]

In his euphoria, Speer may even have ignored Hitler's anti-Semitism, with which he soon became familiar. For many years, he recorded, he had 'regarded Hitler's mad hatred of the Jews ... as a somewhat vulgar accessory, a hangover from his days in Vienna and God only knows why he could not shake it off'. He had soon learnt to make allowances for Hitler's permanent irritability, his violent mood swings from cold fury and outrage one moment to an affable demeanour the next. Like most people he saw such outbursts as a 'tactical device for whipping up the instincts of the masses', possibly also as a means of self-persuasion, rather than as a 'matter of life and death'; some day, he expected, they would come to an end.[10]

However, Speer's ability to talk himself into something went further. He agreed with Hitler on the classical language of architecture but failed to detect any incompatabilities in the dictator's grandiose ideas on buildings. Hitler's vision had not moved on from the end of the nineteenth century, the bourgeois palaces of Vienna's Ringstrasse, the neo-Baroque theatres of Helmer and Fellner, or Charles Garnier's opera house in Paris. It was clear that Tessenow's ideas seemed decidedly contemporary compared with the garrulous eclecticism of these architects. Nevertheless Speer shared Hitler's 'rejection of the modern movement'. This bond enabled Speer to link one strand with the other, no matter

43

how contradictory, without ever feeling the 'break', let alone a 'betrayal' of his teacher. From this perspective Hitler appeared as the 'saviour of the nineteenth-century world from the disturbing world of the metropolis', against which Tessenow had also waged a lone and stubborn battle. Speer persuaded himself that with Hitler as an ally, matters might perhaps be changed at the eleventh hour.[11]

Absurd though it may seem, he worried more at the beginning about Hitler's petit-bourgeois lifestyle, the furnishings of his flat, which resembled that of a 'schoolmaster' or 'branch manager of a savings bank' than he did about all his political excesses. Speer came to know that soulless 'Vertico' taste both in Munich's Prinzregentenstrasse and at the Berghof, complete with a canary in a gilt cage. The room was full of 'richly carved, solid oak library furniture, books behind glass, cushions embroidered with delicate inscriptions or hearty party greetings', Speer recorded. 'A bust of Richard Wagner stood in one corner, idyllic paintings of the Munich school hung on the walls in heavy gold frames … it smelt of baked oil and slightly sour rubbish.'[12] Speer's contemptuous, almost sarcastic description was not so much due to the snobbery of the upper-middle-class son. It disturbed him that these furnishings belied Hitler's alleged artistic taste and negated the notion of an 'aesthetic state' which shaped their dreams and slowly maturing plans.

Each found in the other what he missed in himself, admiring, in a form of transferred self-love, the ideal image of himself. Various observers have described the strangely excited, mutually stimulating harmony which characterized their meetings: Hitler certainly never seemed more relaxed and free from the pose of the 'great man' which he otherwise adopted. Speer later claimed that he had never been sure what Hitler really felt for him, how much sympathy was involved, how calculating Hitler was being, or to what extent it was just his familiar play-acting that turned nearly all his shows of emotion into tactical manoeuvres or unprompted deceit. But during the early years observers already noted that Speer always appeared the cooler of the two and the one who had the upper hand emotionally. He always kept his distance even towards Hitler. Unlike nearly all the members of Hitler's close entourage, Speer was never servile or undignified. In the early thirties the writer Günther Weisenborn saw Hitler with some of his cronies at the Künstlerhaus in Munich. He has left a vivid description of Speer's reserved behaviour:

It was a strange spectacle. When the person they called the Führer and who that evening was playing the simple man of the people with

44

a look of kindly wonderment in his eyes ... spoke a few words, the courtiers sitting around him leaned forward obsequiously, all fixed on the same point: the despot's mouth with that smudge of a moustache above it. It was as though a warm wind of humility had silently bent those proud stalks, so that all I could see were the folds of blubber at the napes of our country's leaders. But that was not all. Chubby-faced Hitler received this wave of servility. He in turn leaned discreetly towards Speer, who sat to his right and occasionally uttered a word of polite boredom. Hitler passed all the homage that billowed his way on to Speer, Speer seemed to be a kind of hero, a beloved; it was he who raked in the tributes as if they were small change.[13]

Hitler may well have noticed the special position which Speer claimed and received in the inner circle from the outset. At any rate he was soon appointed head of the Building Department on Rudolf Hess's staff. In this capacity he was provided with a uniform which not only made him one of the Party's brown-uniformed officials but also put an end to his civilian status. A short while later, on 30 January 1934, the first anniversary of the Seizure of Power, he took over the 'Beauty of Work' office which had the task of providing better hygienic and aesthetic conditions at the workplace. Speer applied himself to the mission with the zeal of one who has unexpectedly risen to rank and influence. The task was not an invention of the Nazi regime. 'Beauty of Work' was based on ideas which had been developed some time ago in several industrial countries, combining them with various notions about the quality of life and, in a wider sense, the aims of the 'garden city' movement. But little had come of these endeavours hitherto and it was only the general feeling of a new beginning, with new men taking the helm, that gave them a fresh impetus. Speer's alacrity was all the greater as the aims coincided with the antipathy that he had felt since his student days for industrialization, urbanization and the uglification of the world. In years to come it was this aspect of his work that appeased him whenever he thought that he might have deserted his much-admired teacher Heinrich Tessenow. For Tessenow was himself associated with the reformist efforts of the period, and had played a leading part in the creation of an extensive garden suburb in Dresden-Hellerau.

In agreement with the 'enterprise leaders', as the entrepreneurs were now called, Speer immediately began to remove clutter from factory yards, bringing more daylight into workshops, designing more attractive tools, simplifying production processes, improving industrial safety and even developing a new factory architecture. In existing factories he set up canteens, showers, break rooms, and sports facilities in fulfilment of all the new drives promoted with slogans such as 'German everyday life must be more beautiful!', 'Let nature into your factories!', or 'Clean workers in clean factories'. The companies that distinguished themselves in this campaign were awarded the title 'NS Model Enterprise'.

The 'Beauty of Work' office was one way in which the new power-holders were redeeming their social welfare promises in a way that impressed the masses. At the same time it lent credibility to the melo-dramatic slogans designed to boost efforts. The same applied to the settle-ment projects, the autobahn construction, the numerous aid schemes and above all the 'Strength Through Joy' leisure organization, which had its own cruise-liners, organized concert and theatre visits for the masses, promoted folklore groups and developed holiday programmes. Initially all these enterprises met with widespread scepticism, a relic of the polemics of political opponents who had been silenced in the mean-time. But the charges against the 'reactionary' Hitlerites were not yet forgotten and the Nazi ideology certainly nourished that scepticism with its muddled emphasis on customs, blood and soil, and its general espousal of pre-industrial patterns. However, the regime also had a manifestly 'modern' side, that aimed at an egalitarian society beyond the anachronistic class struggle and courted the workers with state welfare programmes. Before long, even convinced former left-wingers stopped being refractory and accepted that the rule of the new men could not be seen as the domination of one class over all others. Speer always prided himself on his contribution to 'Beauty of Work'. It met his concept of 'socialism both modern and German', which was gradually taking shape.[14]

The wide acclaim he received for his new tasks made it even more difficult for Speer to be aware of his own errors. In this respect, too, Speer was typical of the muddled thinking to which so many suc-cumbed. The welfare measures, more than anything else, paved the way for the success of the regime. No one could or would see that in reality they were but one facet of the package which promised all things to all people. The regime proclaimed the reconciliation of nationalism and socialism, of the old-established order and mass society; it brought about a revolution under the mantle of tradition and combined its hatred of the Church with the perpetual invocation of the 'Almighty'. It was this reversal of all concepts, which boasted that it had overcome the great conflicts of the century by a 'Third Way', that further confused

46

questions of right and wrong in the minds of the people and almost totally disguised the real drive of those now in power towards war, expansion and 'racial cleansing'. The Third Reich, at least in its first few years, meant many different and even incompatible things to many people. None of the traps set by its leaders proved as effective as this one.

Speer also trimmed his own view. At that time he was profoundly convinced that all Hitler's thoughts and actions were directed towards peace and the crowning of his string of political successes with fame as the social leader of his people and their architect and patron. Whenever Hitler's time permitted, Speer and he visited studios and artists' workshops, Hitler having often worked himself into a state of impatient and excited anticipation for hours beforehand. What impressed Speer most was the reverence which the dictator showed to the architects and sculptors. At that time his favourite artist was without doubt Troost: 'What luck that I made this man's acquaintance,' he declared more than once. Troost had in fact led him away from the pompous cosiness favoured by the *Gründerzeit*, as the period of rapid industrial expansion in the early 1870s was called. Instead he guided Hitler towards the heavy neo-classicism which became the hallmark of public architecture under the regime. But Troost's influence did not last. He died on 21 January 1934 after a short illness. The extent to which Speer's standing had risen over the few weeks that he had been part of the dictator's inner circle is revealed by a small incident. When Speer entered the propaganda ministry on the day Troost died, he met State Secretary Walther Funk, who, 'a long cigar in his round face', greeted him with the words: 'Congratulations! Now you're the number one!'[15]

Troost's death brought Speer even closer to Hitler. Soon he found himself invited to the semi-private gatherings at the Munich Osteria, the Carlton Tea Rooms, or to Hitler's then still modest timber chalet on the Obersalzberg; he was asked to the parties of the Bruckmanns in Leopoldstrasse and the Bechsteins, who had patronized Hitler when he was a young demagogue and remained loyal to him ever since. Much the same applied to Winifred Wagner. Whenever Hitler passed Bayreuth on his way between Berlin and Munich, the convoy of cars stopped at Bad Berneck. In the early evening Hitler would then drive over to the Villa Wahnfried, alone, not returning until the early morning, always 'strangely elated' and even 'blissful', as Speer has recorded.[16] As they continued in the open car, past the crowds lining the roads, Speer was assigned the one spare seat in the Führer's car.

For a long time Paul Ludwig Troost was Hitler's favourite architect. He had designed a number of Party buildings in the Königsplatz in Munich, as well as the 'House of German Art'. When he died in January 1934 Speer's rise began.

Mesmerized, he and the rest of the company registered the cheers which surged up everywhere and the shower of flowers which deluged the convoy. Often it was difficult to get through as Hitler leant far over the windscreen, seizing outstretched hands left and right and shouting encouragements, always condescending and cheerful towards children and old comrades. When they stopped for a break, he would sit on the grass, chatting or lost in thought, while his corpulent major-domo, Artur Kannenberg, played solemn melodies on his accordion.[17]

Cosy images of this kind swept away many lingering doubts and gave the regime the certainty that it was not only in power but that the majority of the population stood behind it. No government had achieved that before, and the powers that be proclaimed their achievement triumphantly. As was observed over and over again with astonishment, they had not only overcome unemployment within a few months, but also generated an economic upswing that was only partly due to the fading of the worldwide depression. This striking turn of events had more to do with an intuitive policy of job-provision programmes and with the psychological atmosphere, which could be convincingly associated with the new masters. The regime could moreover argue that it had liberated the state from its undignified role as the plaything of special interest groups, that it had restored Germany's international reputation and achieved that internal unity which was described, in its own advertisements, as the 'miracle of German *Volkwerdung*', the becoming of a nation. Admittedly all these successes had been achieved at considerable cost: the political ostracizing and harassment of minorities and the loss of freedom. But the misfortune of the minorities was that they were rapidly diminishing in importance, and that a growing majority, especially of the workforce, soon saw the difference from the past 'not so much in terms of lost rights as in gained work'.[18]

That was by no means all. The fundamental change of outlook was underpinned by the psycho-technical skills of the new rulers. With unparalleled powers of invention they created a never-ending chain of great, often idyllic or triumphant scenarios. The theatrical demagogy they invented, or at any rate perfected, created a permanent mood of festivity. There were endless rallies, festive hours, forests of flags, processions and games, and fiery beacons with which the people seemed to be paying homage to themselves when in fact they were paying homage to their leaders. There was a whole calendar of ceremonial feast-days, operated and constantly extended by a specially created 'Office for Festive, Leisure and Ceremonial Events'. The National Socialist Year began on 30 January, the day of the Seizure of Power, and ended on 9 November with a commemoration of the March to the Feldherrnhalle and of the 'Martyrs of the Movement', whose names were read out for a 'Last Roll-Call' in a sombre apotheosis.

The highlight of the regime's calendar were the annual Nuremberg Party Rallies, held in the autumn. After Speer's success with the May Day celebration on the Tempelhofer Feld in Berlin, it seemed only logical to make him the 'Chief Designer' for these spectacles that went on for several days. Once again he demonstrated an exceptional ability to achieve grand effects. In front of the massive platform structures he placed huge blocks of men in brown and black uniforms, arranged to create a suggestive geometrical pattern of narrow and wide aisles. Unsettled as it was by disorder and anarchy, the spirit of the age found it hard to resist these images. The wide flight of steps in front of the main platform was flanked by two Party eagles. Through the middle of these hundreds of thousands ran the stone ribbon of the 'Führer's road' along which Hitler, with the leaders of the SA and SS at a respectful

In 1934 Hitler entrusted Speer with the planning of the entire Nuremberg Party Rally terrain, along with its processional setting. This included the Zeppelinfeld, shown here from the south-east. It was framed on three sides by a total of 34 flag platforms.

distance behind him, strode to the smoking pylons in front of the memorial in the Luitpoldhain (Luitpold spinney), to the sound of a specially composed funeral march honouring the dead. There were flags everywhere: for the rhythmical subdivision of excessively long lines, to break up the scene dominated by hundreds of thousands of monotonous uniforms, or simply as fluttering festoons to heighten the circensian mood.

The Reich Party Rallies also produced what was probably Speer's most ingenious and perhaps his only lasting idea. In order to spare the audience the sight of the unprepossessing office-holders, who had grown corpulent in their new jobs, he had suggested to Hitler that as many of the events as possible be moved to the evening or the night. This enabled him to use on a far larger scale the light beams that had proved so effective at Tempelhof. An official report records how, after Hitler's arrival towards eight o'clock, 'the darkness was suddenly lit in a flood of white' by columns of light surging from one hundred and fifty projectors posted all around at twelve-metre intervals. 'In the night sky shrouded in black-grey' their vertical beams met under the cloud cover 'to form a blazing square crown'. Simultaneously the main tribune was 'plunged into blinding brightness'. On the lateral pillars 'flames licked up from large dishes', while from all sides 'over thirty thousand banners' streamed into the arena, 'their silver points and tassels flashing in the light'.[19]

These famous domes of light, rising as they did eight to ten kilometres into the sky, made Speer one of the 'fathers of light architecture'. Sometimes, he recalled, a cloud would pass at a great height through the cone of the beams, transporting those present into an almost otherworldly state, as if carried by magic to one of the 'crystal fantasy castles of the Middle Ages' or into a 'Gothic cathedral'.[20] The effect of this unusual theatrical device was due not only to the need of all mass societies for spectacular and profoundly memorable images. The reasons for Hitler's admiration lie beyond that. The concentration of an immeasurable host of men in uniform under a massive 'pillared edifice of light' was one of the most telling symbols of the deeper truth about Hitler and the regime he shaped: a sense of being threatened, which kept reality at bay with intoxicating displays of pomp and circumstance and which nurtured its aggressions behind impressive stage-sets. One of the early observers of the movement described its character as 'boastfulness on the run'.[21] But even those who did not share this psychology found themselves, almost against their will, bowled over by the theatrical effect. The French ambassador in Berlin, Robert Coulondre, confessed like many others among the steadily increasing stream of visitors from abroad, that the mixture of military magic, mystique and exaltation had, for a moment, converted him to National Socialism; and the British ambassador, Sir Neville Henderson, spoke admiringly of 'cathedrals of ice'.[22]

Although he was one of the producers, Speer himself was undoubtedly gripped by these overwhelming emotions: seducer and seduced at the same time. 'I was swept away', he admitted, adding that he would not have hesitated to follow Hitler 'blindly … anywhere'. He insisted that the relationship that had developed between them had 'resembled that of an architect toward an admired patron rather than of a follower toward a political leader'.[23] But the one could not be separated from the other, particularly since 'blind' devotion in matters of architecture would be nonsense. Not until much later did he realize that, whenever the regime was accused of persecution or breaking treaties, he

51

subconsciously began to search for justifications and that soon he had joined the chorus of yes-men. It would be more accurate to say that he had completely submitted to Hitler's ideas and goals. And yet he was in a position to be impartial, as Hitler evidently did not regard him as being among the followers who had submitted to his psychological control. He certainly treated Speer as an equal in all building matters, often even bowing to his judgement. Looking back on their conversations on architecture, Speer was unable to recall 'a single case' when Hitler had compelled him to accept his view.[24]

The professional respect Hitler showed him seems to have enhanced Speer's self-assurance still further. No one could fail to notice that Hitler invariably found almost unlimited time for him, especially after he had consolidated his power in the summer of 1934 when, on Hindenburg's death, he had appropriated the prerogatives of the Reich President in a carefully planned coup. Two months later at the Reich Party Rally he proclaimed the end of the 'nervous nineteenth century', adding with the assurance of consolidated power: 'There will not be another revolution in Germany for the next thousand years!'[25]

But the new sense of security dissipated the excitement and stimulation which had emanated from the Chancellorship, his official residence and Bismarck's desk, and Hitler relapsed into the idle ways of earlier years. Particularly on his visits to Munich, which now became more frequent again, he drifted through the studios, restaurants and familiar cafés of the city, and whiled away the hours on building sites and at the opera, always with a trail of half-artists, veterans of the early struggle and uniformed bodyguards in tow, accompanied by his photographer Heinrich Hoffmann, his driver Julius Schreck, Martin Bormann and more often than not Albert Speer. Within six months Hitler attended six performances of *The Merry Widow*, on another occasion he surprised his entourage with carefully coloured stage designs for Richard Wagner's *Tristan* and for all the scenes of *The Ring of the Nibelung*. He could talk for hours about the production problems of *The Master Singers of Nuremberg*, right down to the question of 'what combination of lighting would be best for the moonlight scenes at the end of the second act' and what the gabled houses facing the shoemaker's shop should look like. And then, according to reports, he found time to reread the writings of Karl May which ran to nearly seventy volumes. He was fond of recalling how, in his first few weeks as Chancellor, he had had to devote considerable efforts to free himself from the grip of the bureaucracy, but then he had put an 'end to that nonsense once and for all'.[26] He found

Speer's most effective invention was undoubtedly the 'light domes' produced in the night sky by up to 150 anti-aircraft searchlights, creating an atmosphere of magic, mystery and exaltation. Many guests at the Nuremburg rallies, including foreign ones, were so impressed by the spectacle that they were prepared to overlook some of the regime's more repulsive features.

the routine duties of his office increasingly irksome and frequently spent no more than an hour or two a day on them.

This lax lifestyle of Hitler's, governed by moods and often trivial whims, helped convince not only Speer but the general public that a period of tranquillity and of purposeful, if vigorously enforced, order had arrived after the stormy and unlawful beginning of the regime. Whenever the opportunity arose, as it did with the Olympics of 1936, Hitler made every effort to replace the 'horror image' of a Nazi empire that was frantically rearming with the picture of a peaceful and reconciled nation, headed by a politician who saw his mission not so much in the acquisition and consolidation of unlimited power but in the promotion of works of culture. In November 1934 he told a French visitor that he hoped in this way to establish for himself a more durable memorial than any famous general. That was precisely what Speer wanted to believe. He saw himself as someone who had been able to contribute to the erection of that memorial. When, around that time, Hitler first met Speer's wife he assured her, with some solemnity: 'Your husband is going to erect buildings for me such as have not been created for four thousand years.'[27]

It was a dazzling opportunity, which completely intoxicated Speer, no matter how disciplined his demeanour continued to be. Right to the end he was unable to say why he should have turned it down.[28] The way he saw it, Hitler was indisputably great, a transformer of the world, yet in spite of adulation from all sides not without attractive human traits. In the literature of black Romanticism there is an ambiguous creature that blinds everyone with its seductive powers and its easy victories over men and circumstances. At the same time it radiates a feeling of unrest which no one can explain and a destructive force the purposes of which is a mystery. Only at the catastrophic end does it emerge that this figure is none other than evil itself, which, contrary to well-established iconography, appears not in a monstrous shape but more often in an enchanting, even erotically alluring guise.

It might be objected that this picture does not apply to Hitler during the first years of power, Hitler surrounded by milling crowds, reclining on the grass, or even Hitler the enthusiastic patron of architecture; that despite the winning ways he could adopt he was too vulgar and his almost hunchbacked profile too obvious, however skilfully he disguised it. But his irritable nature, his fits of anger and blind rages have been emphasized all too often, while the 'Austrian charm' that he could turn on at will has been overlooked. Speer, like so many others, only saw the gloss, not realizing that it took but one 'turn of the screw' to reveal the hidden side of Hitler's personality in all its coldness and eccentricity. That was exactly what Speer was talking about when he told Captain Klein – one of the American officers who interrogated him in May 1945 – that he understood nothing of the charisma of a man like Hitler.

As always, things were moving fast. By the beginning of 1934 the commission to design the central flight of steps at the so-called Zeppelin

Field for the Nuremberg Party Rally had been given to Speer, in place of Paul Ludwig Troost. No sooner had Hitler approved his plan than Speer was appointed architect for the entire project. In between he had to do occasional jobs, like arranging a Harvest Festival on the Bückeberg near Hamlyn, model huts for the workers employed on the construction of the Reich motorways, or advise on local Party events. Many of these requests, which flooded in all of a sudden, were unmistakably designed only to attract Hitler's attention. But, no matter how insignificant they seemed, they flattered his ambition and his increasing craving for recognition.

The summer of 1934 represented a kind of caesura. The million-strong army of the SA had grown restless with disappointment at the 'miserable half-measures' of the legal seizure of power. After its violent elimination, referred to as the 'crushing of Röhm's revolt' in the veiled language of the regime, Hitler gave orders for the Supreme SA Leadership to be moved from Munich to Berlin. He wanted to bring it under stricter control after his experiences with Röhm's high-handedness. As the new headquarters of his Practorian Guard Hitler had envisaged the Borsig Palace, which at that time still housed the office of Vice-Chancellor Franz von Papen. When opposition came from those quarters Hitler simply instructed Speer to occupy the building with a team of workmen, move all papers and furniture out into the street and start on the conversion.

Before the eyes of the flabbergasted officials Speer and his men forced their way in. While inspecting the rooms he discovered a large bloodstain on the floor of one of the offices. The blood had barely dried. It must have come from Herbert von Bose, von Papen's private secretary, shot during the indiscriminate murder spree. This was the first time Speer found himself in direct contact with one of the atrocities of the regime, and his own occupation of the palace merely continued the civil-war-like practices of recent days. But already this kind of thing no longer worried him and the black spot in Bose's room was suddenly no longer a trace of blood but a concomitant of a policy which was no concern of his. Even so he felt relieved when soon afterwards he was commissioned to restore the Tannenberg memorial in East Prussia, which commemorated Hindenburg's and Ludendorff's victory over the Russians at the end of August 1914; the restoration was for a ceremony in honour of the deceased Reich President.

One thing led to another. The official commissions which Speer now received without any effort on his part included the refurbishment of the German embassy in London. At the last minute he began to rework the designs for the Olympic Stadium in Berlin, where the games were to open in the summer of 1936. The architect, Werner March, had envisaged a steel and concrete structure with extensive use of glass and enamel, but when he inspected the shell Hitler was beside himself with fury and threatened to cancel the Games. He would not dream of entering a modern 'glass box' of this kind and would not therefore open the Games. Speer thereupon hurriedly removed all the glass, faced the concrete with natural stone and added cornices everywhere until eventually both March and Hitler approved the changes. It is a measure of how Speer's reputation had risen that around that time Göring asked Hitler if he could commission Speer to refurbish his apartment. Although his residence had only just undergone a lavish reconstruction, Göring now believed that he owed it to his rank to employ no less a man than Albert Speer. Without even consulting Speer, he 'dragged the greatest man … Germany has after the Führer', as he intimated not much later, into his apartment behind Leipziger Platz 'like a piece of booty'. 'It must turn out like the Führer's place' was his instruction.[29]

After the many casual jobs which he had declined, time and time again, Nuremberg was the first real commission: he proved himself to be astonishingly adaptable in moving from the formal language of his teacher to Troost's colonnaded façades, rows of pillars, his massive dimensions and angular cornices. Although he later professed that he had sought a synthesis between Troost's classicism and Tessenow's simplicity, he had in fact gone over to Troost entirely, switching from the camp of architects to that of building propagandists.[30]

The Nuremberg terrain measured over sixteen square kilometres, with two deployment areas in the Zeppelinfeld and the Luitpoldhain, as well as the so-called Märzfeld, the *champs de mars* for military manoeuvres, and the Congress Hall, modelled on Rome's Colosseum. It had been commissioned before Speer's appointment from the architects Ludwig and Franz Ruff, whom Hitler had come to know through the Franconian Gauleiter Julius Streicher. In 1926 the Party Rally of the NSDAP had still been held in Weimar. But in the following year Hitler moved it to Nuremberg and announced that this 'annual general meeting' of the Party would thenceforth be held in the ancient Reich city 'for ever'. As the venerable 'symbol of the first Reich of the Germans' the city with its half-timbered houses, its city gates and its Gothic churches would conjure up the image of a familiar German world, far removed from all the horrors of modernity, and serve as a reminder of the pride of an era whose greatness Hitler promised to restore.

This was the starting point for Speer's master plan. Its central feature was the so-called Grand Avenue, a triumphal way, one kilometre long, paved with granite slabs and entered by a majestic portal. It united the buildings and deployment areas into an ensemble, keeping a kind of equilibrium between them. The portal was flanked by two high-pillared obelisks such as were to be erected at some autobahn entrances. Looking ahead into the distance one's gaze would fall on the silhouette of the old Nuremberg Castle. It served as a link between the theatrical parades and the concept of the Reich, giving, as it were, the blessing of the past to the new Germany and lending it legitimacy. After the *Anschluss* of Austria, similar considerations led to the decision to bring the Reich jewels – consisting of the crown, the sceptre and the orb – from the Vienna Hofburg to Nuremberg, where they had been kept until 1796.

The Märzfeld lay at the end of the Grand Avenue. It was surrounded by a steeply stepped enclosure for 160,000 spectators, with a huge goddess of victory, fourteen metres higher than the Statue of Liberty in New York, towering above it. To one side was the Luitpold arena, the scene of the annual ceremony in honour of the dead. Towards the entrance of the area was the Zeppelinfeld, framed by thirty-four towers, each bearing six flags to convey an impression of movement. With the Tempelhof solution in mind Speer had originally bounded the end wall by a wooden tribune with a German eagle between vertically stretched flags. But at the beginning of 1934 he was instructed to replace the construction by a tribune built of limestone.

To one side of the Grand Avenue was a stepped stone massif from which Hitler, surrounded by his generals, intended to take the salute of the Wehrmacht. Opposite stood a pillared hall which also provided access to the huge central edifice dominating the whole area: the exterior of the horseshoe-shaped Great Stadium was faced with red granite. It could hold more than 400,000 spectators and with a built-up space of nearly nine million cubic metres it was more than three times the size of one of the largest buildings in history, the pyramid of Cheops. The total cost amounted to eight hundred million marks, but the sum contained numerous, possibly deliberate, errors of calculation. Thus ten million marks were budgeted for the Congress Hall, but in fact over two hundred million had already been spent when construction was

The centre-piece of the Nuremberg Party Rally terrain was to have been the 'German Stadium', a gigantic building clad in granite. Just before the foundation stone was laid during the 1937 Rally, Hitler, along with Speer (right) and the Supreme SA Leader Viktor Lutze (second from right), inspected the model of the proposed building. As the Nuremberg terrain was to be a 'place of pilgrimage', the Minister for the Churches, Hanns Kerrl, who also acted as president of the 'User Association Reich Party Rally Terrain', was present too.

suspended in the war. It was typical that the publication of building costs was strictly prohibited.[31]

The massive stone blocks, sloping at the pedestals, the flights of stairs and the flanking stone cubes made the structures for the Party Rally seem like oversized altar architecture, and it was no accident these constructions were so often reminiscent of Pergamon or the sacred buildings of the early Middle Eastern world. But they also suggested fortresses, images of unassailable power and the disciplinary effect these had on the masses. The same purpose was served by the ubiquitous symbols of sovereignty, the embrasure-like slits in the masonry and the pillared colonnades, as well as the martial friezes, the cornices and statues, including a Reich eagle with a wingspan of more than eighty metres. The German Stadium, for instance, was bounded on its open side by two stone blocks the height of a house, each of which was to bear a colossal bronze sculpture designed by Josef Thorak and standing twenty-four metres high. All the architectural details took into account the vast geometrical formations that marched past for the military parade, expressing both the elevation of the individual and his extinction as a worthless extra on a set.

In line with the ceremonial view Hitler had of himself and of his regime, the area was a vast temple site, where he would arrive once a year with his followers for a pontifical service. This reading was confirmed by the term 'Place of pilgrimage for the nation', which soon gained currency, as well as by the plan to replace the native spruce and pinewoods between the parade-grounds with extensive oak spinneys and 'all manner of buildings of sacred character'. 'Even the pyramids', Hitler declared in the autumn of 1938, 'will pale against the masses of concrete and stone colossi which I am erecting ... I am building for eternity – for ... we are the last Germany.'[31]

Work began two years after Speer submitted his first designs. From then on, Hitler solemnly performed at least one ceremony of laying a foundation stone during the various Party rallies. The start was made at the Märzfeld surrounded by twenty-six towers of ochre Travertine stone, each about thirty metres high; next came the Grand Avenue, followed by the foundation stone for the German Stadium. The longitudinal axis of the structure measured over six hundred metres. It was twice as wide and five times as high as the Olympic Stadium in Berlin. More than 150 express lifts were installed in the walls and towers, each holding 100 persons, to bring the spectators to the grandstands. Such was the mania for beating records at the time that these leviathan plans were spoken of as 'the biggest building site in Germany and even in the world' as late as 1939, even though they never got beyond the initial stages.[33] The timetable had been meticulously worked out to allow for every possible delay, unforeseen static problems, shortages of material and delivery problems, but it had not reckoned with Hitler's destructive restlessness. The Nuremberg project was to be completed in the autumn of 1945. Already Hitler occasionally indulged in verbose descriptions of the inaugural ceremonies which would last several days. In the end only a few fragmented buildings were finished.

The mammoth effects secured Speer a double triumph at the Paris World Exhibition of 1937. Initially Hitler had refused to take part because he did not like any of the many designs that had been submitted. He was, moreover, annoyed that the exhibition organizers had placed the German pavilion exactly opposite the Soviet site, thereby suggesting some totalitarian link between the two powers. Nevertheless,

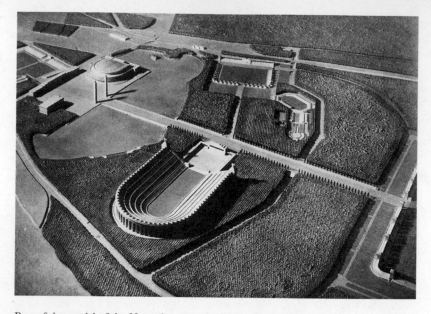

Part of the model of the Nuremberg terrain. In the foreground is the German Stadium with its pillared façade, and facing it the Luitpoldhain. Part of the Märzfeld can be seen on the right-hand edge of the picture; on the left is the Congress Hall and behind it the Zeppelinfeld. The Grand Avenue bisected the terrain, which had a total area of 16.5 square kilometres but was used only once a year, in September, for a week.

at the request of the minister of economic affairs, Speer left for Paris on a reconnaissance trip. Thanks to the indiscretions of a French exhibition official, he lost his way touring the site and found himself in the room where the model of the strictly secret Soviet design was kept. Set on a massive pedestal a group of figures was storming ahead towards the German pavilion, certain of victory, as if anticipating the Soviet triumph over its totalitarian opponent.

With only a few strokes Speer designed a slim pillared building, several metres higher, to create the impression of halting, or even braking the assault. It was none other than Hitler's idea of the Reich as the bulwark against the approaching East translated into a decorative monument, the idea with which he had lulled the suspicions of the Western powers for some time. The cornice bore an eagle holding a wreathed swastika in its claws, looking down with victorious pride on the futile assault by the opposing power. Once again Speer used imaginatively placed searchlights to plunge the finished building into brilliant

At the Paris World Exhibition of 1937 the organizers had placed the German site (right) directly opposite the Soviet building (centre). Hitler found this equal treatment offensive and initially wanted to cancel Germany's participation. Only when Speer, after a secret inspection of the Soviet model, hurriedly designed a counter-concept which seemed to halt, as it were, the onslaught of the Soviet sculptural figures, did Hitler agree. Speer received a gold medal for his work.

whiteness as soon as night fell, so that it stood as a monument of invincibility carved out of the blackness of the night. When the prizes were awarded Speer received a gold medal for the German pavilion, and it was probably a political concession that the Soviet architect was awarded the same medal for his work. To his own and Hitler's surprise, the exhibition management also awarded Speer a Grand Prix for his model of the Nuremberg complex.

During all these years Speer had been working as a freelance architect. His office had expanded steadily and he was almost stupefied by the never-ending flood of inquiries, commissions, journeys and administrative duties, often coming home late in the evening, 'speechless with exhaustion'.[34] To begin with he had refused to accept a fee for his official work, but he increasingly got into difficulties. Only towards the end of 1935, when Göring assured him with his constantly cheerful greed: 'They're all nonsense, your ideals. You've got to make money!', did Speer accept a fee of thirty thousand marks for his work up until then.

He agreed to an annual fee of forty thousand marks for the next few years. Around that time, he moved into a house he had designed in Schlachtensee. He was only able to raise the seventy thousand marks for the building work with a mortgage from his father. With a floor space of 125 square metres it was a provocative rejection of the ostentatious style favoured by the other Party bosses, from whom Speer was always careful to keep his distance. He did not mention his appointment as professor, never used his title and did not even have his academic rank printed on his letter-head. The honour meant nothing to him, he told all and sundry, with a certain degree of arrogance: it had been distributed too generously, he added, since even Hitler's photographer Heinrich Hoffmann had received it.[35]

During the inspection of an autobahn in the spring of 1936, Hitler told Speer that he had one more commission, 'the greatest of all'.[36] He said no more. But it was not difficult to guess that he had referred to the rebuilding of the Reich capital. Whenever the discussion turned to the city and its historical appearance, Hitler had repeatedly objected that Berlin was no metropolis, or words to that effect. Apart from a few superior districts, the visitor would find himself in a 'jumbled sequence of residential and office buildings', a big city, but 'not a world city' like Paris or Vienna.[37]

A few months after seizing power Hitler had therefore used a quarrel between the city administration and the Reich railway to push his own plans forward. The two bodies had long argued about linking up three of Berlin's long-distance railway stations. Hitler seized the chance to discuss the transport issues of the future and introduce his own ideas. In a letter of thanks the state commissar and future mayor Julius Lippert welcomed the Führer's 'majestic plans aiming at the reshaping of Berlin'. They would 'make the Reich capital ... look the most distinguished metropolis'.[38] However, as the profound changes Hitler envisaged for the fabric of the city became more and more clear and it transpired that Berlin would have to bear a substantial portion of the costs, Lippert put up a silent but stubborn resistance. With the self-confidence of an old Party comrade and the tactical cunning of one who for many years had been in charge of Goebbels' militant journal *Der Angriff*, he stalled Hitler by dragging out the bureaucratic process, submitting horrendous estimates or resorting to endless new legal and administrative obstacles. It was assumed that he regarded Hitler's plans for Berlin as going far beyond anything that was compatible with the traditional character of the city. At any rate, even at the preliminary

Julius Lippert, the Mayor of Berlin, considered the plans for the 'world capital Germania' too brutal an intervention in Berlin's traditional city-scape and stubbornly opposed Hitler's and Speer's plans. Lippert's disputes with Speer only ended in 1941 with the former's defeat and removal from office.

planning stage he responded to the proposal that the Grand Avenue planned for the Reich capital as the starting point and central axis of the new government quarter should have a width of at least 120 metres by submitting a design envisaging a width of only one hundred metres. Even when Hitler insisted, informing him that he wished to out-do the Champs-Élysées not only in length but also by at least twenty metres in width, Lippert remained unimpressed. He submitted a second plan where the street was once again a hundred metres wide.

The more Hitler saw his great plan being sabotaged or lost in administrative labyrinths, the more irritable he became. Initially he simply called Lippert 'petty' or 'incapable' of recognizing historical dimensions. But over the years he became increasingly furious whenever his name was mentioned. In one of those wild rages which were so typical of his excitable nature, he angrily called the mayor of Berlin 'an incompetent, an idiot, a failure, a zero'. He did not withdraw the planning of the new Berlin from Lippert and his architectural office probably because he was unsure whom to entrust with this 'task of the century'. Troost, whom, even years later, he still called the 'greatest architect of our day' and the 'schoolmaster' of the future, was no longer alive and 'whether architect

Speer is up to it', as he then observed with astonishing coolness, he 'could not tell yet'.[39] But one day in the summer of 1936 he impatiently swept aside all doubts. Hitler summoned Speer and, without any formality, charged him with the overall plan for the Reich capital. 'There's nothing to be done with the Berlin city government,' he said angrily. 'From now on you make the plans ... When you have something ready, show it to me. As you know, I always have time for such things.'[40]

The ceremonial appointment followed, On 30 January 1937, the anniversary of the Seizure of Power, Speer was appointed General-bauinspektor für die Reichshauptstadt (GBI) (Inspector-General of Building for the Reich capital) by Führer Decree, and furnished with the rank of under-secretary of state in the Reich government. He was also invested with unique powers. Neither a Reich authority nor any Party authority, least of all the Berlin administration, had the right to issue directives to him. And, as if to emphasize his exceptional position, he was freed from any obligation to inform the relevant officials of his intentions. On the other hand, any plans affecting his sphere of work had to be submitted to him for approval. Answerable to Hitler alone, Speer was in fact granted a kind of dictatorial status. Curiously, he was allowed to keep his private office on Lindenallee despite being a member of the government. In order to legitimate this 'impossibility' his office was run not as a civil service department but as an independent research institute under the direction of an under-secretary of state. When Hitler handed him his letter of appointment in an informal ceremony, all he said was: 'Do a good job!'[41]

This was more than just another step up in Speer's career; he had almost reached the final goal. At the age of thirty-one he held almost the same position as Karl Friedrich Schinkel, Frederick William III's Director of the Royal Office of Works about a hundred years earlier; he too had not only been an architect but the 'Decorator-General of Prussia', as he was often called because of his artistic genius. In his restless monologues that roamed through space and time, Hitler extolled his rule as the final reconciliation of art and politics and liked to see himself as the successor of Pericles, calling the autobahns his Parthenon.[42] With his new appointment Speer began to draw similarly extravagant parallels, speaking of his dream to 'become another Schinkel'. At times he even made himself believe that, thanks to Hitler's passion for building and the virtually unlimited powers he now held, he might go further than his great predecessor who had been restricted by a grumpy and tight-fisted king.

At other times he felt 'crushed' by the tasks, the enormity of which only gradually dawned on him: that of world stage designer, property-master-general and First Architect of the Reich. He had conflicting feelings at the time, he later recorded, especially as all the world reminded him that he would be building for 'millennia'. Although his innate scepticism had prevented him from taking such ideas too seriously, he had been gripped by the great fever of those years and had firmly believed in the prospect of a place in the history of art.[43]

Chapter Three
GERMANIA: THE
CAPITAL OF THE WORLD

A few days after Speer's appointment, Hitler instructed that the Academy of Arts building at 4 Pariser Platz be cleared in order to make room for the office of the Generalbauinspektor. This eighteenth-century palace of the Counts von Arnim-Boitzenburg had been reconstructed in the mid-nineteenth century, but the noble modesty of Prussian classicism had been retained. The building, which had until then been used by the minister of education, had the advantage of being separated from the Reich Chancellery only by the so-called 'Ministergarten' and could therefore be reached without attracting attention. In the following years Hitler often went across to see Speer, sometimes almost daily, usually after nightfall. Bent over the drawing tables, surrounded by elevations and countless sketches on the walls, many of them by Hitler himself, they were lost for hours on end shaping the Berlin of the future. The building had the additional advantage of being right next to the office of Fritz Todt, the Generalinspektor für das Strassenwesen (the Inspector-General of Roads), whose autobahns were to be one of the highlights of the 'Gesamtkunstwerk Germany'. They mattered almost as much to Hitler as his building plans.

Now that his position had also been formally secured, Speer felt all the more sure of Hitler's goodwill. He exploited this certainty in a manner that seemed as arrogant as it was resolute. Many of Hitler's leading vassals had registered 'the Führer's favourite' but they had failed to take him seriously politically, regarding him as an 'artist'. For the first time they had a taste of the robust will to power behind the reserved and almost shy exterior. Within eighteen months Speer's planning staff had swollen to eighty-seven, with about the same number working in the so-called implementation section. Speer's talent for moulding young, highly gifted people, with or without a Party ticket, into a team of ambitious employees bound together by a special *ésprit de corps* now became apparent. He appointed people who were both competent and trustworthy to the top posts of the three main divisions into which he divided his department. The Central Bureau, which administered the budget, was taken over by the financial expert Karl Maria Hettlage, the General Building Directorate went to Walter Brugmann, whose acquaintance Speer had made in Nuremberg, and for the Planning Office, which mattered most to him professionally, he enlisted, alongside Hans Stephan, two old friends from his student days, Rudolf Wolters and Willi Schelkes.

The conditions which Speer required at least for his top collaborators attracted a certain amount of attention. Hitler had instructed him to settle the details with Hans Heinrich Lammers, the head of the Reich Chancellery. Speer demanded the best people and the highest salaries, arguing that the Führer's buildings should 'reflect the character of the Movement for millennia' and be a unique testimony to a great epoch.' For himself he claimed the same salary as the Oberbürgermeister, the mayor of Berlin, 'since in terms of its impact on Berlin my work cannot be assessed to be of lesser value', as well as an expense account commensurate with his position, an official car, and other so-called emoluments; all his demands were met, with the exception of insurance for surviving dependants, which raised complicated questions of civil service law.[2]

Inevitably Speer's new job involved him more deeply in the political machine than he ever intended. Knowing that he was answerable to Hitler alone, he had barely noticed most of the Party leaders he had encountered so far and only Hitler's demonstrative favour had suppressed their growing irritation at Speer's offensive remoteness. Now, however, he had to face them. Gauleiters, under-secretaries of state or even the head of the Berlin city administration Julius Lippert, who until then had been faceless creatures to him, suddenly assumed the features of opponents with whom he had to do battle. This compelled him to conclude various tactical alliances which drew him even further away from his specific work. He was not too particular in his choice of allies, although he did not overlook Hitler's personal entourage. Speer improved his contacts with Otto Dietrich, the Reich press chief, who, he thought, might prove useful in some way or other, as well as with Hitler's corpulent adjutant Wilhelm Bruckner and with his physician-in-residence Karl Brandt, who soon became a close friend. But for Martin Bormann, already the most powerful member of Hitler's court, he conceived a violent dislike, which was reciprocated in equal measure.

If his words are to be trusted, Hitler had already conceived the first plans for a new imperial Berlin during his years of loafing about Vienna.[3] The observations of Ernst Hanfstaengl or Heinrich Hoffmann are more plausible: they report that in the early twenties Hitler was mainly designing enormous buildings for representative purposes.[4] There is no tangible proof before his months of detention at Landsberg. The setback he suffered with his unsuccessful *coup d'état* of 9 November 1923 by no means eliminated these grandiose surrogate worlds. Indeed they were a refuge from his disappointments. When at the peak of his life Hitler looked back on the unhappiness of those years, he insisted with the unshaken faith in his mission that was one of the driving forces of his success: 'But in my imagination I lived in palaces.'[5] His surviving sketchbook and numerous drawings show that even then he not only designed parade scenarios, flag decorations and fortified buildings, but also tribunes, pedestals for columns, as well as individual buildings for Nuremberg, Berlin and Munich. In Landsberg he sketched his vision for the Great Hall and triumphal arch on a small card which he later handed to Speer, after appointing him his chief planner for the Reich capital, with the words: 'I made these drawings ten years ago. I've always kept them because I never doubted that some day I would build them. And this is how we will carry them out now.'[6]

Throughout those years of impatient waiting and preparation, architecture remained Hitler's special love. In July 1926 Goebbels made an entry in his diary about a visit to the Obersalzberg, when Hitler finally won over the young demagogue from the left wing of the Party: 'He speaks of the future architectural picture of the country and is every inch an architect. Into it he paints the picture of a new German constitution: And is every inch a statesman!'[7] Hitler never doubted that he would come to power and however far from his goal he may have been at that time, he clung to his determination to give the country a new image by transforming the towns. In April 1929 he gave a speech, explaining the political psychology behind this plan: 'Only a reshaping of the entire thinking and feeling, and of the idea and concept of the state' would preserve the country, he assured his audience.

> We could not imagine a Third Reich which contains only department stores and factory buildings ... only skyscrapers and hotels, but we freely declare that this Third Reich will have to offer documents of art and culture to outlast the centuries ... We see before us the cities of antiquity, the Acropolis, the Parthenon, the Colosseum, we see the

cities of the Middle Ages with their gigantic cathedrals and ... we know that human beings need such a centre unless they are to disintegrate.[8]

Even on the night of 30 January 1933, when the cheers had died down and the crowds dispersed, Hitler returned to this subject. In the company of a handful of faithful followers in the Reich Chancellery he became lost in one of his endless monologues until dawn, recapitulating the innumerable hardships he had had to struggle against, and how everything had eventually turned to victory. He mapped out in eschatological images what would have become of Germany without his intervention, wild visions intermingling with extravagant architectural schemes. His first task, he remarked, would be to rebuild the Reich Chancellery: it was undignified, 'a mere cigar box'.[9]

Initially he only had a vague idea of the future shape of the city. It was confined to individual buildings on a gigantic scale. For that very reason Speer's appointment provided a unique opportunity to devise a planning solution for Berlin that befitted the age. Thanks to his comprehensive powers the new Inspector-General was able to bypass the cumbersome official apparatus and ward off local objections. In fact the master plan submitted at the beginning of the following year aimed not only at the renewal of the official quarters, to which Hitler attached such importance, but also at a fundamental reorganization of the business districts and the residential quarters, right down to the city's transport system. But the freedom Speer enjoyed exposed him to the danger of purely mechanical solutions. This was all the greater as he was in the employ of an opinionated despot set on achieving uniform effects.

By the time Speer embarked on his tasks Hitler had already formed an approximate picture in his mind, which the two men now developed further in close agreement. As at Nuremberg, the plans for Berlin also envisaged a 'grand avenue' as the central axis, extending to more than five kilometres. The subdivision of the urban area south of the old Reichstag into plots at least five hundred metres long produced those heavy, elongated buildings which later appeared in the drafts. They were almost exclusively earmarked for representative purposes, accommodating various governmental and Party authorities, a few big companies, luxury hotels, museums and scientific institutions. Located in between were the so-called cultural buildings, the opera house, the Philharmonic hall, the playhouse, a 'mega-cinema' seating six thousand, a variety theatre, an operetta theatre and several public baths.

Top: Hitler's sketch for the great domed building he had already been planning for
Berlin in 1925. The model of the Great Assembly Hall (below) made twelve years later,
showed how freely Speer interpreted Hitler's ideas. The supporting cube is greatly
reduced in height; the dome is at least three times larger. Speer placed four load-
bearing towers at the corners of the building. In addition he intended to place in front
of the portal two sculptures fifteen metres tall, one representing the 'bearer of the sky'
and the other the 'bearer of the earth'. The incredible proportions are made clear by a
scale model of the Brandenburg Gate in the bottom right-hand corner.

Sketches survive showing that even before Speer's involvement Hitler had set a domed hall and a triumphal arch at either end of the avenue as spectacular focal points. The hall, with a free-vaulted interior 220 metres high and floor-space for 180,000 people, was placed near the old Reichstag in the heart of the old government quarter. It was surrounded on three sides by water, so that the reflections would enhance the impression of size and fairy-tale magic. The space in front was designed to hold a million people for May Day festivities, national memorial days and future victory celebrations. The treatment of the domed hall reveals how self-assured Speer was in his dealings with Hitler even then. Hitler's sketch had envisaged a structure with a shallow curved roof, closely based on the Pantheon in Rome. Speer substantially lowered the bearing cube and added four corner towers. He not only put an out-sized parabolic cupola on the substructure, but also placed two fifteen-metre-high sculptures on the frontage, representing the bearers of the sky and the terrestrial globe. He placed three asterisks below the design to indicate that it was not his work. When Hitler urged him to sign it 'Speer' he simply ignored him.

As a counter-piece to the domed hall Hitler placed a triumphal arch at the southern end of the Grand Avenue, quite near the Tempelhofer Feld. Although 120 metres high and richly decorated with colonnades, a fit of unaccustomed modesty caused the arch to be referred to on the plans as 'Building T'. It was nearly two and a half million cubic metres in volume and it would have been almost fifty times the size of the Paris Arc de Triomphe, against which it had been conceived. The walls were to immortalize the names of all the servicemen killed in action in the First World War, to whom the building offered a promise of rebirth. Nearby was the Soldatenhalle, modelled on Schinkel's Neue Wache but on a vast scale; below it was a cavernous vaulted crypt, built of rough-hewn granite blocks and lit by huge flaming bowls, where the coffins of German field marshals of the past and the future were to be placed.

At the other end of the avenue Speer's design for the Führerpalast, the Führer's palace, further raised the stakes in the order of magnitude. Modelled on the Palazzo Pitti in Florence, it was conceived as a fortress-like structure on a heavy rusticated plinth. Instead of windows, two rows of columns were set into the facade, with bulletproof sliding shutters and a steel portal. At times, when he was in a theatrical mood, Hitler would imagine armoured columns rolling up the Grand Avenue in broad formation to quell a disturbance: no one, he argued excitedly, would be able to resist. The entrance hall led to a series of reception

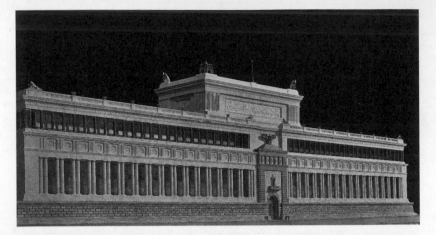

The 'Führer Palace' in the immediate vicinity of the domed hall was a windowless structure, equipped only with embrasures. In addition to offices it was to contain a dining hall of nearly 3,000 square metres and a theatre for some 1,000 spectators.

rooms and long galleries, with a festive hall for thousands of visitors at the end. In addition there were eight salons totalling fifteen thousand square metres floor-space, as well as a theatre for nearly two thousand spectators. The 'diplomats' corridor' leading to Hitler's study was more than five hundred metres long. One need only note that the Führerpalast was one hundred and fifty times larger than Bismarck's premises, which Hitler had moved into at the beginning of his chancellorship, to see what pretentions lay behind these dimensions.

It was a dream, unbridled, confused and born of concepts wholly alien to the city and which was all the less respectful of Berlin's historical buildings for aiming exclusively at monuments of self-glorification. A first step envisaged the pulling down of some fifty thousand residential and business premises in the centre of Berlin. No matter how devoted Julius Lippert and the authorities under him might have been to the rulers' cause as a whole, their silent resistance reflected an awareness of the profound upheavals these plans would inflict upon the townscape. Speer's appointment, however, put an end to all troublesome objections. The new head of planning readily accepted every one of Hitler's ideas, sometimes incorporating an occasional professional consideration, but often outdoing the initial scheme. In his admiration for the dictator, Speer also adopted his belief in the intimidating pathos of magnificent architectural backdrops.[10] Together Hitler and his architect revelled in grandiloquent visions, exhilarated by the prospect of a clean sweep. The plans became more and more extensive until they envisaged nothing less than a comprehensive reshaping of Berlin, combining the plausible with utter madness.

The premiss that geological and historical circumstances had given Berlin a more or less continuous east-west connection, but no similar north-south thoroughfare, was accurate. More than a hundred years earlier Karl Friedrich Schinkel had tried to remedy this unsatisfactory state of affairs, and a study dating from the 1920s had adopted his vision.[11] Ever since, all urban schemes had gone back to the concept of a north-south axis to solve the worsening congestion. One of the basic ideas was to abolish the numerous terminal stations close to the city centre and generally to disentangle Berlin's transport problems. More than a million square metres of land covered by tracks could thus be reclaimed.

In the past these ideas had been much discussed, but they had never been tackled. Speer and his staff used them as their starting point. The overall plan worked out at Pariser Platz also proceeded from the Grand Avenue, but it sought to use the wide aisle which it would carve through the city for a general reorganization of the capital. Accordingly, Berlin was to have two main axes, intersecting just west of the Brandenburg Gate and dividing the city into four sectors. The plan envisaged a system of radial and ring roads designed to save the city from the imminent threat of being throttled by traffic. Immediately behind the row of solemn representational buildings were extensive business districts where the building height was progressively reduced. They gradually merged with lower-built residential districts, eventually leading to the grander residential areas at the extreme edge of the city. These matters assumed increasing importance at the General Inspectorate for Building, while Hitler was more and more concerned with his gigantic toy, the Grand Avenue and the solitary building blocks, the plans for which had been entrusted to Rudolf Wolters.[12]

From then on, the two concepts ran alongside one another. In contrast to Hitler, Speer's office increasingly viewed itself as a successor to the prefect Georges Eugène Haussmann, who had given Paris its modern face around the middle of the nineteenth century. Starting with the requirements of metropolitan structures Speer and his team were gradually swept along by the momentum of their own freedom in planning matters. They reached out further and further, designing an

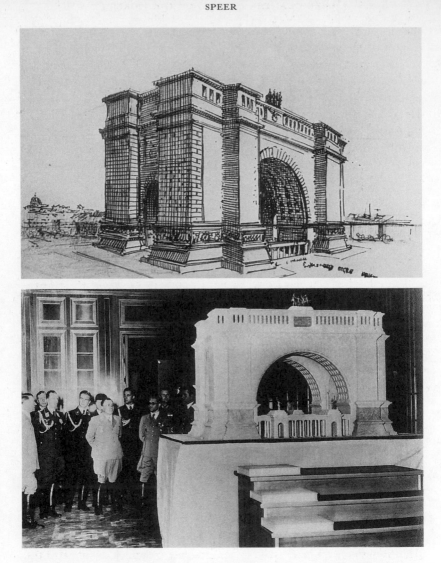

Hitler's sketch for the triumphal arch also goes back to 1925, and here too Speer's model shows that he also took liberties with this design. Hitler had planned an unadorned balustrade inside the arch, whereas Speer envisaged a forest of columns. Those involved in the project never mentioned the monument by name, but somewhat superstitiously referred to it as 'Building T'.

extensively modernized capital right up to the autobahn ring and, in some places, even beyond. The railway system was to be concentrated on two enormous central stations in the north and south of the city, linked by an underground train system, and there was to be an airport at each of the four axial terminals outside the city.

Solving the transport problems of the city, projected to have nearly ten million inhabitants, was by no means the department's only concern. Other programmes envisaged the improvement of the largely down-at-heel residential quarters, hurriedly erected during the period of industrialization, the 'interspersing' of urban spaces with parks, and the creation of new neighbourhoods, such as a university district in the west, at the start of the east-west axis. The transverse route was to be developed following the often crooked street alignment: it was to run from the Heerstrasse via the Victory Column (which was to be moved to the Tiergarten) and then along the avenue Unter den Linden. Several proposals were put forward for its further route eastwards, which was to be decided at a later date. There were also plans to enlarge the museum area on the Spreeinsel by at least three buildings and to establish a medical quarter with institutes, hospitals and labora-tories to the north of the university town. Extensive recuperation areas were envisaged beyond the autobahn ring. And while they were at it, the planners began cutting down the pinewoods of the Mark Brandenburg and planting tens of thousands of seedlings, to restore the former mixed forest which Frederick the Great had cut down to finance his Silesian wars. The Grunewald to the west of the city was, like the Bois de Boulogne, to have wide promenades with restaurants, riding stables and sculpture gardens.

All these projects met with Hitler's acclaim, if only because of his liking for radical solutions. But soon his interest narrowed and he focused with increasing persistence first on the Grand Avenue, its build-ings and squares, and then on individual façades, friezes or decorative cornices. His penchant was exclusively and literally for the building of monuments. Whenever he walked across from the Reich Chancellery, along the purpose-made path, entering Speer's office by the small door specially set into the rear wall of the Academy building, he first had the large-scale master plans shown to him. Although he approved them in principle, he generally turned away after a few minutes. He was only interested in the buildings along the main thoroughfare, which were progressively taking shape on the drawing boards. The Avenue itself formed the southern 'spoke' of the crossing axes but it did little to solve Berlin's town-planning problems, so that a parallel route had to be devised to take the through traffic.

Berlin would 'one day be the capital of the world', Hitler used to say. He was intoxicated by his vision of visitors from all over the Reich and from distant lands arriving at the Southern Railway Station, stepping out into the thousand-metre-long square, modelled on the Avenue of Rams between Luxor and Karnak, lined with captured weapons on granite pedestals, and being virtually 'knocked over' by the power and the glory of the buildings. One day Speer showed him a thirty-metre-long scale model of the Grand Avenue in the famous exhibition rooms of the Academy. Cabinet makers had built it to scale, incorporating every architectural detail. Hitler was ecstatically happy. He spent hours on end in front of his imaginary street. The model was erected on tables equipped with castors, which could be pulled out section by section, so that the viewer could enter the avenue at any point and study every perspective he desired. Specially fitted spotlights imitated the changing position of the sun. As the model was placed at hip height, Hitler and the visitors he often brought along with him had to crouch or even half kneel down to get the impression a pedestrian would have.[13]

Only with such a layout, such buildings, squares and colonnades, Hitler once remarked, could the new Berlin outclass its 'only rival in the world, Rome' and 'make St Peter's with the square in front of it seem like toys'.[14] In *Mein Kampf* he had already mentioned his intention to put the city on a par with the most venerable cities in history, adding that a nation could only achieve world domination if it had a focal point 'with the magical charm of a Mecca or a Rome'. Berlin one day would be nothing less. That domed hall was 'worth more than three victorious wars', he observed on another occasion, returning to his fixation about the psychological power of great works of architecture to overwhelm. He dreamt of addressing the nations of the Greater Germanic Empire from the Führer gallery and of imposing laws on a humiliated world. Similarly, the Triumphal Arch would 'finally and for ever drive out the pernicious idea from the people's minds that Germany had lost the ... World War', he proclaimed. Upon entering the Führer's Palace everyone was to 'have the feeling that he was visiting the master of the world'. Psychological reflections of this kind combined with Hitler's fantasies of omnipotence were similarly at work when, standing in front of the model in the early spring of 1939, he pointed to the top of the dome: 'The eagle should no longer stand above the swastika here,' he said to Speer: 'To crown the greatest building in the world the eagle must stand above the globe.'[15]

The ideology behind all these architectural ideas was far more to blame for the oppressive monotony of the plans for the new Berlin than their uniformly huge size. The fact that they so blatantly represented the will to conquer destroyed them architecturally. Overstepping all the established boundaries of scale had less to do with Hitler or Speer than with the spirit of the age and its ambition to go to the extreme, or beyond, not only intellectually but also technologically. Bruno Taut's glass visions, Mies van der Rohe's design for a high-rise building on Berlin's Friedrichstrasse, Le Corbusier's residential towns or Boris M. Iofan's Lenin Palace and his plans for Moscow, all sprang from the same hubris, as did the competing skyscrapers of New York or Chicago, except that these were not linked to a boundless zeal for world conquest. Instead they were mostly inspired by social Utopias and were therefore in line with the Zeitgeist. Some of these wild architectural fantasies merely expressed ideas which were very unlikely to be realized. They were dreams, or sketches for a kind of manifesto, or even just grandiose examples of handicraft work inspired by a whim and born of the childish spirit of the age. By contrast, Hitler demonstrated here too that he was always ready to take the most eccentric ideas seriously and put them into effect with that fearlessness with which he etched himself so indelibly on the world's memory.

Taken by themselves the objections frequently raised against the 'gigantomania' of that architecture therefore miss the point. Hitler was not alone in aiming at breathtaking and overwhelming effects. The whole epoch was out to impress itself and the world with buildings of cyclopean size. Moreover, Hitler and Speer found inspiring models in the recently rediscovered designs of the French Revolution by architects such as Claude-Nicolas Ledoux and Etienne-Louis Boullée, whom Speer at any rate referred to on various occasions. The gigantic scale was not only a result of Hitler's desire to place hugely impressive buildings in the centre of the measured and severe landscape of historical Berlin. He had also found in Speer a helper who was himself anxious to impress him.

That more than anything else was what drove Speer to aim for the vast dimensions which characterize all his plans. He was certainly free from Hitler's personal and political complex of having to out-do everyone else. He never had a 'crippled psyche', he maintained, and his claim that he occasionally made fun of Hitler's 'record mania' cannot be ruled out. But such reservations did nothing to change Speer's willingness to be part of it all. He had, at the time, been 'intoxicated by the enormous tasks'; the strange rage which seized him at his drawing board did, on one occasion, cause Hitler to express 'alarm' at the lack of moderation in a design submitted to him by Speer, though only for a moment.[16]

In his boundless admiration for Hitler and his aims Speer also shared the deeper motives behind the dictator's desire for gigantic architectural monuments: the ambition of the ancient pharaohs to compensate for the transience of their power by commissioning enduring buildings, as well as the psychological 'flourish' which Hitler believed emanated from great architecture. Just as at Nuremberg he had boasted of the most enormous stadium, so Speer was planning the highest skyscraper for Hamburg, the greatest seaside resort for the island of Rügen, and the world's most powerful radio transmitter for Lower Lusatia. At the Obersalzberg he was fond of pointing to the largest retractable window of all time. Occasionally he would justify this inclination by saying, 'I am not acting out of megalomania, but on the rational consideration that only [thus] can a nation be given the self-assurance it needs for its historic task.' When Hitler was told one day that the Soviet Union was planning a Congress building in Moscow, in honour of Lenin, with an even higher dome, he was 'deeply irked', and only calmed down when it emerged that the building would be twenty metres lower. Even during the Russian campaign he angrily reverted to this subject.[17]

Hitler's architectural ideology essentially consisted of hugeness, of what the world had never seen before. Nothing else counted, nor did he prefer the style of any particular epoch. Contrary to a widespread belief, his predilection was not even for classicism, which is unjustly described as the epitome of the 'totalitarian' style. Despite the general liking for avant-garde experiments between the two wars, the 'classical' style had prevailed internationally for representative buildings since the beginning of the century. In keeping with his Austrian background, Hitler inclined much more towards the imperial Baroque and the neo-Baroque, and it is significant that he returned to it after Troost's death. The ascetic simplicity of classicism, especially in Prussia, was deeply alien to him and contrary to his nature. That chimerical architectural vision of his, which he proclaimed as his guiding idea and the 'style of eternity', was essentially just a hotchpotch of his emotions translated into stone: his desire for theatrical backdrops, his insatiable hunger for stunning symbolism, and his desire to intimidate.

Even so, certain maxims of Troost's remained unforgotten, even if they survived only in the use of classical set-pieces such as columns, gables, axial symmetry and entablatures. Hitler's ideas were helped by the almost unlimited interpretability of classicism which, unlike the modernist games of the 'New Architecture', was immediately comprehensible to the masses and, especially in its vulgar forms, could be interpreted as a testimony both of democratic or of authoritarian rule.[18] In Italy the classical style was naturally linked to the memory of the greatness of ancient Rome, in France to the appeal to national 'grandeur' and in Washington to the republican gesture of the founding fathers. The 'ennobling' effect of classicism began to be appreciated even in Moscow, where, after the experimental efforts of the early revolutionary phase, it was celebrated as the expression of the eternally valid law of history. But when, at the beginning of the 1940s, Stalin expressed his interest in a consultative visit by Speer, combining the invitation with the most flattering compliments, Hitler, half amused and half irritated, vetoed it. Stalin would put Speer in a rat-hole, Hitler suggested, and not let him out again until the new Moscow had arisen.[19]

The constraint of proportion, however, which is the indispensable if arcane law of all classical architecture, was unknown to its contemporary imitators, wherever they were. On closer inspection the designs for Berlin reveal a wealth of arabesques, an over-abundance of ornament and a taste for gilding which were later aptly described by Speer as 'neo-Empire'. But they offered the distinctly unclassical opportunity of exaggerated monumentality. During the Russian campaign, when he believed that victory and world dominion were in his grasp, Hitler indulged in the vision of 'a group of Kirghizians being guided through the Reich capital' year after year 'in order to fill their imagination with the power and greatness of its stone monuments'.[20]

Speer rather boldly called his architectural ideas the 'Doric style'. In fact it was a hodgepodge of bulky historical forms which originated not so much in ancient Greece as in Egypt, Assur or Nineveh. While he may have dreamed of becoming Schinkel's successor, he got much nearer to Cecil B. de Mille.[21] Even in retrospect he did not think the domed hall or the triumphal arch had been too big; he merely regarded the pompous decorations as excessive and tasteless. But for all the pains that were taken to achieve variety he could not overlook the strangely dead world he had produced. Speer attributed his failure to the intoxicating freedom he enjoyed, to the bottomless funds at his disposal and to his arrogant inability to set himself limits. But the spirit of the age and its predilection for mammoth scale also played their part, as well as Speer's eager submissiveness to a dictator who allowed him, and his team, greater latitude than they subsequently admitted.

Significantly, it was not a group of chosen architects, or men close to the Party or to the so-called *völkische* or national style, who produced most of the designs. In principle Speer and his staff confined themselves to the overall planning, inviting well-known or promising young architects to work out the details. These included Peter Behrens and Paul Bonatz, Wilhelm Kreis, Ernst Sagebiel, the office of Hentrich and Heuser, Caesar Pinnau, Friedrich Tamms and even Werner March. Speer confidently ignored 'schools' and 'camps', using his position with Hitler to silence any opposition from adherents of the national spirit or from Alfred Rosenberg, who was responsible for ideological surveillance. More and more commissions and jobs went to 'New Style' architects and close collaborators of the Bauhaus, although the movement was still disapproved of. Those who like Hanns Dustmann and Ernst Neufert took on assignments, realized the unique opportunities the regime's building passion offered them. Their growing influence inevitably weakened the traditionalism of the German nationalist tendency. Only Tessenow was courageous enough to continue to stand aloof and refuse to co-operate, despite repeated invitations to do so. He had lost his teaching post at the Academy of Fine Arts long ago and could not even find the three sponsors he needed for his indispensable acceptance into the Reich Chamber of Culture. Nevertheless Speer stood steadfastly by him. In a respectful letter he once tried to explain to Tessenow why he had abandoned the architectural ideas they had shared; and despite all the hostility from Party officials Speer continued to meet him socially right to the end. Thanks to Speer's intervention Tessenow was eventually reinstated in his teaching post.[22]

It was a trying time for Speer, with building consultations, static calculations, conferences with Hitler and constant examinations of the soil, whose bearing capacity was tested by concrete blocks weighing many thousands of tons. He wanted to recover from these wearying activities,

(*Opposite*) In 1937 Hitler and Speer began to design plans for the rebuilding of Berlin as the 'World Capital Germania'. The picture shows a model of the fundamental changes to the city centre: in the foreground the Northern Railway Station, beyond it the gigantic dome, virtually eclipsing the Reichstag and the Brandenburg Gate; top left the Tempelhofer Feld, in whose immediate vicinity are the Triumphal Arch and the Southern Railway Station. Most of the buildings for the ministries, the Party and cultural institutions were to be located between the Southern Railway Station and the domed hall. In these plans Hitler and Speer gave no thought to the old urban centre of Berlin.

but was also alarmed by increasingly frequent 'feelings of anxiety', accompanied by fibrillations, shortage of breath and turbulent blood pressure.[23] In the spring of 1939 Speer therefore decided to go sightseeing in southern Italy with a few friends. More than three years before he had undertaken a similar trip to Greece in order to overcome the stylistic problems created by the conflicting visions of Tessenow, Troost and Hitler. Speer and his wife had visited Athens and Aegina, the theatre at Epidaurus and the sites of Olympia. At Delphi he believed he had discovered how quickly the purity of the early style had been corrupted by wealth and ostentatious greed. But he still wondered whether there were any essential differences between antiquity, the Renaissance, classicism and his own endeavours. To find out more he now invited a number of artistically knowledgeable friends to accompany him, including the sculptors Arno Breker and Josef Thorak, the architect Wilhelm Kreis, who had designed the Soldiers' Hall on the Grand Avenue, Karl Brandt and a few others.

He also invited Magda Goebbels, the wife of the propaganda minister, who had recently confided to him her unhappiness over her husband's affair with the Czech film actress Lida Baarova. Speer found the decision to help the almost inconsolable woman all the easier as he was at that point involved in a violent dispute with the minister that was even brought to Hitler's attention. Goebbels had opposed Speer's intention to open up the Grunewald with promenades, riding paths and tennis courts. He argued that this would falsify the 'proletarian' image of Berlin by giving that neighbourhood a 'feudal' character.

Matters were further complicated by the fact that Speer's former patron Karl Hanke used the quarrel between Joseph and Magda Goebbels to promote his own social advancement. He began to court Magda Goebbels and to assail her with passionate letters. In her confusion she actually seems to have considered a divorce, and to have toyed with the idea of marrying the simple and rather earthy Karl Hanke, especially after he presented her with a Leporello-like catalogue of her husband's peccadilloes. In order to distract her and stop her from rushing into anything, Speer persuaded her to come to Italy and he reinforced her objection to Hanke's attempt to join the party.

Together they travelled around Sicily, visiting Syracuse and the temple high above Segesta. The monumental ruins of Agrigento and Selinunte led Speer to observe, 'not without inner satisfaction', the extent to which even the Greeks had abandoned classical proportions.

At the tomb of Frederick II in Palermo he decided to suggest to Hitler that the Hohenstaufen emperor be transferred to the crypt beneath the Soldiers' Hall. He also admired the melancholy and noble solitude of Castel del Monte, but nothing equalled his impression of Paestum. 'Paestum overpowered me,' he declared later. 'It simply stood there, magnificent – as if it were the most natural thing in the world.' Although he recognized that it did not resemble his own designs, he thought it encapsulated everything he had pursued and missed 'as though in the dark'. The 'Doric' world, he believed, far outclassed all the architectural heritage of the Italian Renaissance, which, of course, he could scarcely have come across in southern Italy.[24]

Shortly after the party returned, Hanke began to pester Hitler to agree to his minister's divorce and to his own marriage plans. But he was met with total incomprehension. Using no less an argument than *raison d'état* Hitler rejected Hanke's request. After a performance of *Tristan* at the Bayreuth festival, Hitler asked Speer to fill him in on the background to the matrimonial crisis. He then summoned Goebbels and in Speer's presence forbade his liaison with Lida Baarova, demanded a reconciliation with his wife and told the couple to leave Bayreuth at once. Goebbels was noticeably annoyed for some time and, Speer recorded, this always remained 'the cause of a gulf' between them. To the outside world, however, Goebbels concealed his irritation and somewhat later he called Speer an 'old confidant', hinting at the help he had given.[25]

Berlin was by no means the only project of urban renewal, merely the most comprehensive and also the boldest. In October 1933, when laying the foundation stone of the House of German Art in Munich, Hitler had already called it the 'first beautiful building of the new Reich', suggesting that the renewed importance of Hamburg and Bremen, Leipzig, Cologne, Essen and Chemnitz might also give these cities a more forward-looking appearance. The vast Nuremberg building site was not even mentioned in that list. By the following year's Reich Party Rally Hitler was more specific, speaking of the 'tremendous preliminary work' that had been going on for some time. 'Revolutionary construction programmes' were in progress 'in a series of major German cities, the magnitude of which will only be finally appreciated after many decades', Hitler announced. Such things could not 'be conjured up from one day to the next'.[26] Eventually there were over forty so-called 'Führer cities' which were designated for far-reaching reconstruction, often transforming the entire townscape.[27] These building programmes were devised to modernize transport and the infrastructure generally, but with the so-called *forums* they united a large number of meeting halls, parade grounds and cultural buildings in an ensemble of totalitarian community life. Speer accepted the commission to perform this task in Heidelberg, but he later withdrew under the strange pretext that he could not face the idea of pulling down and reconstructing part of the town of his youth, with its alleys, its student taverns and its venerable burghers' houses.[28]

There were so many projects that numerous architects had to be enlisted. Every new name inevitably diminished Speer's influence. In fact he was never Hitler's architect-general; his responsibility was always confined to Nuremberg and Berlin. Any other solution would have contradicted Hitler's principle of 'divide and rule' which meant more to him than any friendship. Spurred on by the power drive that he had acquired astonishingly quickly for all his 'apolitical' clumsiness, Speer tried to overstep the mark. But he was immediately reined in, and after years of intrigue he had to abandon his lofty ambitions.

Within a short time Hermann Giesler, the brother of the future Gauleiter of Munich, had become Speer's fiercest rival. Coming, like him, from a family of architects, Giesler had attracted attention with his plans for Sonthofen, one of the National Socialist elite schools, which he had designed without a commission because he believed in the Party's cause. Thanks to Speer's intervention Giesler had been encouraged soon afterwards to enter a competition for the Weimar Gauforum, one of the complexes of official buildings planned throughout Germany, on the terrain between the railway station and the old town centre, and he had won the first prize. That is how he met Hitler, who recognized in this burly, devoted, though somewhat unimaginative architect an obedient tool for his future plans.

The reconstruction of the famous Hotel Elephant, which had played a part in the life of Goethe and Schiller and in the classical period of German literature generally, was still within the framework of Giesler's work in Weimar. But along with lesser jobs he soon received commissions for another of the increasingly popular *forums*, this time in Augsburg, as well as for the 'High School' of the Party on Lake Chiemsee. His designs, like those of Speer, always evolved in close collaboration with Hitler. Although Hitler clearly showed his appreciation he did not develop a personal relationship with Giesler, whom he found too awkward, lacking in inspiration, and also too petit-bourgeois. Speer nevertheless became increasingly jealous of him. When Hitler appointed his rival a professor and then, in a kind of parallel to Speer, as Generalbaurat für die Hauptstadt der Bewegung (Architect-General for the Capital of the Movement), entrusting him with planning sovereignty for Munich, Speer took it as an open challenge.

He had every reason to feel slighted as Munich originally came within the sphere of Paul Ludwig Troost, as whose successor he saw himself. However, the plans for Munich had not made any more progress than those for Berlin. Hitler felt he had to make a quick decision, and no one seemed more suitable than the servile and energetic Giesler. What may have upset Speer even more was that his rival now had almost as many commissions as he did; some months earlier he had already remarked to his staff, 'we've got to keep an eye on Giesler'.[29]

Filled with alarm, Speer sent a memorandum to Hitler, in which he naturally concealed his private motivations. In view of the numerous building projects everywhere, he argued, a general artistic line would have to be maintained and protected against the presumption of local authorities. Indeed, some Gauleiters and municipal administrations, who were anxious to emulate the Führer's building fever, had set up their own planning teams or had disproportionately enlarged existing ones. On some doubtful authority or other, they had begun to pull down buildings and initiate projects, causing havoc in planning matters. Speer also pointed to the massive costs which this duplication was causing and to the already perceptible shortage of building materials which, as he had recently pointed out, was bound to affect the more significant plans for Berlin and Nuremberg.

Speer's memorandum boiled down to the suggestion that a 'Führer's commissioner for architecture and town planning in the NSDAP' be appointed and there was no doubt that he considered himself the only possible candidate for this post. This would in fact have given him the right to interfere in any building project, as well as a kind of control of the entire guild of architects enlisted for public programmes. He committed the tactical mistake of not discussing his intentions with Hitler in confidence, but of arrogantly using the official channels instead.

This brought Martin Bormann to the scene. Hitler's *Sekretär Wurm*, as he was generally called in allusion to the shifty character in Schiller's play *Kabale und Liebe*, had just begun rising to his dominant position as the central figure of Hitler's court. Quietly and persistently, this burly man in his ill-fitting party uniform had pushed his way up almost unnoticed, climbing step by step, always listening, always assessing with a sly expression on his coarse face. He only really had enemies, but Hitler appreciated his reliability, and, because contempt invariably underestimates its subject, Bormann was proud of the arrogant dislike he usually encountered. With the habitual suspicion that had carried him to the top, he had realized for some time that Speer was trying to get more involved in politics than became an artist. Ever since, he had sensed in him a dangerous opponent. Crude as Bormann was, he was one of the few who never fell under Speer's spell. On the contrary, Speer's charm roused his worst fears. In order to check his growing influence, Bormann had put Giesler in charge of the overall planning for the development of the Obersalzberg. Now he asked him for a 'private' comment on Speer's proposals.

It required little acumen for Giesler to envisage the position of dependence in which he would find himself if Speer were appointed the Führer's Commissioner for Architecture and Town Planning. On the strength of an ill-considered agreement Speer had already denied him various requests for building materials or turned down individual plans. This had made Giesler wary and he therefore rejected Speer's proposal 'on points of principle'.[30]

That was the signal for Bormann. As a born intriguer he knew very well that a thirst for power was best hidden under a show of impartiality. Acting as an unprejudiced mediator loyal to both sides, he conferred first with one side and then with the other, raised factual points, let a casual remark by the Führer drop now and again or a suspicion dressed up as a question, and put off the decision without losing sight of his objective, to contain Speer's influence.

The quarrel dragged on for months. A first step was taken in 1940 when in addition to all his other duties Giesler was invited by Hitler to take charge of the overall plan for Linz, 'my home town, the town of my youth and … of my old age', as Hitler explained on that occasion. He wanted to make this sleepy provincial nest a 'world metropolis', with gigantic halls, towers, galleries and 'a stadium', and he asked Giesler to draw up plans not only for the buildings in which he was personally interested, but also for the whole embankment of the Danube.[31]

This was a special distinction, and it was Speer's first sensational defeat. He later observed that Giesler's appointment had done far more than arouse envy. After years in which his bond with Hitler had steadily deepened, it had marked 'the first crisis' in their relationship. Until then Speer had risen higher and higher, becoming so self-assured that he could no longer see how much offence he was giving to those who

Speer preferred civilian clothing, if only to dissasociate himself from the Party officials. But Hitler disliked Speer's civilian status and in 1934 compelled him to put on a uniform by appointing him to a staff position. Nevertheless, whenever possible, Speer tried to avoid wearing uniform. The photograph shows him inspecting a building site in Nuremberg.

were also bidding for Hitler's favour. Now Speer had been made to realize that there were limits even for him. The shock was all the greater as he could not explain it. It never occurred to him then, he added, that behind Hitler's inscrutable whim there might be a more considered motive.[32]

Speer was hurt, and gave in after a brief tussle. He wrote to Bormann retracting his memorandum and forgoing any further discussion about it. In his letter he complained that 'a large part of me has collapsed inside'. He went one step further and defiantly asked Hitler to relieve him of six, often time-consuming, Party offices, as well as of all 'general building questions'. Speer even laid down the directorship of the 'Beauty of Work' Office, which had meant a great deal to him. In future, he wrote, he wished to concern himself 'exclusively with my real life's work, the erection of the Berlin and Nuremberg buildings'. His disappointment was possibly increased when Hitler 'unreservedly and joyfully' accepted his offer to withdraw. Some compensation came his way a short while later, although it was not particularly attractive. After the conclusion of the Norwegian campaign Hitler commissioned him to take on the plans for the new town which was to arise near Drontheim. With shipyards, docks and a quarter of a million inhabitants it was to be the largest naval base of the future Reich.[33]

This did not help Speer get over Linz. The extent to which this defeat was still troubling him months later emerged on Hitler's next birthday. Speer had arrived at the Führer's headquarters the evening before, in order to convey his personal wishes at midnight. The following morning he submitted a document to Hitler. Speer had ensured that he had the support of several architects and artists who were his friends. Their signatures reinforced his real concern: 'To be allowed, in noble competition, to participate in the rebuilding of the city of Linz on the Danube.'[34]

What clearly hurt Speer most in his quarrel with Giesler was the seeming indifference with which Hitler had watched his setback. But Hitler may well have felt that Speer had risen too fast and that he had been too quick to take liberties and occasionally adopt a tone of command that he was not entitled to. The old Party comrades, who had been hungry for struggle and who believed they had stood up well in that struggle, were not willing to give in to the new man. Each of them had his own body of followers and was skilled in setting traps. Nobody whose position was based solely on Hitler's authority could disregard these people with impunity.

Speer had demonstrated his power drive in the way he organized his department, but also, for instance, in the way he brusquely forbade the independent architects, whom he enlisted for his Berlin plans, to accept other commissions without his consent.[35] Another opportunity for testing his strength was provided by the still unresolved problem posed by Julius Lippert. A decision was pending at about the same time as the quarrel with Giesler. It seems that Speer was so intractable because he wanted to obliterate his defeat by Giesler as quickly as possible. This time he had every reason to feel confident because he knew that Hitler was on his side.

In spite of all the special powers granted him with his appointment as Generalbauinspektor, there were many detailed issues which he had to settle with the municipal administration of Berlin. Accustomed as he was to the commanding tone of the regime, Speer very soon found the need to reach agreements a nuisance, particularly as Lippert continued to oppose any reconstruction of the city. Time and again Speer and his Generalbauinspektion overrode Lippert's office, challenging or ignoring its competence. There could be no arrangements or compromises, Speer informed the city administration, and when a committee was set up to formulate at least some basic rules for the constant squabbles, Speer rejected the proposal as being too petty. 'The unique nature of my task', he wrote to Lippert, 'demands the clear priority of one office responsible for the overall task.' In the manner of a Roman proconsul he added: 'That means me.'[36]

Lippert, however, had no intention of giving in. When Speer sent him a decree which laid down once and for all the powers of the Generalbauinspektor, Lippert replied that binding regulations of that kind could 'only be issued by the Führer personally'. The struggle continued for some time. When Speer decided to enforce the 'decree' regardless, Lippert refused to inform his staff and accused his opponent of nothing less than humiliating the administration of the Reich capital. Speer was indignant. This time he turned to Hitler, who had not forgotten the Berlin mayor's earlier opposition. Angrily he now ordered that 'Reich Minister Lammers be instructed to see to the immediate deposition of Dr Lippert'.

It was a victory, but it meant that Speer had made his first venture into the densest thickets of politics. While he had been prepared to make tactical alliances, he had until then always been careful to avoid the power struggles around him, which struck him as alien and spooky. Ten years later he was still fond of emphasizing his 'unpolitical nature'. Goebbels, who had not forgotten Speer's role in his matrimonial crisis and who regarded the mayor of Berlin as one of his protégés, noted that 'Speer has treated Lippert very unfairly. He will have to pay for this one day.' Another diary entry recorded how Speer had 'tormented' his old friend. Around this time Goebbels formulated one of the principles which determined his actions: 'Let's put the fat on the fire!'[37] All he needed was for the opportunity to arise.

Needlessly, Speer went a step further. He added a kind of postscript to his dispute with Lippert, in which, seen as a whole, he was probably right. Not satisfied with the defeat of his obstinate adversary, he forwarded his entire correspondence with the Berlin city administration to the Reichssicherheitshauptamt, the administrative headquarters of the SS, 'for confidential information'.[38]

The new Berlin was to be completed in 1950 after the victorious conclusion of all the wars already declared and yet to be fought. At an
unprecedented foundation ceremony Hitler would then proclaim the
world empire and bestow on the capital the name *Germania*. In moments
of euphoria when his imagination raced ahead, he already pictured the
victory parade with all the pomp, the salutes and the fireworks that
would crown the triumph. When Speer suspended all building work in
September 1939, at the start of the war, he received a brusque reproof
from Bormann, which had clearly been issued on Hitler's instruction;
and a few months later, after the victory over France, the dictator sent
word that the reshaping of Berlin continued to be a matter of 'maximum
urgency'. A decree, backdated by Hitler to the day of the armistice,
described the realization 'of these vital building commissions for the
Reich ... as the most important contribution towards finally ensuring our
victory'.[39]

But Berlin was to be more than the centre and glory of the new
world empire. In the background there was always the plan of creating
an open cultic space surrounded by an awe-inspiring backdrop. In this
scheme the Grand Avenue was to serve as a processional road, while
'Building T', with the names of those killed in action, suggested itself as
a kind of a shrine; and it was no accident that the assembly hall was
modelled on the domes of Roman churches. It is interesting that when
Speer stood in front of St Peter's at the end of his Italian journey he
was disappointed by the insignificant dimensions of this central building
of Christendom. 'How small it seemed to me!' he remarked later; he
had been 'shocked' by the sight. For he realized that the intended effect
of 'stunning' the observer failed to materialize as soon as a building was
set in relation to the buildings around it. Looking at the balcony above
the main entrance, from where the papal blessing was pronounced, he
asked himself whether the far greater distances which Hitler would be
faced with in the domed hall would perhaps prove unbridgeable, and
whether not only the hundreds of thousands of people in the hall but
also the orator himself would shrink into insignificance. Speer had
shared Hitler's belief that buildings derived their power from their cubic
volume. It dawned on him for the first time that this was a fallacy. But
these were only brief moments of doubt and they did not affect his wonderful exhilaration. Not until he was imprisoned in Spandau, where he
studied books on the architecture of the early French Renaissance, did
he realize 'that something can be great without being massive'.[40]

Taken as a whole the weaknesses of his architectural concepts become apparent. It was despotic architecture which, for all the high aims, never got beyond demonstrating naked power. It was cold, dead and inhuman, but also blatantly devoid of ideas. There was always a Grand Avenue, of the kind Speer planned for Nuremberg and Berlin, and Giesler later did for Munich, always a domed structure, such as the one Giesler was planning for the central railway station in Munich on an even larger scale, always that endlessly monotone sequence of pillars and cornices, the elongated exclamation marks, such as Hitler's own design for the 'Column of the Movement' in Munich, intended to dwarf the spires of the Frauenkirche to the 'dimensions of toys'.

It has been pointed out, in connection with the simultaneous building efforts in Washington and Rome, that these designs represented one last attempt at achieving a grand design. They rebelled against the disintegration of style and the arbitrariness of contemporary aesthetics. Speer himself remarked that the buildings had also been a 'romantic protest' against the unstoppable disfigurement of the modern world that had filled him with 'panic and grief'.[41]

There certainly is some truth in these reflections. But nothing that Speer and Hitler set against this decline had any vitality of its own, it merely reflected a resentment against anything new. By disregarding scale and proportion they missed both classicism and the romantic opposition to it. All they ended up with was another expression of that arbitrariness they detested in modern architecture. One cannot overlook the excessive rage of this architecture, nor the hysterical trait inherent to it, and it only takes one glance at the entrance hall to Hermann Göring's palace with the 'biggest staircase in the world' in order to realize how anti-classical, to the point of caricature, classicism can become.[42]

These buildings not only embodied contempt of the contemporary style. What made them look so strikingly lifeless was in part the theatrical tendency to self-deification. Strictly speaking, they got by without people. They were in fact no more than the shapeless lines or dots in the building sketches, what Hitler once significantly referred to as 'the planet's bacilli'. This architecture knew nothing about life and certainly placed death high above it. That is why the temples, the pillared halls, the candelabra and the façades decorated with statues inevitably conjure up images of mausoleums, with the shadow of death hovering above and each stone colossus representing a sarcophagus with a strange aura of Hades. The full impact of the picture suggested by these symbols can only be appreciated if one knows that general traffic was to be banned from the Grand Avenue.

Model of the staircase in Hermann Göring's palace, designed by Speer's office. When shown a photograph of it, the famous Italian architect Luigi Nervi said: 'Incredible! They must have gone mad!'

Speer may unwittingly have revealed something of the hidden truth of his buildings when, at the beginning of his work for Nuremberg, he invented the 'theory of the value of ruins'. The sight of a tram hangar being demolished made Speer realize how unsightly the ruins of modern buildings were. It struck him that shapeless fragments of con-crete and rusty steel rods were incapable of producing the historical frisson which lent special dignity to the ruins of the ancient world. On further reflection it occurred to him that by using materials predating the modern age and by applying statics modelled on antiquity it would be possible to create buildings which could look like the remains of the Palatine or the Baths of Caracalla when they fell into disrepair.

To illustrate his theory he had a large drawing made, showing the Zeppelinfeld with collapsed walls overgrown with ivy. Nearly everyone voiced doubts, suspecting that the durability of the Thousand-Year Reich was being called in question. Speer cast them aside and decided to show the sketch to Hitler. There was no furious outburst. Hitler was calm and reflected silently, before pointing to Italy which had recap-tured the spirit of past centuries thanks to the architectural heritage of ancient Rome. Hitler believed that great architecture could make time stand still. In a speech at the laying of the foundation stone for the Nuremberg Congress Hall he said: 'But if the Movement were ever to fall silent, then this witness here will continue to speak even thousands of years later. Amidst a sacred grove of ancient oaks people will be admiring in respectful astonishment this first giant among the buildings of the Third Reich.'[43]

In order to ensure the 'eternity value' of his buildings Speer obtained durable granite from all over the place and stored enormous quantities of it. But ancient building methods involved enormous costs, so he only applied it to a few important structures: the stadium and the Märzfeld in Nuremberg as well as the Soldiers' Hall and the Führer's Palace in Berlin; Hitler thought that a steel framework would be indispensable, for the dome of the great assembly hall at least, even though Speer wanted to do without it. There were doubts too about the statics of the triumphal arch, so that its construction by the 'ruin method' was regarded only as 'probable'.[44]

Looking back, Speer 'vividly remembered a swarm of utopians and planners' who 'came crawling out of the woodwork and crowded all the ante-rooms' after Hitler's rise to power in 1933. 'All of them had something to offer on which salvation, or at any rate progress depended ... Dilettantism flourished.' Sometimes, Speer concluded self-critically, he asked himself 'whether the building projects for Berlin and elsewhere don't belong to the same category.'[45]

One day, during the years of dreaming and being carried away making plans, Speer's father came to Berlin. The famous son proudly showed him through the Academy. He looked through the countless drawings which had accumulated, and his son explained the buildings on the model avenue. Shaking his head in obvious astonishment, the old man's eyes wandered between the plans and his enthusiastic son. In the end he just shrugged his shoulders and said: 'You've all gone completely mad.'[46]

Chapter Four
ENTANGLEMENTS

At the beginning of 1935 Speer had bought a small hunting lodge in a high valley of the Bavarian Alps. He wanted to retreat there occasionally to spend more time with his family. Although it was cramped, there was just room enough to erect a few drawing boards and to put up the occasional colleague or two. It was another attempt to escape from the hectic life of the big city, into which he was being increasingly drawn by his political offices and the growing workload. Looking back, it was 'a happy period', he observed.[1] But no sooner had it begun than it came to an end.

In his enthusiasm Speer told Hitler about his refuge. The timing could not have been worse as both of them were just discovering their mutual interests and feelings for each other. Hitler spontaneously proposed to Speer that he should give up his hunting lodge and move instead into a summer cottage on the Obersalzberg, a short distance away from the Berghof. The family of the piano manufacturer Bechstein had given it to Hitler years ago. Although he felt a twinge of regret at the thought of giving up the idyll in the Ostertal, Speer accepted the offer without much reflection. He realized that he was being offered promotion to Hitler's most intimate circle which included Göring and Bormann, and Speer was not the person to turn down this invitation to the 'Mountain of the Grail'.[2] The Bechstein house soon proved too small, and immediately after moving in Speer began to design a studio house for himself and his family, at the same time as Hitler was having his simple Berghof converted into an imposing property, according to his own plans.

It was a time of great harmony, all the more so as it coincided first with the plans for Nuremberg and then for Berlin. In the end Bormann was instructed to have both houses built, and in the spring of 1937 Speer moved for a second time.

The temporary circumstances of those months had brought a certain degree of unrest into his life that soon made him question the advantages of his new place of residence. Furthermore crowds of visitors streamed through the fence of the high-security compound every day in order to see 'the Führer', who would indeed appear on the terrace of his house from time to time to receive their homage. Bormann, tireless as ever, had taken nearly all the building activity on the Obersalzberg into his own hands and was progressively turning the site into an extensive and increasingly lavish complex. He bought up farmsteads and forestry plots in the neighbourhood, often applying pressure, he had the woodland paths asphalted and built barracks, servants' quarters, guesthouses and garages. Labour squads were at work day and night, up until the last years of the war, converting the quiet mountainside into a gigantic, noisy building site.

Speer may have found the company in which he now moved even more trying. Hitler would often spend weeks on end on the Obersalzberg, invariably surrounded by a *camarilla* of personal followers and a few chosen Party veterans, who had been in his circle in Berlin or even in the Munich days. These included his personal photographer Heinrich Hoffmann, who had brought Dr Theodor Morell with him one day, the commander of the Leibstandarte (personal bodyguard) Sepp Dietrich, Hitler's physician-in-residence Dr Karl Brandt, Ambassador Walter Hewel, a few Wehrmacht adjutants and Party officials, and Martin Bormann, who was usually present. Unlike Berlin, women were admitted on the Obersalzberg. Once he had joined the circle Speer met Eva Braun and a friendship soon developed. She still seemed unsure of herself then, addressing Hitler as '*Mein Führer*', even when among intimate friends. But she gradually learned to fulfil her difficult role in an attractive natural manner, patiently enduring the frequent slights resulting from her position as Hitler's mistress and making no demands. Speer soon noticed the 'insultingly modest' jewellery which Hitler had given her. Whenever the company set off for the Berghof, mostly from Munich, Eva Braun was packed into a small car, Speer recorded, and great pains were taken to see that it never came into contact with Hitler's official motorcade.[3] When less intimate guests or official visitors were present she always had to withdraw, and even when Göring came over from his nearby property she was banished to her room on the upper floor. At all other times, however, she sat at Hitler's side, trying to enter into the spirit of his conversation. When he fell to brooding and stared silently into the fireplace she tried to keep the conversation going in a lowered voice. Sometimes he would hold her hand.

Discussion of a sketch in one of Hitler's private rooms on the Obersalzberg. 'I always have time for you and your plans,' Hitler said to Speer.

When Hitler re-emerged as if from a stupefied sleep, he always expressed his thoughts in a sudden torrent of words: oft-repeated political declamations alternated with recollections from the legendary days of struggle, how he had overcome thousands of obstacles and egocentricities to forge a Party from the initially uncertain followers who had joined the movement from all over the place. Some cue or other would make him think of Henry the Lion, of dietary recipes or of the breeding of German sheepdogs, or he would formulate diplomatic maxims such as that one must never be embarrassed to start a war. Any treaty with a rival power must leave a few questions open, which might provide a pretext for war, he explained, pointing to the example of

Rome which had always built the trigger for a new war into its peace treaties. 'That's Rome! That's statesmanship', he exclaimed, before the 'stiff and respectful circle'.[4] Then he often switched to details.

Speer once tried to map the abrupt character of these monologues that jumped from one subject to the next. Beginning for example with a criticism of the lighting regulations for motor vehicles and a complaint about the driver of an Obergruppenführer – an SS general – whose driving licence was withdrawn on his orders after an accident, Hitler went on to threaten that in future he would lock up even Gauleiters for traffic offences; next he demanded that the Niederwald monument and Kaub Castle in the middle of the Rhine be floodlit at night; then all of a sudden he wanted to know the best method for manufacturing artificial honey and then without any transition he gave his opinion of the latest film he had seen, followed by a smoking ban for all official premises of the Party, and so on *ad infinitum*. In between he would make some aggressive anti-Semitic remarks.[5] Even the most unimportant matters were uttered with an excited, strangely disjointed intensity as he drifted from one emotive word to the next without ever coming to an end. The only diversion occurred when he exposed particular followers to ridicule, such as the Labour Front leader Robert Ley, the Party philosopher Alfred Rosenberg, whom Hitler regarded as a 'narrow-minded Balt', and even Heinrich Himmler with his 'enthusiasm for pottery shards'. Then, in turn, he would worry and frighten others, such as Ernst 'Putzi' Hanfstaengl, his old comrade-in-arms and foreign press chief, who was so upset by one of these crude pranks that he promptly decided to go into exile.[6]

Speer later admitted with some embarrassment that he had joined in the laughter at these humiliating and offensive jokes, even though they were not to his taste. But they created a sense of complicit agreement and could also offer tactical advantages in the tangled power struggles of an entourage where each person was everyone else's secret opponent. He might not have been aware of it, but Speer gradually advanced from outsider to team player. In retrospect he himself spoke of the 'depths' to which, inevitably, one descended with every step towards the pinnacles of power.[7]

The days passed in a regular, almost ritual, pattern, beginning in the late morning on the terrace of the Berghof. The guests would stand around in small groups or lounge on the wicker deckchairs until Hitler's arrival was announced towards noon. After lunch the company always walked on the same path to the so-called Little Tea House, situated

higher up. There the flagging conversation was resumed. Towards
evening the party set off on its way back in no particular order, and a
mere two hours later they all met again for dinner. Sometimes, if he
was in a good mood, Hitler would throw a flower to one of the ladies
before leading whoever was his dinner partner by the arm into the spacious living room to watch one or sometimes several films, most of them
recent productions. He was fond of quick-witted social comedies with a
happy ending, of Heinz Rühmann's *Quax, the Daring Pilot,* of Hans
Moser's impersonations of grumpy porters or of Willy Forst's entertain-
ing revues, but he also liked disaster melodramas such as *San Francisco* or
King Kong. Hitler asked to see some of these films up to ten times.

When the performance was over and the company struggled out of
their chairs there was usually more to come. With leaden limbs the
exhausted guests gathered in front of the fireplace at Hitler's insistence.
There conversation resumed again. It dragged on, impeded chiefly by
Hitler's presence. Nearly everybody's face betrayed the effort it took to
help the discussion along by interjecting some new idea. Rarely did the
exchanges rise above the level of the small-talk which had already characterized lunch and tea, and soon it dried up from a mixture of respect-
fulness and exhaustion. Often Hitler would sit there, lost in thought.
Between two and three in the morning he would formally say goodnight
to Eva Braun, and shortly afterwards he himself would leave the room.
Only then did the company revive briefly in a spirit of nervous jollity
before finally breaking up.

Although almost all the participants suffered from the relentless triviality of those meetings, no one ever dared absent himself from the
monotonous procedure. Speer spoke of how a prolonged period in
Hitler's presence had 'made him tired, exhausted and drained'. At least
in winter he was able to get away for a few days by going on a skiing
trip with Eva Braun and others, but Hitler was invariably irritated by
such 'extravagancies' and spoke of his hatred for cold and snow. Now
and again Speer succeeded in replacing the evening film by an opera,
but the repertoire of records was soon exhausted: it was always Richard
Wagner, the *Merry Widow,* or *Fledermaus*; once, after *Tristan,* Hitler
remarked that this was what he would wish to hear 'in the hour of his
death'. Sometimes Speer would try to invite a famous scientist, an artist
or a musician to the Obersalzberg, but he did not get far with it.
Indeed, when he repeated the suggestion, Hitler turned it down 'almost
irritably'.[8]

Presumably Hitler needed the idleness of those empty days, Speer remarked, to make up for the pressure to which he was exposed by his countless public appearances. Besides, as one observer put it, he used those periods of drifting and dozing 'like a crocodile in the mud of the Nile' to prepare for the next drama he would inflict on the world. From time to time he would draw the attention of his visitors or guests to the Untersberg across the valley, where, as legend had it, the emperor Frederick II was sleeping his sleep of centuries until the day that he would come back and liberate the people. It could be no accident that he had found his place of residence opposite it, Hitler was wont to say. Here he was reminded every day of his mission to liberate his country and make it powerful: 'The old legend will be fulfilled from here.' Before leaving the room, he would sometimes go to the large window and gaze at the dark face of the mountain.[9] All in all, the routine of the days and evenings on the Obersalzberg spent in trivial conversation was the inevitable consequence of a system which tolerated no difference of opinion. By making everyone think the same way the art of dispute was lost, until there was nothing more to argue about.

Once Speer's mother came to the Obersalzberg to look after the children for a few days. Hitler often invited her to the Berghof. He obviously liked the spirited and imperious woman who was still a convinced follower of his. He mobilized all the charm at his command to demonstrate his admiration, but she was too shrewd and socially experienced to be impressed by it. Instead she changed her opinion of Hitler and the company he kept, finding the circumstances '*nouveau riche*' and his hospitality 'crude'. Hitler was 'terribly nice', she thought, but it was a '*parvenu* world' which he had created for himself.[10]

Speer stood aloof from the intrigues at court as much as he could. In retrospect he pleaded that his ambitions had been exclusively artistic and technocratic. Some observers have felt that this was just an excuse, but it was strong enough to prevent him from attending most Party events. He increasingly neglected the links he had to the Party, although they might have helped him extend his influence. Speer could afford to do so. As Hitler's confidant he was throughout most of the period in possession of the magic ring which eliminated all obstacles. Hitler also appears to have seen him as the non-political artist. He never spoke to Speer about the manoeuvres he was then beginning to initiate and which largely belonged to the realm of foreign affairs. In spite of his workload Speer felt that he was being sidelined: 'Evidently I lacked some mysterious consecration,' he observed, revealing how much this neglect had hurt him.[11]

Days on the Obersalzberg were a strange mixture of holiday and nerve-racking triviality for the participants. Hitler's monologues, strolls to the Little Tea House and film performances alternated in never-ending monotony. The top picture shows an architectural discussion on the terrace of the Berghof; the bottom one shows Speer with Dr Karl Brandt, Hitler's physician-in-residence (left, next to Speer). Against the railing is Max Wünsche, an aide. Opposite Speer is Walter Hewel, a representative of the Foreign Office. Both pictures were taken in the late 1930s.

Why, one might ask, did he nevertheless remain so close to Hitler? For apart from these slights, it was not only the days filled with tedious ceremonial and the triviality of the endless conversations that made him suffer. He still had an unfailing social eye and for all his conviviality he was well aware of the undistinguished company on the Obersalzberg.

Nothing could prevent him from having a sense of not quite belonging anywhere. Neither the temptations of power, perhaps not even the architectural fame that beckoned as he continued throughout all those years to dream of Hitler as a modern Pericles or Cosimo de' Medici and of himself as a second Schinkel, could compensate for the sense of humiliation that often came over him. What held him in that strange thrall and made him accept the many unacceptable demands that contradicted everything that his origin, his interest and his lifestyle stood for, was above all the 'magic' power which Hitler had over him ever since 'he took possession of me'.[12] It even survived the break he decided to make at the last moment.

The more uneasy he felt, the more energetically he devoted himself to his building projects in the fragmented time that was left to him in Berchtesgaden. Speer managed his office with the same mixture of discretion and professional distance which he maintained towards everyone. This earned him deep admiration among most of his staff. They respected his authority and his incorruptibility and they were proud of his closeness to Hitler, which also increased their importance. Speer shielded his colleagues from any Party influence. He increasingly saw himself as the leader of a more or less free artists' association which had nothing to do with 'those people outside'. When the architect Wilhelm Kreis asked him through Rudolf Wolters whether he could obtain an official uniform for him, Speer haughtily rejected the idea: 'Tell him that if he identifies himself by the velvet jacket of an artist, he is more than any Obergruppenführer and has no one above him.'[13]

'We will create a great empire ... it will begin in Norway and extend to Northern Italy,' Hitler had said to Speer on one occasion.[14] In the late autumn of 1937 he thought he was ready to begin the great game. Hitler's first actions were only the opening moves on the chessboard: Austria, the Sudetenland and possibly Czechoslovakia, the Memel territory and eventually Danzig. But he never lost sight of the whole scene. At the end of January 1938 he summoned Speer. Standing in the middle of the room, he asked him with almost fervent solemnity whether he could build a new Reich Chancellery in time for his diplomatic New Year's reception on 10 January of the following year. The building would be 'of great importance for the further development of his policy'. At first Speer was speechless. He had seen a sketch Hitler had made in 1935 for the extension of the Reich Chancellery and only a few months ago Speer himself had submitted a provisional draft. But

In January 1938 Hitler charged Speer with building a new Reich Chancellery in less than a year. Initially Speer was dumbfounded, regarding the project as impossible. But he was so excited by the challenge that he agreed, and the building was in fact completed on schedule. The picture shows the so-called Court of Honour, with two sculptures by Arno Breker.

there had never been any mention that the new construction was imminent and, as far as one could see, it would be impossible to meet the date. Nevertheless Speer was tempted by the offer and the excessively tight schedule made the challenge all the greater. He asked for a few hours to consider it, consulted his staff and gradually attuned them to his own ambition. In the evening he reported to Hitler and presented him with 'the most reckless promise of my life'.[15]

That same night he held the first planning talks and gave the signal for the start of a feverish race against time. While demolition work started on Voss-strasse, the whole of which was given over to the new building, hardly any of the plans were completed and not even the sequence of rooms had been decided. And that was how it remained from start to finish. The actual construction work took barely nine months. Throughout, the final shape of the building was always limping alongside the state of construction at any moment. Material and individual parts were ordered as soon as even a provisional idea existed of numerous rooms. Nearly 4,500 building workers were enlisted within a short time and employed in two shifts. As Speer was also responsible for the interior design, he placed advance orders for the furniture, the hand-knotted wall hangings, the mosaics, the decorative doors, the bas-reliefs above the doors and innumerable other objects of craftwork. Disregarding his staff's advice, he did without a schedule, which could not be met anyway, and for the first time he displayed the brilliant improvisational genius with which both followers and opponents have always credited him.

As far as the public was concerned, the project was shrouded in secrecy so as not to feed rumours about extravagant expenditure. But when the building had its formal topping-out at the beginning of August, Hitler felt he had to face the critical rumblings head-on. In an address to the architects, engineers and builders he declared: 'I am too proud to go into former castles ... This new German republic is neither a lodger nor a bed-renter in former royal rooms. If others reside in the Kremlin, at Hradčany or in some castle, then we will ensure a represen-tation of the Reich in buildings that spring from our own period.'[6]

The greatest architectural difficulty was posed by the narrow elongat-ed shape of the plot with its front extending over the whole 360 metres of Voss-strasse and which, moreover, had to be broken at the axis to achieve the required width. The visitor went through the main entrance in the Wilhelmsplatz into the stone-flagged 'Court of Honour' dominat-ed by four heavy columns. At the end a flight of stairs rose up to the building, its sides flanked by two over-lifesize bronze sculptures by Arno Breker, 'The Wehrmacht' and 'The Party'. The access behind the columns led, via a continually rising sequence of corridors and imposing rooms, up a few steps to the Circular Hall subdivided by fluted pillars. The empty walls were to be filled with a number of large sculptures.

In the plan the rotunda took up the broken axis of the building, opening onto the so-called marble gallery. It was modelled on the famous Hall of Mirrors at Versailles, but with a length of nearly 150 metres it was nearly twice as long. At the extreme end were the 'Great Reception Room' and the 'Reich Cabinet Room'. The floor and the walls were lined with dark red stone, speckled with deep green lights. It created an impression of solemnity and prepared the visitor for the holy of holies: Hitler's study, located to the side of it. The entrance, about halfway down the gallery, was emphasized by a heavy marble profile decorated with a cartouche bearing the initials A.H. The room mea-sured nearly 400 square metres. Speer had placed the furniture, the

The garden façade of the new Chancellery, with two equine sculptures by Josef Thorak.

groups of chairs, the map table and the huge globe, all designed by himself, near the walls in order to heighten the sense of size and spaciousness.

About fifteen metres lay between the double entrance door and Hitler's writing desk on the opposite side, the purpose being that any visitor not sufficiently filled with awe by the endless gallery, would in approaching the Führer finally be reduced to a kind of paralyzing despondency. In *Inside the Third Reich* Speer mentioned the four statesmanlike virtues of 'Wisdom, Prudence, Fortitude and Justice' that he incorporated in the gilded panels above the doors of the study in a kind of symbolic *Fürstenspiegel*, or book of guidance for the conduct of princes. But Hitler showed far greater interest in the inlaid woodwork which decorated the front of his desk. The depiction of a sword half drawn from its scabbard was a much more fitting image for the deliberately intimidating character of the building as a whole. 'Good, good,' Hitler said when he inspected the work; 'when the diplomats sitting in front of me at this desk see this, they'll learn to shiver and shake.'[17] The walls were faced with red marble and lined with paintings of the Italian school. A portrait of Bismarck by Franz von Lenbach hung above the fireplace. The open long side of the room was broken by five french

View of the writing desk in Hitler's study, where the furniture was designed by Speer.
The intarsias on the front side of the desk show a sword drawn from its scabbard.

windows leading to a terrace with sculptures of horses by Josef Thorak at each end. Steps led down from the side to the lower garden and across to the greenhouse.

Surprisingly, the building was largely devoid of the megalomanic features that made Speer's by then partially completed plans for the World Capital Germania seem so overwhelmingly excessive. It suggests that Speer may, if only in a gesture, have wanted to recall the more severe classicism of Paul Ludwig Troost, as whose liaison man he had initially met Hitler during the reconstruction of the old Reich Chancellery. But it seems more likely that, unlike with the huge projects for Berlin and Nuremberg, Speer drew inspiration from the very constraints imposed by the elongated building site. Of course, the architecture was garish and straining for effect, but no more so than the representative buildings of other ages, be it the Palatine, Versailles or the palaces of St Petersburg and countless other places. Even if Hitler was clearly exaggerating when, in his preface to the festive brochure published after the completion of the building, he described the old Reich Chancellery as 'mouldy through and through' with 'all its load-bearing beams consisting of rotten tinder', he was undoubtedly correct in claiming that the old building no longer met the administrative and representational needs of the Reich. For all its mannered magnificence the Reich Chancellery was without doubt Speer's most impressive building, even though he himself preferred his plans for Nuremberg.[18] The proportions were more modest and the blustering manner of the regime was less in evidence than in any other work of his design.

The race against time became increasingly breathless as the date for completion approached. In the midst of all this there occurred an event which Speer scarcely noticed and, for that reason, landed him in great trouble. On the evening of 9 November 1938 SA commando squads set off throughout the country and abused Jewish citizens, smashed the windows of their shops, wrecked numerous apartments and torched the synagogues, under the eyes of the police who stood idly by. The pogrom was a unique event staged and organized by Goebbels. He had travelled to Munich that day for the annual commemoration of the unsuccessful November coup of 1923. After a conversation with Hitler ('His views are totally radical and aggressive'), he had called on the assembled Party bosses to mobilize the 'people's wrath'. In his diary he wrote: 'I immediately issue appropriate directions to the police and the Party ... Tumultuous applause. Everybody rushes to the telephones. Now the

The so-called Marble Gallery, inspired by the Hall of Mirrors at Versailles but twice as long.

people will act.' When the allegedly 'seething soul of the people' was called back to order the following day, some 270 synagogues had been destroyed, over 7,500 businesses had been devastated, 190 Jews had been murdered and a few hundred more had put an end to their own lives. 'That's shown them!' Goebbels noted in the tone of cheerful infamy that he was fond of displaying.[19]

Driving to his office on the morning after the night that was soon sarcastically dubbed the *Reichkristallnacht*, or 'Reich Night of Crystal', Speer passed the smouldering wreckage of the Berlin Central Synagogue on Fasanenstrasse. It had been destroyed on Goebbels' specific instruction. Although Speer saw the collapsed façade and the charred beams scattered around, there is no telling whether, pressed as he was by a thousand deadlines, he even took in what he saw and whether he received more than a fleeting impression of it. At any rate the first version of *Inside the Third Reich*, which he admittedly described as a provisional draft, does not mention the experience at all. And even when the advisers he had enlisted for his memoirs insisted that an event such as this, occurring as it did in peaceful times and within a civilized nation, could not be allowed to pass unmentioned, Speer at first contradicted them.

SPEER

Not even the question why the middle-class instincts he was so fond of citing had not rebelled against it, could make him change his mind. He had nothing to say about it, he objected and, in a later conversation, he added: that was his real problem, he no longer understood the person he had been then. Only the suggestion that he should discover and, if possible, describe why the event had left him so unmoved, eventually made him comply.[20]

This resistance shows more clearly than anything else how rigidly Speer still insisted on the time-honoured distinction between the political and the private or even the artistic sphere to which he felt he belonged. As an architect not only his professional responsibilities but also those as a human being were narrowly defined, and the 'compartmentalized' thinking so strongly encouraged by the regime further strengthened this attitude. For those in power it was the most effective way of ensuring obedience and preventing conflicts of conscience. Moreover, it provided everyone with an alibi for human lethargy. Speer's remark that 'political events did not concern me'[21] was in a sense the key statement about those years. It set him apart from events in the streets, which had been born of the seemingly noncommittal tea-party talk at the Berghof; it dispelled any understanding of the moral dimension that is essential to politics in general, and it kept his self-esteem intact. In short, it helped him, and countless others, to escape any doubts in the confused life under a dictatorship. It also lies at the root of the paradoxes which characterized the actions and omissions of so many right to the end: the notion that one could 'blindly serve' Hitler and yet despise his henchmen and tools, that one could admire his strategy and celebrate its successes without feeling responsible for its instruments, that one could sit at the table of power and yet remain aloof.

This was one side of the self-appeasement practised by Speer. His wish to preserve the idealized picture he had concocted of his friend and patron despite all the conflicting experiences may have been a stronger motivation. When Hitler uttered a few words of regret after the events of 9 November, speaking once again of 'excesses', Speer's few doubts evaporated. Of course, he did not know of the silent agreement between Hitler and Goebbels whereby the Führer's person was on no account to be linked to the events. But he also had almost daily contact with the secondary figures, who had been active as scene-setters or accomplices. And even if, as has been argued, he somehow failed to notice the smouldering ruins on Fasanenstrasse because he was so

On 9 November 1938 SA commandos went into action, smashing the windows of Jewish shops, arresting Jewish citizens and setting fire to many synagogues. The following morning it was impossible not to notice the devastation, but Speer claimed to have no recollection of it.

exhausted, he was reminded of them soon afterwards. Hans Simon, one of his closer colleagues, handed in his notice on the grounds that: 'I don't work for people like that!'[22] Speer once distanced himself from Hitler's violent followers with the remark that they were nothing but 'repulsive bourgeois revolutionaries', adding that he himself was 'more typical' of the other side of the regime, of those 'whose idealism and devotion sustained Hitler'.[23] Where was the difference?

On 7 January 1939 Hitler came to Berlin from Munich to move into the new Reich Chancellery. To avoid any conceivable problems Speer had allowed for a few extra days, so that the building was finished two days ahead of schedule. This time Hitler had kept away from the planning work altogether and was therefore all the more expectant. He was deeply impressed, and perhaps it was the admiring glances which he repeatedly directed at Speer during the inspection that justified his office chief Karl Maria Hettlage's remark to him: 'You must know that you are Hitler's unrequited love.'[24]

Hitler organized a rally at the Berlin Sportpalast for the 4,500 workmen who had carried out the construction, as well as for the thousands of suppliers and he gave a festive banquet in the dining hall of the new Chancellery for the architects, artists and craftsmen. He proudly spoke of the 'first building of the great new German Reich', not forgetting to point out that it would 'last many centuries'. In an unusual tribute he called Speer an 'artist and architect of genius' several times. Moreover Hitler awarded him the Gold Party Badge and gave him a watercolour from his early days. It represented the Minoritenkirche in Vienna, painted in a pedantic manner and from the conventional perspective typical of picture postcards. The sober Tessenow was the only one to contradict the praise from all sides. When Speer showed him the documents and pointed out that the building had been erected in a mere nine months, Tessenow replied drily: 'I would have preferred you to have taken nine years over this task.'[25]

One incident occurred that could not have been foreseen. During the removal, a few days before the building was handed over, one of the workmen dropped Bismarck's bust by Reinhold Begas, which had for decades been part of the inventory of the Reich Chancellery. In great haste Speer commissioned the sculptor Arno Breker to make an exact copy of the original. When it arrived a few months later, Speer used a pot of tea to give it some patina. He also instructed all those involved to maintain the strictest silence about the affair. Fortunately the accident remained unnoticed when the building was handed over. But Speer was filled with uneasy premonitions which he could not shake off.[26] Eight months later the Second World War broke out, and when it was over Bismarck's Reich had gone too.

Hitler's fiftieth birthday was celebrated with a great gala held in the middle of the East-West Axis opened only the day before. There were splendid parades and a concluding trooping of the colour. In addition Speer had arranged for an almost four-metre-high model of the triumphal arch to be set up in the exhibition hall on Pariser Platz. When he told Hitler about it at midnight, during the congratulatory reception, the Führer instantly left the party and hurried across to the Academy. He stood in front of the monument with shining eyes, inspected it from all angles and pointed to a few details. In the end he shook Speer's hand, silent and overcome. During the course of the night he returned to the model several times; on one occasion he fell into a gloomy mood. 'If only I were in good health!' he remarked.[27]

The strange alternation of apathy and feverish restlessness had first been observed in Hitler towards the end of the twenties and since then had never left him. He was filled with anxiety that his life-span might elapse before the 'enormous tasks' he had to discharge were completed: the shaping of 'our people ... into a single block of steel', the conquest of vast spaces and the embodying of all the victories in enduring buildings. Over the years this had been the motivation which drove him forward. From the summer of 1939 at the latest, it was this that had made him steer ever more resolutely towards open conflict. The country was not ready for it. But Hitler argued that the war would itself have to create the necessary conditions: psychologically, by tempering the public into that resolute unity which he still painfully missed, and materially, by providing the Reich with the resources it needed. After his pact with Stalin he also felt sufficiently secure politically. A week later, on 1 September 1939, he started the war by attacking Poland.

In the chaos before the outbreak of hostilities Speer had sided with the radicals who were in favour of war, even though he realized that resorting to arms might threaten his life's work. On the evening of the day Britain and France declared war on Germany, he suddenly appeared in Wolters' office. Pointing to the plans scattered on the tables around them and 'pale in the face' he said: 'It's all over.'[28] But the 'idealism' on which he prided himself demanded that all personal interests be subordinated to the alleged solution of the fateful national issues. During the preceding weeks he had accused the supporters of the 'peace party', such as Göring and Goebbels, of being 'weaklings who had degenerated in the luxury of power'.[29] As a result he now felt obliged to contribute his share to the outcome of the struggle. He instructed the head of his ante-room to assemble a technical squad for the construction and repair of bridges, roads and runways from the staff of the major building projects. On the very day of mobilization he offered the unit to the High Command of the Army.

To his surprise, however, Hitler declined the offer as soon as he heard of it. He probably saw it as another instance of Speer's highhandedness. In his irritation he instructed that Speer be informed that no one was entitled to put aside the work they had been assigned to choose new tasks at their own discretion. But Speer was overwhelmed by the gravity of the situation and moved by Hitler's announcement of the 'life-and-death struggle' that lay ahead, and simply ignored the reproof. 'This was the first of Hitler's orders that I bypassed', he noted later.[30]

When war broke out, Speer clearly receded into the background. Hitler asked to be shown the latest plans whenever he could snatch a few hours from the pressure of time and invariably urged the remaining designs to be completed, so that Speer occasionally gained the impression that the military operations were no more than unavoidable preliminaries for the construction of triumphal structures and that he was the secret addressee of those victories. His admiration for Hitler was boundless; he seemed to him 'like a hero of ancient myth who unhesitatingly and fully aware of his strength, embarked on the wildest undertakings and confidently held his own'.[31] Speer was all the more hurt that he was not even admitted to any consultations as a member of Hitler's inner circle. He only learned about the French campaign towards the end of 1939 when he was instructed to extend an old manor at Ziegenberg near Bad Nauheim for use as the Führer's headquarters in the West. But when the work was completed Hitler refused to use the extravagant building; in wartime, he let it be known, even he would have to manage with modest circumstances. Soon afterwards a new headquarters for the Führer was set up in the Eifel mountains.

Such was the power of the German attack that Poland was defeated on 28 September. It was only a matter of a few days or at most weeks until the campaigns against Denmark, Holland, Belgium and Luxemburg were completed, and even France surrendered after brief resistance. Three days before the armistice took effect on 25 June 1940 Speer received a telephone call from Hitler's adjutant, asking him to come to Hitler's headquarters at Bruly-le-Pêche, a small place near Sedan. There Hitler informed him that he intended to visit Paris on one of the next few days and that he had decided to take him and Giesler along: he was going to drive to the city not as the victorious general but as a lover of architecture.

Speer was both flattered and alarmed by the invitation. Hitler's decision to take himself and Giesler along as his only companions apart from his usual entourage of Keitel, Bormann, Karl Brandt and a number of adjutants, was bound to greatly raise the prestige of his rival Giesler as Hitler's other favoured architect. For that reason he requested that Arno Breker, who had spent many years in Paris and was regarded as an expert on the city, be included. It was a strangely undignified manoeuvre, but it shows how fierce was the struggle for the dictator's favour. When Hitler agreed to the proposal the nature of the trip changed: he would now be accompanied not just by the two architects he clearly favoured but it could be said that he was coming 'in the company of artists'.[32]

Between four and five o'clock in the morning of 28 June, the aircraft landed at Le Bourget airport and the waiting motorcade set off for the centre of Paris in the first light of dawn. The first stop was Charles Garnier's much admired Opéra. As they walked up the ceremonial staircase and through the rooms shining in golden splendour Speer observed how Hitler 'went into ecstasies which struck me as uncanny'.[33] At the same time Hitler used the opportunity to present himself to his startled entourage as a great expert on the building. He proved that according to the ground plan a small *salon* was missing behind the left-hand stage box, and indeed an elderly box attendant recalled that the room had been blocked off in the course of a renovation years ago. The convoy drove past the Madeleine and across the Place de la Concorde down the empty streets to the Champs-Élysées and up to the Arc de Triomphe. Hitler found the dimensions 'too small' and thought that they might possibly be justified by its elevated position; the avenues all round 'positively assailed it'.[34] The motorcade then proceeded to the Trocadero and to the terrace of the Palais de Chaillot. In the Invalides Hitler stood for a long time in front of Napoleon's sarcophagus; as he left, he told Giesler that he had chosen him to build his tomb.

The second part of the tour took them past the Louvre to Notre-Dame and on to the Place des Vosges. Hitler found every one of these places disappointing for some reason or other. Only when they reached the arcaded façades of the Rue de Rivoli did his interest revive: evidently they reminded him of the long chain of columns of the buildings for Berlin. At the end he demanded to see the Opéra once more, this time in bright daylight. He concluded the trip with a detour to Montmartre, where he wanted to have a panoramic view of Paris, from the elevated terrace of Sacré-Coeur. Numerous worshippers were just coming out of the church; they recognized him but ignored him. By nine o'clock the sightseeing tour was over and the cars drove back to Le Bourget. In the evening Hitler, still content with the fulfilment of 'his life's dream', said to Speer: 'Wasn't Paris beautiful? But Berlin must be made far more beautiful! … When we are finished in Berlin, Paris will be but a shadow.' He was deeply impressed and gave orders that all designs for the reshaping of the German towns be once more examined in the light of Paris.[35]

In the course of the same conversation he urged Speer to push the

After the French campaign Hitler visited Paris in June 1940, not as a victorious general but as a lover of French architecture. The planned victory parade down the Champs-Élysées never took place. The picture shows Hitler leaving the Invalides after visiting Napoleon's tomb. On his right: Albert Speer; on his left, in long overcoats: Hermann Giesler and Arno Breker.

building plans on more forcefully, confident that nothing was impossible after his rapid victory over France. He handed him a prepared document which assured him of every support and which he had antedated to the day of the armistice in his own handwriting. Only four weeks later Hitler issued a decree significantly entitled 'For safeguarding victory', ordering that the suspended work be resumed at once. In his reply to Lammers Speer gave the document a very free interpretation, to say the least. In his view it did not demand that 'the practical reconstruction of Berlin' should be resumed 'as long as the war was still going on'. But Hitler issued express orders for both planning and building preparations to be continued.[36]

Speer still did not yield. At a time when all resources were strained, it seemed to him both inappropriate and psychologically disastrous to create a hugely extravagant new Berlin or an area for the Reich Party Rallies in Nuremberg, which were not being held during the war anyway. At the same time he experienced his first vague doubts as to whether the buildings would ever be built. During the early days of the war a pensive Hitler had casually spoken the words, '*Finis Germaniae*'. It was one of the Führer's remarks that was for ever engraved in Speer's memory. Later he described how, in his thoughts at least, he had sometimes called Berlin 'my beautiful ghost town'.[37] 'He devoted greater efforts to his building projects again, but he continued to employ his technical staff in urgent tasks for the army and later also the Luftwaffe. Moreover, within a few months he set up three extensive production sites for the JU-88 newly developed twin-engined dive bomber in Graz, Brno and Vienna, as well as a large shipbuilding yard in Norway.

In so doing Speer proved himself to be far more realistic than Hitler, who always wanted to have his cake and eat it. Speer soon extended his activity to the construction of air-raid shelters. By the early autumn of 1941 he had already completed some thirty thousand units in Berlin and over eighty thousand further projects were in preparation. To meet these demands he set up several transport units which soon had hundreds and later thousands of trucks at their disposal. In addition he established a 'Speer Transport Fleet' with nearly three hundred freight barges and thousands more being built at specially established yards. They were designed to ship stones, granite and other building materials to Berlin and remove the debris from the demolition work. When the air war became more intense they were, without Hitler being properly aware of it, increasingly used to clear rubble from bomb sites.

Thus Speer inevitably left the 'ideal world' in which he had lived for so long. He now found himself in the 'depths' he had once spoken of. The problems this entailed were worse than anything he had experienced. The preparatory measures for the reshaping of Berlin included the demolition of buildings and entire residential neighbourhoods to make room for the Grand Avenue and the urban structures along it. Already in January 1939 Speer had therefore extended his Bureau by a Central Department for Resettlement, putting at its head Dietrich Clahes who had recently joined him. The department was given the task of registering the tenants within the designated area and allocating new accommodation to them. In practice this work was directed predominantly against the Jewish population of the city, either because they lived in the streets concerned or because they had to vacate their flats for so-called 'demolition tenants' who were not Jewish and had been living in the 'redevelopment zone'.

Anxious as ever to establish legal foundations even for its arbitrary actions, the regime had, towards the end of April 1939, followed up the Nuremberg Laws with a 'Law on rental contracts with Jews', under which any Jewish tenant of a flat could be given notice if 'alternative accommodation' was possible. When a flood of notices ensued, many of them issued under pressure from Party authorities, so-called resettlement departments were established at the housing offices of nearly all major towns. They were responsible for ensuring that the evictions ran smoothly and for allocating new accommodation to the evicted, usually in co-operation with Jewish welfare organizations. This procedure was referred to in the bureaucratic terminology of the time as the 'de-tenanting' of Jewish tenants and their 'boxing up' in existing Jewish accommodation. In Berlin the Central 'Department for Resettlement' under the Generalbauinspektor was responsible for this task.

It was a step from the supposedly non-political sphere of architecture into the executive sphere. Until then Speer's office had dealt with building enterprises, delivery firms or municipal administrations. Now its representatives were dealing with delegates of the Jewish community, senior officers of the SS Reich Central Security Office and not least with Joseph Goebbels, who had always been regarded as the most vehement persecutor of the Jews. Even before the outbreak of the war he had commissioned the film *Jud Süss*, in order to identify those responsible for all international conflicts. For the première in September 1940 he had drummed up a 'veritable chorus from hell', accompanied by an unprecedented clamour in the press, of the kind which was required to mobilize the people, according to a note in his diary.[38]

In mid-March 1941 when it was reported that Vienna would 'soon be cleansed of Jews', there was no holding back his ambition. Only three days later he called a conference at his ministry which was instructed to work out proposals for the solution of the 'Jewish question' in the Reich capital. Along with the top officials of his own ministry, those present included representatives of the Berlin Gauleitung, as well as Adolf Eichmann and, representing the Generalbauinspektor, Dietrich Clahes. With growing impatience Goebbels also assailed Hitler and in August had several talks alone with him. It was not least as a result of these meetings that the decree of 1 September 1941 was issued, making it compulsory for all Jews over the age of six to display a yellow star on their clothes.

Berlin was faced with particular difficulties, one of which being that, according to Goebbels' diary, some 30,000 of the more than 75,000 Jewish inhabitants of Berlin were employed in the armaments plants of the city. They had all been compulsorily enlisted because of their special skills, especially in precision engineering, and their elimination would have resulted in major production losses. Hitler himself had conceded this in his talks with Goebbels and had therefore put off the idea of cleansing Berlin of all Jews for the time being. However, Goebbels informed the conference in his propaganda ministry through his representative Leopold Gutterer that 'a suitable evacuation proposal would certainly meet with the Führer's consent'. Thereupon Clahes eagerly remarked that the Generalbauinspektion needed the roughly 20,000 flats still occupied by Jews, as 'a reserve for relocations should major bomb damage occur', he added, 'and later for relocations from apartments that will have to be torn down as part of the urban renewal of Berlin.' In the end Eichmann was instructed 'to work out a proposal for evacuating the Jews from Berlin for Dr Goebbels'.[39]

A little earlier Wolters had suggested to the Generalbauinspektor that, in view of their increasing tasks and responsibilities, an official Chronicle should be kept, recording all the major events in the department. Speer not only gave his approval, but actually instructed his departmental heads to supply Wolters with the necessary information. An entry of April 1941 reads:

> Since the beginning of the year the clearance of the demolition areas and the resettlement of tenants from that area in Jewish flats had

SPEER

proceeded on a larger scale. The Jewish flats rented by the tenants of the area were cleared and the Jewish tenants boxed into Jewish accommodation in Jewish properties. In terms of the war the purpose of these measures was to make the evacuated flats in that area of the Reich capital available in the event of catastrophes (air-raid damage). Over the period from 1.1.1941 to 15.4.1941 ... altogether 366 tenants were asked to be resettled.[40]

In accordance with the law of self-radicalization that governed the regime, this was the beginning of a chain of measures which resulted in the extinction of Berlin Jewry within two years. By August 1941 an entry in the Chronicle stated: 'According to a Speer direction a further action for the clearing of some five thousand Jewish flats is being started. The available apparatus is being suitably enlarged so that in spite of all the difficulties arising from the war the Jewish flats can be restored as quickly as possible and filled with demolition tenants from the areas that must urgently be cleared.' And a few weeks later: 'During the period from 18 October to 2 November roughly 4,500 Jews were evacuated. As a result, a further 1,000 flats were vacated for bomb-damaged tenants and made available by the Generalbauinspektor. The flats will be made available for demolition tenants again later.'[41]

The revealing word in this note is 'evacuated'. Until then the term 'resettlement' had been used. This concealed the fact that the Generalbauinspektion had meanwhile surrendered its administrative responsibility for 'resettlement matters', either because it could no longer cope with the enormous administrative tasks or because it was weary of the countless unpleasantnesses connected with them. At any rate Goebbels now took charge of the measures for the expulsion of the Jews himself. He had long felt that they had proceeded much too hesitantly or, as he suspected, with deliberate delay, and immediately changed the policy from one of resettlement to one of 'deportation'. Although some eyewitness reports state that the delegates of the Generalbauinspektion behaved, as one record put it, 'in a correct way',[42] Goebbels proceeded with terrorizing directness and handed over the whole proceedings to the SS and Gestapo. On the evening of 15 October their squads burst into the flats for which notice had been given the previous day, ordering the tenants to hurry up and pack up a few belongings and to follow them. They were taken to a collecting camp duly set up by the Jewish community in the synagogue on Levetzowstrasse. Two days later, a pitiful procession, under heavy

118

```
             - 4 -

S p e e r /Wg.                    Obersalzberg, den 27.11.1940


         Herrn  C l a h e s :        Eingegangen am:


         Was macht die Aktion der Räumung der 1 000 Juden-Wohnun-
         gen ?
         Besonders Räumung Lichtenstein-Allee ?


                              gez.  S p e e r

                                     F.d.R
```

Preparatory measures for the construction of the Grand Avenue in Berlin involved the evacuation of tens of thousands of apartments, many of them Jewish-owned. Speer's department took on this task, as shown by the minute reproduced here. Speer later said nothing at all about these measures which, as they progressed, led to deportations to the camps in the east.

guard, moved in pouring rain past embarrassed or indifferent pedestrians through the streets to Grunewald railway station. On 18 October the first transport left for Lodź; others followed, first for Riga, then for Minsk and elsewhere. Instructed by Goebbels, the newspapers reported: 'Over the past few days many Jews have hurriedly left Germany, leaving debts behind them.'[43]

The final report submitted by Dietrich Clahes on the activity of the Central Department for Resettlement for the period from 1 February 1939 states in sober bureaucratic language:

It was the task of the Resettlement Department to identify all Jewish flats existing in the Reich capital, to clear them and to allocate them to tenants who had lost their flats as a result of rebuilding measures. In all, 23,765 Jewish flats were registered. The scope of those who were to be cared for was extended, by Führer Order at the suggestion of the Generalbauinspektor, to soldiers disabled in active service, bearers of the Knight's Cross, and other ranks and noncommissioned officers decorated with the Iron Cross (first class). Of the Jewish flats registered, 9,000 flats were assigned. The number of persons resettled amounted to 75,000.[44]

Taken in isolation, the events underlying this document are lost in the greater criminal context of the time. Even Clahes's note soon sounded like a report from another age, especially since the Austrian-born Sturmbannführer Alois Brunner, who had been in charge of the expulsion of the Jews from Vienna, had appeared on the Berlin scene in 1942 with his SS unit. With manhunts in the streets, 'house searches', the 'unfurnishing' of collective accommodation, and the brutal practice of 'wagon-loading', he made the deportations, which often proceeded slowly, seem like 'a mass expulsion of herds'. As suicides increased among those affected, he angrily demanded that the representatives of the Jewish community should take all possible steps 'to prevent this flight into suicide'.[45] After only nine months a Gestapo official turned up at the community office on Oranienburger Strasse to announce that the Jewish community in Berlin had ceased to exist.

As head of department Speer certainly had nothing to do with these incidents, having relinquished his responsibility in this field. Importance has been attached to them because he never mentioned his initial participation. There cannot, on the other hand, be any reasonable doubt that he knew of the 'de-tenanting measures'. In a memo to Clahes dated 27 November 1940, he inquired urgently: 'How is the action for the clearance of those thousand Jewish flats going?'[46] But neither in *Inside the Third Reich* nor in *Spandau: The Secret Diaries* did Speer mention the events. And although an entire chapter of his book *The Slave State*, which deals with his 'disputes with the SS', is devoted to the expulsion of the Berlin Jews, there is not even a hint that the transports resulted from the resettlement practice of his own department. There are several mentions of Goebbels' increasingly categorical demands for the removal of the Jews from Berlin. Speer also mentions attempts to stall the process by labelling them as 'indispensable to the armaments effort', in view of the prevailing shortage of skilled workers, and he relates how it was eventually possible, by secret warnings, false documents and other means to save at least four thousand of the remaining eleven thousand Berlin Jews from the Gestapo and thus from deportation. But on the whole, for all the self-accusations, the account remains vague:

When I recall the fate of the Jews in Berlin [he says in conclusion], I am overcome by an unavoidable feeling of failure and inadequacy. Often, during my daily drive to my architectural office I saw ... the crowds of people on the platform of the nearby Nikolassee railway station. I knew that these must be Berlin Jews who were being evacuated. I was certainly overcome by a feeling of oppression as I drove past; presumably I had a sense of sombre goings-on. But I was rooted in the principles of the regime to an extent that I find hard to understand today.[47]

Speer once spoke of the uncanny ability of the ruling powers to stifle conflicts of conscience or even to prevent them from arising. Without doubt the regime used this method to make countless right-thinking people do things or omit to do things in which they later did not recognize themselves. Speer was one of them. But what more could provoke a conflict of conscience when neither the wreckage on Fasanenstrasse nor the pitiful scenes at suburban railway stations triggered any emotion? One can accept Speer's repeated assurances, at least as far as that period is concerned, that he had not even a remotely accurate notion of what awaited the deportees in the camps in the East. But did the unlimited disenfranchisement they were subjected to even before being deported, the 'resettlements' and the 'boxing up' not provide sufficient grounds?

The truth is probably that he had long been more or less totally absorbed by the world of official responsibilities and specific aims, a narrow world which no human appeal could penetrate. In his *Diaries* Speer declared that he never was, not even faintly, an anti-Semite, pointing out, with some satisfaction, that 'not a single document turned up that incriminated me in this regard' during the Nuremberg trials.[48] But this assertion is even more puzzling. In the morbid 'world of Streicher', to which Speer contemptuously referred, there was at least some emotion which, no matter how twisted and repulsive, at least reveals traces of a motive; in Speer's world there was no motive whatsoever to be found. The state of total dependence into which he had placed himself transformed everything into administrative procedures, and for him the fate of the 75,000 in whose lives he tragically intervened boiled down to a purely administrative guideline for 'building policy measures'. Added to this was his sense of privilege as an artist, which became more and more marked, and he would no doubt have regarded it as a sign of unforgivable weakness if he had sacrificed the 'historic task' assigned to him to any legal or human objections. Rudolf Wolters accurately characterized their attitudes with the words: 'We were, in a sense, standing in the middle of the sun and could not, and did not even wish to, notice what was happening in the shade around us.'[49]

There was a complicated postscript which makes the issue even more confusing. Of the eight hundred pages of the Chronicle which Wolters had kept from the beginning of 1941 until 1944, there existed two complete versions as well as three further ones for the years 1942/43 only. To be on the safe side Wolters deposited the copies in different places shortly before the end of the war. Most of them were in fact lost, but in 1946 Wolters recovered one of the complete versions. Without the knowledge of Speer, then imprisoned at Spandau, he had a transcript made a few years later, having improved it stylistically and added an index.[50]

But he also made a number of editorial changes and deleted 'a very few passages ... which unfortunately were not entirely unimportant in terms of contemporary history', as he later wrote to Speer. These included all passages relating to the resettlement and deportation of the Berlin Jews. After Speer's release, when the two met again for the first time in October 1966, Wolters gave this 'expurgated' version to him together with copious other material. In spite of always receiving a carbon copy of the entries, Speer had never checked them during his time in office. Therefore he naturally did not notice the deletions, especially as Wolters later conceded he had only 'briefly' mentioned 'slight amendments'. Without giving it much thought Speer had a photocopy made and in July 1969 passed it on to the Federal Archive in Koblenz 'for future use by historians'.

Some time earlier the British historian David Irving had discovered the Chronicle for the year 1943, which had reached the Imperial War Museum in London through some unknown channel. Although the entries for that year had scarcely been changed by Wolters, Irving nevertheless identified a few discrepancies between the London and the Koblenz version. He wrote to Speer asking for an explanation and, if possible, to be provided with the manuscript covering the other years. Still ignorant of the extent of the expurgations made by Wolters, Speer, who was then on holiday in South Tyrol, suggested to his friend that he clear the matter up. 'Fortunately', he wrote to him, this part of the Chronicle showed only 'insignificant divergencies which I enclose. But even so: wouldn't it be better if we took the first step of our own accord and if I replaced the copy of the Chronicle now deposited in the Federal Archive by a photocopy of the original in your hands?'

In a lengthy letter of 10 January 1970 Wolters came clean. He dealt in particular with the deleted passages about the evacuation of the Jews, referring to his right to edit the text as he was, after all, the author of the journal. Wolters justified the cuts by explaining that he had made them out of consideration for Speer as well as for one or other of their colleagues and their families. When he had made the alterations in 1964 a series of 'witch trials' had just started again, he wrote, and, although still detained at Spandau, Speer had been in danger of being arraigned once more since the evacuation of the Jews had not been part of the charges levelled against him at Nuremberg. Wolters also made it clear that he was not at all in favour of handing the original over to Koblenz. He had arranged for everything to be made public later, he continued. For the moment, however, it would be best simply to tell the Federal Archive that 'the fellow won't part with the original'. He confidently added that he would 'be delighted to give his reasons' to the gentlemen at the Archive.

It was one of Speer's most imprudent mistakes that he not only went along with this suggestion but that he went even further. Although he immediately informed the Federal Archive, he wrote to Wolters from his holiday location: 'I suggest the pages in question no longer exist. I mean, contrary to your letter, not at all. Postponement to a later date would be undesirable; who rejects a distorted interpretation which is made worse by having been withheld for many years? It will be seen as entirely legitimate that you have omitted a few pages from a series of documents ... I hope that, in spite of the swathes of mist surrounding this house, I have expressed myself clearly enough.'

But Speer had failed to do so. He had not made clear what was to be done with the original of the Chronicle, in other words whether Wolters was to destroy the volumes or merely continue to keep them locked up until none of those concerned could suffer any harm. For the time being Wolters replied with a letter to be forwarded to the Federal Archive, saying that he and his secretary Marion Reisser had searched high and low for the original of the Chronicle. 'To put it bluntly: it has disappeared without a trace, is no longer there, it simply does not exist any more. And I believe that to be a good thing ...' In a covering letter to Speer he also wrote: 'In case there is any follow-up, just blame it all on me – and on Marion; she is an artist and accordingly untidy in the keeping of documents.'[51]

We can only guess at the reasons that induced Speer to suppress this document. One factor, no doubt, was carelessness over and above the acquiescence that had so often misled him. Despite his ironical tone towards the 'great arms boss', as he was fond of calling Speer, Wolters had made it clear more than once that he would have to regard any disclosure of his expurgations as rank disloyalty, and Speer was aware of how much he owed this closest of friends. He had no wish to disregard this. It also seems that he still failed to understand properly the role he had played in the Berlin evacuations or that he had completely suppressed it. At any rate one is struck by the guilelessness with which he first proposed handing over the complete Chronicle to the Federal Archive, only to agree readily to the deception suggested to him by Wolters.

In view of these contradictions, the many inaccuracies in his response to Matthias Schmidt's intention to uncover these facts in his doctoral thesis years later, are even harder to understand. Admittedly Schmidt was anxious to prove that none other than Speer himself had been the author, or at least the agent, of this 'falsification of history', concluding from the documents that, in spite of all his protestations, he knew early on of the fate awaiting the Berlin Jews. But the first conclusion contradicted the facts that had been clarified meanwhile, the other merely arose from it. Schmidt had obtained the material for his accusation from Rudolf Wolters who had been outraged by Speer's 'penitential attitude', first on the publication of *Inside the Third Reich* and at every further publication or interview and had finally broken with his erstwhile friend once and for all.[52] The whole truth came out when Wolters carried out his threat and handed over most of his documents, including the original of Chronicle, to the Federal Archive in Koblenz. In July 1983, Rudolf Wolters' literary executrix, Marion Riesser, left those papers to the Archive that had been held back.

On 22 June 1941 Hitler started his campaign against the Soviet Union under the codename Operation Barbarossa. Once again he revealed his inability to put his own intentions into effect step by step. He had always regarded the avoidance of war on two fronts as a basic law of German foreign policy. But now he convinced himself otherwise. Although the war in the west was still in progress, he assured the Wehrmacht leaders in early January 1941 that the campaign in the east would, as by a stroke of magic, solve all strategic embarrassments and make the Reich 'unassailable'. 'The vast Russian space contained immeasurable wealth,' he went on to say, and would also enable Germany 'to wage war against continents'.[53]

As always he was thinking not only of victories which would confirm his fame as a general, but also of his halo in the form of buildings and enduring monuments. On the evening before the attack he walked over to his living room after dinner with Speer and played a few bars of Liszt's *Les Préludes* to him: 'You will get to hear this often in the near future,' he explained, 'because it will be our victory fanfare for the Russian campaign.' But in his next sentences he had already moved on to his building plans: 'We will get as much granite and marble from there as we want.'[54]

As on several previous occasions, Speer remained sceptical. Six weeks after the opening of the campaign, while German troops were still storming ahead, Speer approached Fritz Todt, the Commissioner for the Construction Industry, and proposed to him that all building that was not of immediate importance to the war effort be suspended for the time being. But when Hitler heard about it he again insisted on the continuation of the construction programmes. Against Speer's opposition he even increased to about two hundred the number of tanks and heavy weapons that were to be positioned along the Grand Avenue as trophies. In a conversation towards the end of November 1941 he demanded that 'building be started while the war was still on'; he was not to be 'prevented by the war from ... realising his building plans'.[55]

At any rate Speer managed to get the name of the General-bauinspektion, which was almost exclusively linked to the plans for Berlin, changed to 'Baustab Speer' (Speer Construction Staff). When a transport and supply crisis arose during the unusually early Russian winter because of the destruction wrought by the retreating Soviet troops, Speer offered half of his 65,000 building workers for the restoration of the transport network. In spite of the daily flow of bad news from Russia Hitler only agreed after a fortnight's hesitation, and even then he made it clear that the building projects must not be delayed. At the same time he used this opportunity to feed Speer's jealousy by demanding that Giesler's building team be employed for a similar task. Todt thereupon assigned the repair of roads and railways throughout the Ukraine to Speer, while Giesler was entrusted with the same task for the territory of Army Groups Centre and North.

Towards the end of January 1942 Speer flew out to inspect his construction teams in the Dnepropetrovsk area. Steady blizzards meant that he kept having to postpone his return flight from one day to the next.

On one occasion an advanced Soviet armoured group got within a few kilometres of his quarters. An attempt to make at least some headway towards the west by train faltered in the endless waste where the banks of drifted snow were four metres high. Several attempts to reach the airfield also failed in spite of hundreds of helpers. On one occasion they stumbled about in the dreadful whiteness for so long that Speer suffered second-degree frostbite. Not until 7 February did a plane, bound not for Berlin but at least for Rastenburg in East Prussia, take him aboard as an extra passenger.

This was the first time that Speer saw the Führer's headquarters. Two days later when he left for Berlin on the night train everything had changed.

Chapter Five
MINISTER AND
ECONOMIC DICTATOR

When Speer unexpectedly turned up in Rastenburg on 7 February 1942 his first impression was that he had come at an inconvenient time. Although his arrival had been immediately reported and he had not seen Hitler for more than two months, he was not even invited for that short handshake for which Hitler had always made time even when he had urgent business. Dr Todt was with the Führer, it was said, and later Speer was told that there were noisy goings-on in the room. As insiders were aware, tensions had arisen over the past few months between Hitler and the minister, which had produced more than one heated clash.

Fritz Todt was without question one of the most important figures in the leadership of the Reich even though he had never belonged to Hitler's closer circle. Like Speer he came from a wealthy middle-class family in Baden. He had been an officer in the First World War and had then completed his engineering studies. Todt had joined the NSDAP at the beginning of 1922. His professional abilities had led Hitler to appoint him Generalinspektor für das Strassenwesen (Inspector-General of Roads) only six months after the Nazis seized power. This post mainly involved the construction of the Reich autobahns, a task which Todt assumed with organizational skill, technological understanding and a feeling for nature. Over the years he held many leading posts, but he particularly made a name for himself with the 'Organization Todt', set up in 1938, which constructed the West Wall and, with the outbreak of war, grew into an army of millions. In March 1940 Hitler appointed him 'Reich Minister for Armaments and Ammunition' and a year later Generalinspektor für Wasser und Energie (Inspector-General for Water and Energy).

Todt's standing, however, was due not so much to his numerous posts as to the 'respect bordering on reverence' which Hitler had for him, as well as his warmth and personal integrity. With the 'Roman medallion head' his admirers credited him with, he was a widely respected figure amid the petty plebeian Machiavellians at the top of the Nazi regime.[1] Self-assured as he was, he kept out of all power struggles and never let his genuine admiration for Hitler develop into the competitive servility of his court. Significantly, he lived in an exceedingly modest former toll-house by the Hintersee in the Berchtesgaden area throughout those years, and although he was one of Hitler's neighbours he kept away from the Berghof to protect his independence and self-respect. Todt was an 'unpolitical technocrat' to a far greater extent than Speer, who also liked to think of himself as such, but they had enough in common to ensure a close working relationship. During Speer's dispute with Giesler, Todt had, on his own initiative, written a mediating letter to him:

> Perhaps the point of view which I have gradually arrived at would have given you a little psychological help: that in the course of such great events ... every activity meets with opposition, everyone who acts has his rivals and unfortunately his opponents also. But not because people want to be opponents, rather because the tasks and circumstances force different people to take different points of view.[2]

In contrast to Speer, however, Todt was wholly unsentimental in character and it was his sense of reality which particularly distinguished him in Hitler's entourage. When the early onset of the Russian winter not only halted the German advance but also revealed the hopeless over-extension of forces, Todt immediately drew firm conclusions from a visit to the front. He repeatedly urged Hitler to find a political solution to a war which had been lost in military terms and, following the failure of the *Blitzkrieg* strategy, also in terms of armament. He did so most emphatically in a frosty discussion at the Reich Chancellery on 29 November 1941 in the presence of Field Marshal von Brauchitsch. Todt had followed the judgement of the industrialist Walter Rohland ('Panzer Rohland'), who had declared that the war could no longer be won.[3] But Hitler had responded to their joint proposal by pointing out that he saw 'hardly any way of reaching a *political* conclusion', and that victory was not just a matter of armaments but chiefly of will. When Todt did not yield, Hitler simply ended the discussion. His decision to intensify the war at all levels shows that he was not prepared to be swayed by the minister's arguments. In this context even his decision some two weeks later to declare war on the United States, although he was under no pressure to do so, seems like a spiteful reaction to the quandary Todt had put him in.

On that 7 February Todt did not return to the officers' mess of the Führer's headquarters until shortly before midnight. He seemed exhausted and dejected as he sat down with Speer. Although he had recently confided his differences of opinion with Hitler, Todt made no mention of the disagreement he had just had. In the course of a 'sluggish conversation' he offered Speer a seat in the aircraft that was to take him to Berlin early in the morning, and Speer gratefully accepted. When Todt retired Speer did not follow him, in spite of his fatigue, as if he were still waiting for a sign from Hitler. Towards one o'clock an aide arrived to say that the Führer wished to see him.

Hitler, too, was clearly exhausted and out of sorts. He listened in silence to Speer's report on his impressions of Dnepropetrovsk and only when the conversation turned to the Nuremberg and Berlin building projects did he revive. The shadow-land of the architectural projects again did its trick, so much so that Speer began to be confident once again that the plans might yet get beyond the drawing board. It was nearly three o'clock in the morning when Hitler dismissed him. Before retiring Speer therefore cancelled his flight in Todt's plane. In the early morning he was rudely awakened by the telephone. In a state of great excitement Dr Brandt informed him that Todt had just been killed as his aircraft took off for Berlin.

Even in the first moments of shock, suspicions arose that the crash might have been the result of a plot. There were too many oddities: the troublesome view that the war was lost, about which the minister had been adamant ever since the failure before Moscow; Speer's 'coincidental' presence at headquarters, the first for many months; his prolonged 'wait' for an audience with Hitler long after midnight, despite his own exhaustion; the cancellation of his flight and the circumstances of the crash itself. It was soon established that the aircraft had taken off. While still in view the pilot had abruptly turned back and tried to land with the wind behind him, as would occur only in an emergency. Just before he reached the runway a vertical jet of flame had shot out from the fuselage, evidently from an explosion, so that the plane fell some twenty metres and hit the ground, where it broke up with several explosions. Only a few charred remains of the occupants were found.[4]

The cause of the accident has never been established. Although

Fritz Todt, the creator though not the inventor of the autobahns, came, like Speer, from a middle-class background. Although he had joined the Party in 1922, he retained his independence from Hitler's court. After the failure of the Russian campaign outside Moscow he regarded the war as lost and expressed this view to Hitler himself. On 8 February 1942 he was killed in an air crash that was never fully explained. Hitler appointed Speer to succeed Todt in all his posts.

Hitler had immediately instructed the Reich Aviation Ministry to investigate the crash, the commission set up for the purpose never got beyond an account of the accident, any more than did the party of criminal experts sent to Rastenburg by the SS. The report concluded with the sentences: 'The possibility of sabotage has been ruled out. Further measures are *therefore* neither requisite nor intended.'[5]

The most frequent assumption was that either the pilot or possibly Todt himself had inadvertently activated the self-destruct lever with which all aircraft operating near the front were equipped in the event of an emergency landing in enemy territory. But Todt had come to Rastenburg in a Heinkel HE-111 as his own aircraft was being serviced; the Heinkel had been put at his disposal by his friend Field Marshal Hugo Sperrle. Unbelievably, the question as to whether the self-destruct mechanism had been set off by mistake was never thoroughly investigated. A few months later it emerged that the plane did not have such a mechanism.

The suspicions which soon began to circulate were directed against Hitler, against the SS, and also against Speer himself, at least as one who was in the know. Hitler can hardly be exculpated by pointing out that he was one of the first to speculate that there was something fishy about the accident or that he immediately ordered the introduction of flight recorders. This could have been the move of an experienced cheat. Nor is he freed from suspicion by the distress he displayed at the news of the crash, and even more so a few days later at Todt's funeral in the Mosaic Hall of the Reich Chancellery, when, on the verge of tears, he struggled to speak. Mourning and acting in cold blood were not mutually exclusive. As the murder of his intimate friend Ernst Röhm shows, these traits were part of the tragic image of the great man who did not permit himself any human emotion and followed only the imperative of his historic mission. At any rate Speer recorded that Hitler adopted a 'stoic' attitude soon after the accident. *Hitler's Table Talk* reveals that Todt was not even mentioned by a single word on 8 February over luncheon and dinner in the presence of the two guests, Himmler and Speer. Instead the conversation was about the usual everyday topics, the judiciary, priests and the 'cultural disgrace' of the Christian Churches. It is just as strange that, a few days after the event, Hitler, 'irritable and often distinctly nervous,' refused to tolerate any doubts about the credibility of the investigation findings, using the curiously contrived justification: 'You know, this loss still affects me too deeply for me to want to talk about it.'[6]

One cannot rule out the possibility that Himmler's SS caused the accident, with or without Hitler's knowledge. It may even have assumed that it was doing a service to Hitler, who was clearly affected by the first major setback of his life, by removing his pessimistic admonisher. Significantly, the SS was then trying to gain control of armaments. It may have wished to get rid of Todt, whose over-powerful influence had made him the most serious rival in that field. In the days before the crash Himmler was alone with Hitler on the evening of 1 February, and then again three days later, on the evening of 4 February, and on 8 February, both at lunch and in the evening, he spent many hours in the Führer's room, this time in the company of Speer. Contrary to usual practice Himmler contented himself with the inconclusive findings of the investigations, in which the SS had had a part. It is also curious that Todt had deposited a large sum of money in his safe shortly before the accident. It was to go to his long-standing secretary if anything happened to him.[7]

Speer must surely be acquitted even of the suspicion of privity. For all the ambition that he had by then developed, the 'idealistic' streak in his make-up had not been completely buried. It made him incapable of such 'cold-blooded infamies'. Besides, the accusations are based on nothing more than a few vague indications and on the alleged advantage he gained from Todt's death. But it is questionable whether he saw any advantage in taking over Todt's posts. In the spring of 1939, and then again after the French campaign, Hitler had already approached him with the question whether, in view of the overburdening of the 'treble' minister, he wanted to take over some of Todt's tasks, especially construction, along with responsibility for the Atlantic Wall. But Speer had declined on the grounds, which seemed logical enough to Hitler, that construction and armaments should remain in the same hands and that, moreover, Todt would feel deeply offended by having such duties withdrawn. Years later Speer dismissed the suggestion that he had been in the know as 'utter nonsense'.[8]

When Hitler received news of the disaster he scarcely showed any emotion, as his Luftwaffe adjutant has recorded: 'He was very shocked and remained silent for a long time.' Then he decided 'instantly to entrust Professor Speer with Todt's succession'.[9] When he was summoned by Hitler towards one o'clock in the afternoon Speer naturally suspected that a major or minor part of Todt's tasks would fall to him. But he was surprised when Hitler received him standing up, in order to emphasize the formal nature of the meeting, and, after stiffly accepting his condolences, declared in a solemn tone: 'Herr Speer, I appoint you successor to Minister Dr Todt in all his posts.' Then, as if not expecting any contradiction, he extended his hand in dismissal. Speer made a half-hearted attempt to change his mind. He would do his very best, he stammered, to replace Todt in his construction tasks. But Hitler cut him short, almost impatiently, and assured him of his boundless confidence, adding that he could refer to him at any time. At that moment Speer, as he later said, had 'one of the best and certainly the most useful ideas of my life'. He demanded a Führer Order containing 'nothing less than an unconditional promise of support' which 'also bound Hitler'. After brief, barely perceptible, hesitation, during which he evidently 'quickly considered the consequences', Hitler agreed.[10]

Nearly all observers regarded this decision as probably Hitler's most risky and at the same time his most inspired appointment, whilst wondering why he chose Speer of all people. There were indeed a number of young and eager armament experts, especially in Todt's ministry, whose appointment would have been all the more obvious as they enjoyed Hitler's confidence. Speer, on the other hand, was a layman in nearly all the spheres which had now been assigned to him, from civil engineering to armaments, power supplies, and much else. But that was precisely what was in his favour, for Hitler had an almost insuperable mistrust of experts and was fond of singing the praises of the imaginative dilettante. Another advantage was that he had no power base, so that Hitler could say to himself that in future no one would be able to interfere and that he himself would have the final say in armament matters, as had long been the case in military affairs. His expectation was confirmed by the impression he had formed of Speer. By then he had come to know him well enough and believed that, unlike the troublesome Todt, his successor would be 'a willing tool'.[11] Moreover, Hitler had admired Speer's planning skills ever since he had completed the Reich Chancellery ahead of schedule. Hitler had also come to realize that the difficulties of the war economy were due in large part to the confusion over responsibility that had arisen over the years and become a serious threat to operational efficiency in the East since the winter disaster at Moscow. He was confident that Speer would bring about the decisive turn in the war, particularly as far as organization was concerned, supported not least by the authority he had given him.

Speer himself was by no means sure of his new job. He was worried about his unsociableness, his weakness as an orator, and also by the thought that Hitler's demands would, for some time at least, mean bidding farewell to his architectural dreams. Nor had he forgotten Todt's well-founded judgement about the hopelessness of the war, which was supported by statistical evidence. Yet in the end his ambition overrode all misgivings. Although he later declared that he had not entered politics until the beginning of August 1943, in reality he did so on 8 February 1942, if not before. He yielded not only to Hitler's overwhelming power, but also to his own desire to 'be one of the makers of historic events', a desire which had been aroused by his dealings with the dictator: 'I still remember', he noted, 'the elation that filled me when my signature enabled me to dispose of billions of marks and to dispatch hundreds of thousands of people to the construction sites.'[12] Although he was accustomed to thinking in signs and symbols, it did not seem to worry him that, for the second time, he owed his advancement to a death. That was part of his pact with the Devil, one of his critics wrote, and Speer expressly agreed with him.[13]

As Speer turned to leave, Göring's arrival was reported. Without wasting any time he had hastened to the Führer's headquarters from his hunting lodge in Rominten, East Prussia, in order to be first in line when the dead man's estate was shared out. As Commissioner for the Four-Year Plan he had always felt responsible for the whole war economy and, as a result, he had inevitably clashed with Todt on various occasions, especially as Todt's numerous posts also included responsibility for construction within the Four-Year Plan. Now Göring saw the opportunity for retrieving at least that responsibility. No sooner had he embarked on his great condolence and booty tirade than Hitler turned away and curtly announced that he had already appointed Speer to succeed Todt in all his posts.

On the evening of the following day Speer travelled to Berlin. Even before he left it became clear to him on what slippery ground he now found himself. One of the well-established officials of the ministry, Konrad Haasemann, turned up at headquarters unannounced in order to fill him in on the intrigues and the power games in the department. But Speer impatiently fended off the visitor. The next morning, when he arrived at Todt's office in Pariser Platz, nervous and exhausted from lack of sleep, he immediately provided a taste of his unconventional style. It was customary to receive the top officials, individually, strictly according to their rank and official position. Instead Speer walked from door to door to introduce himself. But he could not overcome the reservations of the top officials in particular, by such transparent gestures of modesty. His decision to incorporate the Baustab Speer into the Organisation Todt was more effective. Nonetheless, nearly all of them, as they later testified, missed Todt's warmth. On one of his first days in office Speer presented himself to the staff in the courtyard of the ministry during a heavy snow storm and tried to win their trust. In his response to Speer's address, Xaver Dorsch, the head of the construction organization and one of Todt's close advisors, informed him sharply: 'Dr Todt had our unlimited trust. Trust does not come by itself, it has to be earned.'[14]

During his first few days Speer had to fend off attempts to divide up Todt's responsibilities in spite of Hitler's decision. The Ministry of Economic Affairs sought control of power generation, and Ley wanted the Party's Central Office for Technology back. Even before Speer's appointment a meeting for a fundamental discussion of armaments problems had been fixed for 13 February at the Ministry of Aviation. It

After being appointed Reich Minister for Armaments and Ammunition, Speer introduced himself to his staff in the courtyard of the Todt Ministry in Pariser Platz in a snowstorm.

was to be attended by representatives of the three armed services and top industrialists. Having tried unsuccessfully to postpone the date, Speer had called on Hitler to remind him of his recent promise of support. Hitler advised him simply to break off the conference if any difficulties arose and to invite the participants over to the Reich Chancellery, where Hitler would tell them whatever was necessary.

On the evening before the meeting Speer was asked to go and see Göring. In a surprise attack conducted with exquisite courtesy the Reich Marshal presented the young minister with an agreement such as he claimed to have had with Todt; this, he explained, established that Speer was not entitled to take any decisions affecting the Four-Year Plan. Since the Four-Year Plan concerned the whole of the economy, the suggestion implied nothing less than total surrender. Indeed Speer knew that Göring's arrangement with Todt had led to bitter quarrels. Being shrewder than his predecessor, he therefore talked around the subject at length, just as courteously as his interlocutor; but whenever Göring tried to be specific he avoided any kind of commitment and he never signed the prepared agreement.

The next day he drove to the nearby Ministry of Aviation on Leipziger Strasse at the appointed time for the conference on armaments. Field Marshal Milch, the state secretary responsible, opened the meeting and the participants complained about the confusion over who was responsible for what, the muddle of orders and counter-orders, the rivalry of the three Wehrmacht branches and the continuous change of priorities. There followed a series of carefully measured interventions, which had evidently been pre-arranged, demanding a firm direction of the war economy. While the discussion was still in progress, Walther Funk, the Minister of Economic Affairs, suddenly got up and declared 'in the name of all those present' that none other than Erhard Milch was suited to take on the difficult task. Even before Funk had finished, Speer whispered to the Field Marshal sitting next to him that Hitler had asked all those present to come to the cabinet room and Milch had enough presence of mind to reject Funk's proposal. Speer then conveyed Hitler's invitation to the assembled company, adding that their concern was unnecessary: the decision about who controlled armaments matters had already been made with his appointment, 'since that is surely my task'.[15]

This was presently confirmed by Hitler, who had quickly asked Speer to give him a few cues as the party came in. In a speech lasting an hour he advocated an unprejudiced attitude towards the economy and its engineers, free from the narrow interests of the Party. Hitler emphasized the difficulties in armaments policy which, he said, had failed to make the necessary simplifications both in organization and in weapons and he called for an increase in production: it was outrageous, he said, that it had not yet been possible to bring in labour from the occupied territories, all that was needed were 'rough yokels'. He went on: it 'is possible. Otherwise I would shoot myself.'[16] He then commended Speer and the achievements of his Baustab and appealed to those present to support the new minister in every way possible. After the participants had left, he advised Speer not to pay too much attention to the difficult civil servants and to follow the practices of industry instead. Speer used the opportunity to point out to Hitler that some of the experts he intended to enlist were indeed often politically aloof; but he could only succeed if they were left in peace by the Party. Hitler showed himself to be understanding and uttered his usual 'Agreed!' Almost incidentally, Speer had eliminated his fiercest opponent Bormann, who wanted to ensure Party control in industry as in all other affairs.

But that was by no means all. As if to extend the special position he enjoyed to his entire apparatus, Speer went a step further. The Minister of Justice and the chief of the Reich Chancellery objected and Göring was outraged when a few days later Speer submitted to Hitler the draft of an 'Order for the Protection of the Armaments Industry'. Henceforth those who made false statements about requirements in manpower, raw materials and machinery or who hoarded materials, could incur the most grievous consequences, from prison to the death sentence. The decree laid down that prosecution would ensue at the behest of the armaments minister alone, which meant bypassing the Ministry of Justice. In a later supplement Speer extended the order, which used an unprecedentedly sharp tone towards the armaments industry, to the entire construction industry. It should be added, however, that its provisions never apparently led to any criminal proceedings.[17]

Within a few days the politically inexperienced minister had thus, in a sense, completed his novitiate. From then on, Speer certainly showed no diffidence. His awkwardness as a speaker also disappeared, and, as one of his top 'economic commissars' observed, he 'seized the reins with lightning speed and authority'.[18] He instantly knew how to handle the cabals of power politics, outmanoeuvring most of his potential adversaries at one stroke. Moreover, he won the respect of the industrial leaders with his unexpectedly rough self-assurance. At the time, as he himself put it, Speer cunningly practised the arts of 'dissimulation, mock innocence and hypocrisy ... conspired [and] took Hitler's capriciousness into his reckonings',[19] so that it seemed as if the power that had dropped into his lap had made him a different person. Others believed that his true nature had now been revealed.

At the first conference he called to resume the meeting of 13 February five days later, Speer surprised those present with a demand that was as startling as it was presumptuous. He circulated a text around the table which announced in few words that he was 'herewith given a mandate for full authority'[20] to direct armaments and requested that all those present countersign the document. Despite his astonishment Milch was the first to comply after a brief moment of reflection, next came Friedrich Fromm, the Director-General of the Reserve Army, followed by General Georg Thomas, the head of the War Economy and Armaments Branch (WiRüAmt) in the High Command of the Armed Forces (OKW), and General Ritter von Leeb, the head of the Army Ordnance Department. With progressively shorter pauses for consideration Walther Funk and the big industrialists Albert Vögler and Wilhelm Zangen added their names, as did all the others. Only Admiral

Karl Witzell, the head of the Navy Ordnance Department, hesitated for a while and eventually signed with reservations. With feigned naivety Speer pleaded his unfamiliarity with the rituals of bureaucracy, as he was to do when faced with other unusual situations. In order to contain the flood of correspondence he had a rubber stamp made saying: 'Return to sender! Not vital to the war effort!' After obtaining these signatures, he remarked to one of his collaborators that he already had 'more power than Todt ever had'.[21]

Speer realized that his task demanded nothing less than the transformation of a relatively small and not very influential ministry into the authority that directed and controlled the entire war economy. First of all he had to put Göring's mind at rest. The Reich Marshal had been outraged by the 'spineless wretches' around him. By their signature they had withdrawn important responsibilities from him and sabotaged both his position and prestige, he complained. In a laborious conversation, the course of which was dictated by Göring's vanity, Speer assured him that he had not the slightest intention of reducing the Reich Marshal's responsibilities and eventually declared that he would perform his duties '*within* the Four-Year Plan'. On paper that was more than Göring had demanded but in fact it amounted to less, and it revealed the principle which guided Speer from now on, as if he had adopted Hitler's maxims on the art of statesmanship: to yield on mere formalities and pay whatever price had to be paid to vanity and complacency. It was far more important to avoid defining rights and competences precisely, leaving room for unimpeded action.[22] Deeply satisfied, Göring signed the decree which set his loss of power in motion on 1 March.

Armaments were indeed in a bad way when Speer took over the ministry. There were numerous omissions and aberrations, which mostly sprang from two causes. One of these derived from Hitler's '*Blitzkrieg* concept' of conducting the war as a sequence of swift and drastic strokes. Initially this policy had indeed yielded a number of much-admired successes. As a result, production had never been fundamentally reorganized. Instead, priorities had been shifted with cutbacks here and an increase there, depending on requirements. Hitler had even stuck to this armaments strategy during the preparations for his eastern campaign, particularly as he believed that he would smash Russia within a few months in that proverbial 'sand pit game' that was much discussed at the Führer's headquarters. That was why the armaments machinery was still operating at about one-third of its production

No one felt the edge of Speer's will to power more than Hermann Göring, the second man in the Reich. Step by step Speer wrested from him one competence after another, until Göring was left with a few meaningless titles and some honorary offices. The photograph shows Göring and Speer in May 1942 in the Court of Honour of the Reich Chancellery during the presentation of a decoration. In the background are Field Marshals Keitel and Milch.

capacity at the beginning of 1941. When the onset of the winter catastrophe forced Hitler to acknowledge that this concept had failed and that the *Blitzkrieg* had become a long war with entirely different armament requirements, the flexibility and the will for the necessary reorganization were lacking.

The second cause was closely connected with the first. It stemmed from Hitler's permanent fear that he might ask too much of the people. This was a relic of the traumatic experience of 1918, when the combat-weary masses went out into the street and brought down a centuries-old order. In addition Hitler probably had an intimation of how fragile and, in a wider sense, 'illegitimate' his regime was, and of how difficult was his intention of 'forcing' the reluctant German people 'into greatness', as he put it. All this was intensified by a fear of fluctuating popularity, since public favour had been artificially created by constant propaganda campaigns.

Apart from minor readjustments the armaments industry continued to work according to the principles established before the war. In marked contrast to Britain, on whom Churchill had grimly imposed ever greater demands, and soon also the United States, manufacture of consumer goods had hardly been cut back in the Reich. In spite of the growing manpower shortage, female labour had only been introduced to a limited degree and was still a long way from the level of the First World War. Even in munitions factories it had been impossible to introduce shift work until early 1942. One evening when Speer visited the production shops of one of Berlin's major armaments plants he found the premises empty and the machines unmanned.

The lack of co-ordination and the impenetrable disputes between conflicting authorities were probably even more disastrous. Five 'Supreme Reich Authorities' each claimed their own competence in the armaments field, starting with Göring's Four-Year Plan authority, followed by the Ministry of Economic Affairs, the Ministry of Labour and the High Command of the Armed Forces, and finally Speer's own organization. Moreover, each of the ordnance departments of the three services was pursuing a different programme, making sure above all that its own needs were met. Things were, as Speer observed, 'like in a baker's shop' with everybody wanting something different and wanting to be served first.[23]

This confusion of responsibilities reflected a similar muddle at all levels of the regime, which was far from being the monolithic block it pretended to be. It was far more like 'chaos goose-stepping in unison',[24] as a shrewd observer had earlier described the Kaiser's Germany. There was no central authority to regulate the distribution of raw materials, to set priorities or to prescribe the standardization of ammunition or weapons systems. Even the transport system was left to the discretion of the Ministry of Transport. One economic manager has related how at times it seemed that the Reich was waging a world war without a government.

This muddle had not arisen accidentally. It corresponded to Hitler's social Darwinism, according to which the strongest prevailed in internal power conflicts. In that sense the chaos promoted the dissolution of the state apparatus, as well as all its regulatory channels, in a regime whose only law was the Führer's own will. It is significant that he hardly ever went to the central office of government, that he never held cabinet meetings, and that again and again he gave chance callers conflicting responsibilities on a sudden impulse, so much so that he himself would sometimes wonder where a particular decision came from. On the other hand he refused to receive an official who had lost his favour, such as Walther Funk, the weak Minister of Economic Affairs or even Göring, who as chief of the Four-Year Plan was in charge of a kind of 'general economic command centre' but had become absorbed by his costumed tomfooleries and other diversions. Hitler often made his ministers feel his displeasure even when there was no reason. The conclusion that the entire 'territory ... was a swamp' was therefore not far from the truth.[25] By November 1941 the Ministry of Economic Affairs had declared that existing conditions did not permit an increase in production. Todt's increasingly open resignation stemmed not least from the realization that he was wearing himself out in a hopeless struggle.

It is astonishing how quickly Speer found his way through the chaos of competences, figures and reports. 'The principles were clear to me from the start', he recorded: basically it was a case of reorganizing the country into a war economy.[26] He also knew that radical measures could only be implemented at the beginning, before his authority was spent, and that time was working not only against him but against Germany as a whole. After the heavy losses of the winter and America's entry into the war, any further delay would be disastrous. Speer openly stated that the war could only be concluded before the onset of the second Russian winter with a total mobilization of all manpower and resources, otherwise, he added, adopting Todt's view, 'we will have lost the war once and for all'. In the plan which he submitted a mere ten days after assuming office Speer took up a few first attempts at reform for which Todt had obtained authorization at the end of January.[27] Unlike his predecessor, Speer was helped by the fact that he had Hitler's full authority. Just as the Führer had watched the bold measures of the lover of architecture earlier on, he was now filled with a mixture of happiness, admiration and even greater affection as he observed the energy with which Speer got down to work, as though he had done this all his life.

The fundamental idea was to divide the whole field of armaments according to weapons systems, such as tanks, aircraft, artillery and track vehicles. Each section was to be headed by a *Hauptausschuss*, a central committee responsible for the final product. Soon there were thirteen of these central committees; attached to each of them were so-called 'rings' responsible for delivering the raw materials, spare parts, fuel and special equipment. Speer appointed Karl Otto Saur head of the central committees. Saur was a man of rigorous temperament who had already held a key position under Todt. Walther Schieber, who also came from

Todt's staff, was given responsibility for the rings. According to his colleagues he had 'the strength and energy of a bull'.[28]

More importantly Speer placed not civil servants or desk-bound generals at the head of these departments, but experienced industrial leaders, technicians or engineers, men who were accustomed to thinking exclusively in terms of results. Almost at a stroke the bureaucratic lethargy, the quarrels about competence and departmental selfishness were replaced by an open exchange of experience and by inventive rationalization, which prevented needless duplication by implementing comprehensive standardization. The basic idea of Speer's method was to avoid the time-consuming detours via ministerial approval and control systems, as well as via the bureaucratic ordnance departments of the military, in order to achieve greater flexibility for industry. He also made sure that no departmental head was older than fifty-five, when, as he used to say, 'routine and presumption' began to prevail. A deputy departmental head could be forty years old at most.

The new principle of organization, which Speer called 'self-responsibility of industry', was also not his invention. His predecessor had already introduced the first stages along with Generalluftzeugmeister (Director of the Air Force Economic Branch) Milch, who had in turn taken the scheme over from Walther Rathenau, the organizer of the German war economy in the First World War. But the forceful way in which Speer put it into effect was new. The impetuosity with which he abolished and established responsibilities stunned all those involved. A reflection of this may be found in the minute of a conference at the Economy and Armaments Office of the Wehrmacht High Command on 23 March 1942: 'It is only Speer's word that counts nowadays. He can interfere in all departments. Already he overrides all departments ... head of department stresses that we have to be drawn into and pull along with the Speer organization, or else Speer will go his own way. On the whole Speer's attitude is to the point.'[29]

As the minute suggests, Speer went beyond his sphere of competence from the start. He used the committee of three which he called 'Central Planning' as his instrument. As he was not entitled to issue directions to the other ministries, he had originally thought of creating a large steering committee transcending ministerial powers. This would have been responsible for the allocation of raw materials not only within the armaments industry but also between the war economy and the civilian sphere and against whose decisions there would have been no appeal. As for controlling this 'last instance' he had relied on the belief that his own greater dynamism would prevail over the other members. But this concept had been changed in the further course of discussion, and Speer eventually decided to involve only Erhard Milch and run 'Central Planning' jointly with him.

Before putting this plan into effect he had to pacify Göring once more. Until the beginning of the war Göring had, after all, performed a comparable function as chief of the Four-Year Plan but he had squandered it with lethargy and indolence. On 3 March Speer appeared with an impressive entourage at Karinhall, Göring's hunting lodge in the Schorfheide not far from Berlin. Coming straight to the point he informed Göring that Hitler had instructed him to create a central planning authority. To this day it has not been established whether such an instruction ever existed; there is certainly no mention of it in the records.[30] But Speer had meanwhile achieved the deception necessary for success, and eventually the mighty Göring, who saw his economic powers dwindle one after another in a matter of weeks, had no choice but to give in. In the end he merely insisted that at least his state secretary Wilhelm 'Billy' Körner be included on the committee and after some tough negotiations Speer agreed, on Milch's advice. He told General Thomas that Central Planning was to play the same role in the economy as the general staff did in the conduct of the war. A few days later Hitler issued a decree confirming Central Planning as a 'super-ministerial body'.

By and large the system developed by Speer was scarcely more transparent than the *status quo ante*, especially as it contained numerous posts occupied by two people as well as a number of experts active both in the 'central committees' and in the 'rings'. The indistinct separation of armaments and civilian manufacturing also produced endless new confusions over competence. But meanwhile Speer had learned that lesson as well: the more muddled his organization seemed from the outside, the more effectively was he able to fend off all objections, hold the reins himself and distribute his decisions like 'signs of favour' in one direction and another. For this reason he appointed no state secretary under him but personally dealt with all requests, allocated tasks, checked, controlled and kept his ministry small and flexible. Throughout most of the period he employed a staff of no more than two hundred who were, however, assisted by a huge army of more than ten thousand, mostly honorary managers and technicians. He described this principle, which he soon developed to perfection, as 'organized improvisation'.[31]

With his curious mixture of central control, diminished bureaucracy and extended responsibility Speer created a counter-model to the over-organized command economy of the regime. He went even further and called for the abolition of the entire suspicion principle on which the state's administration was based, showing greater trust not only in industry but in the public generally. In this way he hoped to reduce the labyrinthine surveillance apparatus with its staff of roughly three million and thus to gain a major resource of manpower for armaments. However, in the end he did not succeed with these ideas, which questioned the very nature of the regime. At least he was later able to claim that with the 'self-responsibility of industry' he had adopted a different method to Germany's adversaries in the war: while Britain, and to a certain extent also the United States, were developing planned economies or at least authoritarian structures, he had tried to reinvigorate stagnating enterprise and inspire entrepreneurial fantasy, reviving a kind of 'democratic economic leadership'.[32] In reality the self-responsible organs were subordinated bodies, their advantage being that they were now subject to Speer's ministry alone, instead of being ruled by the chaos of directing authorities.

Although Speer very soon declared that the reorganization of the armaments industry had been completed, he impatiently reached out further and further. Initially only the army came under his central committees. Arguing, however, that a perceptible improvement in the armaments situation could be achieved only if the system were applied to all the services, he partly extended 'self-administration' to the navy on 20 March. Only the Luftwaffe created difficulties. In terms of expenditure its armaments accounted for nearly forty per cent of overall costs. But by establishing an 'industrial council' it had in a way already anticipated the system developed by Speer, or Todt to be precise.

Instead Speer continued his drive to extend his responsibilities to many other areas: he deprived Funk's Ministry of Economic Affairs of further rights, gained control of the 'armaments inspectorates' in the occupied countries – he already controlled most of them within the Reich – and, this time in his capacity as Inspector-General of Roads, he wrested first transport and, as chief of Baustab Speer, construction from the 'Eastern minister' Rosenberg. On 7 May he achieved the disbandment of the Finance and Armaments Office of the Wehrmacht High Command in its existing form and seized its essential tasks for himself. Things were no different for the Minister of Transport. Speer imposed his own man, Theodor Ganzenmüller, on him as state secretary and a

Even more than during his time as an architect, Speer's life was one continuous rush after he took over the armaments ministry. Everything was happening under enormous time pressure. Speer later admitted that his obsession with work may also have been an escape from the doubts which sometimes assailed him. This picture shows the minister studying papers on a flight to the Führer's headquarters.

little later he applied the same measure to the office of the Commissioner for Iron and Steel, which was part of the desperate Göring's domain. So it went on. 'Speer, I'll sign anything that comes from you,' Hitler declared around that time. It was a *carte blanche* such as no one else had ever received.[33]

Inevitably Speer's administrative insatiability and his success attracted all kinds of opposition. Göring was resentful, so was Funk, and Rosenberg, too, was deeply offended, not forgetting Bormann who had never got over his defeat on 13 February. The Wehrmacht was incensed, and the navy was angry at not having been included in 'Central Planning'. Even within Speer's own ministry there was some grumbling at the restrictions which the self-administration concept had brought upon them. Todt's former collaborators, in particular, felt discriminated against, so much so, as Wolters confided to his Chronicle, that at a 'social evening' designed to eliminate these tensions in the ministry he expected a 'brawl'.[34] Within the Party there were quite a few who remembered its socialist beginnings and who vented their irritation at the freedoms the 'intruder' Speer was granting to industry.

Speer noticed hardly any of this. His militant mood intensified, and perhaps also his hubris, each time he saw powerful organizations yield to his grasp. A mere fortnight after assuming office he had faced 'the most difficult forum' of all in Munich: the meeting of Gauleiters. He knew how powerful they were and he also realized how important they were for his plans to mobilize the public for an all-out effort. He therefore described to them the critical situation, arguing that in future the war had to be waged not only at the front but also in the homeland. Speer demanded that all 'peacetime building' be abandoned as well as the system of privileges, and finally, referring to the Decree for the Safeguarding of Armaments, he threatened to report to the Führer any incident that would impede the conduct of the war. But instead of the approval he had expected there was only feeble applause, and when the event was over those present besieged him with requests for special exemption for Gau forums, hunting lodges, domestic servants, luxury cars and so forth. The occasion was a severe setback. Bormann was the first to be gratified. He persuaded Hitler to issue a counter order, authorizing the continuation of building work on the Obersalzberg, and the other Gauleiters soon successfully followed suit. Speer later called his performance a 'beginner's mistake'.[35]

His Munich experience not only showed him how corrupt the leadership of the regime was and how much the formerly radical corps of Gauleiters had changed into an interest group of parasitical local princes. It convinced him that in future he would have to proceed more cautiously. For the time being, however, his opponents fell silent when, in the summer, transport conditions had already been reorganized and the much-lamented log-jams in the carriage or distribution of armaments goods and supplies for the forces were eliminated. They were even more astonished when the new production figures were announced. Merely through better organization and stricter control, the same labour force had increased the performance of the armaments industry by about sixty per cent; with a ninety-seven per cent increase, production of munitions had almost doubled. Nevertheless the figures were still well below those of the First World War and, especially in the munitions sector, they never reached those earlier figures even by the end of the war.[36]

At the very start of his activity Speer had identified shortage of manpower as one of the key problems. In March 1942 he therefore got Hitler to sign a decree suspending nearly three-quarters of all future building, thereby hoping to gain several hundred thousand building workers for munitions. But again the Gauleiters, who were responsible for regional manpower employment, opposed him, refusing to hand over manpower for enterprises in other provinces. In order to avoid such blinkered quarrels in future, Speer approached Hitler with the request to appoint a 'General Plenipotentiary for Manpower Employment'. With feigned innocence he suggested that one of the Gauleiters be appointed to that post and immediately put forward a name: Karl Hanke, who had left the Ministry of Propaganda after the affair with Magda Goebbels and been made Gauleiter of Lower Silesia. Hitler readily agreed, but when Speer called on him again a few days later he was told that, after consultation with Bormann, the person chosen was Fritz Sauckel, the Gauleiter of Thuringia. It was Speer's second defeat within a short time, both inflicted on him by Bormann.

There was one more to come. Speer had based his proposal on the assumption that the General Plenipotentiary for Manpower Employment would merely provide the manpower and then offer it to him or, at any rate, to Central Planning. This time Lammers, alarmed by Speer's rapid rise, objected and Bormann was quick to side with the head of the Reich Chancellery. Hitler himself did his part in removing the new post from the sphere of influence of the Minister for Armaments by extending Sauckel's responsibility beyond the armaments industry to the economy as a whole. Both these changes not only led to endless squabbles, but, when everything had blown over, they turned out to be lucky for one and unlucky for the other. Sauckel, who had viewed Speer as his principal rival from the day of his appointment, insisted that he would not respond to any demand, no matter who made it, and that he would not even give priority to the armaments industry in the allocation of labour. Instead he would at most take note of the wishes expressed by the various applicants and then decide on them. After all, he was not subordinate to anyone but had, like Speer, been appointed by the Führer himself and, if he was under anyone it was Göring, again 'within the Four-Year Plan'. For that reason he almost always stayed away from the meetings of Central Planning.[37]

All the experts shared Speer's view that the labour requirements of the armaments industry in Germany itself could be met with better organization, more accurate registration of unused manpower and, in particular, by extending female labour. But Sauckel objected, especially to the demand for employing more women. Time and again he invoked the 'moral dangers' of factory work which would affect not only the 'spiritual and emotional life' of the women but also their 'ability to bear children'. In vain did Speer point out that, for instance, the number of women employed in domestic work had hardly decreased even by the fourth year of the war, whereas in Britain, where the initial figures had been almost the same, two-thirds of domestic staff had been called up for war work. Again he made comparisons with 1914–18, when more women had been enlisted for factory work than in the present war, although the population had been smaller then. But Sauckel rejected all these objections with ideological arguments.

Driven by blind energy, this stocky, peasant-like man insisted on the disastrous idea of providing the required manpower from the occupied territories. With his combination of 'heart', boastfulness and brutality, Sauckel was the epitome of the 'old fighter', invariably signing all his letters to Hitler 'your always obedient and faithful Fritz Sauckel'. For years he had served the Party in various functions, mainly in Thuringia. Significantly he took up the cues provided by Hitler himself in his address on Sauckel's appointment: 'The area working directly for us embraces more than 250 million people. Let no one doubt that we will succeed in involving every one of these millions in the labour process.'[38] Unlike Speer, Sauckel believed that German manpower reserves were exhausted. He therefore took Hitler's words as a licence for any form of recruitment, deportation and compulsory labour.

On 20 April 1942 Sauckel announced a 'gigantic' employment programme with a 'colossal number of foreign civilian workers'. Until then the required contingent had been recruited on a 'voluntary' basis, though not without pressure. Sauckel now went over to the forcible recruitment of anyone born in certain years. In the ruffian style of the Party satraps, Sauckel spurred on his own department as well as the special commandos setting out on their manhunts throughout occupied Europe with the slogan that 'the last vestiges of our humanitarian dopeyness should be dropped'.[39] Without warning his hordes burst into villages and towns, arrested all those capable of work, be they male or female, in the street, dragged them out from churches, cinemas and homes, and burned down entire villages on the pretext that the draft figures had not been reached. By August 1942 Sauckel had brought 700,000 workers to Germany, his 'richest hunting ground' being the part of Poland which formed the Government-General.

Fritz Sauckel (left) at the Atlantic Wall in France in June 1943. Sauckel, General Plenipotentiary for Labour Employment, regarded Speer as his main rival. Applying the most brutal methods, Sauckel rounded up hundreds of thousands of slave workers in the occupied territories.

Once the counter-thrusts, by which the Soviet formations had responded to the failure of the German winter campaign, had been halted in early 1942 Hitler immediately began preparations for the summer campaign. It was only in the planning stage that the full truth emerged about the enormous German losses during the winter. In the end the German forces which mounted the second offensive in May and June were not even half the strength of the formations which had launched Operation Barbarossa a year previously. To bring up its units to anything like full strength the Wehrmacht intensified its enlistment of supposed reserves within Germany, and Speer had his work cut out protecting the workers in the most important munitions factories from the military recruitment drive. Month by month the growing demands of one side increased the difficulties of the other. While the Wehrmacht High Command extended its call-up within the Reich, combing through all industrial establishments, in November 1942 alone Central Planning demanded some 600,000 additional workers whom not even

Sauckel was initially prepared to promise. But Speer and Milch pressed on impatiently, and in the report Sauckel submitted on 15 April 1943 on the first year of his activity he put the number of foreign workers brought in at over three and a half million.[40] Meanwhile he had greatly stepped up conscription in the western occupied territories, notably in France, not only provoking the protests of the local military commanders but also driving young people into the underground movements in droves.

Speer, however, continued to urge a total extension of the war. He had allied himself with Milch, with whom he had grown increasingly close since his spontaneous gesture of renunciation on 13 February. Their professional agreement on nearly every issue had gradually developed into a kind of friendship. As the older of the two, Milch had far more experience and his admiration for the young minister, then just thirty-seven years old, always included a touch of indulgent irony. But his broad view and his quick repartee provided Speer, who was still somewhat inhibited in the conference room, with valuable support. Indeed, Milch's choleric temperament, which spared not even Göring, and his occasional parade-ground roughness, often helped overcome opposition. When, in August 1942, General von Gablenz, one of Milch's closest colleagues, was killed in an air crash, Speer called on the field marshal in the evening, offering himself as a 'substitute' for his lost friend. Moved by this gesture, Milch stood by him even more firmly, and only aerial armaments, whose independence Milch jealously guarded, remained a contentious issue between them.[41]

Together with Milch, Speer increased his demands on Sauckel step by step. But while the airforce industry found itself in real difficulties because it almost invariably came off worst when competing for manpower with Speer's industry, it is quite possible that Speer was also trying to create difficulties for the unloved Sauckel. At the same time Speer demanded that entire civilian plants be closed down in order to fill the gaps which the armaments industry had suffered as a result of conscription. He also made plans for thorough administrative reform and for self-declared tax returns; the traditional mistrust of the state, he repeated, was inappropriate in a war such as this. Speer calculated that hundreds of thousands of civil servants could be made available for munitions in this way. He accused Funk of being too soft and declared his determination to 'drastically cut the living standard of the upper classes' even if, as he added 'quite crudely', this would 'proletarianize' the country.[42]

Although this kind of initiative had initially run aground on Hitler's opposition and, even more so, that of the Gauleiters, Speer had new hopes of getting his radical course accepted, now that the country was reaching a turning point in the war. Admittedly Hitler's territorial power was now greater than ever before, extending from Hammerfest to Tunis and from Bordeaux to the Caucasus. But Speer knew that the map was deceptive. For an armed conflict on three continents, on the seas and in the air, there was a basic shortage of everything from raw materials to transport and supplies, not to mention human beings. In fact towards the end of the year, one proud position after another crumbled in a matter of weeks. First North Africa was lost, then, almost simultaneously, the U-boat war; next the British air offensive began and, soon after, the Americans followed suit. On 20 January 1943 Field Marshal Paulus, the commander of the Sixth Army encircled at Stalingrad, stated: 'All that is left of us is what the chronicles will report about us.' A fortnight later the remnants of his army surrendered.

The unexpected collapse on all fronts hit Hitler as a body blow. The spectre of defeat, which, after years of continual triumphs, had first appeared before Moscow, now became a regular guest at the Führer's headquarters. In the summer of 1941 he had 'suspended' the inconclusive war against Britain in order to smash the island empire by waging a lightning campaign against its 'continental sword', the Soviet Union, before the United States joined the war. Now the advance in the East had come to a halt, the Red Army had mounted a counter-attack and America had appeared on the enemy side. The turning point had been reached in all theatres of war. It marked the beginning of the war of attrition, which Hitler had always feared and regarded as hopeless.

'There were days when my nerves snapped,' Hitler had remarked in connection with the winter battle of the previous year. Now they went completely to pieces. Those near him have all recorded the choleric outbursts with which he reacted to the collapse of his strategy and all its assumptions. In addition his whole lifestyle, which had always been characterized by hectic spurts of activity and prolonged phases of inertia, disintegrated under the pressure of the war. More so even than the reverses, the unremitting stress may well have induced the increasing paralysis which was also recorded. Hitler certainly lost the flexibility that had so often helped him over crises in the past. These two moods, the wild fits of rage and the increasing petrifaction, governed his behaviour right up to the end. A nervous irritability, expressed by the dressing-down of the men around him, the sacking of top brass, and eventually his own withdrawal from the communal meals, went hand in hand with a radical hardening of his overall policy.

Surprisingly, however, contrary to all pronouncements about 'total war', Hitler could not be moved to ask of the German population those incisive restrictions which he had proclaimed as the 'dictates of the hour'. Now and again, especially in conversation with Goebbels, he gave his entourage the impression that he would at last agree to their demand for mobilizing every last resource and to sharing the burdens fairly in a 'socialist war'.[43] But then, mainly under Bormann's influence, he would revert once more to his hesitant state and shy away from decisions. Goebbels had good reason to observe that the seriousness of the situation was due not only to a long apparent 'leadership crisis' but also to a 'leader crisis' which was increasingly diminishing German prospects of victory.[44]

Speer later asserted that Hitler's almost blinkered obstinacy had driven him to desperation.[45] To lend his views greater weight Speer allied himself to Goebbels and even included in his party the loose-cannon Robert Ley, who had for some time faded into the background because of his notorious drunkenness. Like everybody else Speer knew that the leader of the labour organization was ruthless and took a class-conscious pleasure in his coarse plebeian attacks on the grandees whom, like Speer, he regarded as the real opponents of any intensified war effort. This grouping was, moreover, intended as a counter-front against Bormann, who, along with Lammers and the Wehrmacht chief of staff Wilhelm Keitel, had set up a kind of cordon around Hitler in order to screen him not only from any importunity but also from the depressing reality. It was they who determined his daily routine, who decided who was granted or refused an audience, and in the longer term even who was in or out of favour. They had an advantage over all the other rivals simply because they enjoyed the privilege of daily access to the Führer. The only exception to this privilege was Speer, who continued to have Hitler's confidence. Besides, as armaments minister, he belonged to the military sphere whose meetings with Hitler were fixed by his Wehrmacht aides; the other exception was Heinrich Himmler, for different reasons. There was some justification to Goebbels' suspicion that the 'triumvirate' around Bormann was trying to establish 'a kind of cabinet government'. 'This', he added, 'cannot be tolerated under any circumstances.'[46]

To this day it is not clear who was the driving force of the counter-alliance, but both Speer and Goebbels had a largely practical interest, and Ley at least a demagogic one, in intensifying the war. On tactical grounds they considered reviving the existing but half-forgotten 'Ministerial Council for the Defence of the Reich' headed by Göring, in order to induce the irresolute Hitler to take 'decisive action'. After Speer had settled a long-smouldering dispute between Goebbels and Göring, the group met on the Obersalzberg to discuss joint action. But the 'power struggle' they had decided upon failed even in the opening move because Göring's position had been shaken much more than they had realized: the 'incompetent Reich Marshal', Hitler angrily sneered, when a devastating air-raid on Nuremberg was reported on the very evening that Goebbels and Speer put forward their plan.[47]

It is against this background that Goebbels' speech of 18 February 1943 in the Sportpalast should be viewed. There he put the famous ten leading questions to a chosen audience of followers and demanded their consent for total war 'in a confused and feverish atmosphere', as he himself recorded. He used gloomy images to invoke the disaster of Stalingrad as a 'great alarm call of destiny', and seemed almost to revel in painting new horror-scenarios of the 'onslaught of the steppe' and the 'Jewish liquidation commandos' advancing behind it. Then came his real message: in future, he exclaimed, rank, position or occupation would no longer be of any consequence, and everybody, whether poor or rich, exalted or low, would be expected to make the same sacrifices when the 'people's community' was finally realized.

No less important than the attack on the upper ten thousand headed by Party bosses was Goebbels' attempt to expose Hitler himself to the pressure of the street by addressing a passionate appeal to the masses. He smugly put about his view that the event had been something like a 'silent coup d'état'. Contrary to a widespread presumption, it was not really an offensive proclamation of total war. For, despite the authoritarian 'lack of direction' Goebbels complained about,[48] that war had long started on the German side and had also been set in motion by the Western Allies with the air war against the civilian population and, more officially, at the Casablanca Conference three weeks earlier, when Roosevelt and Churchill voiced their demand for 'unconditional surrender'. But unlike Hitler and most of his followers, Goebbels realized that a total war was hopeless without the total mobilization of all resources; it was for that very reason that Speer, who was more determined than anyone else, had joined him.

However, the wave of applause for Goebbels' concluding slogan,

'Now people arise, now storm break loose!', ebbed away even before it crested. And if the people did not rise, then its Leader was even less ready to do so. Göring was outraged at the suggestion that he should close down his favourite Berlin restaurant Horcher, Bormann as ever sensed some kind of an intrigue, so did Lammers, while Ribbentrop suspected Goebbels of trying to wrest the foreign ministry from him. As Goebbels noted in his diary, the 'by then rather recalcitrant' Gauleiters were furious at the attack by one of themselves. Everyone had a different motive, but they all began to urge Hitler not to yield to Goebbels' dramatizations. To that extent the speech led to nothing and remained simply a remarkable example of rhetorical rabble-rousing.[49]

Some time later Speer, too, made his first speech to a mass audience at the Berlin Sportpalast. Although he also spoke of the mobilization of all reserves, he scarcely touched on the impending efforts and, strangely enough, even avoided the current formula of 'total war', which he used in his official dealings. Instead, in a stiff tone, he read out figures, percentages and production increases, explained the 'self-responsibility of industry', justified the importance of 'gaining additional manpower' and uttered a few dry notes of assurance. When he had finished, Goebbels mounted the rostrum again. He praised the will to resistance of the 'sorely tested population', vehemently predicted the 'radical elimination' of the Jews ('This time, too, Lucifer will fall!') and ended by invoking the 'new era of a German socialism' that would dawn with victory. This time he did not display the whipping verve of 18 February. But then the purpose of his speech was different. Like Speer he was clearly less concerned with rousing emotions than with demonstrating their unanimity as champions of total war.[50]

Despite subliminal irritations, Speer's collaboration with Sauckel soon worked more or less smoothly. In a speech to armaments workers he thanked the General Plenipotentiary for increasing manpower by twenty-three per cent. Although they were very different people, they suited one another in a remarkable way. Both were obsessed by statistics and their deceptive magic. But what in Speer was a cold fever, derived in Sauckel's case from his predilection for bombast and 'gigantic programmes' and Goebbels was right to speak of his penchant for megalomania.[51] Whereas Speer saw statistical data as a starting point for continuous calls for greater efforts, Sauckel viewed them as symbols of success, regardless of their implementation. As a result Sauckel promised everything and, despite occasional hesitation, kept agreeing to the most extravagant demands because, as he declared, the 'believing

Speer was a reluctant orator. However, his position demanded that he occasionally
appear in front of large audiences. At the beginning of June 1943 he and Goebbels
spoke at the Berlin Sports Palace. As a champion of total war, Speer demanded the
mobilization of all available forces.

and unconditional National Socialist' could 'completely solve' any
task.[52]

That was the trap into which Sauckel soon fell. The source material
reveals little and, as nearly always, gives no indication of people's ulteri-
or motives, but one may assume that Speer had a hand in his failure,
for he never lost sight of his ambition to get manpower under the
control of Central Planning. Even so, Sauckel was by no means always
fighting a lost battle in the disputes which arose on countless issues. On
one occasion when Speer repeated his demand for an increased enlistment of German women at a conference at the Führer's headquarters,
Hitler had 'sharply' opposed him. He had, as Sauckel gloatingly recorded, declared 'that our long-legged, slender German women could not be
compared to the "short-legged", primitive and healthy Russian women'.
But when in the spring of 1943 Sauckel promised, and not long afterwards actually reported, approximately one and a half million foreign
workers, Milch recorded after examining all the data: 'Speer is searching, I am searching …' and arrived at a shortfall of 800,000 people.[53]

Central Planning only had to increase its requirements again. In fact it persuaded Hitler to demand more than four million workers for the following year. Again Sauckel promised to provide the required reinforcements 'with fanatical will'. In the end he arrived at a figure of approximately 100,000.

Speer, however, far superior to him intellectually and tactically, had by then, in a sense, dealt him a fatal blow. In view of the unpleasantness and opposition accompanying the increasingly brutal business of 'Sauckeling off' slave labour from France, Italy, Norway, Holland and Belgium, Speer had developed a new concept. He saw this as a means of diminishing the numerous tensions in the occupied countries and as the first step to a co-ordinated direction of European production, no matter how far off that seemed. The basic idea was not to bring the people to the jobs, but to bring the jobs to the people. In France this was not even necessary: production facilities already existed where they needed to be, or at any rate there were a host of factories not used to full capacity for the production of armaments.

After several preliminary talks in Paris, Speer invited the young French production minister Jean Bichelonne to Berlin. He received him like a state visitor from an allied power and spent the weekend with him at Arno Breker's country house near Berlin. They soon agreed on the mistakes and continuing resentments of the older generation, marked as it was by the First World War, and finally arranged to establish some so-called 'protected enterprises' in France. These were to produce locally for the German economy and in return they were to be guaranteed exemption from all deportation measures. Within a few months more than 10,000 French factories were already delivering products for armaments and civilian needs to Germany. Before this had been accomplished Speer even succeeded in getting Sauckel, who was too simpleminded to grasp the significance of the arrangement, to agree and, as a result, to gain Hitler's consent. Once the agreement had been reached Speer again displayed his lack of concern for administrative niceties. He impatiently put an end to the meticulous work of the lawyers and sealed the arrangement with Bichelonne with a mere handshake, without a written contract. As he kept strictly to his promises there was no cause for disagreement afterwards. The price had to be paid by Sauckel. No sooner had the arrangement come into force in the latter half of September 1943, and been extended to Italy and Germany's western neighbours shortly thereafter, than Sauckel's whole system of forcibly recruited foreign labour quickly and quietly collapsed.

Sauckel was only one example. Wherever Speer reached out, he gained the upper hand and extended his powers. He no longer even asked Hitler for support in particular cases, but only for approval in principle, which he used as cover for his own power games – until Hitler discovered this and occasionally refused his approval. The time in which his wishes were readily fulfilled had gone by the end of 1942, Speer noted.[54] Sometimes he simply steamrollered his adversaries, on other occasions he cornered them or undermined their position step by step, like the species of wasp which settles inside a body and consumes it from within. By reducing steel quotas Speer made the navy, which had retained some of its independence in armaments, agree to surrender it at the end of 1942. Moreover, he did all he could to see to it that the stubborn Grand Admiral Raeder was pensioned off, as he would later do with the 'armaments' general, Georg Thomas. A few weeks after Dönitz was made commander-in-chief of naval forces early in the following year, he asked Speer to take over naval armaments. Speer used Dönitz's inquiry to get Hitler to order further cuts in consumer goods production and even to close down entire enterprises which were of no importance to the war effort. Only then did he agree to Dönitz's request.

He had scarcely achieved one success before he extended his tentacles towards a further accretion of power. In the same conversation in which he had obtained Hitler's consent to the take-over of naval armaments, Speer also expressed interest in taking over the entire civilian sector. When Hitler did not oppose this, he met with Hans Kehrl, the head of the civilian sector in Walther Funk's Ministry of Economic Affairs, who combined organizational acumen with a firm grasp and shirt-sleeve dynamism. For some time Kehrl had leaned more to Speer than to his own weak minister, and the two now agreed to work together. As soon as Hitler had approved Kehrl's transfer to the Ministry of Armaments, all concerned were summoned to the Reich Chancellery, where Funk, surprised and worried despite preliminary talks, had no choice but to deliver his own 'funeral oration'.[55] A final intrigue by Bormann against Speer's victorious advance having failed, Hitler signed a decree 'On the Concentration of the War Economy' on 2 September. Funk was left with little more than the distribution of consumer goods and a number of formal functions.

Speer immediately embarked on a fundamental redistribution of tasks in his gigantically enlarged ministry. Above all, he established a 'Planning Office' which would prepare the decisions of Central Planning and supervise their implementation. Soon this became the most important authority of production. Two days later Speer drove out to

Speer and Karl Dönitz at a naval exercise towards the end of 1943. At the turn of 1942–3 Dönitz was appointed to succeed Grand Admiral Erich Raeder, who had successfully resisted Speer's attempts to control naval armaments. Dönitz, on the other hand, soon asked Speer to relieve him of that task.

Karinhall to obtain Göring's signature for these changes which, technically, fell 'within the Four-Year Plan'. The once-so-powerful master of the German economy who had been equipped with full dictatorial powers was by then hard put to conceal how pleased he was that Speer had even come to see him.[56] By signing his name he endorsed nothing less than an exchange of powers.

Combining threats, subtle machinations and bold tactics, with a vigour which left even Hitler's old-established entourage bewildered, Speer had brought nearly all economic affairs under his control and reorganized them in little more than eighteen months. Only the Luftwaffe, which continued to go its own way, had escaped his grasp. But Speer felt sure that before long it too would surrender to his superior power. 'In view of his extended tasks,' Hitler's decree of 2 September 1943 stated, the Reich Minister for Armaments and Ammunition would in future have 'the title of Reich Minister for Armaments and War Production'.

On closer inspection, however, it was production as a whole that now came under Speer's control. His sphere of activity also extended beyond the Reich proper to the incorporated regions. Even in the occupied territories he was entitled to give instructions to the military and civilian authorities. Thanks to his power over 'protected enterprises' and millions of workers, he had in fact become nothing less than 'the manager of the European production apparatus'. In an appeal to the vast army of his employees he declared, with an undertone of triumph: 'The entire production of the Greater German Reich is now being operated and directed from one single central post.'[57] All in all it was a revolution no one would have believed possible. Hugh Trevor-Roper has written that Speer complemented the revolution by which Hitler had overturned all political and social circumstances in Germany with the overdue industrial revolution. Not until the 'Speer-Revolution' had the Führer state been accomplished.[58]

Speer never asked himself what the purpose of the 'Speer revolution' was or what it set out to achieve, nor did he face up to any of the many questions raised by his actions. He explained this by the hectic pace that drove him on, the 'thrill of the chase' and his ambition. But when circumstances gave him the opportunity to stop, the doubts he had were only passing ones and they never extended beyond a world to which he belonged more than he himself liked to admit.

Chapter Six

STATIONS OF
AMBITION

By the middle of 1943 Speer was at the peak not only of his power but also of his reputation. He wielded great influence, enjoyed Hitler's trust and was that rare thing among the top cadres, an excellent administrator. These qualities had earned him unprecedented public prestige. Whatever he put his hand to seemed to be successful. He had effortlessly taken the great Göring to pieces and then toppled, like skittles, anyone in his way, ministers, generals and even a few 'old Party fighters' who were thought to be invulnerable because of Hitler's sentimental attachment to them. Goebbels, who like others had watched his rise with jealous unease, soon concluded that it was wiser to ally himself with Speer. After initial doubts, his diaries reveal a note of undisguised hyperbole about the 'genius' of the new minister, the 'veritable miracles' he was working in armaments, and how he was 'riding roughshod' over the distinguished gentlemen. After a year he noted that Speer had proved 'a good exchange for Todt'. As an outsider, the new minister was not in awe of big names and, being a civilian, did not stand to attention before every general, unlike Todt who had been 'too much of a soldier'.[1] The only bastions which had proved unassailable for Speer were held by Bormann and by Heinrich Himmler, who was keenly observing the scene from the background.

At the same time Hitler's deep feelings for Speer had grown even stronger. Almost resuming the adulatory tone of earlier years he had on one occasion described Speer's achievements as 'epoch-making'.[2] Their relationship was much more formal than it used to be, lacking the bohemian camaraderie of earlier years. In order to emphasize the official nature of their relationship Hitler would normally address him as 'Herr Minister', and the only thing that recalled their past friendship was the occasional invitation to Speer after his quarrel with the generals to join him for a lonely lunch at his headquarters, where they ate their meal in 'tortuous' silence. However Speer had now received that 'mysterious consecration' he had missed years ago: whenever he was at headquarters he participated, as if it were a matter of course, in the situation conferences, where he was the only civilian.[3]

Speer formed a close alliance with Goebbels because of the aims they shared. Quite apart form the brilliance and energy of the propaganda minister, Speer admired the will to 'ruthlessness' with which he was manoeuvring for 'total war', like himself, though for other reasons. Goebbels was driven by the calculated conviction that there was no going back: 'triumph or disaster' were all that remained. Speer on the other hand believed with a mixture of ambition and 'romantic' dedication in a higher task. 'He is not only a cool calculator,' Goebbels noted, 'but also a real enthusiast', adding that with the 'radicalization of methods' he was proving himself to be 'a real National Socialist'.[4] Together with Ley they pressed for increased efforts, supervised, tracked down overlooked or concealed reserves and schemed with one another. In order to avoid any stoppage of production Speer proposed the introduction of a 'flexible Sunday' in the late summer of 1942, and Goebbels promised him every propagandist support against the expected opposition, particularly from the Churches, which promptly came. They also joined forces on Speer's plan to assign the students of the technical colleges to armaments, and only when Speer announced his intention of establishing a 'Propagandastandarte Speer' (a Speer propaganda squad) did Goebbels feel challenged on his own home ground and curtly refuse.

The propaganda chief was mistaken if he thought his agreement with Speer was evidence of the latter's firm ideological position. Nothing mattered less to Speer than the ideological exegeses which led Hitler to indulge in endless monologues and which Goebbels appreciated at least as a stimulant.[5] What had made Speer susceptible to National Socialism was the aesthetic side of the new beginning, the grand gesture, ostentation and self-glorification, along with the theatrical opportunities it offered him. Apart from serving 'the great man' there was the enormous exhilaration of the daily rush, the drug of exerting all one's efforts. Speer looked on the convoluted justifications concocted by men such as Himmler, Rosenberg or the blood-and-soil philosopher Walter Darré, with an astonishment which had always struck Hitler's faithful followers as arrogant and which had escaped only the similarly conceited Goebbels.

In the long run even he noticed Speer's ideological indifference. It became most apparent in the disagreement which emerged between them about the treatment of the Jews from Berlin. Whereas Goebbels complained that even after the 'de-jewing drives' of autumn 1941 and spring 1942 there were still tens of thousands of Jews living in the Reich capital, Speer insisted that they were indispensable as armaments workers and kept pointing to the huge amounts of material consumed by the campaign which had faltered in the Russian winter. Indeed he succeeded in getting Bormann to issue a circular on 13 March 1942, suspending deportations for the time being or at least slowing them down.

Nevertheless Goebbels did not give in. His efforts at persuasion having failed, he even tried to force Speer to change his mind by a special order of the Führer; but again he foundered on Speer's stubborn counter-arguments. Goebbels eventually achieved his aim 'to totally cleanse Berlin of Jews by the end of March [1943] at the latest' by simply calling the Leibstandarte to his aid. On Saturday, 27 February, it surrounded the armaments enterprises and raided the workshops in order to track down and arrest the remaining Jewish workers. In an argument with Speer a few days earlier Goebbels had been more than usually fierce, telling him 'emphatically' that he had 'finally had enough' of his perpetual references to the indispensability of Jewish skilled workers, especially as he had just received from Sauckel 'the definite promise' to 'provide Polish substitutes'. When the last transports had left Goebbels spoke of one of his 'greatest achievements'.[6] Sauckel, incidentally, never provided the promised workers.

As Speer's resistance had been based solely on the needs of armaments policy, he declared that 'in these circumstances' he would 'no longer raise any objections'. The documents reveal no other motives, certainly no humanitarian ones, and there is reason to believe that Speer never raised any considerations of this kind. His opposition was largely governed by expediency. Apparently disturbed by his clash with Goebbels, Speer confided in Hermann Bücher, the chairman of the board of AEG, who had been something of a friend over many years. Bücher was disappointed by Speer's compliance and observed several times: 'We will never be forgiven for this.' It made Speer think. Later he also spoke of a 'pincer movement' which Goebbels had mounted against him.[7] Soon, however, he recovered his professional blinkers and continued to stare only at numbers, manufacturing capacities and production figures. Even so, it may be said to his credit that the 'colder' motivations gave him, for a time at least, remarkable determination, the same determination he

In the summer of 1943 Speer had reached the peak of his power. Occasional remarks by Hitler led him to expect that he might be chosen to become the 'Second Man in the State' and some of the generals at the Führer's headquarters supported that belief. The picture shows Speer boarding a Ju-52, which he temporarily used as his official plane.

showed in the face of Himmler's repeated attempts to grant him an honorary rank in the SS, first on his appointment as Generalbauinspektor and next as minister. Almost offensive in his indifference, Speer rejected these approaches or simply failed to respond to them.

It was plain to everyone that the summer of 1943 had brought the great turning point in the war. Until then the over-extension of forces had been hidden or drowned by propaganda. Now it forced the army into retreat on nearly every front. Following the loss of North Africa, the Allied conquest of Sicily in July had resulted in a *coup d'état* in Italy and in Mussolini's overthrow. In the same month Operation Citadel, the last German offensive in the East, had collapsed with heavy losses after ten days and only three weeks later the Soviet counter-offensive had begun. 'Bad news is simply beating down on our office,' Goebbels wrote at the beginning of August.[9] A month later came the landing of British and

American troops in the Gulf of Taranto near Salerno.

Italy's elimination from the Axis alliance initially led to a further extension of Speer's power. On 13 September Hitler signed a decree placing the entire industry in the occupied part of Italy under the Minister of Armaments. Speer also received the right to dispose over all manpower in the country, including the 'military internees', as the disarmed and captured Axis allies of yesterday were referred to. While the rapidly retreating German formations were establishing a line south of Naples, the removal of machines and raw materials started in the north. Ten days later the local army command stated with unusual frankness: 'Italy's betrayal now enables us to utilize this country, too, in every respect for the further German conduct of the war.'[10] The dreaded war on two fronts had begun.

Strictly speaking, it was a war on three fronts. At the turn of 1941-2 Britain had already gone over to 'area bombing', the systematic destruction of the military and industrial centres of the Reich in keeping with Churchill's instruction to Arthur Harris, the new chief of the British Bomber Command. But Harris soon widened this strategy into one of wearing Germany down psychologically by extensive attacks on residential areas. Towards the end of March 1942 he had opened that theatre of war with a major raid on Lübeck. The ancient Hanseatic town 'burnt like matchwood', according to one British airman. In retribution Hitler recalled two bomber groups with around one hundred aircraft from southern Italy. Over the next weeks they selectively bombed old towns in England. But the change in the ratio of strength became obvious when the Royal Air Force responded on the night of 30 May with its first thousand-bomber raid on Cologne. From 4 July onwards the Americans also attacked with their Flying Fortresses. Together the Anglo-American forces stepped up the aerial terror against the civilian population, stage by stage, to 'round-the-clock bombing'.

The expectations raised by this policy revealed destructive rage and strategic short-sightedness in equal measure. Rather than discouraging or disheartening the population, the horror of ceaseless bombing further hardened it and, as though seeking protection, it closed ranks with the regime as never before. Today it is clear that abandoning the strategy of 'selective air war' – that is to say, the bombing of a few selected and vital war industries – was both nonsensical and costly. Furthermore it considerably prolonged the war.

In the middle of May 1943 it seemed as though Harris had recognized the principle of paralysing industry across the board after all. One night a small formation of fewer than twenty Lancasters, each with a special rotating bomb, attacked the dams in the Ruhr, which were full to the brim and glittering in the light of the full moon. Although the Möhne and Sorpe dams supplied almost three-quarters of the local economy, as well as nearly five million people, with water and power, the defences were so inadequate that the few anti-aircraft guns on the walls of the dams were unable to deal with the low-flying aircraft. As a result both plants were destroyed or badly damaged with comparatively little effort, as was the Eder dam which was not part of the Ruhr system. To the amazement of the Germans, the remaining Ruhr dams were spared.

This mistake, and the half-hearted nature of the undertaking, cost the British their success, even though the effect of this 'dambuster raid' was still far greater than all the previous attacks on residential areas. The next few days revealed how little Harris had thought the programme through. Not only did he fail to attack the neighbouring barrages, he never carried out the expected incendiary raids in the Ruhr which would have wreaked havoc in the area because the fire brigades had no water. With his improvisational skill Speer had restored the barrages and arranged for two hundred batteries of heavy flak to be posted between Dortmund and Düsseldorf by the second half of September. But there were no further attacks on the dams. Speer spoke ironically of the powerful ally he had in the enemy's general staff.[11]

The same lack of method in Allied strategy manifested itself time and again. Speer later stated that, despite the horrors of the bombing war for the civilian population, he soon had no reason to worry about any short-term effects on the armaments industry; Harris had been pigheaded, relying less on a carefully designed plan than on a primitive 'killer instinct'.[12] What worried him far more was the thought that the Americans might bring about a change in the air war and direct it at the few indispensable nerve centres of the economy or, as he put it, attack the headwaters of armaments instead of the estuary. Destruction of just one of four or five vital production branches would, he believed, have had incalculable consequences.

Apart from the hydration plants his anxieties were focused on the steel industry and the most crucial traffic junctions, mainly the town of Schweinfurt, where roughly half of the German ball-bearing industry was concentrated. His repeated demands to provide better protection for the factories had been unsuccessful. Göring in particular had felt affronted by them. With his usual grandiloquence he declared that his

Demonstration of new weapons behind the front. Hitler insistent and clearly annoyed, Speer relaxed, even haughty, the picture reveals something about the nature of their relationship. In the centre is Karl Otto Saur, chief of the Technical Office.

fighter formations would sweep the enemy machines out of the skies. But when on 17 August 1943 the American 8th bomber fleet bombed Schweinfurt it encountered no significant opposition and German ball-bearing production dropped by nearly forty per cent at a single blow. Not until after the war did Speer learn that the Allied airforce chiefs had recognized the importance of a rapid second strike, but had failed to overcome Harris's opposition. Had the attacks been maintained and included the remaining ball-bearing plants, Speer believed that it would have taken only four months to bring armaments production 'to a complete standstill' and the war would have been over.[13]

Not until the middle of October did the Flying Fortresses appear over Schweinfurt again. Meanwhile, however, air defences had been strengthened and one of the most dramatic air battles of the whole war was fought above the city, with the Germans summoning up all their strength. The American formations suffered such heavy losses that Schweinfurt was spared for some time to come. But instead of switching to other vital industrial targets, the Americans followed the British practice of bombing the civilian population for several months and it was only in February 1944 that the Schweinfurt factories, along with ball-bearing plants in Erkner, Bad Cannstadt and Steyr, were bombed twice within a span of four days and largely destroyed. After that the Combined Command went back to random attacks, and at the beginning of April bombing of the ball-bearing industry, which had meanwhile been partially relocated, ceased altogether. The chance of ending the war then was wasted once and for all. As a result of the inconsistent Allied strategy not a single tank, aircraft, submarine or motor vehicle was lost because of a shortage of ball-bearings.[14]

A similarly uncoordinated muddle existed on the German side. Speer had demanded early on that the principle of paralysing industry be applied also to Germany's adversaries, especially the Soviet Union. But before the time-consuming decision process got going, the distances to the Soviet targets had become too great because of the rapid German retreat in the East, making the proposal redundant. Even the idea put forward by the Luftwaffe of using volunteers as sacrificial airmen for a 'mission without return' was soon discarded.[15]

More disastrous still was the failure of the German Luftwaffe, which had operated so spectacularly at the beginning of the war. Göring's loss of prestige and the confusion of his management made Germany increasingly impotent in the face of the enemy's domination of the air. To begin with there was the multiplicity of over-hastily designed aircraft types, repeatedly modified or delayed as strategic thinking swung first one way and then another. Moreover most designers, especially Willy Messerschmitt, developed an unrestrainable liking for new and bolder aircraft, whilst neglecting the production of completed designs. In 1943 alone there were twenty-three separate aircraft programmes with ten variants and more than forty further models for development: twin-engined fighters, night fighters, freight gliders, dive bombers, long-distance reconnaissance aircraft and long-range bombers, and almost as many engines, power units and other parts. This chaos not only brought aerial armaments into discredit, but also moved it down to sixth place in the list of priorities.[16] Its weakness was to some extent due to Göring's deep antagonism to Milch. For weeks the Reich Marshal refused to speak to Milch, left his submissions unanswered, and when in one of their arguments Milch reminded Göring of an inspection report he had sent him, he snapped: 'You don't imagine that I have read your rubbish!'[17] In between his extended journeys to Rome and Paris, or after prolonged hunting trips, whenever he had seen Hitler and been showered with reproof, Göring pulled himself together and summoned his top officials. Having given them a complete dressing-down, accused them of

SPEER

mistakes and of ruining his reputation, and even threatened them with 'instant courts martial', he invited them all to a sumptuous meal in one of his favourite restaurants.

Towards the end of 1943 the Allies had almost total superiority in the air and their hold was steadily being increased by sophisticated electronic detection systems. The only logical response should have been to strengthen the fighter programme at all costs, especially as the Me-262 jet fighter, developed at the Messerschmitt works in Augsburg, was almost ready to go into serial production, thus providing the German airforce with an aircraft of superior speed and climbing ability. But Hitler applied his veto, even though he had until then been receptive on armaments matters. But under increasing pressure he, like Göring, became more and more set on the idea of devastating retaliatory strikes against hated England. 'Terror is only broken by terror,' was his constant refrain.

Having first ordered all work on the Me-262 to be suspended, he then overrode the opposition of the experts and ruled that the aircraft should be reconstructed as a super-fast bomber, regardless of the delays involved. For weeks Speer, Jodl, Milch, Guderian and others implored him to revoke what was patently a wrong decision, which undid all the advantages of the new weapon. But Hitler was not to be moved. 'A town a week is being smashed and we must act quickly,' ran the desperate arguments from many sides who believed that even as an interceptor the Me-262 could achieve the great turning point in the air war.[18]

Hitler remained deaf to such appeals. He was guided by the kind of psychology of embitterment which at Stalingrad had made him refuse the establishment of a reserve position behind the eastern front. The more hopeless a situation, the more stubbornly the forces would resist, he argued, citing as an example the way the Greeks burnt their ships during the Persian wars. Eventually he put an end to all discussions about the Me-262 by simply forbidding any further mention of the subject. Instead he ordered the anti-aircraft artillery, which had anyway grown to 20,000 barrels, to be extended, even though they had long been proved ineffective: they were providing little more than a 'tranquilizing fireworks display' for the frightened but defiant population. There is much to support Speer's view that, notwithstanding all the mistakes made by the enemy high command, the air war had been the 'greatest lost battle on the German side' of the whole war.[19]

The enormous rise in armaments statistics was all the more surprising. To the amazement of military staffs on all sides, a stream of new

168

In spite of intensified Allied air attacks, German armaments production was increasing until autumn 1944. The supreme directing authority was Central Planning, set up by Speer together with Field Marshal Erhard Milch, the Generalluftzeugmeister of the Luftwaffe. The photograph shows Milch and Speer at a meeting of General Planning in 1943. Left, next to Milch, is state counsellor Walther Schieber, head of the Armaments Delivery Department in Speer's ministry.

successes were reported from the rubble of the towns and industrial enterprises. In the ammunition sector, for instance, the previous year's figures more than doubled again in 1943; aircraft production increased from about 14,000 to over 25,000 planes; in submarine construction the relatively low growth rates of about fifteen per cent were made up for by shortening production time from nearly one year to two months. As for armoured vehicles, production rose from 140,000 to just short of 370,000; the figures for medium and heavy tanks alone rose from 5,500 to approximately 12,000 in 1943. This increase was particularly astonishing as Hitler, who had revealed a special regard for that weapon early on, possibly in remembrance of his triumphant French campaign, had by a never-ending series of interventions totally disrupted all production schedules even at the development stage. Significantly, he also progressively saddled the tanks, which had been designed to be light and mobile, with so much firepower that he ended up with vehicles the size of the existing Tiger or, in the case of the so-called Mouse, a monster weighing 188 tonnes.[20]

Even though they have to be taken with some reservations,[21] these impressive figures, which increased yet again in the following year and reached their peak in the second half of 1944, revealed not only the failure of the Allied air war concept, but also the absurdity of Speer's armaments efforts. In the final phase of the war his organization was producing equipment and instruments for some 270 army divisions, whilst the Wehrmacht had just over 150 divisions in action. Moreover, the traffic situation was causing insuperable difficulties. The collapsing fronts led to a confusion of troop redispositions and supply transports which the proudly proclaimed system of 'organized improvization' could no longer cope with. While some replacement units in the home country were supplied with weapons and equipment of the latest manufacture, the front was frequently short of the most important items and, as time went on, of absolutely everything.

Speer's reputation initially remained unaffected by such paradoxes, which indeed were due more to the disorganized state of political power and Hitler's lack of an overall war concept. On the contrary, many saw Speer as the man whose clear vision and cool, rational mind might yet halt the course of events. In the late summer of 1943 Hitler's adjutant in the Wehrmacht high command, General Schmundt, approached Speer. He spoke about Göring's increasingly obvious incompetence and called his interlocutor 'the great hope of the army'. A similar remark was made to him by the chief of the general staff, Kurt Zeitzler, who passed on to him a remark by Hitler that he was the newly rising 'sun'. Around that time, when Speer entered the situation room at the Führer's headquarters together with Himmler, Hitler came up to them and welcomed them: 'You two peers'.[22]

Predictably Himmler showed his displeasure at this remark, and it may be that Hitler had intended just that, using this well-tried psychological trick to sow discord among his leading ministers. As the head of police, supreme controller of prisons and camps, and as a general with troops of his own, the Reichsführer SS had long regarded himself as a power without rival or equal. Pedantic as he was in questions of protocol, he had therefore never called on Speer in the past but invariably summoned him to his office.[23] But Hitler's remark surely went beyond the purely tactical intention of letting Himmler feel the limits of his power. The burden of the war and the growing uncertainty about its outcome had visibly marked Hitler, and it is significant that from 1942 onwards there were increasingly frequent remarks about how much he was longing for the end of the countless ills and for his retirement from politics.[24]

Such moods inevitably raised the question of a suitable successor. Göring, whom Hitler had named as his deputy in a speech at the beginning of the war, had deprived himself of power, Bormann was without doubt too servile, and Goebbels was ruled out because of being crippled, leaving in effect only Himmler. But Himmler was narrow and schoolmasterly, as well as completely unartistic, and there is much to suggest that Hitler also measured his successor against the ideal of the 'artist politician' he liked to consider himself as. At any rate he is said to have assured Speer that he 'was planning great things for him' and had 'placed him after Göring on the list of successors to the Führer'.[25]

Speer was both alarmed at this unexpected prospect and dazzled. He felt he had been promoted to higher things. Indeed he now saw the great, all-transcending goal beckoning his unfulfilled ambition. Despite his initial reserve, he fed the rumours that were circulating, taking close colleagues into his confidence. Speer discussed at length with some of them whether he was regarded as 'Führer capable'; and when Hans Kehrl, the chief of his ministry, confirmed that he was evidently Hitler's first and preferred choice, 'he nodded with satisfaction'.[26]

Everyone doubted Speer's assertion that he had remained an unpolitical artist or technocrat. But the awkwardness with which he set about becoming the 'second man in the state' could not have made his point more convincingly.[27] He had not the slightest notion of the real power games he would now have to play. Otherwise he should have been aware that Hitler's open display of favour and all the talk, which he encouraged, was bound to arouse Himmler's anger and revive Bormann's enmity.

Bormann had only been promoted to 'Secretary of the Führer' in April 1943 and, in view of this increase in his own power, he regarded it as a unequivocal defeat that the debate about the succession was pointing towards one of his sworn enemies. His perpetual machinations against Speer had ended in conspicuous failure, and he was not prepared to take this lying down. His instinct for danger, developed in countless petty power squabbles, made him instantly sense the threat which emanated from a man who had the aura of the Führer's successor, and who moreover, stood outside the Party hierarchy and was therefore not subject to his authority. His first defensive move was to put it about that Speer was not only 'a fundamental opponent of the Party', but that he was also aiming at Hitler's succession with all the ruthless ambition for which he was known.

No matter how inaccurate such suggestions may have been, they nevertheless produced considerable irritation. Even Speer's old friend Karl Hanke was upset and tried several times to get through to Hitler to inform him about Speer's insidious aspirations.[28] Goebbels, for his part, unexpectedly switched his alliance to Bormann, despite a prolonged hostility hardened by many tough conflicts. Critical remarks about Speer appear again in his diaries around this time, and one day he drew the armaments minister's attention to the fact that 'he was not at this moment in great favour at the front'.[29]

Himmler, Bormann, Göring and Goebbels represented the most powerful coalition of opponents that Speer could possibly have. All he had to confront them were a few generals dependent on Hitler's whim, from Zeitzler to Guderian and Friedrich Fromm, the Director of Recruitment, and a few heads of department such as Milch and Kehrl. And, of course, he had Hitler's hints. But no one could be sure whether the allusion to Speer being the chosen one was just a casual remark, nor how the succession would work once the real weights were thrown onto the scales.

Speer failed to see this. He was unaware of how hopeless his situation was. Having no power base, he had lost the battle before it even started. It took just the briefest of moments, and the combined forces of his adversaries saw to it that the first cracks began to appear in his much celebrated image, not without a little help from Speer himself.

However, as long as Speer produced one stunning armaments success after another he remained hard to attack. The first to oppose his high-flown figures were the Gauleiters. They argued that the war could clearly also be waged 'without big sacrifices'.[30] And if such appeasing views were sharply rejected by the fighting front, the Party officials like almost everyone at the top began to question reality more and more openly. When in the autumn of 1943 the War Economy Office submitted a memorandum about the Soviet Union's exceptionally large reserves, Hitler was outraged for weeks on end. Eventually he simply forbade the Wehrmacht High Command to prepare such analyses. Much the same happened some time later to a study of Allied armaments capacities produced by Speer's planning office; and soon afterwards Hitler altogether prohibited information on the enemy's war

A bitter struggle for power and influence was waged in Hitler's entourage right to the end, with Martin Bormann, the 'Secretary of the Führer', pulling the strings. To counteract his influence, Goebbels, Ley and Speer formed a kind of alliance. After the beginning of 1943 they tried to get the still hesitant Hitler to agree to the total mobilization of all forces for the war effort. The photograph shows Speer, Ley and Goebbels at a demonstration for armaments workers in 1943.

industry to be passed through official channels. Göring went further still. He issued a special 'official order' forbidding Adolf Galland, the much-decorated Inspector-General of the Jagdgeschwader (Fighter Wing), from disclosing that American escort fighters protecting the attacking bomber formations had been sighted over Reich territory.[31]

The most conspicuous symbol of this denial of reality were the windows of the Führer's headquarters: they were always closed and had their curtains permanently drawn, even on fine days. After the heavy air-raids on the Ruhr and those seven days at the end of July when bombing waves, shrouded in dense clouds of aluminium foil, devastated Hamburg in a series of attacks culminating in a huge firestorm, Speer tried in vain to persuade Hitler to visit the ruined cities. Goebbels, too, applied all his eloquence to the same end. But Hitler turned down this suggestion time and again, as if he suspected how brittle the belief in victory was, which required so much effort to invoke. Instead he used his consultations to indulge in tirades about impending successes.

Speer's arrogant behaviour was reflected, among other things, in the way that he took out his papers and started working on them or even drawing during this idle talk. To his amazement Hitler endured the affront in silence. But the Führer may have concluded from this and other indications that his ministerial friend no longer had that unwavering and boundless optimism with which he deceived himself, and with which everybody in his entourage deceived everyone else. Indeed, after the destruction of Hamburg Speer remarked: 'If the air raids continue on the present scale ... we shall be going downhill smoothly and relatively swiftly.' And to Hitler he said that, if the same catastrophe were to befall another six cities, the war would be over.[32]

The steady rise in production figures which persisted until the autumn of 1944 seemed 'like a miracle' even to one of the cool heads in Speer's ministry.[33] But there was no disguising that the armaments race against Germany's opponents could not be won in the long run. After all, the ratio was two to nine in the area of ammunition alone. There were still those at the Führer's headquarters who talked themselves into believing that there was a chance of that 'intermediate success' which Hitler had made a condition for a political solution to the war. He could not negotiate from a position of weakness, was the argument he repeatedly used to silence the warning voices around him. The tiny margin of hope was based on the belief in the Reich's superior weapons technology. It was contended again and again that Germany would always be one step ahead of the enemy, thanks to its engineers. New developments, not least the legendary 'miracle weapons', would help achieve the saving pause for negotiations.

These included not only the V weapons, news of which was first rumoured and then announced with ever greater clamour, but also the Me-163-B rocket-propelled aircraft, the Me-262 and the remote-controlled Hs-293 bomb; in addition two 'hydrodynamic' submarine types, the Waterfall surface-to-air rocket, the Orkan aircraft rocket, and a number of other constructions such as the mysterious V3 and V4. But all these systems suffered from some defects which had still to be eliminated. Many came too late or went into operation without adequate testing. This applied even to the Me-262, which still lacked acceleration, mobility and sufficient armament. Some of the new weapons provided all too easy targets for the air war, such as the Walther submarines, one-third of which were destroyed in their pens. As for the rockets, the problems both with the thermodynamic remote control and with the ignition mechanisms had not been satisfactorily solved. Often the expenditure of scarce material and manpower was not justified in relation to the military value of the weapons, as was the case with the thirteen-tonne A4 rocket, later known as the V2, already developed by the young Wernher von Braun in the mid-1930s. Other matters fell victim to the constant interdepartmental squabbles, and many things were simply the subject of legends which Speer himself helped create, as he later admitted. In his memoirs he dated his realization that the war could no longer be won, if only on grounds of production technology, to the end of 1942. But then he stated that promotion of the V2 at the expense of the Waterfall rocket and the jet fighters had been one of his 'most serious mistakes in leading German armaments'. He even went so far as to claim that had they been employed in a co-ordinated way, both weapons would have 'caused the air offensive of the Western Allies against our industry to collapse'.[34]

The contradiction is all the more striking as Speer never pinned great hopes on these miracle weapons. Although he was impressed by the demonstrations on the Peenemünde testing grounds, he made no secret of his reservations. After a first warning in September 1943 he declared that the country 'had no miracle weapon and probably never would have one'. There was 'technical progress', he observed, 'but there are no miracles'. In contrast, Hitler had placed his hopes for the decisive turning point in the destructive power of the new weapon: 'This will be the retribution against England,' he repeatedly exclaimed after the research team of Walter Dornberger and Wernher von Braun had visited the Führer's headquarters. 'With this, we will force England to her knees.'[35] Speer, however, was unmoved by this euphoria. Nevertheless, by assigning a high priority to the rocket programme he yielded not only to Hitler's hopes of victory but also to his power of persuasion; even if this was not, as he later maintained, 'the last time' he succumbed, his doubts about the effectiveness of the weapon, publicly stated in speeches to the heads of propaganda departments or the armaments commission, show that Hitler's power over him was waning.[36]

However, the energy with which Speer promoted rocket armaments set him back in the increasingly open internal power struggle. For he provided Himmler with the opportunity for penetrating the war economy that he had long sought. When the Royal Air Force destroyed the army research establishment at Peenemünde on 18 August 1943, the night following the American attack on Schweinfurt, Himmler was immediately on the spot and, as had occurred several times before, offered to provide concentration camp inmates to rebuild the plant and continue rocket production. This, he reported to Hitler, would not only be the most practical way of overcoming the shortage of manpower for large-scale production but it would also solve the problem of 'strict secrecy', since the prisoners were cut off from all contact with the outside world.

Speer had every reason to fear Himmler's influence on his sphere of responsibilities, especially when the discussion about the succession was just beginning. But some time earlier Himmler had made greater concessions to him than he would have liked by agreeing that 'concentration camp inmates be made available for armaments enterprises'. In view of the priority he had himself given to the rocket programme and following the consent Himmler had now obtained from Hitler, Speer had no choice but to accept the offer. It was the first time since his appointment as a minister that he was losing an area of responsibility. Contrary to Hitler's instruction that all measures were to be taken jointly, Himmler informed Speer on the very next day in a domineering tone that he would 'take charge' of the production of the A4 from now on, and that he would 'carry out the promise to supply 5,000 A4s in the shortest time to the letter'.[37]

The determination with which Himmler grabbed rocket production for himself had a twofold motivation. For one thing the 'miracle weapons', possibly because of the word miracle itself, held a magical fascination for him, given as he was to wild fancy and pseudo-scientific humbug. For years he had been approaching research institutes with requests to examine the technical feasibility of bizarre ideas, beginning with the 'non-combustible' material 'durofol', which he proposed for motor-vehicle construction, to a fuel he hoped to derive from fir-tree roots, and alcohol to be obtained from bakery fumes, all the way to the 'Gerloff miracle pistol' or the *Zischboot* (Hiss boat) developed by Fritz Wankel, which was supposed to reach fabulous speeds in attacking naval formations. What the planning office of the Reich Research Council had said about Himmler's proposal to turn the atmosphere into a conductive element through ionization, applied to these and many other illusions: they showed 'a lack of any deeper understanding of the technical and physical processes in question'.[38] The proposals that he pursued with desperate zeal until the spring of 1945 were pipe-dreams, and often quite simply insane.

But his endeavour to build up that 'chimerical SS economic empire', which he had long regarded as the foundation of the shadow state that he proposed to establish with the SS, was at least as important to him. His virtually unlimited authority as chief of police had just been rounded off, in August 1943, by his appointment as Reich Minister of the Interior. Besides these positions Himmler regarded the economy and production as the most promising doorways to power, particularly as he could thus harass Speer – who had stepped, however awkwardly, into the arena as an unexpected rival – and demolish his standing.

Thus motivated he therefore systematically undermined the already weakened ministry of economic affairs and increasingly the whole Speer organization by attempting to infiltrate his own followers into key positions or by making senior officials compliant by awarding them honorary SS ranks. The same purpose was served by the SS's own manufacturing facilities, which he set up inside the concentration camps. At Buchenwald and Neugamme near Hamburg he had infantry weapons made, at Ravensbrück high-frequency equipment, at Brandenburg motor vehicles and elsewhere trench mortars. Despite the generally amateurish administration and low productivity of these SS enterprises, the SS Economic Management Central Office under SS Obergruppenführer Oswald Pohl controlled over forty enterprises with some 150 different firms by the end of the war. In addition to armaments they manufactured furniture, textiles, tinned food, mineral water, pharmaceuticals and other things. Every one of these enterprises withdrew responsibilities as well as manpower from Speer's official sphere. At the same time Himmler started a covert war of attrition against his rival by setting the Sicherheitsdienst (SD), his security service, against certain highly placed collaborators of Speer's, such as Wernher von Braun, and having them arrested on trumped-up charges. Even Speer's telephone was monitored and there was talk of an SD report to the effect that mistakes made by Speer's organization had 'so far caused unbelievable damage to the growth of German armaments production'.[39]

Since the spring of 1943 the widening of the air war, which filled Göring with 'towering rage',[40] and the ever present threat of the Allied strategy of paralysation, had led to the suggestion that vital war industries be

The increasing Allied superiority in the air forced the German leadership to move some armaments production to underground locations, into mountain caves and bunker systems. An extensive production facility was established at Nordhausen in the Harz mountains, the so-called Mittelwerk, where V-weapons were manufactured. At the end of the war 40,000 prisoners were working at the related SS-operated concentration camp.

moved into mountain caves or specially constructed bunkers protected by concrete ceilings several metres thick, especially for the production of the V weapons. This intention was entirely in line with Himmler's nightmare fantasy, because it not only met his 'security' complex but also banished the foreign workers to a lemur-like underworld. They would be 'new cavemen', as he wrote to Pohl.[41] It also satisfied his need for unblemished environments by making neither the armies of slaves nor the industrial complexes visible. Even for the 'paradise gardens' in the east he had refused to permit any evidence of the ugliness of the technological world and had given orders for electric cables, generators and telephone wires to be buried.

With such considerations in mind Himmler instructed the 'Cave Identification Department in the Military Scientific Institute for Karst and Cave Research of the SS' to prepare a record of caves immediately after the destruction of Peenemünde. But even before the results were available one of his 'evil angels', the 'cold ruthless schemer'[42] SS Gruppenführer Hans Kammler, a single-minded careerist who was head of the SS construction administration, had discovered a cave system in a remote valley near Nordhausen in the Harz mountains, which had been used in the 1930s for the storage of war-vital chemicals. Besides the workshops hewn into the mountain, the labyrinthine tunnels included a makeshift camp, consisting of kilometres of ramified tunnels with narrow sleeping niches cut into the walls. Because Kammler constantly urged haste, the prisoners, most of whom were brought in from the nearby Buchenwald camp, were already installing machinery while, with an ear-splitting roar, a hail of stones and stifling dust, vast catacombs were still being blasted in the far part of the massif for the construction of V2s.

While this work was still in progress Speer received from the head physician of his ministry a report on conditions at Dora or Mittelwerk, as the plant was soon called. He had seen 'Dante's Inferno', the doctor wrote.[43] A few days later, Speer himself set off to inspect the plant together with Kammler and his office chief Karl Otto Saur. As he arrived preparations were underway for the execution of one of the prisoners, as was evidently the custom in order to intimidate and discipline the rest. Speer succeeded in preventing the executions.[44]

His grim expectations were confirmed in every other respect. Hygienic provisions were indescribable, there was no medical attention, and mortality among the prisoners, wasting away in permanent darkness lit only by a few dim bulbs, reached a disastrous rate of seven

per cent a month. 'The prisoners were under-nourished,' Speer recorded, 'the air in the cave was cool, damp and stale and it stank of excre-
ment. The lack of oxygen made me dizzy too.' Some of his companions
were so shaken after the inspection that, as Wolters's Chronicle
recorded, 'they had to be sent on forced leave'.[45]

The shock of what he had seen remained with Speer for some time.
It was the unsuspected collision with reality which he had deliberately
hidden from himself in the hectic rush of his office, behind piles of
papers, conferences, journeys and production directives. At the beginning of the year he had first seen one of the notorious concentration
camps when he visited Mauthausen near Linz. But this had been a
guided 'VIP tour' with neat rooms, flowers and contented inmates, so
that he had returned home 'reassured'. The Mittelwerk, on the other
hand, represented the hidden side of the regime. Speer later referred to
the 'sombre notions of certain monstrosities' which he had previously
formed from hints and casual remarks. But how could these have
become certainties unless he had seen Kammler's dungeons with his
own eyes?

The horrible images pursued him for some time. No sooner had he
returned to Berlin than he gave instructions for the construction of a
hutment town for the 10,000 prisoners outside the mountain. He angrily
rejected the protests of Kammler and subsequently of Ley, who pointed
to his responsibility as head of the 'Labour Front': he saw no reason, he
wrote, to deal with their objections since the armaments industry had
the greatest interest in looking after the camp workers satisfactorily. The
protracted to and fro of official correspondence paradoxically meant
that Speer's complaints further delayed the improvements of conditions,
which were minimal anyway. In June 1944 the newly established hutments went into use; a little later the connection between the Mittelwerk
and Buchenwald was discontinued, and the Mittelwerk was run as an
independent concentration camp. At the end of the war it numbered
just under 40,000 prisoners.[46]

Despite his concern about Himmler's increasingly threatening machinations, Speer, with a mixture of innocence and ambition, placed considerable hopes in him, and at times it seems as if he was not properly
aware of the power struggle which the leader of the SS was waging
against him. He received more and more warnings that there was open
talk within the SS of establishing an industry of its own with the aim of
progressively eliminating the Minister of Armaments.[46] But instead of

fighting back he let Himmler carry on and even considered him a comrade-in-arms in pushing for total war, which had become something of a fixed idea. As Reich Minister of the Interior, Himmler was now also responsible for the Gauleiters in their capacity as Reich Defence Commissioners. With his help it would therefore be possible not only to mobilize the civilian population, but also tame the regional Party leaders. At any rate, Himmler had assured Speer that he would enforce the powers of the Reich against anyone; moreover, unlike Speer, Himmler also had in the SS an executive tool with which to frighten the provincial potentates. For a while therefore Speer saw Himmler as a powerful ally whose support, after so many lost battles against Bormann and the Gauleiters, would yet help him to succeed.

However much one tries to put oneself into Speer's position, his concessions to Himmler remain difficult to understand, regardless of any tactical aims he may have pursued. He was aware of Himmler's reputation and he had long had his reasons to steer clear of him. Besides, more recently he was not only the designated rival of this man who was fighting him with such cold determination, but he had just returned with horrific impressions from the Mittelwerk camp, which came under Himmler's authority.

At times it seems as though, even in retrospect, Speer was hardly aware of the compartmentalization of his own thinking. It enabled him to come to terms with the sharpest contradictions, and it explains most of the riddles of his life. Speer's dichotomy not only affected fundamental decisions. It also emerged, far less conspicuously, in his everyday behaviour and at times greatly confused even those members of his staff who knew him well. Even at the confidential conferences of Central Planning or of the armaments commissions he would, according to one of the participants, be more optimistic than the propaganda required, denying emergencies or brushing them off with 'cheerfully ironic' platitudes.[48] But in the autumn of 1943 in a conversation with Walter Rohland, the industrialist responsible for armoured vehicle production, he reverted once more 'with greatest frankness' to the pessimistic truth which he had long accepted and painted the approaching end of the war in gloomy colours.

The purpose of the conversation was to prepare for a conference called by Bormann for 6 October 1943 in Posen with all the Reichleiters and Gauleiters, as well as Alfred Rosenberg and Speer himself, who, like some of his top officials, was to give a report on the state of armaments. 'The first to speak were a number of Speer's staff,' Goebbels

At Nuremberg and later, Speer always denied having known about the regime's extermination practices. Yet he clearly knew enough to want to know as little as possible. The picture shows him at the beginning of 1943 at Mauthausen, on his only visit to a concentration camp. On Speer's left is August Eigruber, leader of the Gau Oberdonau.

noted in his diary, Walther Rohland among them. It sounded like an echo of the preparatory talks when Goebbels added: 'They paint a little too black on black.'[49] Next Speer stepped up to the lectern.

In his address he outlined the crisis in which the country found itself, without glossing over anything. He emphasized that because of the air-raids the monthly production increases in munitions now only amounted to 3–4 per cent instead of the planned 15–20 per cent, and he used sharp words to attack the officers' armaments ambitions. He then shattered whatever hopes those present may have had of the imminent employ-ment of the 'miracle weapons' and thanked Ley that 'during these very days a few thousand loafers' had been 'arrested straight from the facto-ries and sent to the concentration camps'. He referred to a Führer Order stating that he would have to provide a million workers for armaments production within a short period; as things stood, however, that man-power could only be found in the civilian sphere, where countless useless products were still being made, such as the two million brooms manufac-tured for the Luftwaffe every year, the hundreds of thousands of service bags for the signals-communication women auxiliaries, the addressing machines, heating pads, as well as 300,000 electric meters or the refrigerators which, as he observed, only served as bribes. As for consumer goods, 'I hear one lie after another,' he continued; 'everything I am told is a lie.' He would therefore have the controls carried out by his own people in future, and they were sure to behave like 'real hellhounds'.

These remarks were directed at his favourite adversaries, the Gauleiters assembled before him, who were particularly interested in the regional production of consumer goods. But, once in full flight, he attacked them and warned them even more directly: 'We cannot have one Gau pursuing a tough line while another is doing the opposite. Unless therefore the Gaue follow my call within a fortnight I shall myself decree the closing-down [of civilian industries], and I can assure you that I am prepared to enforce the authority of the Reich whatever the cost! I have spoken with the Reich Führer SS Himmler and I will from now on deal accordingly with the Gaue which fail to implement these measures.'[50]

No one had ever dared to utter such a threat before and the excitement was indescribable. The Gauleiters had not forgotten earlier pronouncements by Speer, including his inaugural speech of 24 February of the previous year, nor had they forgotten the extortionate pressure which he had applied in the allocation of fuel, coal or building materials to get them to comply. But now they cried 'blue murder', as Goebbels recorded, himself reproving Speer for his 'harsh tone'. Led by Josef Bürckel, the former Gauleiter of Vienna who was then Governor of the 'Westmark' (Lorraine), they stormed up to Speer, 'shouting and gesticulating', accusing him of having threatened 'the Führer's guard' with the concentration camp. Amidst the clamour Speer turned to Bormann and asked for the floor again in order to correct that assertion. But with 'feigned friendliness' Bormann declined with the assurance that there were no misunderstandings. However, he made immediate use of the incident to reduce Speer's standing with Hitler, putting it about that the non-Party Minister of Armaments simply did not have the confidence of the Führer's old comrades-in-arms and did not know how to handle the Gauleiters. From then on, Speer recalled later, he 'could no longer count on Hitler's support as a matter of course'.[51]

The Posen conference was held only a few weeks after the debate about the succession had begun. Speer's dismissive tone was due not least to the sense of power of the elect. But he was to discover how little his candidacy counted against the solid front of the Gauleiters when he asked his friend Karl Hanke to have his Posen speech printed for distribution to the lower formations of the Party. With unusual sharpness Hanke rejected the 'shameless' request, adding that Speer should 'take care not to provoke the solid corps of the Gauleiters'.[52] Without being aware of it, Speer had passed the zenith of his career. The Posen conference marked the beginning of his descent.

In the afternoon Himmler addressed the meeting. Two days earlier he had spoken to senior SS leaders in the same Golden Hall of Posen Castle, apparently using the same cues as in his present speech. All the evidence suggests that he had decided to expose to a wider circle the extermination policy which until then had been kept secret or thickly veiled in euphemism. The two speeches differed only in the more vicious tone of brutality which he used to the SS leaders as the executors of the murder programme. Some time later he repeated his remarks to the senior officers' corps.

His motive was not difficult to understand. It had probably been agreed with Hitler and aimed at turning those present into accessories or even accomplices of the hard-pressed regime, which was being forced into retreat on all fronts. By admitting to the gigantic crime in which they would all be more or less involved, Himmler hoped to impel them to exert all their energies. He wanted each and every one to realize the hopelessness of his position now that the Allies had announced that they would put the entire leadership of the Reich on trial. There are many remarks by Hitler and Goebbels to prove this.[53]

In a memo Himmler made of his conversation with Hitler about the 'Jewish question' on 18 December 1941 there is a note: 'To be exterminated as partisans.'[54] That was one of the prescriptions for the mass murder. Other codenames, maintained even in secret correspondence, spoke of 'evacuation' or 'labour employment'. In his Posen speech Himmler dispensed with these and other fictions for the first time, at least to a wider circle of the leadership.

After some introductory words about the partisan war, the Slav 'auxiliary nations' and the struggle against sabotage, he said: 'The sentence with its few words "The Jews must be exterminated", is easily spoken, gentlemen. For he who has to implement its demands it is the hardest and most difficult task there is.' It is, moreover, obstructed by the 'millions of people who have their own famous decent Jew' and 'this number is already greater than the number of Jews' actually living in the country. Then he continued:

The question arose for us: What about the women and children? I have decided to find an entirely clear solution here too. The fact is I did not feel entitled to exterminate the men – that is, to kill them or have them killed – and to allow the avengers in the shape of their children to grow up for our sons and grandsons. The difficult decision had to be taken to make this people vanish from the earth ... It was carried out, without – as I believe I am able to say – our men and our leaders suffering injury to spirit or soul.

Himmler next spoke about the danger of 'becoming crude, heartless and no longer to respect human life', to which every single man in his cohorts was exposed, of the 'nervous breakdowns' which had occurred, as well as cases of corruption: 'In the past few days I have therefore ... signed about a dozen death sentences,' he claimed, finally announcing: 'The Jewish question in the countries occupied by us will be settled by the end of this year. Only residual numbers of individual Jews will be left in hiding.' He ended this part of his speech with the words: 'With this I should like to conclude the Jewish question. You now know the facts and you will keep them to yourselves. Perhaps at some much later date one will be able to consider whether the German people should be told more about it. I believe it is better that we – all of us – have borne this for our nation, we have taken the responsibility on ourselves ... and we will take our secret with us to our graves.'[55]

While Himmler was speaking 'the silence in the room was leaden', according to one of his audience. 'He spoke in the same icy way about the extermination of men, women and children as a businessman would about his balance sheet. There was nothing emotional in his speech, nothing that pointed to inner involvement ... Bormann rose and closed the meeting with the words: "Party comrades, may I now invite you to the room next-door for a meal."'[56]

Himmler's speech is crucial to Speer's life because he always vehemently denied having known about the extermination of the Jews. Yet at the Posen conference Himmler had spoke of it with terrifying frankness. Although Speer mentions the meeting and more especially his own attack on the Gauleiters in *Inside the Third Reich*, he says nothing about Himmler's speech and its key message. This is all the more striking as the short-sighted Himmler at one point specifically turned to Speer. In the Warsaw ghetto, he said, 'fur coats, clothes and similar things' had been manufactured for years, but whenever he had wanted to 'reach out there' he had been told that such interventions would upset the war

One of the most horrendous documents of the time was Himmler's speech in Posen on
6 October 1943 about the extermination of the Jews. Whether or not Speer was
actually present during that speech has never been resolved. The photograph shows
Himmler with his daughter Gudrun and the SS general Karl Wolff.

economy. Then came the sentences: 'Of course this has nothing to do
with Party comrade Speer. You', he addressed Speer directly, 'are not
responsible.'

The American historian Erich Goldhagen pointed out this discrepancy in 1971, using it as the basis for a fundamental attack on Speer's
credibility. Although in his memoirs Speer had not denied having taken
part in the conference, Goldhagen observed, he said 'nothing, absolutely nothing, about Himmler's speech, or even about Himmler's presence.
He secretly washed his hands of the blood of those to whose death he
contributed and, with seemingly clean hands, his heart beats in repentance: "I am a murderer even although I never saw, heard or knew
anything about the death of my victims." It is, to put it mildly, a
contemptible performance.'[57]

Goldhagen's accusation affected Speer, as he repeatedly admitted, 'in
his innermost being' and raised profound doubts about his memory:
'Suddenly I was seized by the suspicion that I could no longer believe
myself.'[58] After extensive research he eventually established that on

6 October 1943 he left Posen around noon, shortly after his own report on the armaments situation, whereas Himmler did not begin to speak until around 5.30, by which time Speer had long been en route to the Führer's headquarters. Speer was also able to name several witnesses to confirm his assertion, including Erhard Milch, who had attended the afternoon event and like Dönitz had spoken before Himmler, as well as the organizer of the meeting, Harry Siegmund, and, most importantly, Walter Rohland, who declared under oath that he had accompanied Speer on his journey to Rastenburg. Rohland moreover gave the reason for Speer's immediate departure. As the Gauleiters had been summoned to Hitler's headquarters for the following day, Speer had been afraid that they or Bormann would give Hitler a misleading account of what had happened in Posen, especially Speer's sharp remarks, and weaken his demands. He wanted, Rohland wrote, to 'induce' Hitler 'to remain firm vis-à-vis the Gauleiters'.[59]

Goldhagen's accusation would certainly have been more convincing had he not used a few sentences in his article which he tried to make readers believe also came from the text of Himmler's speech. In fact they had been freely invented. They were intended to give his indictment of Speer a truly devastating finality and they read as follows: 'Speer is not of the wood of a philo-Semitic politician obstructing the Final Solution. He and I will jointly snatch the last Jew living on Polish territory from the hands of the Wehrmacht generals, send him to his death and thereby conclude the final chapter of Polish Jewry.' Goldhagen later claimed that the addition was simply meant to make clear what Himmler really thought and his agreement with Speer. But this does not explain his using the first person singular for Himmler's remark. Asked why he had passed off the passage as a quotation, Goldhagen came up with the somewhat unusual explanation that he had wanted to remove the quotation marks at the beginning and at the end of the alleged remark by Himmler, but had 'not got round to it'.[60]

On closer examination it is clear that with all the circumstantial evidence, invented quotations and affidavits, the controversy misses the core of the problem and that it assumed disproportionate importance only because Speer was so adamant about not having known anything. The extent of his guilt remains unaffected by it and his protestation of ignorance does not diminish his culpability for monstrosities to which he claims to have closed his eyes. Speer certainly conceded this. Both before the tribunal and in his writings he admitted his responsibility and, later, even his guilt. But he would not give up the distinction between the certain knowledge of a deliberate and systematic murder programme and a general fear based on conjecture and the darkest suspicions. Legally mere knowledge did not incriminate him. But morally it made a difference, and to that he clung with all his might.

This picture demands a certain amount of credulity: how can a person belong for years to the inner circle of the dictator and to a *camarilla* which he described as a 'bunch of murderers', albeit only late in the day, and yet present himself as an *anima candida*, a pure soul? No sensible person could have regarded the endless tirades about war, subjection and extermination as meaningless metaphors, the less so as Hitler's entire political career was one merciless demonstration of his readiness to take even mere phrases literally. In *Inside the Third Reich* Speer vividly described the goings-on at Hitler's table:

> Between the soup and the vegetable course he could say quite calmly and casually: 'I want to annihilate the Jews in Europe! This war is the decisive confrontation between National Socialism and world Jewry. One or the other will bite the dust, and it certainly won't be us …' And the entire circle, not only the lower ranks, but generals, diplomats, cabinet ministers and not least I myself, all of us would sit there looking grave and gloomy. But there was also, if I recall rightly, something akin to awkwardness in our behaviour, as if we had caught someone close to us making an embarrassing self-revelation. No one ever said a word … Perhaps I thought he did not mean it literally, indeed, that is what I thought. But how could I doubt that his ideological fanaticism would stop at the Jews of all things?[61]

The account came very close to a confession, but it avoided the actual confession to having heard of the mass executions and the factory-like annihilation of human beings. One might accept Speer's assurance that Hitler never spoke of the methods of 'racial cleansing', at least in the semi-private circle of his guests at the Berghof. But what about Himmler, Oswald Pohl or Hans Kammler whenever they were filled with base feelings of triumph, having just read the latest statistics on victims? Or Goebbels, who so prided himself on his barbaric dash and was fond of boasting of the number of Jews expelled? Or Sauckel, or the chief of *Einsatzgruppe D*, Otto Ohlendorf, whom Speer saw frequently during the month-long debate about 'self-responsibility of industry'? Even before his appointment as minister Speer had repeatedly been to the Ukraine as head of *Baustab Speer*, and was he claiming not to have seen or heard anything there too?

And, one is bound to go on asking, what about the generals who placed such high hopes in him? What about the Gauleiters whom he saw again on the morning after the Posen event, if not before, after they had drowned the horrors of Himmler's disclosures in one of their 'alcoholic excesses'?[62] On one occasion Karl Hanke had drawn his attention to a camp in the 'Gau Upper Silesia', which he did not name. Later Speer concluded that he must have meant Auschwitz. 'I did not investigate', he wrote and added, 'I did not want to know what was happening there ... for fear of discovering something that might make me turn from my course.'[63] But how is this ignorance compatible with Hitler's and Himmler's intention to use the mass murders as a psychological way of cutting off any means of escape by turning accessories into accomplices.

Similarly, one should not disregard the men around Speer. They included a number of sober people capable of drawing conclusions from a few grisly facts, and they were not all stricken with blindness. Not a word from them either? Speer's extended area of responsibilities included transport, and on his own recommendation Hitler had appointed young Dr Theodor Ganzenmüller a state secretary. Despite countless difficulties with military supply trains, he then directed the crowded wagons to the extermination camps, from where they regularly returned empty. Did he never say anything? Speer has rightly pointed out that under Hitler's rule knowledge was a risky business, adding that one of his occasional drivers had admitted after the war to having known something about 'what went on in the camps'; but it never occurred to him, a man of 'low rank', to report such hearsay to his 'powerful minister and confidant of the Führer'.[64] This sounds plausible enough for a lower member of the staff. But what may have applied to him and his like certainly did not apply to the senior ranks, to men like Bücher, Kehrl, Milch, Rohland and others. Were they too so intimidated by official secrecy that they did not permit themselves a single remark about the horrors in the East?

That was one argument in his defence. Speer also pleaded that the exhausting and numbing workload had screened him from anything that did not belong to his immediate area of responsibility. Running his super-ministry was undoubtedly an exacting business. He was responsible not only for the organization and supervision of the armaments industry throughout the domain of German rule, for supplying it with raw materials, energy and millions of workers, but also for providing transport between factories and between the home country and the fighting fronts right across the continent. In addition, as the war went on, Speer travelled more and more frequently to the cities that had been hit by Allied bombing in order to show himself to the people and to get production going again. His life was an endless series of dates, discussions, deadlines, directives, Führer conferences, plant visits and mountains of reports. For one of these days Speer listed seventeen important meetings, and anyone who has seen the dozens of memoranda he drafted for Hitler gets an idea of the extent of his tasks. Looking back, he spoke of a 'narcotic frenzy of work' which had taken hold of him and dominated him like a drug.[65]

This noticeable obsession with work which increased by the month may well have had the anaesthetizing effect that Speer sought. His need for it grew with his misgivings about the dark side of the regime which haunted his dreams; occasionally he admitted that the sixteen or eighteen hours which made up his working day had, among other things, been a ceaseless 'attempt at flight'.[66] But what was he fleeing from if he did not even suspect that boundless atrocities were taking place?

The persistence of this flight motif emerges also from the way in which he concerned himself with countless problems of detail over and above his official duties. Thus on a train journey to Rastenburg he unscrewed all the clothes hooks, water taps, watch holders and reading lamps in his compartment because he regarded them as a waste of non-ferrous metal vital to the war effort, at a domestic goods fair he protested against the multiplicity of models of pots, pans and cutlery; and he took the time to attend a fashion show, where he criticized the number of young men who were displaying the latest collections instead of serving at the front. Nothing was unimportant to him so long as it kept at bay the thoughts that were crowding in on him; in a sense he was suppressing one kind of unrest by another.

It was an abstract world in which he sought refuge, filled with file numbers, minutes and columns of figures behind which no real person and none of the individual destinies over which he had control were visible. 'Statistics don't bleed,' he once casually quoted.[67] In fact the frenzy with which he performed his duties served only an end in itself. Under pressure of work his veneration for Hitler had given way to a more businesslike official relationship where agendas were discussed, successes and reverses reported, and disputes settled. The ideological obsessions that sustained and drove many of those alongside him were as alien to him as ever. He had turned into one of the machines which he had produced: high-rev, insensitive and purely mechanical. It was a kind of autism that had taken hold of him. Incapable of seeing things in perspective, he no longer questioned the goals he was so feverishly working towards and stifled all moral doubts, if indeed any arose, in the ethos of pure functioning. To that extent, too, he represented a common type of those years. Speer repeatedly remarked on Hitler's predilection for curtained windows, interpreting it as a revealing sign of his fear of seeing things as they were and thinking them through to the end. Now he too was sitting behind them.

Even so, the question of how much he knew of the crimes of the regime has never been resolved. Speer himself called it the 'cardinal problem' of the years after his release from prison. Despite all his protestations it has remained the dark point in his biography and no one can tell whether his persistent denials have something to do with the truth or merely with the art of, or perhaps even the need for, repression. Generally speaking his assertions almost seem like litanies and have not met with credence, neither from his Nuremberg counsel nor from his publishers and the few friends left to him, nor from his critics. But regardless of a good many reservations and in contrast with the other highly placed followers of Hitler's, a note of understanding and even sympathy quite often comes through, as though there was an inkling of how much desperation lay behind his denials. Somewhere Speer had picked up Nietzsche's remark that one cannot look into an abyss for long without the abyss looking into one. 'That describes me and my situation,' he commented.

When he had finished writing his memoirs and the Spandau diaries, one of Speer's advisers once more raised the question. Was it not the case, he asked, that before the tribunal Speer had denied having known about the mass crimes in order to secure an extreme line of defence? Had he taken it up not only because it had then been quite simply a matter of life and death, but also in order to preserve, under the impact of the frightful revelations made in the course of the trial, that remnant of self-esteem without which no person can cope with his life? Years later, after his release, he had had to maintain that position unless his credibility were to be sacrificed for good. 'Was it like that?' the questioner urged, offering him one more bridge: 'Perhaps it was like that. It would be entirely understandable and would resolve the enigma of your evasive actions.' After a lengthy pause Speer, as if suddenly worn out, came up with a reply which, while no proof that he was abandoning his long-held line of retreat, nevertheless lifted a corner of the veil behind which the whole truth was hidden: 'Oh,' he said, 'you should not go on asking me such unanswerable questions.'[68]

He never went further than this in his admissions.

Chapter Seven

CRISES AND INTRIGUES

The defeat in Posen had immediate consequences. No sooner had the Gauleiters departed from the Führer's headquarters than Hitler's dealings with Speer changed perceptibly. He treated him 'coolly and irritably', criticized his sober sums for 'lacking the element of hope', and one day, without a word of explanation, he asked for the monthly armaments figures to be passed on to him not by Speer but by Karl Otto Saur, whose permanently inflated confidence was more in line with Hitler's wishes.[1] When, shortly afterwards, the army's Chief of the General Staff, Kurt Zeitzler, asked Speer for a memorandum on manganese stocks, he experienced the full extent of Hitler's wrath for the first time. In a state of great agitation he told him off and prohibited him from sending any memoranda whatever to the Chief of the General Staff. While Speer had arrived at a more favourable figure, he himself had described the manganese situation as extremely critical, Hitler went on. Speer had now made him look 'like a liar'. Outraged, he forbade him 'once and for all from addressing any memos to anybody but himself' and, beside himself with fury, screamed at him: 'Do you understand that? I forbid it!'[2]

Hitler had behaved as he normally did only towards certain stubborn generals, Speer later recorded. It was the first open clash between them and it abruptly removed Speer's certainty about his privileged position. Added to his human disappointment was the realization of the fragility of his power and the extent of his dependence on the mood swings of the dictator. At the first signs of disfavour a mere five days after the Posen conference Speer tried to revive the old intimacy by drawing Hitler into a lengthy conversation about their architectural projects. As if there had been no ill feelings, Hitler willingly followed him once more into the fantasy world of the past. They were soon back among their former daydreams, laying down principles for future building projects, and in the end Speer asked for and obtained a Führer-decree appointing him chief planner for the reconstruction of Germany's destroyed towns.

Although Speer had mainly engineered the conversation in order to placate Hitler, he also had a hidden agenda. He secretly hoped that his appointment as chief building planner would be a new weapon in his continuous struggle against the Gauleiters. In the meantime he had discovered that they had drawn Hitler over to their side not only because of Speer's alleged threat of sending them to concentration camps. Some of them had also fallen back on the old assertion, stemming from the socialist repertoire of the Party, that Speer was a man of big business and that his plans for stopping supposedly unnecessary manufactures had nothing to do with the requirements of the war but only with the wishes of powerful company directors. Speer's new powers, of which he notified the Gauleiters in an arrogant circular of 18 December, were bound to hit them even harder as most of them regarded the rebuilding of wrecked cities as their most important postwar task. Already some of those on the radical wing of the Party, such as Florian in Düsseldorf, Murr in Württemberg and Wagner in Baden, had begun to pull down town palaces, churches and other buildings, including the National Theatre in Mannheim, which they regarded as 'bulwarks of reaction', when Hitler's Decree, confirmed by Speer in repeated circulars, called a halt to these activities. The strength of their hatred of the past was revealed at the beginning of 1945, in Robert Ley's jubilation over the destruction of Dresden: '[We] almost draw a sigh of relief. It is over now,' he wrote. 'In focusing on our struggle and victory we are now no longer distracted by concerns for the monuments of German culture … Now we march towards the German victory without any superfluous ballast and without the heavy spiritual and material bourgeois baggage.'[3] After the war this Gauleiter attitude prevailed in the west as well as in the east – with an apparently different justification.

There was a third motive for Speer's discussion of architecture with Hitler. Faced by mounting difficulties, intrigues and increasingly open hostility, he felt a first, slight touch of resignation. The terrifying experience of his visit to the Dora camp, which happened in those weeks, and many a worse certainty, may all have made him think, if perhaps only occasionally, of retiring from politics. On his appointment as Todt's successor he had already obtained from Hitler the assurance that, his 'war service' completed, he would be allowed to return to architecture. While fighting Bormann and the Gauleiters, enduring Göring's presumption and Sauckel's bumptiousness he enviously watched Giesler turning up more and more frequently at the Führer's headquarters to submit his latest designs, especially for Linz, where Hitler, beset by thoughts of death, wished to be buried in a kind of crypt on top of the Party Forum tower, high above the City.[4] Much as the importance, influence, reputation and whatever else he had earned for himself may have flattered his ambition, he sometimes began to wonder if he had not taken a wrong turning. But, as he later admitted he hurriedly dismissed such ideas. His attachment to Hitler still outweighed everything and, besides, he did not wish to be accused of 'deserting'. However, in agreement with the finance minister and without informing Hitler, he quietly wound up the account for the world capital Germania, which had accumulated over three hundred million marks.[5]

Meanwhile he had also failed in his attempt to align Himmler, the Reichsführer SS and newly appointed Minister of the Interior, against the Gauleiters. Although Himmler had accepted Speer's complaints he had then, as if to expose him, asked Bormann, of all people, for an opinion. A few days later Speer received a letter from Hitler prohibiting him from taking such unfounded steps against the Gauleiters.[6] It was also a new experience for Speer that more and more frequently he had to defend his top officials against an angry Hitler, and soon also against attacks by various Party leaders. Towards the end of the year he found to his surprise that he had begun to avoid the Führer's headquarters and at times even Hitler himself.

On the night of 22 November 1943, during one of the heaviest air-raids on Berlin, a bomb hit the ministry in Pariser Platz. Speer had watched the never-ending waves of enemy formations over the city from the roof of a nearby flak tower. He saw his Reich Chancellery and most of the ministries in the government quarter being hit, as well as the Zeughaus, the old Prussian armoury, the Gedächtniskirche and parts of the old Reich Chancellery. Later, when he crossed Wilhelmsplatz the entire neighbourhood was as bright as daylight because of roaring flames. Early estimates indicated that well over 300,000 people had been made homeless. In Pariser Platz the British and the French embassies were burning. As Speer walked across to the badly damaged ministry accompanied by some of his staff, he found it difficult to retain his composure. In a brief ironical address he thanked the British for having taken a workload off him and facilitated his fight against bureaucracy by destroying mountains of papers. Secretly, however, he wondered whether the destruction might have a 'deeper significance' and whether the rubble was perhaps a symbolic reflection of the setbacks and unpleasantnesses of the past few weeks.[7]

Speer did not spent Christmas and the New Year with his family on the Obersalzberg, where he would inevitably have met Hitler. Instead, he once more sought the remoteness of nature, as though remembering his youthful escapes into the solitude of the mountains or the remote forest lakes of Mecklenburg, except that now he was not fleeing from the big city but from the affronts, court intrigues and power squabbles of Hitler's world. His decision to visit Lappland, the remotest northern corner of German territory, revealed his need for distance in the most literal sense. His wife as always submitted without complaining. With their six children she provided him with a domestic setting, which, given the rat-race of his life, he did not usually make much use of.

Speer deliberately chose unpolitical companions. He invited the violinist Siegfried Borries and a conjurer who later became a great attraction under the stage name 'Kalanag'. They traversed the waste of endless forests on skis and in the evenings they stood around great pyres of burning wood while Borries played some bravura piece by Paganini. They spent their nights in smoky tents, wrapped in sleeping bags of reindeer skin or in the open under the cold sky. They visited Rovaniemi near the Arctic Circle, the mines of Kolosjokki, where Germany's entire nickel production came from, the airport of Kirkenes and some remote outposts. At a few hurriedly organized 'comrades' evenings' they distributed the presents they had brought along. A haphazard band played Christmas carols, followed by *Glocken der Heimat, Gute Nacht, Mutter* and *Lili Marleen.* One morning, on waking, Speer felt a piercing pain in his left knee, as had occasionally happened ever since his youth.

In spite of increasing discomfort he concluded his trip and on the morning of 31 December flew out to Rastenburg, where a conference was to be held over the next few days on the armaments programmes of the new year. Again there was a dispute, principally with Sauckel, about the employment of women and the untapped reserves in the home country, and again Hitler remained aloof towards Speer and repeatedly sided brusquely with his opponents. When a swelling appeared on Speer's leg a few days later he consulted Hitler's attending physician Dr Brandt, who diagnosed numerous symptoms of physical and mental stress. He urgently advised a rest in hospital and suggested that he consult the orthopaedic specialist Professor Gebhardt about his knee.

Speer had met Gebhardt once or twice in the past and knew that he belonged to Himmler's circle of acquaintances. But he claimed that he only learned after the war at Nuremberg that Gebhardt was not only an intimate friend of Himmler's but also the highest SS medical officer, with the rank of an SS Obergruppenführer and lieutenant-general of

To escape the intrigues in Hitler's entourage, Speer spent Christmas 1943 with a well-known violinist and a conjurer in a distant corner of German territory – in Lappland. He visited remote outposts of the Wehrmacht and spent the evenings with his companions in the forests near the Arctic Circle.

the Waffen-SS. The clinic he ran at Hohenlychen, a few kilometres north of Berlin, thus came under the SS and, as emerged in the trial of the doctors, Gebhardt had performed various experiments on prisoners there. However, Speer's initial refusal to visit that hospital had nothing to do with these circumstances, even if one is prepared to believe his later assertion that he was 'reluctant to receive any medical attention from the SS'.[8] What worried him more was leaving his ministry without a head, particularly since his adversaries, headed by Bormann, had already used his brief absence at Christmas to stoke Hitler's irritation. Nevertheless, on 18 January he was admitted to Hohenlychen in a state of total exhaustion and collapse.

The assumption that Speer's breakdown was an 'escape into illness', or an evasion from the 'end of his lifelong illusion', is too obvious not to have been made.[9] But despite the depressing experiences of recent times, Speer was far from either. No sooner had he been admitted than his knee was put in plaster and he was given strict orders to rest in bed. Characteristically, Speer immediately asked Gebhardt to make three nearby rooms available. On the very next day he called his two secretaries in and had a separate telephone line installed; his ministerial office was thus, in a sense, transferred to Hohenlychen. He instructed his closest collaborators, Willy Liebel, the head of the central office, and his deputy Karl Maria Hettlage, to channel all official business through him personally as usual. Speer received visitors every day, had consultations which, to Gebhardt's annoyance, often dragged on well beyond midnight, and he did not even neglect his extensive correspondence. The four submissions to Hitler, dictated by him on 25 January 1944, testify to his determination not to give up the struggle for Hitler's favour.[10]

In line with his working practice, Speer had given his ministerial heads of department a great deal of independence over the past two years. 'Now I realize', he wrote to Hitler some time later, 'that this was undoubtedly a mistake.' As he was now in disfavour, some of his adversaries thought the time had come to exploit his weakness and perhaps even bring him down. Within a short time 'the whole pack was after him', Milch remarked: Bormann was anyway, then Robert Ley, who had for some time reckoned that he had a good chance of succeeding Speer and who, though overloaded with offices, let it be known that he could 'take that job on as well', and also Göring, who admittedly proceeded with more finesse. Shortly after Speer fell ill the Reichsmarschall gave his bruised rival a considerable sum of money from a disposal fund to enable him to purchase a property from the forestry office at Freienwalde, not far from Berlin, either to distract Speer's attention or perhaps to make him inclined to return to him some of his responsibilities."[11] Then there were one or two of Speer's officials who had been close to his predecessor, such as the chief of the Organisation Todt (OT), Xaver Dorsch, and his deputy Konrad Haasemann, who suddenly magnified a trivial promotion matter, bringing it to Bormann's attention. And finally there was the ghostly figure of Ilse Todt, making sinister allusions about the divisions in the ministry between the followers of her unforgotten husband and Speer's people.[12]

Needless to say, Goebbels, or at least the Berlin Gauleitung, also became involved and it was basically its *démarche* that uncovered an intrigue initiated by Dorsch some time before. Possibly by arrangement with Bormann, the Gauleitung attempted on 26 January to take the political profiles of every employee of the armaments authority away from Speer's ministry, where they were kept under lock and key, and bring them to Dorsch at the OT head office. Alerted by his head of personnel, Speer had the papers secured at the last moment. By telephoning Goebbels' state secretary Werner Naumann he succeeded, first of all, in having the action postponed and, secondly, in agreeing with him that the steel door of the filing cabinet be sealed by Party officials. Having learned something of the tricks and manoeuvres of his opponents, he instructed his trustworthy departmental head to open the cabinet from the rear and to bring all the compromising papers to Hohenlychen. There he discovered that a number of his long-standing collaborators were being accused of an 'anti-Party attitude' and that Gestapo surveillance was being demanded for some of them. The documents also showed that Dorsch had long been one of Bormann's informers and had repeatedly fed him with information to discredit his own minister.[13] It was a case of the 'murkiest backstairs policy', as Speer later wrote to Bormann,[14] and as in all shoddy plays his efforts to shed light on the matter initially came to nothing. Goebbels pretended to have 'no idea' and called it an 'impossible situation' if any Party agency tried to set up a kind of ideological 'shadow government'; Naumann let the investigation into the initiators drag on.

The string of furious letters which Speer sent from his sickbed show not only his growing nervousness but also reveal how, unable to free himself from his blinkered ideas, he was still far removed from reality. In a letter contradicting all his experiences of the Gauleiters, he spoke of the 'dignity' of the Party which was damaged by such incidents; he demanded that Bormann's state secretary should rein in their informers, and protested to Funk and Sauckel about their attempts to profit from his absence. The person he embarrassed most was Dorsch, particularly as he had also discovered that the head of the OT, albeit pressed by Bormann, had spoken of the 'worries' which Speer's ministry was causing him and the Organisation Todt in a conversation with Hitler. Having high-handedly kept Haasemann 'in custody' through his transport brigade and posted him to the road construction directorate for Saxony, Speer now threatened to send all 'rumour mongers' to a concentration camp. He angrily informed Dorsch that he did not consider him indispensable in the OT head office.[15]

Speer even showed his irritation towards Hitler. The doubts about their friendship further strengthened Speer's resolve to go the whole hog. In a fifth memorandum to the Führer, dated 29 January, he informed Hitler about the 'camarilla' of Todt people in his ministry, as well as about Dorsch's 'breach of trust'; he would, he wrote, insist on an official inquiry, leading to the most severe punishment. He not only demanded Dorsch's instant dismissal but also proposed two suitable successors. He was aware that he was breaking the rule under which, formally at least, Hitler alone could dismiss or appoint top officials. Of course he realized that his chances of success were exceedingly slight, since Dorsch belonged to the Party's 'old guard' and, as a participant in the legendary march of November 1923 to the Feldherrnhalle, enjoyed Hitler's particular respect. But he wanted to force a decision at long last. In retrospect he called his action 'either foolish or provocative'.[16]

Of course all this was not just about his position, his competence or his influence, but about a sense of rejected affection. Unlike Speer, however, Hitler was too skilful a tactician even in his emotional relationships to allow himself to be pushed into an impasse. While Speer was waiting at Hohenlychen, his disquiet growing by the day, Hitler persistently delayed his response, sent placating messages to his sickbed and eventually forgot to reply altogether. If the matter were ever raised, he could explain his deliberate affront by saying that Speer's memorandum was to serve as a basis for a personal conversation when the minister visited the Führer's headquarters. But things turned out quite differently, as the patient's condition took a sudden turn for the worse.

Speer had spent three weeks in bed, unable to move or do anything about his anger and growing disappointment at Hitler's silence and lack of sympathy. He discovered that Hitler had regularly kept himself informed of his condition through his personal physician Dr Morell; once or twice he had even telephoned and they had exchanged a few meaningless words; on one occasion he had even sent flowers, but only with a typed, unsigned cover note, as if to hurt Speer. On 10 February, though still very weak, Speer's impatience drove him to try to walk. But after only a few steps he felt dizzy and exceedingly limp; a little later a fever set in, as well as a violent chest pain. Professor Gebhardt was hurriedly summoned. He diagnosed muscular rheumatism and prescribed sulfonamide and applications of bee's poison.

Over the preceding days Speer had repeatedly voiced his dissatisfaction with Gebhardt, but now his diagnosis and the evidently inadequate treatment also alarmed those around him. Speer's agitated secretary informed his wife, and together with Dr Brandt they decided to consult Professor Friedrich Koch, the specialist in internal medicine at the university and, for many years, a colleague of Ferdinand Sauerbruch. When Koch arrived at Hohenlychen late in the evening he found the patient extremely short of breath, with 'strong cyanosis', a dry cough, haemorrhages and other symptoms which he regarded as clear signs of a pulmonary embolism. On Brandt's instruction a room was prepared for Koch. As the patient continued to deteriorate during the following night, Koch took Frau Speer out into the corridor and told her she must prepare herself 'for the worst'.[17] Dejected, the small group stood or sat around the patient while doctors and nurses came and went, and Speer lay in a state of extreme stupefaction, hallucinating, and filled with a sense of 'euphoria'. Two days later, however, the crisis was overcome, the medical reports were more confident by the hour, and Speer's condition was improving so rapidly that he was beginning to make plans for the immediate future. Koch was of the opinion that the damp winter climate of Hohenlychen would impede Speer's recovery and therefore recommended a fortnight of strict rest, followed by a few weeks at Merano.

This apparently straightforward case-history has acquired a certain biographical interest because of a series of strange circumstances. Gebhardt's obviously false diagnosis might just have been the mistake of an orthopaedic surgeon not very well versed in internal medicine. But during the weeks that Koch was at Hohenlychen he had constantly had 'serious quarrels' with Gebhardt about Speer's illness and the appropriate treatment. Koch never disclosed the reasons for these differences of opinion, but the fact that, as later emerged, Gebhardt kept the findings of the clinic's own specialist in internal medicine from him may have

The SS physician Karl Gebhardt, an intimate friend of Himmler's and chief of the Hohenlychen clinic near Berlin, treated Speer during his prolonged illness at the beginning of 1944.

contributed. One of Speer's friends, who visited him at his bedside, recorded a confidential remark by Koch, according to which Gebhardt had tried to persuade him to perform a nonsensical and life-threatening lung puncture. Twice after Gebhardt's rounds Speer himself said: 'I think he's trying to kill me.'[18] During these weeks, moreover, the SS doctor continuously spoke to Himmler on the telephone. Koch also reported to Speer a remark by Gebhardt that he largely saw himself as a 'political doctor'. When, during the latter half of February, Speer began to prepare for his stay in Merano, the head of the clinic, referring to Himmler, stubbornly obstructed him, finding a succession of pretexts for preventing his departure until mid-March. Finally, as Koch stated in an affidavit after the war, Speer felt that he had 'had enough'. He personally turned to Himmler and made sure that the minister could leave Hohenlychen.[19]

Even an observer with a sense for the often fantastical features of the Nazi regime will find it difficult to believe that Himmler was able to keep a ministerial colleague as if under arrest and then demand the final say in his place of convalescence. He was certainly exceeding his authority, but he also knew that Speer was virtually helpless so long as Hitler's displeasure lasted. Having been forced to yield in his conversation with Koch, he then took it upon himself to find accommodation for Speer, instructing SS General Karl Wolff, who was responsible for South Tyrol, to investigate the resort 'scrupulously', particularly 'from the point of view of the State police'.[20] He also assigned to Gebhardt responsibility for Speer's security and gave him sole medical charge, thereby eliminating the troublesome Koch. He further posted a twenty-five-man guard under Gebhardt's command in and around Goyen Castle near Merano, which had finally been chosen for Speer's convalescence. Every one of these measures was designed to give the economic dictator, who Himmler thought had risen far too high, an overdue lesson in where the real power lay.

It seems that Himmler was prepared to go even further. In Spandau Speer learned from his fellow prisoner Walther Funk that, in the autumn of 1943, when the succession to Hitler was being discussed, in the presence of senior SS leaders Gebhardt had let slip a remark by Himmler to the effect that Speer represented 'a peril' and that 'he has to disappear'.[21] At the beginning of February 1944, one or two days before the patient's collapse, Himmler had turned up at Hohenlychen, and, hidden behind a door, Speer's secretary had overheard a few sentences which greatly alarmed her. 'Well, then he'll just be dead,' she had heard Himmler say to Gebhardt in the corridor of the ward and when the doctor objected, he cut him off: 'Enough! The less said, the better.'[22]

The story has the hallmarks of the worst trashy novel, but it was typical of the regime. Internal power relationships may have been presented to the public as a solemn spectacle. But once the sets were shifted a fraction, these relationships all too often turned into the cheapest blood-and-thunder drama. Even if, as some critics suggest, Speer had read more into the evidence than the facts warranted, the grounds for suspicion are too numerous to be written off as a 'product of paranoia or persecution mania'.[23] One point emerging from a letter from Gebhardt to Himmler dated 21 February 1944 is not only unexplained, but probably inexplicable. According to the letter Speer himself requested Gebhardt, whom he had accused only a few days previously, to accompany him to Merano and look after him 'until he had safely adjusted to the climatic conditions there'. It is plausible that Speer might have preferred the devil he knew over another opponent who would undoubtedly have been assigned to him.[24] He may also have reflected that Gebhardt's presence would have made the plot more obvious and limited the circle of suspects. Besides, he kept as far away as possible from the doctor, who was put up with his family a few kilometres away at a Merano hotel and scarcely saw him over the next few weeks. But in order to demonstrate that he retained a scrap of independence, despite everything, he invited Professor Koch to Goyen Castle as his 'private guest'.

On 17 March Speer set out for Merano. His confused mood of barely diminished affection for Hitler, defiance and disappointment led him to travel via Berchtesgaden. However, he had no intention of visiting his own home on the Obersalzberg, where the Führer's headquarters with its noise and bustle was then housed. In view of their strained relationship Speer also felt that it would not be appropriate to stay near Hitler. Speer therefore had the baroque pavilion of Klessheim Castle near Salzburg assigned to him. On the very evening after his arrival, Hitler came to welcome him in person.

The conversation got going with difficulty, even though Hitler clearly tried to recapture the personal and friendly tone of times gone by. He made thoughtful and sympathetic inquiries about Speer's progress, asked after his family, brought up shared memories and spoke of the buildings they would erect after this 'damned war'. 'Everything was as always,' Speer remarked, 'and yet it was quite different.' Even as his visitor stepped through the door Speer, in a sudden flash of disenchantment, had spotted Hitler's 'ugliness', his common forehead, his broad nose and the vulgar shape of his face generally; each one of these repulsive details, which he had never noticed before, was reinforced by his pale, pasty skin. 'Suddenly the veil had been lifted.'[25]

They had not met for nearly three months, longer than ever before, and during that period Speer had not only been removed from Hitler's influence but also subjected to continuous humiliations; the two factors together had more or less weaned him from the drug to which he had become addicted. Hitler, he recalled, had talked at him as though 'from a great distance', but whereas 'in the past he had managed to release in me ... exceptional energies, with a few words or a gesture, I now felt weary and exhausted ... in spite of Hitler's cordiality.' Several times Speer caught himself only listening to the flood of words 'with half an ear', at times he heard himself interject some phrase or other, and only once had he come to life – when he demanded from Hitler the release of Wernher von Braun and two of his colleagues whose arrest by

Himmler had principally been directed against himself. Then he relapsed again into apathy and, as Hitler kept talking, Speer felt gripped by painful 'thoughts of futility'. 'What am I doing, sitting here?' he asked himself, now that everything was lost, 'the war as well as the great buildings I had designed for him.'

But his depressed mood ended the next day, his thirty-ninth birthday, as he observed his rivals and the greed with which they were carving up his skin, over the telephone, by courier and by means of surprising alliances. In the morning Göring telephoned to convey his good wishes, and when Speer told him about the satisfactory diagnoses, Göring cheerfully interjected his usual 'You don't say', adding that only the previous day he had been informed by Professor Gebhardt that Speer was suffering from a serious and incurable heart condition. Like all objections he did not wish to hear, Göring dismissed Speer's assurances that his cardiological examination by Professor Koch had not revealed the slightest pathological feature. In the end he uttered a few retrospective words about Speer's 'fine and successful time as a minister'. In the course of the day, as numerous visitors arrived to convey their wishes, it emerged that Gebhardt had misled everybody, indeed describing Speer to Hitler as a 'wreck no longer capable of work'. At a champagne reception Hitler was heard to remark sadly, in the presence of Speer's wife, that 'Speer has had it'. In the afternoon he suddenly appeared outside the pavilion with a huge bunch of flowers and Speer had the impression that he had come to say a last goodbye.

To his own amazement he accepted this gesture with indifference. And when, four days later, Hitler paid Speer another visit, just before his departure for Merano, he even behaved with terse formality. Over the past ten years a relationship had developed between them which was inspired by friendly affection, far beyond Speer's work as an architect and later as a minister. Now a few weeks of absence and the transparent intrigues of his rivals had sufficed to undermine these feelings on Hitler's part. In view of the excessive burden and almost unendurable pressure on Hitler, Speer was prepared to accept the offhand treatment to a certain extent. What he found more difficult to understand was how a short meeting could have been enough to revive Hitler's sentiments, and he began to ask himself what kind of a friendship it was that would come and go depending on whether the other party was present. As Speer suspected, Hitler had noticed the reserve of his 'willing admirer' at his first visit and had mobilized all his skills of persuasion to win him back. But Hitler failed to realize that, in keeping with the strange algebra of human relations, he was merely pushing him further away.

Speer and his family spent the 'best six weeks' of his time as a minister at Goyen Castle. For a while Hitler, the war and armaments were almost forgotten. He scarcely paid any attention to the fact that Bormann and Himmler had started a campaign of suspicion against three of his departmental heads and he even disregarded rumours that Göring was already looking for a new minister of armaments. But then matters took a surprising and, he felt, outrageous turn as Hitler openly sided with Speer's declared opponents.

The episode followed on from the dispute with Dorsch. As soon as it was clear that Speer's request to relieve Dorsch of his duties would not be granted, Göring got hold of the Organisation Todt chief and began to use him as a pawn in his game. Initially, the attack was directed at Speer's building activity, but Göring was hoping to strike at the entire radius of power of the armaments minister and bring Speer down for good. With this in mind he now took Dorsch along to the Führer conferences as an expert, and, above all, revived a project which had been discussed the year before in connection with underground production but had then been sidelined. The idea came from Dorsch and envisaged an unusual but simple method of constructing underground manufacturing facilities. Sizeable hills were to be covered with a concrete layer about six metres thick; once the concrete had set, the soil underneath would be excavated and used for making concrete for the next project. Hitler was so taken by the idea that he immediately ordered six of these large-scale bunkers to be constructed, each with a surface area of 100,000 square metres.

Speer, however, had been sceptical about the idea. He not only questioned the short construction time predicted by Dorsch, but also pointed out that the quantities of concrete required could never be supplied and that, moreover, the project would paralyse all other construction efforts required by the air war. He therefore delayed the start of work, eventually authorized the establishment of two of these so-called mushrooms for fighter production, but was then compelled by a lack of labour and materials to postpone the work again. In a conversation with Hitler, to which he had again brought Dorsch, Göring complained about the failure of cement deliveries to arrive. When Dorsch contradicted him, at least as far as the Organisation Todt was concerned which, he claimed, had invariably met its promises and which, besides, was only authorized to build in the occupied territories, everybody blamed the slow progress of the project on the absent Speer.

Hitler angrily ordered the immediate resumption of work. When Dorsch pointed out with a gesture of apparent loyalty that the sick minister should not be bypassed, Hitler promised to settle the matter with Speer himself. But he failed to inform the armaments ministry or even the minister himself. On 16 April he placed the Organisation Todt chief directly under himself and ordered him to build ten bunker systems by the proposed method. It was the first time since Speer's appointment as minister that Hitler had deprived him of a substantial part of his responsibilities. Göring was triumphant. And Dorsch received Hitler's assurance 'that anyway the Organisation Todt would also have to carry out the great building projects in the Reich of the future'.[26]

For Speer this was a question of principle. In a letter of 19 April, which he asked one of his staff, Gerhard Fränk, to deliver to Hitler, he scarcely veiled his indignation. Once again he voiced his doubts, indicated his surprise at Hitler's actions, and finally sketched out a system of organization which, he believed, would remove points of friction between the Organisation Todt and his ministry's building department. He envisaged that Dorsch remain responsible for construction work in the occupied territories; within the Reich, however, he wanted to entrust the department to an experienced member of Todt's staff; both officials were to come under the direction of his colleague Walter Brugmann. Through Göring and Milch he offered Hitler his resignation in the event that he was unwilling or unable to accept his proposal.[27]

Hitler was clearly stunned when he received the message on the eve of his birthday. To his entourage he said that Speer's letter not only contained factual errors, but also lacked the tone that was appropriate towards him. He could only regard the offer of resignation as 'impertinent'. Moreover, he continued, the letter confirmed Bormann's complaint that Speer was a stranger to the Party and failed to understand the rules of the Führer state or possibly even thought that they did not apply to himself because he was an artist. Hitler's reaction may in part be explained by the growing impression that Speer regarded the Führer's orders as mere recommendations to be implemented according to his own judgement. This had emerged not only in the case of Dorsch's concrete caves. In February Speer had already contradicted a strict instruction by stopping the construction of bunkers for the foreign diplomatic missions, so that Hitler felt compelled to ask Bormann to remind him of the principle that 'commands of the Führer ... [are] to be carried out by every German and may not just be ignored or suspended or delayed'. Now Hitler remarked that 'even Speer must know there is such a thing as reason of state'.[28]

During Speer's illness in early 1944 some of his colleagues, in collusion with Göring and possibly also Goebbels, started an intrigue which so embittered Speer that for a while he thought of resigning. The leader of the cabal was Xaver Dorsch, head of the Todt Organization. This photograph shows Dorsch and Speer in May 1943 at an inspection of German fortifications on the French coast.

Informed by his few friends at court about the excitement caused by his letter and his offer of resignation, Speer became increasingly discouraged at his castle near Merano. While he was still considering the circumstances of his departure from office, Göring telephoned. Feigning outrage he told him that no one was entitled to throw his job at the Führer. After a certain amount of toing and froing they agreed that Speer must not cause a sensation by the manner of his resignation. The critical situation, Göring explained, made it necessary for Speer to vanish quietly, perhaps by prolonging his recuperation until his disappearance would scarcely be noticed. Speer readily agreed, even though he doubted that his resignation could be kept secret even for a few weeks.

On the afternoon of 20 April Walter Rohland appeared in Merano unannounced. He came from Hitler's birthday party, which was being held at Klessheim Castle, culminating in a spectacular demonstration of new tank models. Speer was in an exceedingly bad mood. A few hours previously he had said goodbye to his private guest Professor Koch, who, after several clashes with Gebhardt, had been declared as 'undesirable' by Himmler and been forced to depart from one day to the next.[29] Rohland explained his unexpected visit by saying that Speer's plans to give up his office had spread like wildfire, causing exceptional disquiet everywhere. He referred to a conversation they had had at Hohenlychen and argued 'gravely' that Speer had a duty not only to his country but also to industry, which had always been loyal to him and should not now be handed over to some radical Party figure who would undoubtedly succeed him. There was also a need, now that the war was clearly lost, to preserve a remnant of economic substance for afterwards to ensure at least some hope of survival for the population. In short, Speer should abandon his resignation plans and stay at his post, however difficult this might be for him.[30]

While Rohland was speaking Speer was aware as he had not been for some years of a fleeting thought that had nothing to do with greatness, war, a hero's life and all the other ideological baggage in Hitler's proximity, nor indeed with the anaesthetizing abstractions into which he had always escaped, or the mountains of statistics with which he held reality at bay, something that related only to life and perhaps to the responsibility which he bore. At first his visitor did not convince him and he stuck to his intention to resign. But as they continued talking about the dangers threatening the country, the spectre of 'scorched earth' appeared before him for the first time; he had an idea that it would be hard to avoid seeing it in future and equally difficult to dismiss the impending catastrophe as mere 'politics' which did not concern him.

The eventful day was not over. Towards one o'clock in the morning Milch, Saur and Dr Fränk, the departmental head who had handed Speer's letter to Hitler, arrived at Goyen Castle after driving for several hours over the icy Brenner Pass. They informed the minister about the birthday celebrations and Milch told him about a conversation with Hitler during which the Führer had made unusually derogatory remarks about Speer. At his request, Milch continued, he had then spoken to Hitler privately. Milch had not only expressed his regret for the clouded relations between Hitler and Speer but had also predicted the probable collapse of armaments if the former trust were not immediately restored. Hitler had became thoughtful. He had stepped to the window, stared at the tanks ranged below the terrace and drummed his fingers against the window pane. After a 'sharp searching look' at him, Hitler had become more friendly, even finding a few words of respect for

Speer. At any rate, it had been clear that Hitler did not, at this point, wish a break with Speer. Encouraged, Milch had in a sense increased the stakes and, with Göring, Dorsch and Bormann in mind, he had 'told Hitler the plain truth': the ill feeling had only arisen 'because of the intrigues of those rivals of dubious value'. After a lengthy pause he had asked Hitler for a conciliatory gesture, merely a word or a sign that Speer might take as a token of continuing favour, and which he, Milch, would personally convey to him 'that same evening'. Relapsing into his sulky mood, Hitler had hesitated at length and the field marshal had had to ask several times before he was given such a message.[31]

This was the background to the nocturnal scene in the drawing-room of Goyen Castle, which it is difficult to describe. It is significant because it reveals the emotional and touchy nature of a relationship which persisted despite all the ill-humour and which, with its childish traits, was for Speer as much as for Hitler the only 'affair of the heart' of their lives. It also shows how much posturing the role of the historic leader demanded of Hitler. For a brief instant his message to Speer removed the curtain that hid the sentimental and petit-bourgeois side of his nature. While Speer was still looking at his visitors expectantly, Milch said: 'The Führer asked me to tell you that he holds you dear.'[32]

Speer's reply was no less characteristic. It showed him as the 'abandoned' party and revealed the measure of the despair which seized him after Hitler's 'betrayal'. 'The Führer can lick my arse!' he exploded, and Milch had to reprimand him: 'You are much too insignificant to use such language towards the Führer,' he told him. For some time they continued to argue loudly. The three visitors urged Speer to return to his office and restore the relationship, while he maintained that it had irrevocably broken down. Although Rohland's arguments had made him waver, his signed letter of resignation was lying on a table in a far corner of the room. After five hours Speer gave in, on condition that Dorsch was again placed under his authority, and he drafted a letter ordering the Organisation Todt chief to construct six 'mushroom bunkers'. After a cursory glance at the sheet of paper, Hitler put his signature to it the very next day.

Speer's vacillating state of mind became evident shortly afterwards. No sooner had his nocturnal visitors left than he began to wonder if he had perhaps given in too quickly and fallen between several stools. In view of the shortage of manpower and resources he was bound to have either all the authorities concerned with construction, or at any rate the hostile Dorsch, ranged against him in the impending quarrels about distribution. He was familiar with this dilemma, but in the past he could count on Hitler. That was no longer the case. After prolonged reflection Speer therefore prepared a kind of countermanding letter, proposing that the entire sphere of construction be detached from his ministry and that Dorsch be in a sense appointed his successor as 'Inspector-General for Building'. Even before the letter was finished he decided to break off his convalescent leave and seek out Hitler in person.

There were more difficulties with Gebhardt who suddenly raised medical objections to his flying, but in fact he was merely following Himmler's orders to detain Speer wherever that may be and not to let him near Hitler. After prolonged argument Himmler eventually intervened in person and approved the flight on the medically dubious condition that Speer would present himself to him before seeing Hitler. When on 24 April Speer called on Himmler, even before going to his own house on the Obersalzberg, it soon emerged that he had only wanted once again to demonstrate to his rival the extent of his own power and superior position. He grandly informed him that it had been agreed months ago in a talk with Hitler, at which Göring had also been present, to detach Dorsch from the Speer ministry and to transfer all construction projects to him as a separate authority. He was talking about 'facts', Himmler pointed out, 'which could not be revised' and he could only advise Speer to stop resisting plans worked out by the highest powers, among which he evidently included himself. He accused his visitor of having countermanded orders and delayed Hitler's programme of relocating German industry under concrete or in caves. As Speer was determined to recommend the very same solution to Hitler, he let Himmler talk without contradicting him.

No sooner had he got home than he found himself invited by an impatient Hitler to the daily tea party at the Berghof. However, to emphasize the official nature of his visit, Speer curtly declined the invitation. Even in retrospect he was startled by this outrageous temerity. When he was summoned to an audience a few minutes later, Hitler received him outside the entrance, with cap and gloves, as though he were an official guest. During the ensuing conversation he outdid himself in courtesies and was so attentive that Speer had the impression of being wooed in the most flattering way. To Speer's amazement Hitler rejected his suggestion of detaching Dorsch and construction from his ministry; he had, he explained, no one he could entrust with 'our building work', thus disavowing not only Himmler but also dismissing Dorsch and his sensitivities with a disparaging gesture. He also discarded the suspicions against three of Speer's staff, who were faced with mounting difficulties, as trivial. Instead every movement and every word reflected his pleasure at having eliminated the annoyances of the past few weeks and found his old friend again. When, before dismissing him, Hitler once more reached for his official cap and gloves, Speer made a gesture to show that this was not necessary. Although he had every reason to reflect again on the nature of a friendship which came and went depending on whether the friend was present, that evening Speer was back among the virtually unchanged group at Hitler's fireside, allowing the tirades about smoking, artificial honey, the Churches and whatever, along with the agonizing jokes and the false merriment, to wash over him, secretly counting the lost hours – but happy.[33]

News of Speer's triumph spread like wildfire, and he himself made sure everyone took it in. He let it be known that his adversaries had intended to bring him down over construction, but that Hitler had now assured him that in future he would agree, unseen, to anything Speer considered right. In order to savour his success to the full, he officially presented Dorsch to Hitler on the following day as the new head of the building sector under his, Speer's, authority. Göring accepted the defeat with monosyllabic fury, Himmler nodded silently as if he knew Hitler's vacillating moods, and only Bormann readjusted overnight to the new situation by assuring Speer of his old unshakable comradeship, denying any participation in the 'hunt' against him, even offering him the familiar '*Du*' a little later, which Speer accepted and forgot again on the following day, not without wishing to offend.

On the evening of 25 April he returned to Merano. As his trial of strength with Himmler was, for the time being, over, he dispensed with an aircraft and took the night train. Filled with the euphoria of having returned to favour and power he disregarded not only medical advice but also the requests of his family and immediately hurled himself into his work, dictating, attending conferences and telephoning. Since the beginning of the year the Allies had greatly intensified their air war and the effects were now felt in all spheres of life. Towards the end of February, Operation Big Week had begun, making German aircraft plants the exclusive targets of Allied bomber fleets. For a moment it seemed as if the Allies had adopted the strategy of targeting resources after all. By the end the British and Americans had lost some 300 aircraft, but losses on the German side amounted to over 1,100 fighters in

January and more than 1,200 in February. In addition, the greater precision of the attacking formations led to the destruction of over 700 fighters while they were still in production, as well as all night fighters and three-quarters of all manufacturing facilities. It was very nearly the end of the German fighter defence.

To Speer's relief the Allies had once again broken off operations half-way through and, moreover, directed their attacks solely against the production facilities for fuselages and not against the more vulnerable and more important engine works. Besides, General Spaatz, the commander of the American air forces in Europe, had not, for the time being, succeeded in getting his plan passed to smash the German fuel and synthetic-rubber industry in an uninterrupted air offensive lasting fifteen days.[34] Instead, no doubt with a view to the impending invasion, the focus switched to the destruction of transport routes.

While Speer was still hospitalized at Hohenlychen, Karl Otto Saur had been charged with the creation of the so-called 'Fighter Staff'. This was to ensure not only the development and production of an effective fighter force, but also to discover ways and means of mitigating the worst consequences of the enemy's air superiority. It was based on the model of the Ruhr Staff set up in 1943, which had successfully united defence measures for the Ruhr area under the leadership of the industrialists Albert Vögler and Walter Rohland. Strictly speaking, however, these new bodies merely increased the existing muddle of responsibilities since they were given prerogatives and special powers without this same authority being removed from the existing organizations. Speer was aware of this and, despite his preference for improvised solutions, he would have proceeded more circumspectly with the creation of still more new bodies had he not simultaneously been pursuing tactical objectives. While the Ruhr Staff had been designed to provide him with the power base he had sorely lacked in conflicts with his opponents, he saw the Fighter Staff as a means to pay Göring back for his intrigues over the preceding weeks.

Circumstances favoured Speer. He returned to Berlin on 8 May and a mere four days later nearly a thousand American daytime bombers attacked the fuel industry dispersed throughout the Reich territory. This was the long-feared blow at one of the nerve centres of armaments; in retrospect Speer believed that 'the technological war was decided on that day'.[35] No sooner had he got production more or less going again with his feverish efforts than Allied air formations repeated the attacks. Twenty-four days later they came for the third time, and shortly afterwards for the fourth and fifth time. Instead of the planned 6,000 tonnes, the plants were soon producing a mere 120 tonnes of aviation fuel per day. Speer thereupon sent a memorandum to Hitler on 30 June and another on 28 July. On the basis of existing reserves, he explained, the most urgent requirements could be covered until September. After that, however, an 'unbridgeable gap' would arise, 'which would inevitably have tragic consequences'.[36] At the end of his memorandum he again broached the idea of total mobilization, although this time only for the restoration of the fuel industry, demanding material and even skilled workers from other armaments branches to be made available. Hitler was dumbstruck: 'In that case we'll immediately have fewer tanks,' he protested. Only when Speer had convinced him that the tanks would be useless without fuel, and when Saur had promised to maintain a high rate of tank production, did he consent. From the late autumn of 1944 onwards 350,000 skilled workers, some of them highly qualified, were involved in constant repairs to the hydrogenation plants.

Furthermore the American formations were employing long-range fighter escorts which, meeting with less and less opposition, accompanied the bombers right up to their targets and, if only by their numerical superiority, largely eliminated the German fighter defences. During an attack on 20 June 1,000 fighters protected an armada of 1,500 'Flying Fortresses' and Liberators. This proved a further, almost fatal, blow to Göring's standing and Speer wasted no time exploiting it. Through Dorsch's mushroom bunkers, which were predominantly to serve fighter production, he had already penetrated into the realm of the still independent aerial armaments; now he went one step further. Together with Milch, who increasingly despaired of Göring's lethargy and was eventually willing to give in, Speer, without informing Hitler, the Reich Marshal or the aircraft factories concerned, concluded an initially confidential arrangement designed to bring together the tasks of both sides. When all the details were worked out, Speer went to see Hitler on 4 June and, using a prepared plan of organization, proposed that the entire air armament be incorporated in his ministry, thus adding the missing cope-stone to his economic empire. In order not to make Göring's humiliation too obvious, he suggested that the decision should, if possible, be presented to the outside world as originating from the Reich Marshal himself. This seemingly conciliatory gesture made it easier for Hitler to approve the plan unreservedly.

Göring failed to realize that the apparent concessions to him really amounted to an act of extreme self-mockery. By signing the decree of

Victims of an air attack in a Berlin sports hall in 1944. By the summer of 1944 Allied air supremacy over Germany was virtually unchallenged; in May of that year Speer had stated in a memorandum that the 'war is decided'.

20 June he virtually issued his own death certificate, proclaiming to all the world that Speer had robbed him of his last responsibilities in the field of armaments policy. As if to justify the transfer of power, the Fighter Staff immediately scored considerable successes. By July production of fighter aircraft more than doubled. But Göring, who was deeply offended, had some cause to grumble: the high production figures merely proved that Speer had, over the past years, deliberately discriminated against air armaments in order to get control of them. Even Milch had, some time before, remarked on the state of aircraft manu-

facture: 'Not a soul helps us ... Everyone expresses deepest sympathy and promises to lay a wreath on our coffin.'[37] A mere six weeks later Speer again dissolved the staff which had done its duty with the final elimination of the Reich Marshal. He replaced it with a larger 'Armaments Staff' responsible for the weapon programmes of all the Wehrmacht services. When Göring relapsed some time later into his old habit of issuing directives to the air force industry, Speer rudely put him in his place in writing: he, the Reich Marshal, had no business to interfere in air armaments, because 'in matters of the armaments industry ... everyone obeys my command'.[38]

However, the intrigues continued even after Göring had been sidelined. Nothing reveals more clearly how far the top leadership was removed from reality than the growing bitterness of the in-fighting, at a time when it was increasingly obvious that they were heading for destruction and there was no real power to be won. Alarmed at Speer's regained status and influence, Himmler intensified his counter-measures, mobilizing his whole arsenal from police threats to surveillance and denunciation, from intimidation to the 'preventive detention' of some of Speer's staff. He was more and more open in pursuing his claim to further areas of armaments production. Bormann soon returned to his policy of insinuation, encouraging the Gauleiters to obstruct the armaments ministry, and mobilizing Sauckel and Ley. Soon after returning to his office, still in May, Speer was compelled to ask Hitler for help against these intrigues.[39] However, his attempts to draw at least some of the Gauleiters to his side by means of a 'Reconstruction Conference' for the years after the war were unsuccessful and the meeting scheduled for June at the Plessenburg near Kulmbach had to be cancelled. His halo of invulnerability was gone.

Similarly his feelings of friendship for Hitler did not return. Ever since Speer had first openly opposed a confused Hitler and compelled him to give in, their relationship seemed curiously unbalanced, despite the renewed formalities of closeness. The romantic feelings which had inspired and driven him over the years had distinctly cooled. Speer commented that the unmistakable moral depravity of the leadership, the intrigues mounted against him by Himmler, Gebhardt, Bormann and others had aroused in him, albeit much too late, the 'first doubts about the fundamentally questionable nature of this system of rule'; it was then that his painful process of detaching himself had begun, accompanied as it was by the need to lean on someone, by dark anxieties and a fear of betrayal.[40]

There was a slight change in Hitler too. He had responded to Speer's request for help against the Gauleiters by refusing to support either him or the people from the Party. When Speer made a renewed effort to win the Gauleiters over and asked for Hanke to be appointed head of the Fighter Staff, Hitler rejected the proposal by pointing to Sauckel, of all people, whose example, he objected, had reduced the authority of all the Gauleiters. If the crisis with Speer had been due to Speer's persistent refusal to gloss over the upsetting facts of the war, Hitler soon had further cause for complaint. In a conversation with his Luftwaffe adjutant Nicolaus von Below he let it be understood that he had recalled Speer to office because he had seen no other way. Although, he observed disapprovingly, Speer was showing a 'lack of confidence in victory', he was the only person with 'a clear overview of the entire field of armaments and its entanglements'.[41]

In Speer, however, the automatisms that had ruled him for so long continued to operate, soon suppressing or mitigating any doubt. Added to this were his growing worries about the war. Day after day he studied reports about production losses, about sudden delivery problems or the desperate fuel situation, trying to provide replacements in one place and restarting production on a makeshift basis in another. With the new strategic concept behind the Allied air war, the transport disasters never stopped; the chaos on roads and railways was being made worse by the retreat of machinery and manpower as the German fronts were driven back in the east and in the south.

In between, Hitler came up with ever more nervous and often absurdly detailed demands. Speer later calculated that in his ministerial years he had nearly one hundred personal conferences with Hitler, at which 2,221 individual items on the agenda were discussed or settled, many of them 'of minimal importance'. Just as Hitler had formerly jumped from dietary recipes to the floodlighting of the Niederwald monument and from there to the breeding of sheepdogs, he now made decisions on the heating or the hatch covers of tanks, moved seamlessly to the contracts of foreign workers, then on to a railway project and 'in the next breath' laid down 'the cruising speed demanded by the army' for various types of vehicles and their deployment.[42]

Completely misjudging the circumstances, Hitler was equally abrupt in demanding 'the establishment of self-sufficiency in fuels within eighteen months', then an increase in tank production and a tenfold expansion of the anti-aircraft programme. The change in Speer's self-assurance is proved by the way in which he first ignored an order by

On 6 June 1944 the Allied invasion of Normandy began. The ratio of forces is reflected in the fact that for every mission flown by the Luftwaffe that day, there were 47 flown by the Americans and British.

Hitler soon after his return from Merano and even succeeded in persuading Saur to do likewise. Then again he, Milch and others 'implored' Hitler not to fritter away all the two thousand fighters produced each month at the numerous fronts, but to deploy at least some of them within Germany's own air space. Otherwise, they pointed out, not only would one city after another be lost, but transport and, due to the lack of aircraft fuel, any effective defence against the bombing war would ultimately grind to a halt. When, around that time, Milch said that 'Hitler could no longer be regarded as normal', Speer agreed without much ado, as if he had long come to the same conclusion.

After tough and protracted arguments, during which Hitler once more put forward his favourite image of the burnt ships, he was eventually prepared to make a limited concession. But matters were now slipping from his hands and he was compelled to withdraw his assent again. On 6 June the Allies landed in Normandy and the fighter aircraft were needed at the new invasion front. The ratio of strength, however, became clear that day when the German Luftwaffe flew 319 missions as against about 15,000 by the British and Americans.[44]

Only two weeks later, on June 22, the third anniversary of Hitler's invasion of Russia, the Red Army opened its major offensive on the central section of the Eastern front, outnumbering the enemy by three to one. The war had entered its final stage.

Chapter Eight
SCORCHED EARTH

Despite the unmistakable signs of approaching collapse, armaments manufacture reached its peak between June and August 1944. This level was more or less sustained for the next three months, when it suddenly became clear how deceptive the figures were. But before this happened they produced a feeling of euphoria.

At the same time the contradictions in the armaments strategy emerged. In keeping with his nature and his lack of realism, Hitler continued on the one hand to call for weapons of attack, even though these could no longer meet the demands of the moment. Advised by a short-sighted military entourage, drilled to automatic agreement, he broke off the development of fighter aircraft and anti-aircraft rockets, sacrificing them to a few 'sensational weapons' of dubious strategic value. On the other hand, defensive weapons and equipment, from anti-aircraft guns, mines, and anti-tank bazookas to temporary bridges and emergency equipment, accounted for an increasing share of production in order to meet the increasingly urgent demands of the armed forces.

Amidst all this wrangling, concrete became the real symbol of the changing situation, a symbol that reconciled the many differences. 'Fortress Europe' was surrounding itself with concrete on all sides. More than thirteen million cubic metres was swallowed up by the Atlantic Wall alone, which was soon to prove totally useless because the invention of artificial harbours made landing possible almost anywhere. Almost the same amount was employed along the open flanks, in Dorsch's subterranean production sites, in submarine bunkers, as well as at the hastily erected command posts in France, Silesia and western Germany. Even the move of the Führer's headquarters to the Obersalzberg, which dragged on all summer, had became necessary because the 'Wolf's Lair' in Rastenburg was being turned into a concrete refuge. The conqueror was crawling away and hiding in caves and concrete bunkers.

The delirious visions of an imminent turning point in the war were rekindled once more when the 'retaliation weapons' were finally deployed. During the night of 12-13 June, a week after the Allied landings had begun, the first VI rockets were fired from one of more than fifty launching ramps in the Pas de Calais. The complicated procedure had been completely disrupted because the order to fire had first been repeatedly delayed and then hastily brought forward on Hitler's constant urgings. 'Twenty days of that will have them all trembling,' Milch had predicted of the effect of the rockets.

In fact even the first salvoes ended with a serious reverse, as Goebbels recorded in his diaries.[1] Instead of the planned 500 rockets, only ten were fired; six exploded on launching or crashed into the sea, and it soon became clear that the enterprise had also failed on a strategic level. Nearly 10,000 VIs were fired over the next few months, mostly at London. Each of them could carry about one tonne of explosive, while the V2s, launched from September onwards with even greater hopes, carried a quarter less. The entire production of five months, not counting the frequent malfunctionings, did not exceed some 3,700 tonnes of explosives, compared to the 8,000 tonnes dropped by the more than 4,000 British and American bomber fleets over Germany in a single day. In the end the expected psychological impact, which had been triumphantly proclaimed by Goebbels and his propaganda machine, failed to materialize. As in the air war over Germany, the unpredictable rockets, which came crashing down at any time of the day or night only seconds after an ominous hiss had announced their arrival, merely strengthened the British people in their defiant resistance.[2] As production of these weapons was tying up skilled labour, materials and energy urgently needed elsewhere, the damage to Germany turned out to be greater than the benefit.

Speer had not changed his sceptical stance. Once again he distanced himself from exaggerated expectations of a weapon whose production he had vigorously promoted, in spite of his reservations. When the failure of the rocket warfare had become obvious, he declared to an assembly of generals, 'after all, the propaganda did not come from me,' and demanded an end to 'that propaganda'.[3] But this was only one of the contradictions in which Speer was getting increasingly entangled. 'One part of my consciousness acknowledged that everything must now come to an end,' was how he later described his state of mind.[4] At the same time he spoke not only in public but also before specialized audiences, such as an armaments conference in Linz, predicting similar production increases for the following year as during the past few months. In between he wrote Hitler one memorandum after another, warning that all armaments efforts would soon dry up. To the outside world he spoke of the 'restoration of the situation', while on the other hand distributing with sarcastic solemnity green neckties to leading members of his staff who had expressed some confused hope.[5] These contradictions were soon to be put to the test.

On 17 July 1944 Colonel von Stauffenberg, recently appointed chief of staff of the Commander of the Reserve Army, called on Speer. On behalf of his superior, General Friedrich Fromm, Stauffenberg invited Speer to lunch followed by a discussion at the command centre in Bendlerstrasse for the following Thursday. As Speer had long promised to give a lecture that morning to members of the Reich government in Berlin and leading industrialists, he refused the invitation. Even when Fromm, unusually, approached him again and repeated his request, Speer declined. That Thursday was 20 July.

Goebbels had offered Speer the still undamaged Schinkel hall in the propaganda ministry for his lecture. After his speech he was sitting with Funk and Goebbels, when a loudspeaker announcement urgently called the propaganda minister to the telephone. Reich Press Chief Dr Dietrich was on the other end from Rastenburg, to where the Führer's headquarters had returned about a week earlier. He told Goebbels that an attempt had just been made on the Führer's life, during the *Mittagslage*, the conference regularly held at noon. However, Dr Dietrich was able to add, the Führer had escaped with only slight injuries, unlike some of the others present. First suspicions were directed against the workers of the Organisation Todt still engaged on the site. Then the line went dead.

At first Speer may not have grasped the significance of the news. Stunned by the enormity of the event, it may not have dawned on him how close they had come during that brief historic moment to the point where the uncontrollable horrors and the hopeless situation might have been brought to an end. Certainly, as emerges from his memoirs, he gave no thought whatsoever to the wider implications. Instead, in a reflex typical of totalitarian regimes, he was concerned solely with the personal consequences the news might have that a worker of the Organisation Todt, for which he was responsible, was under suspicion.

Speer also omitted to make his own inquiries about Hitler's condition or about the state of affairs at the Führer's headquarters. After leaving

Goebbels, he returned to his own office as though nothing unusual had happened, dealt with a few routine matters and then had a late lunch with Colonel Engel, Hitler's former army aide-de-camp who had meanwhile been ordered to the front. Speer wanted to sound him out about a recent memorandum on tightening the organization of the Wehrmacht. Later, while he was receiving a foreign ministry official to hear a report on safeguarding Romanian oil supplies, Goebbels telephoned. In a voice that was 'excited and hoarse' he asked him to come to his residence as a matter 'of extreme urgency'. There Speer learned that an army *coup d'état* was in progress throughout the Reich. Not long afterwards they both watched from the window as troops in battle equipment took up position in Pariser Platz and outside their building, where a machine-gun was mounted at the entrance. As soon as Goebbels realized the seriousness of the situation he went across to his bedroom and returned with a few cyanide capsules. 'Just in case,' he said.[6]

One of the reasons for the failure of 20 July was that General Thiele, the chief of staff of army communication and one of the conspirators, had not ordered a news blackout or cut the telephone lines, because of the vague reports from Rastenburg. While Goebbels was constantly gathering news and sifting the often confusing torrent of information, Speer, as he himself recorded, stood around with a 'strange feeling of being present but unconcerned'. On his arrival he had, admittedly, declared his position by describing the *putsch* as 'a disaster in our situation'. But in that hectic atmosphere any inactive aloofness must have seemed an affront. It is therefore far more likely that he involved himself to a greater degree than his memory suggested in the efforts to clarify the situation. Indeed, a note from an unknown source to Rudolf Wolters, who was still keeping the ministry's Chronicle, recommends: 'Our minister's participation in the elucidation of the enigma of 20 July was so active that it should be recorded in our Chronicle – what do you think?'[7]

Another fact contradicts Speer's account. The more names cropped up, the more suspicion fell on Speer. Stauffenberg, Fromm, Olbricht, Fellgiebel and others all belonged, as Goebbels knew, to Speer's circle of closer acquaintances. When Speer summoned up courage and telephoned Bendlerstrasse in the early evening, General Olbricht informed him that he had only been detained in error; the matter would be put right at once, he said, and hung up. Speer passed this on to Goebbels, possibly strengthening his suspicions. Some time later, when news came through that Speer's name was on a ministerial list found in Bendlerstrasse, both men burst out laughing, according to an eyewitness. Speer's laughter may well have been even louder than that of the propaganda minister.[8]

Goebbels, who increasingly became the real opponent of the officers' faction, had already tried to gather information about the political reliability of Major Otto Ernst Remer, who commanded the battalion guarding the government quarter. The findings being satisfactory, Goebbels asked him to his residence. But faced with the instant torrent of words about 'the greatest infamy of history', Remer insisted that he had to obey the orders of his superior, the city commandant von Hase. For a moment everything hung in the balance. But then Goebbels played his trump card. He informed the dumbfounded Remer that Hitler had survived and pointed to the historic role that fate had placed on his young shoulders. Goebbels suggested that Remer speak to the Führer. A few seconds later Hitler was on the line. He granted Remer all military powers in crushing the conspiracy and ordered him to obey any instructions given by Goebbels. Next Goebbels called the guards battalion together in the garden of the residence and addressed them briefly in flaming words of outrage. This was the turning point in the *coup d'état*. Matters now took their course.

Shortly before midnight Speer learned that General Fromm, who had been temporarily detained, but then released by the conspirators, intended to hold a court-martial and sentence the leaders of the rebellion to death. As this decision was bound to create the impression that Fromm was trying to eliminate all those who knew about the coup, Speer drove to Bendlerstrasse with Remer and the commanding officer of an armoured brigade that had arrived in the meantime. As the white Mercedes drew up in front of the floodlit building, which seemed surreally festive in blacked-out Berlin, Speer glimpsed the spectral figure of Ernst Kaltenbrunner, the chief of the SS Reich Central Security Office, a little way away in the shadow of buildings and trees. Kaltenbrunner stood there as if he were waiting. Now and again he whispered a few words to his large entourage, before relapsing into his uncanny silence. When Speer told him he had come to prevent the court-martial, Kaltenbrunner, with strange equanimity and in a muted voice, refused to intervene. The army, he said, had started the coup and the army would now have to end it. Besides, the execution appeared already to have taken place. An hour later Fromm was arrested.

This was not the end of Speer's worrying experiences. The very next

Because of his reputation for personal integrity the conspirators of 20 July 1944 had requested Speer to come to the Bendlerstrasse command centre at noon. However, he had an appointment that day at Goebbels' ministry and it was there that he learnt of the attempt on Hitler's life. During the day Goebbels proved the driving force in crushing the *coup d'état*. This photograph shows him and the commander of the guard battalion, Major Otto Ernst Remer (right); between them is General Lorenz.

day a congratulatory reception was held in Rastenburg. As if to make clear to him how uncertain his position was, Speer, unlike any of the other ministers, was asked to bring along his highest-ranking officials, Saur and Dorsch. Hitler was noticeably 'curt and cool'. While he received Speer's congratulations almost absent-mindedly, he put his hand on the shoulders of each of the minister's two companions in an almost intimate gesture. Nobody overlooked the scene, and as soon as the gathering dispersed, every member of the puppet world at head-quarters imitated Hitler's coldness towards Speer.[9] Wherever Speer appeared, conversation stopped and he sensed furtive glances following him from every direction. The following day, when Hitler was more friendly, his entourage followed that cue as well. But no sooner was Speer back in Berlin on 24 July than Kaltenbrunner called on him.

The Gestapo chief showed him the ministerial list from the safe at Bendlerstrasse and demanded to know how much Speer had known of the whole business. Speer received him lying down, as his knee problem had returned. When Speer assured him that the mention of his name was a surprise to him too, Kaltenbrunner accepted this, not least because an unknown hand had added a question mark to his name with the remark, 'To be won over'. Doubtless any intention of appointing Speer minister in a government of Hitler's opponents was due not to any conspiratorial pre-arrangement but merely to his reputation for complete and non-ideological integrity.[10]

In the afternoon Speer summoned some two hundred of his leading officials in his large conference room for one of those demonstrations of loyalty that were then being staged in all ministries, authorities and offices. The departmental heads sat in a long row on either side of their minister, just like the apostles in Leonardo's *Last Supper* – as the Chronicle recorded – and Speer gave a short, unusually faithful, address about the Führer's new 'vigour', his 'unbroken confidence' and everyone's duty to emulate his example. Although he avoided the by then customary vilification of the conspirators, he ended by uttering 'Sieg Heil!' – 'for the first time in my life', as he recorded.[11]

Such exaggerated gestures were no doubt due to his insecurity, especially as rumours were circulating that he had already been arrested or even shot 'because of his links with the clique of traitors'.[12] But his worst fears evaporated when Hitler, obviously swept this way and that by his emotions, invited him through Bormann to address, at a Posen meeting scheduled for 3 August, those very Gauleiters who had recently refused to be schoolmastered by him. Although the figures he presented were again impressive, the reservations against him persisted and even Hitler's praise for him in his introduction made no difference. Goebbels, who had initially cast aside his suspicions, now noted that Speer was 'not entirely of our old National Socialist blood' and 'more vulnerable than the real Nazis' in a crisis situation.[13]

But Speer did not worry for long, and he soon appeared to have regained his former nonchalance. He was not to be prevented from intervening with Himmler or the minister of justice Thierack on behalf of those among the accused who had been more or less close to him, such as Fromm, the generals Zeitzler, Speidel and Heinrici, as well as Count Schwerin, the industrialists Vögler, Bücher and Reusch, and the publisher Peter Suhrkamp. Later Speer gave some of their families financial support. He even offered to appear as a defence witness at the trial of General Fromm, who everyone, particularly Hitler, thought was guilty. Hitler certainly interpreted the offer as a sign that Speer was attempting to distance himself from their former friendship, which indeed it was, and angrily refused him permission to testify. Kaltenbrunner, who evidently had no idea of the depth of the friendship between Hitler and Speer, never stopped distrusting the minister, and as late as December 1944 Speer was compelled to write a letter of justification to the Gestapo chief. In retrospect Speer observed that he thanked God that the conspirators had not invited him to join their cause – because he 'couldn't have done so'.[14]

Before long, another shadow of suspicion fell upon Speer. In countless memoranda, mostly about the mobilization of the war effort, he continued, in spite of the general feeling of resignation, to champion the idea of total war which, he believed, was still 'only an empty phrase'.[15] A decree of mid-June had already given him authority to concentrate production. A further memorandum to Hitler now proposed that dictatorial powers be given to a 'sub-dictator' for the military and the civilian sector respectively. Finally, a third memorandum, dated, of all days, 20 July, deplored the squandering of forces in all areas. While armaments employed a little more than six million workers, he explained, public administration, commerce and the banks employed half a million more, and of the ten and a half million soldiers less than a quarter were deployed at the front. In order to remedy this oft-criticized state of affairs Speer not only proposed that all factories, staffs, offices and even the Party organizations be sifted through more radically than ever before, but also that the Wehrmacht branches be unified. In so doing Speer was adopting a policy which the perpetrators of 20 July had long advocated and which he had indeed developed in discussions with them. His memorandum also contained the compromising sentence that the 'younger officers' all shared his view. Moreover, it corresponded in every detail to the draft of a decree that had been found in Bendlerstrasse.[16]

All the same, as a result of the attempted *coup d'état* Hitler decided to proclaim total war for Germany itself too, and Speer thought that he had finally reached his goal. He had failed to consider that these matters were in fact backfiring on him. For the two people who were now equipped with greater powers, as he himself had advocated, turned out to be two adversaries who had always been jealous of his career and had opposed him two-facedly or openly. It was not long before they went over to the attack, and this time they actually brought him down.

The first of these adversaries was Heinrich Himmler. On the very afternoon of 20 July he had gained command of the Reserve Army and shortly afterwards been instructed to drive forward the reform of military organization. His new powers enabled him to penetrate numerous positions fiercely defended by the Wehrmacht and the armaments ministry,

During the weeks following the *coup d'état* of 20 July far more people lost their lives in Germany than during the entire period since the beginning of the war. Many towns, until then only partially damaged, were destroyed – such as Stuttgart, Darmstadt, Braunschweig, Hildesheim, Mainz, Dresden and Potsdam. The photograph shows the destruction in Würzburg in April 1945.

especially as he was now also responsible for weapons requirements and allocation. The suspicions of Speer, certainly kindled by Himmler, also gave him a pretext for 'drawing the net of the Gestapo and the SS Security Service ever more closely' both around the official scope of the armaments minister and his principle of the 'self-administration of industry', which had always been distrusted.

Denunciations, accusations and arrests soon multiplied. Sauckel declared in public speeches that armaments would not be sorted out until some of the economic leaders had their severed heads placed in front of their feet. The campaign of suspicion against three of Speer's departmental heads, begun a few years ago, now reached it climax. Walther Schieber, the head of arms deliveries, was recalled and soon afterwards Speer had to drop General Waeger, the head of the munitions office, as well as Willy Liebel of the Central Office. At the same time Dr Karl Brandt, Hitler's doctor-in-residence and for many years one of his closest circle, who had watched over Speer's interests at court, was overthrown by Bormann – all signs that Speer's influence was waning and would soon collapse.[17]

The other adversary was Goebbels. A fortnight before the Allied invasion he had summoned all his skills of persuasion and spent three hours trying to talk Hitler into proclaiming total war. Despite his 'passionate' objections Goebbels had been told in the end that the present crisis did not yet warrant 'pulling out the last stops'.[18] The officers' rebellion, however, had been a shock to Hitler, raising his fears that he might have lost more support than he was able to gauge in the seclusion of his headquarters. He therefore instructed Goebbels to mobilize the state and all civilian life 'by a total national employment of men and materials', thus, as the minister recorded, establishing a 'virtual internal war dictatorship'. On 25 July Goebbels was appointed 'Reich Plenipotentiary for the total war effort'. 'The effect on the German public', he noted, 'is colossal.'[19]

Goebbels got down to work at once. As a first step he ordered a series of meetings the course of which he prescribed down to the smallest detail. In a speech broadcast by all transmitters he also laid down the guidelines. His address began and ended with an extensive verdict on the 'treasonable clique of generals'; it proclaimed total war and referred to new weapons, the sight of which 'made my heart stop ... for a moment'. In his mind he had, Goebbels maintained, seen 'apocalyptic images' of a vast 'to us still wholly unimaginable disaster', and he praised with 'gratitude of near religious devotion' Providence which had so obviously taken the Führer under its protection and given a sign to everyone that his work 'must be completed, can be completed, and will be completed'.[20] With his instinct for sensational gestures he had well-known factories closed down, as well as most theatres, variety stages and concert halls. He also reduced the size of daily papers to four pages, introduced the sixty-hour week and took relentless action against exemptions from active service, which were still being generously granted.

Goebbels was anxious to limit excessive administrative costs and restricted the size of his own office to a minimum, employing a staff of not more than twenty in his new role. For the enforcement of many of his measures he therefore had to fall back on the Gauleiters, who, as Reich Defence Commissioners, wielded the decisive power within their regions. This meant that he inevitably had to deal with the very Party corps that had, in the past, succeeded in undermining similar attempts by Speer and who were again trying to pursue their own particular interests. True, Goebbels was one of them. But over the years they had more or less fallen prey to self-important greed, and the local interests of their Gaue meant more to them than the fate of the country. As they were fully aligned with Bormann, Goebbels' total-war efforts ultimately ended up with the Führer's secretary. His shrewd instinct for intrigue made Bormann instantly realize the danger from this new rival. He controlled Hitler's favour with well-measured remarks and made sure that too much goodwill was not shown towards Goebbels.[21]

Inevitably this – albeit partial – backing from Goebbels strengthened the presumptions of the Gauleiters, and Speer soon had to ward off a pack of opponents acting 'arbitrarily', as he explained to his staff towards the end of August: the 'double line of command,' he added, was causing 'a confusion that stinks to high heaven'.[22] In addition, he clashed with Goebbels himself. With the radical verve which Speer had so long admired in him, the 'total warrior' – as the propaganda minister was called, with a mixture of irony and respect – extended his recruitment measures for the 'great man-eater', the Wehrmacht, to armaments enterprises. Goebbels' ambition to shine with ever higher figures, soon exceeding hundreds of thousands and presently well over a million, was bound to conflict with Speer's demand for increasingly high production levels. Soldiers or munitions workers was the increasingly irreconcilable dilemma, which could not be resolved by Hitler's slogan of 'soldiers *and* munitions workers'. At least this 'Führer's will' enabled Goebbels to disregard agreements time and again in his recruitment drive. In a conversation with Speer, conducted 'in a very hard and severe tone', he dropped all camaraderie and informed the armaments minister that he would also make 'unrestricted use' of his comprehensive powers against him. When Speer thereupon became 'very stuffy' and repeatedly hinted that he might put his office at the Führer's disposal, Goebbels accused him of 'totally un-National-Socialist behaviour', declaring that Speer had 'still not learned anything'. In his diary he noted: 'I believe we allowed that young man to get too big.' Speer had to give in. With a hopeless gesture of outrage he turned to the propaganda ministry and 'gave orders' that henceforward 'my name is no longer to appear in the press'.[23]

On 20 September Speer addressed a memorandum in his defence to Hitler. Full of self-deception and resignation he began by writing: 'The task I have to fulfil is an unpolitical task. I felt happy in my work so long as my person and my work were assessed solely on my professional achievement ... I do not feel strong enough to carry out the technical work assigned to me and my associates unhampered and with any promise of success if it is to be evaluated according to the standards of Party policy.' Speer pointed out that his ministry was being more and more frequently accused of being 'a gathering place of reactionary captains of industry or even of being hostile to the Party'. He reminded Hitler of the Führer-command for the Protection of the Armaments Industry, issued immediately after his appointment, which decreed that criminal prosecution of his staff could be initiated only upon Speer's own application. Next he demanded that if the Gauleiters and Goebbels were to continue their unreasonable interference in armaments, they should also be made to bear 'a substantial part of the responsibility'. Although he did not consider that to be the right path, he wanted 'a clear decision'. When he presented his memorandum, Hitler handed it unread to his aide with instructions to pass it on to Bormann. The game, Speer realized at that moment, was 'finally lost'.[24]

What hit him most was the realization that he was completely isolated. Liked and celebrated as he had been all his life, he suddenly found himself without a single influential ally. He had even lost the support of Milch when the quarrel about the Me-262 had erupted again a few weeks earlier. At a conference on the Obersalzberg Milch had brusquely declared that the plane would continue to be built as a fighter and not as a fast bomber, whereupon Hitler had shouted to his entourage in a sudden rage: was anyone still obeying his orders? When the officers present, Korten, Petersen and Galland among them, had been silenced one after the other, Milch had tried once more to change Hitler's mind. But no sooner had he begun to speak than he had been interrupted by 'a torrent of abuse'. Outraged by Hitler's unreasonableness, the short-tempered field marshal had screamed back: 'My Führer, the smallest infant can see that this is a fighter, not a bomber aircraft.'[25] Speechless, Hitler had left him standing there. Soon afterwards Milch had to assemble his staff to take leave of them.

By the autumn the whole system of precarious mutual support began to disintegrate and its collapse became more and more apparent. The persistent shortage of fuel made the fighting troops virtually immobile; in the army it meant continual operational restrictions and in the Luftwaffe it impeded operational flights and even training. From one day to the next, explosives had to be eked out with twenty per cent of salt. Deliveries of chrome ore from Turkey and nickel from Finland had already run out some time earlier, and the railways had reported that their rolling stock was reduced to one half. At the same time there were increasingly prolonged interruptions in electricity supplies. Soon new Allied air tactics threatened to cut off the Ruhr from all means of transport. The few goods trains which still left the territory were confiscated by Gauleiters as they passed through their own territories, and the coal was used to supply the local population. The other great industrial region, Upper Silesia, was already within reach of the Red Army. Goebbels again complained that 'the bad news is beating down on us like a cloudburst'.[26] Far more ominous was the fact that one prerequisite for the continuation of the war was now undermining the basis of the other.

At the same time the internal order collapsed, and it was obvious that the process of dissolution would hit Speer first as the weakest link in the chain. Kammler seized control of V2 production, Sauckel tried to set up an aircraft factory in Thuringia, and a few Gauleiters, all too readily assisted by Bormann, Goebbels and Himmler, succeeded in snatching entire sections of munitions from Speer's responsibility. Since his quarrel with Milch, Hitler also seemed to be giving way in the conflict about the Luftwaffe, especially as the target area of Allied bomber formations was constantly shrinking as the fronts drew closer. Whereas Hitler had declared to Speer and Galland only in August, 'the fighter arm is to be dissolved. Stop aircraft production! Stop it at once, understood?', he now added to the prevailing confusion by suddenly demanding that 'fighters and still more fighters' be built. Driven by the desire to act once more as the master of life and death, Göring reinforced the demand by threatening to have anyone shot who did not obey what, the day before, had still been an act of extreme insubordination.[27]

The camps were beginning to separate. Hitler stood on one side with Goebbels, Bormann, Ley, Kaltenbrunner and Sauckel, obsessively steering towards the spectacular catastrophe; on the other side was the paralysed troop of the downhearted, seized by fear and confusion, realizing for the first time, now that the end was nigh, what those triumphs of past years were really worth. Speer himself had championed the radicals, well beyond the point when hope was still justified. Now he began to admit that any radicalism was a form of madness in the current state of affairs. No doubt this realization was triggered by his realism as well as his much criticized sobriety or even 'coldness'. These traits now led him to observe the twilight-of-the-gods fantasies of those around Hitler with incomprehension. He saw them as nothing more than the mixture of selfishness, hatred of the world and destructive pleasure which indeed they were. On the other hand, without his experience of Hohenlychen and Merano, and without the weakening of his position, Speer might not have turned away, or at least not for the time being.

Hitler seemed to sense that Speer was eluding him. The mere fact that Speer kept sending him one memorandum after another in increasingly rapid succession indicated that he was avoiding him. Moreover, the dejected and − Hitler believed − 'cold and pedantic tone' of these memoranda rekindled his doubts in Speer's confidence in victory. After Milch's dismissal, Speer was anxious to find a few reasonably sober minds, unaffected by the hysterically charged atmosphere of the Führer's headquarters. He therefore occasionally met with some of the members of the cabinet which had long since been discharged. These meetings with the ministers Dorpmüller, von Schwerin-Krosigk, Backe and others, took place privately. But they were of short duration. Speer later suspected that it was his joining this circle of powerless and half-forgotten ex-politicians that so annoyed the jealous Hitler that he instructed Bormann to prohibit those 'defeatist club evenings'. At the same time Speer's deputy Saur was moving to the fore, imperturbably declaring as late as the autumn that 'by Christmas we'll have air supremacy!' Venting his irritation Hitler announced to a large gathering at a situation conference, 'we have the good fortune to have a genius in our armaments industry. I mean Saur. All difficulties are being overcome by him.' When one of the generals drew his attention to the fact that Speer was present, he added irritably: 'Yes, I know. But Saur is the genius.'[28]

Meanwhile the war was approaching Germany's frontiers both from the west and the east, and from the seething atmosphere of doom there arose, louder and louder, the authentic voice of National Socialism. In one of their songs the stormtroopers had proclaimed that they would smash the world to pieces. This voice had long been drowned out, first by the slogans of restored national honour, then by the series of impressive political and social successes, and finally by the booming trumpets of war. But it had always been perceptible, even though Speer, like countless others, had pretended not to hear it – at the cosy tea parties on the Obersalzberg, in front of the overwhelming stage-sets of his world capital and in his breathless armaments drive. With 'profound shock' he had therefore heard Hitler declare at the Gauleiter conference in Posen: 'If the German people were to be defeated in the struggle, it must have been too weak, it would have failed to pass the test of history and would therefore only be destined for destruction.'[29]

Speer's responsibility covered not only production, but also the dismantling and destruction of factories and power plants which might fall into the hands of the enemy. During the retreat in the east this principle of 'scorched earth' had repeatedly been applied. Now that the Allies had broken out of the invasion pocket, flight and retreat also began in the west. From then on Speer opposed the destruction orders more and more openly. While the Allies were still deep in France he had begun to persuade the occupation authorities and front commanders to leave the plant behind undestroyed wherever possible, inducing General von Choltitz, the Wehrmacht commander of Greater Paris, for example, to postpone all demolitions. As the enemy was approaching the German frontiers he travelled more and more frequently to the western areas of the country, trying, by cautious and ambiguous talk, to win over the local authorities, including the Gauleiters, to the idea of merely 'paralysing' the industries rather than destroying them. On occasion, as for the Minette ore mines in Lorraine, he received Hitler's consent, but this had only been granted case by case, a fundamental decision not having been forthcoming. In order to avoid continuous requests to Hitler, Speer took it upon himself to extend this single authorization, justifying his procedure by a 'surprisingly simple trick' which at first even disarmed Hitler himself. There could be no reasonable doubt, he argued, that these only temporarily abandoned territories would shortly be reconquered and that the factories and supply bases would then have to be available again for German requirements.[30]

Hitler must soon have noticed that he was being duped. In mid-September, at any rate, on returning from one of his trips, Speer was surprised by the news that Hitler had issued a number of orders which, while speaking of 'defence', 'relocation' and 'blocking', had in fact extended the 'scorched earth' principle – which was not proclaimed as such until later – to the Reich territory. On closer inspection these orders stipulated that the advancing enemy be left only a 'desert of civilization' and that all installations necessary for maintaining life be demolished – factories and sewage systems, food stores and telephone exchanges, and the records of notification authorities, banks and the land register. Even art monuments, in so far as they had survived the air war, were to be destroyed, along with churches, castles and historical buildings. Every bridge was to be wrecked and every farmstead burnt to the ground. It was the ancient destructive urge, temporarily concealed by ideological theories of 'saving the world', which Hitler could at last realize, disguised as the strategy for the final decisive battle. This wilful destruction was not simply prompted by the desperate situation. All his life Hitler had invoked the alternatives of 'to be or not to be', of 'world power or downfall' and there was no reason to believe that he had meant downfall any less literally than the dream of world power, which had now been shattered. Should Germany fail, he had already said at the beginning of the 1930s, 'then as we ourselves go under, we shall drag half the world with us into the abyss'.[31] Now that moment had arrived.

It presented Speer with a dilemma. The disputes of years past had not been about principles but about the extension of his own power, the repulsion of intrigues and about Hitler's favour. Now he had to ask himself whether his principles did not clash with each other, because Hitler was equating the existence of the country with his own existence. It meant that if Hitler went down, then Germany should go down too. Speer believed that to be a decision of such wild insanity that he found it hard to comprehend. However, the indications that Hitler was serious about it soon left no room for doubt. Everything that had determined Speer's life was wiped out – the hopes that had filled him, his projects for the future, postponed but never abandoned, and, as he saw it, his unselfish dedication to the war effort, as well as his emotional friendship with Hitler.

On the other side was his sense of responsibility, of which he had been reminded in Merano by Rohland and by others since. For all his sobriety Speer had always preserved a naive enthusiasm for the 'great tasks' and had 'felt behind the trite, sentimental sayings the whole weight of a categorical imperative'.[32] Some of this had been buried over the years or displaced by the compromises demanded by his office and ambition. Now, as Hitler was preparing to turn the increasingly senseless continuation of the war into the destruction of the country, some of these characteristics emerged again, plunging Speer into 'the crisis of his life'.[33]

It was not only tactical caution that induced him to adopt a two-pronged strategy for the time being. In spite of their gloomy *leitmotif* of the lost war, the memoranda and reports Speer continued to send to Hitler too often referred to a resolute determination to resist and to fight to the end, and one of his senior officials has said that, even in the autumn of 1944, Speer's exhortations to hold out had 'swept us all along'.[34] But while he was using his entire energy to squeeze the last reserves out of the collapsing armaments industry, he soon applied an equal determination to opposing Hitler's destruction orders.

It was a life-or-death gamble. But he was not afraid of the risks, indeed he appeared to seek them out. Walter Rohland, who probably knew Speer better than anyone else, regarded Speer's inclination to throw the dice for the highest stakes as one of his most striking traits, and the fearlessness with which he contradicted Hitler, to the horror of those around him, confirms Rohland's judgement. Rohland also described a low-level air attack in which they had been caught on one of their trips to the front: while everyone else had taken cover in the ditches by the road, Speer had remained standing upright, as if challenging fate. With the same mixture of cold-bloodedness and fatalism he now decided to follow what seemed to him a higher calling. All the other top leaders were hiding behind orders or were nowhere to be found. Although, as Speer rightly remarked, they had all justified their plans of world conquest by arguing that they were safeguarding the survival of the nation, when it came to the crunch, they had shown only fear and cowardice.[35]

In August Speer had the opportunity of a personal conversation with Dietrich Stahl, the head of the main committee for ammunition. Stahl felt an obligation towards his minister, who had once saved him from the clutches of the Gestapo. 'To my complete surprise,' Stahl testified at Nuremberg, 'I found, for the first time, a leading and responsible figure who viewed the actual situation soberly and clearly and who had the courage not only to conduct such conversations, by which he was risking his life, but also to act with determination.' Speer told him that nothing would have been easier, after the attacks on him during his illness, than not to return to his post; but he had resumed his activity 'to erect a dam in industry so that the lunatic idea of total destruction of all industrial and supply plants – and sacrificing the last man – could be prevented'.[36]

When, on returning from the west, Speer had learned of Hitler's 'scorched earth' intentions he had not protested. Instead, on the following morning he dictated a letter to the Gauleiters, which he submitted to headquarters for approval. In a sense it simply disregarded Hitler's

Hitler at the map table with the Hungarian prime minister, Sztojay. Behind him, from left to right: the foreign minister, von Ribbentrop, and Generals Korten, Warlimont, Göring, Keitel and Jodl, as well as an unidentified Hungarian general. After the Allied invasion, meetings at the Führer's headquarters often seemed unreal. The fronts were breaking up and planned operations were almost unthinkable.

recent orders, stating that, 'the Führer has declared that he can shortly reconquer the territories now lost. Since the Western areas are vital for the armaments and war production needed to continue fighting, all evacuation measures must be geared to the possibility of restoring the industry of these areas to full function ... Not until the last moment are the industrial installations to be rendered useless for a considerable time by "paralysation"...' Then he gave some details. Shortly afterwards Speer was astonished to be told that Hitler had approved the text and passed it on. He had merely added a sceptical reservation to Speer's opening sentence. It now read: 'Recapture of part of the territories now lost in the West is by no means ruled out.'[37]

Like everything he did, Speer's counter-measures grew at a restless pace over the next few weeks. He was permanently on the move; between January and April 1945 alone more than seventy trips with over a hundred conferences have been recorded.[38] To avoid the enemy's ground-attack aircraft he usually set out at dusk, along roads hopelessly congested by troops, supply convoys, fleeing civilians and evacuees. Whenever he set out in daylight he had to spend hours seeking cover in patches of woodland or roadside ditches. He was mostly accompanied by his liaison officer to the general staff, the young Major von Poser, for whom he soon developed a feeling of amicable trust. Together they drove all over the Ruhr mining area and the other western regions, organizing, negotiating and trying not only to get production going again on a makeshift basis, but also to keep the radical Gauleiters from implementing the destruction which had in many cases already been prepared. Speer appointed so-called immobilization commissioners to keep an eye on them. Occasionally he also took Theodor Hupfauer along, whom he had appointed to succeed Liebel as chief of the Central Office. In spite of his background in the SS leaders' corps, Hupfauer soon saw eye to eye with Speer about the hopelessness of the situation and proved extremely useful in his dealings with Himmler and the Party.

As always, Speer steadily extended the scope of his activity, not only disregarding Hitler's orders but acting against them with such temerity that those who found out about it were paralysed with amazement and horror. 'Once again I had what I always wanted or needed,' he said, 'a task, and what is more, the only meaningful one.'[39] When Hitler ordered that supplies for the population in the west be suspended and that all transport capacity be reserved for the troops, Speer sent out food trains instructing them to run, as though blind, 'as far as possible into the fighting zone'. In order to prevent the destruction of factories that were still functioning, he set up armed protection squads and had the prepared explosive charges buried in the mine-shafts. Finally he stopped the production and delivery of industrial explosives altogether. Asked if he had not been afraid that Hitler would find out about his counter-measures, Speer later observed: 'I wanted to offend and throw my weight into the balance.'[40]

Over and above these unauthorized measures, Speer also ignored Hitler's express order to step up poison gas production by every means and instead ordered that manufacture of the chemicals required be stopped. When, on one occasion, he confided in Göring, explaining that he could no longer obey Hitler's destruction orders, the Reich Marshal replied that if this was so he had better go abroad. He himself would keep silent. Jodl, on the other hand, tolerated Speer's unauthorized actions without a word and Guderian, recently appointed chief of the army's general staff, actually encouraged Speer. Covered by the general chaos in command structures, Speer issued six instructions in the name of General Winter of the Wehrmacht High Command for the preservation of bridges and transport installations, and eventually, along with Colonel Baumbach and a few Luftwaffe officers, made preparations to foil the plans of leading Party figures to escape responsibility by fleeing abroad.[41]

Around the middle of October Hitler decided to play his 'last card' and to try to bring about a change in the fortunes of war by launching an offensive in the west. He rejected all arguments about Germany's inferiority in troops, weapons and fuel, just as he ignored warnings of the crushing Allied air superiority. Basically this foray was no different from the destruction orders, it was just the military variant of his increasing blatant revenge against his own people. In vain did the general staff draw his attention to the troop concentrations beyond the Oder, pointing to an imminent large-scale offensive by the Red Army. In a conversation which revealed the manic system of the past few months, Hitler explained to Speer that the recent reverses and destructions meant nothing. 'What does it all matter, Speer!', he said in one of his endless monologues. 'I only laugh at them ... The enemy's advance is actually a help to us. People fight fanatically only when the war reaches their own front doors. That's how people are ... No city will be left in the enemy's hands until it's a heap of ruins! ... It is those who are ruthless, not the cowards, who win! Remember this: it isn't technical superiority that is decisive. We lost that long ago. I know that too!' Then he continued, possibly giving a warning hint: 'I won't tolerate any opposition, Speer. When the war is over, the people can vote on me, for all I care. But anybody who disagrees now is going straight to the gallows! If the German people cannot understand me, I'll fight this fight alone. Let them go ahead and leave me! The reward only ever comes from history. Don't expect anything from the populace!'[42] But whereas some hopes of victory still flickered behind this declaration of destruction, Nicolaus von Below also heard him say about the same time: 'The war is lost. The superiority is too great.'[43]

The so-called Ardennes offensive began under low cloud on 16 December 1944 with some thirty divisions and 1,400 tanks, and initially it scored an impressive success. But only a few days later the sky cleared and enemy aircraft appeared over the combat zone in dense swarms. Within hours they smashed the German formations, paralysed supplies and caused traffic chaos that put an abrupt end to all military operations. In the end the shooting-down ratio between the German

In December 1944 Hitler struck his final blow. The Ardennes offensive, which began
with thirty divisions under low cloud cover, initially produced impressive results. But
then the skies cleared and Allied aircraft appeared in huge numbers above the battle
area. Within a few hours the operation was over. This photograph taken on 29
December 1944 shows destroyed vehicles abandoned by German troops.

Luftwaffe and the enemy air forces was nearly one to ten. A week later,
on 23 December, Field Marshal Model pronounced that the offensive
had 'finally failed'. Despite his profound doubts about the sense of the
enterprise and its success, Speer had once more made every effort to
'squeeze out of production' whatever was possible. Hitler had said that
this was to be 'our last effort', and, Speer told himself, 'if it fails we shall
at least have it all behind us.' But now, to the minister's consternation,
Hitler ordered that battle continue. This time von Below heard him say:
'We may go down. But we shall take a world with us.'[44]

On New Year's Eve, when he arrived at Ziegenberg, the Führer's
western headquarters near Bad Nauheim, known as the *Adlerhorst*, the

Eagle's Eyrie, Speer found the euphoric, almost drunken atmosphere in Hitler's entourage all the more disturbing. For more than a week he had followed operations on the Ardennes front. Wherever he went he had met with scattered units, tanks that were stuck or burnt out, and dead and wounded. Deeply depressed and still stunned by the images of devastation and a sense of total impotence, he now found himself in a spectral company of carousers. Uniformed orderlies were scurrying about, serving champagne, staff officers, secretaries and Party leaders were standing around, listening to Hitler lecturing them with growing intensity about the impending year of victory. Most of them looked straight ahead, serious and silent, but the longer Hitler spoke the more their features lit up. Speer observed Hitler's magic taking effect once more and, for a moment, even sweeping him along. In the end the mood almost became frivolous or at least carefree, as if the New Year would bring new hope.

Early the following morning the Luftwaffe mounted a last desperate large-scale attack. To support the bogged-down Ardennes offensive all operational fighters and bombers, more than a thousand in all, were concentrated in the west to destroy enemy airfields, command posts and radar installations in a surprise strike. Again, the German formations initially scored impressive successes, in spite of enemy opposition. But they had taken off two hours later than originally planned. Because the rules of secrecy had been tightened for this engagement, it was impossible to communicate the delay to the ground troops. As they turned back, the German formations therefore found themselves in the fire of their own anti-aircraft batteries. More than three hundred planes were lost that day, sealing the fate of the Luftwaffe.[45]

Three days later Goebbels appeared at Ziegenberg. At the big conference which, as always, met at the beginning of the year, he demanded additional reinforcements for the Wehrmacht, 'because otherwise', he explained, 'we cannot continue the war'. He dismissed Speer's retort that, with the exception of the civil service, practically all available manpower had long been assigned to front-line action, and called for a '*levée en masse*'. When Speer stuck to his view and mentioned the foreseeable end of entire categories of manufacture, Goebbels, as Speer reported, stared at him aghast and then, addressing Hitler rather than him 'in a solemn voice', exclaimed: 'Then you ... will bear the historic responsibility that the war is lost because of a shortfall of a few 100,000 soldiers! Why don't you say yes at last? Consider! Your fault!' In the end Hitler sided with Goebbels and the army was promised 240,000 men for the first quarter of 1945, which of course could never be raised. During the ensuing armaments discussion Hitler pointedly ignored his armaments minister, addressing himself exclusively to Saur, so much so that Goebbels was astonished at the indifference with which Speer reacted to his loss of power. But when Goebbels spoke to him about it, Speer did not answer. Goebbels then walked over to Hitler, who was so upset by the quarrel that his left arm was trembling violently. The following day Goebbels returned to Berlin to judge the epic film *Kolberg*, just finished and designed to turn the defence of that Pommeranian town against Napoleon's armies in 1807 into an inspiring example of the will to resist.[46]

On 12 January 1945 the Soviet formations opened their full-scale offensive from the Baranov area north-east of Cracow. The very next day they went over to the attack along the entire front from the Carpathians to the Bay of Danzig, crushing the battle-weary German units and cutting off contact between them. All proposals to check the thrust by flexible movements failed in the face of Hitler's obstinacy. Soon familiar German place-names cropped up in the Wehrmacht communiqués for the first time – Oppeln, Gleiwitz, Ratibor, Rominten and Insterburg, and not long afterwards Breslau too. A fortnight later the Red Army had more or less cut off East Prussia from the Reich and reached the boundary of the Upper Silesian industrial region. At the middle of the eastern front its armoured spearheads stood some seventy kilometres from Berlin.

Hitler had returned to the Reich Chancellery in Berlin and the increasingly obvious end did not seem to impair his delirious mood. Although the Führer now decided to suspend offensive operations in the west, which were anyway bogged down and had almost all been thrown back to their starting positions, Guderian was horrified when he learned that Hitler had directed the SS Sixth Armoured Army not to the Oder but to the Budapest area. A letter from Speer, urging him to deploy the Luftwaffe, now hopelessly outnumbered in the west, against the Red Army, only made Hitler laugh – even though he remarked that Speer was entirely right, before turning to the order of the day with a shrug. When Speer returned a few days later from a trip to Katowice, already in the battle zone, and showed Hitler a series of photographs of the destruction in the city and especially of the inhabitants fleeing in panic in icy temperatures, Hitler angrily pushed the pictures aside.[47]

During the weeks that followed, whenever Guderian recommended a tactical withdrawal or the shortening of a front, he met with Hitler's bitter opposition. In their combination of omnipotence mania and lack of realism on one side and intransigency on the other, these clashes, some of which the chief of the general staff vividly depicted in his memoirs, resembled a dialogue from the theatre of the absurd. When he informed Foreign Minister von Ribbentrop of the war situation and suggested the opening of armistice negotiations with the Western Powers, Guderian once more encountered Hitler's wrath. He referred to his 'Fundamental Order No. 1' which decreed that no one was permitted to pass any information from his own sphere of activity to a third person. Anyone who offended against this, he added with a glance at Guderian, and for instance 'called on the Reich foreign minister to inform him of the situation in the East', would be regarded as a traitor to his country, and his family would bear the consequences as well as himself. Over the next few days a number of tightened regulations were issued and they all referred to the principle of '*Sippenhaftung*', liability of the whole family for the actions of one of its members. Henceforth Ernst Kaltenbrunner attended the situation conferences more and more frequently. He was a stony guest, keeping to the background and silently observing the scene. 'For he had no business there, nor was he ever asked anything.'[48]

For a fleeting moment Speer was troubled by the thought that the head of the SS Reich Security Central Office was present not least because of him. The drive for destruction had steadily increased since Hitler's return to Berlin, but Speer had not abandoned any of his counter-measures, although there were now some indications that Hitler's entourage, at least, had knowledge of them. On 27 January Speer had presented a kind of final report of his ministry's work to some three hundred of his closest staff, which besides listing another overwhelming number of success rates included a thank-you and goodbye. At the same time Speer left Saur in charge of the technical leadership of his authority and from then onwards he no longer participated in any armaments conference. He instructed the remaining staff from the distant days of the General Inspectorate for Building to collect photographs, drawings and architectural sketches and keep them in a safe place. Three days later, on the anniversary of the Seizure of Power, he addressed another memorandum to Hitler; in stubborn contravention of the prohibition on passing critical evaluations of the situation to third parties, he had six copies made and addressed them to the leading military figures. Speer's memorandum stated that, in the field of armaments for which he was responsible, the war was at an end and there was no

The exposure of the conspiracy of 20 July 1944 was largely directed by Ernst Kaltenbrunner, chief of the Reich Central Security Office of the SS. Speer, too, was under intense surveillance, and Kaltenbrunner went on suspecting him to the last.

chance of 'even remotely covering ... the front's requirements of ammunition, weapons and tanks'.[49]

Hitler waited for a few days, and Speer later asked himself whether this was a sign of indecision or another attempt to unsettle him. On 5 February Hitler summoned him to his private office in the Reich Chancellery, as in the years when they were close, but this time he also asked Saur to be present. Without at first taking any notice of Speer he discussed the armaments problems of the next few months with Saur, thereby providing him with an opportunity to disprove, point by point, his immediate superior's memorandum of a few days before. Then Hitler broke off abruptly and turned to Speer. Without a trace of emotion, he accused him in a low cutting voice of infringing Fundamental Order No. l, of which he had recently reminded him, adding that even Speer was not permitted to draw and disseminate any conclusions from the armaments situation. He did not use many words. But his tone struck Speer as eerier than any explosions he had ever witnessed, and on leaving Hitler he felt that this was his final warning.[50]

Although Hitler had not mentioned the minister's opposition to his destruction policy, Speer felt he could not continue his game of dissembling and ambiguity. But no sooner had he returned from the Reich Chancellery than his 'fatherly friend', Friedrich Lüschen of the Siemens concern, who was responsible for the electricity industry, called on him and handed him a sheet with a few sentences from *Mein Kampf*. Among other things they stated: 'There can be no state authority as an aim in itself since in that case any tyranny on earth would be unassailable and sanctified. If a nation is led to ruin by the behaviour of the government then rebellion is not only the right but the duty of any member of that nation.'[51]

His response to these grandiloquent words instantly freed Speer from the helplessness into which Hitler's rejection had thrown him. For a brief moment his romantic inclination, which like all romaticism made him susceptible to vagueness, led him to indulge in reflections which, in their way, were no less removed from reality than the absurdities he condemned among Hitler's entourage. For a while he considered taking Hitler at his word from *Mein Kampf*, and proposing to him that, together with his ministers, the Party leaders and the Wehrmacht High Command, he address a proclamation to the enemy powers, declaring that they were ready to surrender themselves, provided that, in return, the German people were granted tolerable conditions for their continued existence. Later Speer himself admitted the operatic nature of this plan with its Wagnerian idea of self-sacrifice and redemption.[52]

The consternation he met with everywhere quickly made him give up the idea. He got a little further with a second, equally impracticable consideration. During an air-raid in the middle of February, he came across Dietrich Stahl in the ministry's air-raid shelter. He was the colleague with whom he had recently discussed the dwindling prospects of the war. The two men withdrew to one of the small, separate rooms of the bunker. When the heavy door of the cell had closed behind them, Speer said he could no longer stand being 'governed by madmen'. The German nation would be totally destroyed unless 'some decisive action' were taken 'against these insane plans of destruction'. After much soul-searching he himself had come to the decision 'to put an end to this business, by violence if need be'. But there was 'no point in removing a single individual; the whole most dangerous, immediate entourage must go,' he added.[53] After a brief hesitation he asked Stahl if he could get hold of the new poison gas 'Tabun', explaining that he wanted to introduce it through the ventilation shaft into the bunker underneath the

Reich Chancellery. Stahl declared himself ready to help in any way he could and collected some information the very next day. However, the information was that Tabun consisted of two separate components which only acquired their deadly effect through an explosion. Since an explosion would rip off the thin metal air-shaft covers, allowing the gas to disperse in all directions, the plan was dropped.

Speer and Stahl therefore decided to use 'a traditional kind of gas' and Speer turned to the chief engineer of the Reich Chancellery, Johannes Hentschel. He told him that Hitler had recently complained about the stale air in the bunker and instructed him to replace the filtering plant. In this way he hoped to have unimpeded access to the air-shaft for a few days. But when shortly afterwards, even before Stahl got hold of the gas, Hentschel inspected the area, armed SS sentries were posted everywhere and a chimney-stack, almost four metres high, had been built on top of the ventilation shaft, making the inlet inaccessible. The general scepticism which met his plan of action when it became known after the war is indicated by the sneering remark that 'the second most powerful man in the state did not have a ladder.'[54] Anyway, the plan, which sprung more from a romantic cops-and-robbers impulse than the kind of perfectionism Speer normally upheld, had finally failed.

In conversation with the (meanwhile dismissed) General Galland and the Luftwaffe colonel Werner Baumbach, the idea next arose of arresting and detaining Hitler's entire entourage – Bormann, Himmler, Goebbels, Ley and many others – on their way home to their mansions around Berlin and perhaps even handing them over to the Allies. Speer himself, as Dietrich Stahl testified, was willing to lead one of the commandos of this coup. But when the plans were worked out, the weapons provided and the squads won over, one of the generals privy to the plan succeeded in talking Speer out of this adventure. A later idea was to use a seaplane, which had, from Norway, supplied a German weather station in the Far North, for an escape to Greenland and there to await the end of the war. The necessary foodstuffs had already been prepared, as well as medical supplies, tents, weapons, a kayak and several boxes of books, when Speer had misgivings and called off the operation significantly codenamed 'Winnetou', after the Red Indian hero of Karl May's novels. These fantasies, with their confused, partly ridiculous and partly romantic elements, glowed briefly, produced a few days of hectic activity and then fizzled out. All that remained was the more enduring concern that they might accidentally come to light in retrospect.[55]

Instead, Speer once again turned to more promising tasks. When Hitler demanded that all available transport be made available for the conduct of the war, directing Speer to issue a decree setting out the order of priorities for goods that had to be transported, the minister ordered that foods and other supplies for the population be safeguarded first and foremost. To avoid an impending famine, he provided his ministry's trucks for the transportation of seedstock and farm machinery. Through the planning office he gave instructions that destroyed nitrogen plants, indispensable to the production of artificial fertilizer, were to be rebuilt even before hydrogenation plants. Armaments were put at the very bottom of his list and soon disappeared from it altogether.

Around this time Hitler conceived yet another horror programme. In a series of decrees he ordered that the population be evacuated from threatened regions both in the West and the East; an instruction issued through Jodl and Bormann stated bluntly: 'No consideration of any kind can at this time be shown for the population.' A fortnight earlier, at the beginning of March, Goebbels had noted that 'some seventeen million people [had been] evacuated' in the meantime. Although he found the figure 'downright terrifying' and urged that the matter 'be left to its own devices … at least in the West', Hitler was not to be deflected from his decision. On 14 March Goebbels' diary states:

> The Führer has now decided that, despite the extraordinary difficulties involved, evacuation is to continue in the West. The evacuation cannot even be carried out because the population simply refuses to leave its villages and towns … The decision taken by the Führer is based on totally mistaken assumptions. I gather this also from a report which Speer has given to me after a trip to the West about the situation there, according to which evacuation is no longer possible. Speer speaks very angrily about the measures taken. He takes the view that it is not the task of a war policy to lead a nation to heroic doom, which, after all, the Führer himself has clearly emphasized … in his book *Mein Kampf*.[56]

There is probably no clearer indication of Hitler's waning authority than this note by the propaganda minister who, after years of strenuous, often almost bigoted veneration, is for the first time openly critical of Hitler. The very next day Goebbels went further by agreeing with Speer's 'correct view' that the policy of 'scorched earth', as it is called there, 'cannot be our task but the task of our enemies'.[57]

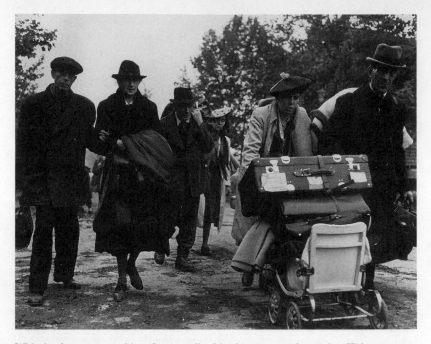

With the fronts approaching, Speer realized in the autumn of 1944 that Hitler was
increasingly intent on turning Germany into a wasteland. At the same time he ordered
the threatened regions to be evacuated, until finally – according to Goebbels' diary –
seventeen million people roamed the roads, as in this photograph of refugees near
Aachen.

However, when Speer tentatively hinted that they might now join
forces in mitigating the war and its sufferings, just as they had done in
stepping up the war effort, Goebbels pretended not to hear. Speer
himself meanwhile continued acting against Hitler's orders more and
more openly. He later remarked that he had observed with growing
astonishment how Hitler, 'that destroyed person resembling a ruin', was
still displaying an extraordinary degree of suggestive power and was
perhaps more compelling than ever before. In his impatience Speer
addressed another memorandum to him on 18 March which violated
the recently tightened prohibitions in more ways than one. It declared
that the point had been reached when civilian needs deserved to be
granted priority over military necessities; it predicted 'the final collapse
of the German economy' within four to eight weeks, and concluded
with the observation that in future the basis of people's existence must
be preserved even when 'reconquest no longer seems possible'. With a

touch of didacticism and condescension he then came to the core of Hitler's 'hold out' strategy, reminding him that 'no one has the right to take the view that the fate of the German people is tied to his personal fate'.[58]

Speer knew that this time he had gone to the limit or even beyond it, and he therefore deemed it advisable to present his memorandum via an intermediary. When he left his office in the evening with two copies and walked across to the deep bunker under the Chancellery he seemed unconcerned, but his secretary later said: 'We thought he was mad.'[59] Speer approached von Below and asked him to deliver the memorandum to Hitler. In order to contain the expected outburst of fury he instructed him to wait for a suitable moment and to hint at the contents verbally before handing the paper over. Next Speer went to the Führer's personal aide, Julius Schaub, and asked for a dedicated photograph of Hitler, to be dated the following day, Speer's fortieth birthday; after all, he added, he was the only one among the Führer's close collaborators who had never asked for, or received, such a photograph. He was hoping that his request would put Hitler in a conciliatory mood and indicate that, while he opposed his policy of destruction, he continued to revere him. Speer then prepared to leave the immediate danger zone of the headquarters by flying overnight to Königsberg, which had been cut off.

Things worked out differently. At the evening situation conference Hitler had overridden all objections and ordered the compulsory evacuation of the Saar territory. Speer therefore decided to travel to the west. Towards midnight he received the congratulations for his birthday, and as Hitler handed him the red leather case with his photograph he said: 'I find it so difficult to write a few words myself. You know how my hand shakes.' But when Speer had deciphered the dedication which expressed gratitude and perpetual friendship, he forgot all caution and handed Hitler the second copy of his memorandum.[60] While he was preparing to set off he was summoned back to Hitler's office.

Hitler had evidently read the memorandum in the meantime, but he made no mention of it at all. Only his voice was strangely angry as he pressed Speer to undertake the trip with his, Hitler's, personal driver, Erich Kempka. Speer immediately sensed the trap behind this seemingly thoughtful offer. Kempka, who held an SS rank, would not only make any confidential talk with his permanent companion von Poser impossible, but also complicate his 'treasonable' efforts. He therefore resisted for a while. Only when he noticed that his objections were merely arousing Hitler's mistrust did he finally agree. He had got to the door when Hitler suddenly called after him: 'This time you'll get a written reply to your memorandum!' Then, after a short pause, he added, 'in an icy voice', the words which Speer had heard at the Gauleiter conference in Posen the year before and had not forgotten since: 'If the war is lost, the nation will also be lost. It is not necessary to worry about the basics which the German people will need for its most rudimentary survival. On the contrary, it is best for us to destroy even these things. For the nation has proved to be the weaker, and the future belongs solely to the stronger eastern nation. In any case only those who are inferior will remain after this struggle, for the good have already been killed.'[61]

Immediately afterwards Speer set out. In order to reach the head-quarters of the Commander-in-Chief West near Bad Nauheim before daybreak and before the appearance of enemy ground-attack aircraft, they tore down the motorway with a roaring compressor and full head-lights and fog-lights. But Kesselring refused to meet Speer's demand to save human life or manufacturing plants, hiding behind his military duty to obey commands; he had received his orders from the Führer and was not prepared to negotiate on them. Even the Party representa-tive on Kesselring's staff, to whom Speer turned next, as well as, a little later, the SS General Hausser and the Gauleiter of the Saar, proved more understanding, regarding the orders both for evacuation and for destruction either as impossible to implement or as irresponsible.

At his next stop Field Marshal Model, whose headquarters were in a Westerwald village, promised to preserve the transport facilities of the Ruhr. As their conversation was drawing to a close an officer entered the room with a teleprint message. Model glanced at it and then ner-vously handed it to Speer. The Field Marshal's expression had suddenly petrified. It was Hitler's 'written reply' to Speer's memorandum of the preceding day.

The telex has come down as the 'Nero order'. It was a reply in the sense that, sentence by sentence, it ordered the opposite of what Speer had been demanding for months. Even the opening passage directly opposed him, though without mentioning his name: 'It is a mistake to believe', Hitler reprimanded him, 'that destroyed or temporarily para-lysed transport, telecommunication, industrial and supply installations can be started up again for our own purposes after the reconquest of lost regions. The enemy will only leave us with a scorched earth on his retreat and drop any consideration for the population.' The command

Around the turn of 1944–5 the Allies reached the German frontiers, both in the east and in the west. Taken in December 1944, this photograph shows a warning notice on the German-Belgian frontier.

then brusquely ordered the total destruction of anything that 'the enemy might in any way make use of for the continuation of his struggle immediately or in the foreseeable future'. At the same time it annulled all orders to the contrary and stripped Speer of his power by charging the Gauleiters with the implementation of the destruction orders.[62]

The talk with Model had thereby become pointless. As soon as dusk fell, Speer set out for Berlin. Towards five o'clock on the morning of 21 March he arrived exhausted in the small flat which he shared with Hupfauer in the half-destroyed ministry. He woke Hupfauer, pulled up a chair and after a long weary silence simply said: 'Hitler is a criminal.' When Hupfauer sat up, 'shocked', as he later reported, Speer without a word handed him the teleprint he had received a few hours earlier.[63]

He finally seemed to realize how far he had strayed. But he was still plagued by doubts, and the weeks of impending collapse showed clearly how heavily the break weighed on him, which he had now carried out both in thought and deed.

Chapter Nine
END WITHOUT END

Everything was heading for collapse. There were no cohesive fronts left in the west or in the east. By the beginning of March the Allies had overrun the West Wall along its entire length from Aachen to the Palatinate. They had crossed the Rhine at Remagen and before long at other points. When Speer walked across to the Reich Chancellery on 21 March he learned that Kolberg had fallen two days previously, but that Goebbels had demanded that its fall not be mentioned in the Wehrmacht communiqué because the 'psychological shock' was not 'convenient for the Kolberg film'. In one of the corridors Speer had suddenly bumped into Hitler, who was monosyllabic and only casually asked how his trip had gone. Strangely embarrassed, he made no mention of the memorandum or of his reply to it, and Speer thought it wiser not to bring it up. 'I was shaking a little,' he later wrote.[1]

He called on Guderian and, as if Hitler's orders no longer concerned him, handed him a copy of his memorandum; Keitel, on the other hand, for whom another copy was intended, rejected it with dismay. Speer observed how the atmosphere of anger, confusion and will to destruction was steadily thickening. A few days earlier Hitler had ordered the execution of the four officers who had been posted at the Remagen bridge and had been unable to set off in time the explosive charges which had been damaged in a low-level air attack. He also ordered the death sentence against Friedrich Fromm to be carried out now. At the situation conferences, Speer was told, Hitler referred more and more frequently to the hardships of the Time of the Struggle and how they had been overcome. Whenever Saur submitted his production programmes Hitler set him dates which were far in the future, announced schedules for December 1945, and fixed the beginning of production of the new jet bomber for the 'end of the year'. He also gave way in the months-long quarrel about the Me-262 and ordered the machine to be built as a fighter after all.[2] When Speer was invited to the armaments conference the following day, he declined. Instead he met with a few industrialists and leading generals to agree a common line against the 'scorched earth' policy. How unsafe the situation had become for him emerges from the fact that General Thomale made a number of reliable officers available for Speer's personal protection.[3]

As he was largely condemned to inactivity in Berlin, Speer set off again for the west two days later, on 23 March, alarmed by news of a British thrust towards the Ruhr where the three Gauleiters of the region were determined to carry out Hitler's destruction orders. Rohland, who was still in charge of the Ruhr Staff, informed him that the expertly prepared demolitions were due to begin the following morning. Speer hastily summoned some twenty trustworthy managers of the major mines and invited them to seize any explosives still in the factories or the Organisation Todt and either destroy them or pass them on to Model. From the remaining stock of an arms factory he obtained fifty sub-machine-guns, to be issued to reliable workers with instructions to prevent any demolition work, if necessary with maximum violence. The sub-machine-guns, he added by way of reassurance, represented even greater firing power as the police and Party authorities had recently been ordered to surrender their weapons to the army. But although the Gauleiters were thus prevented from implementing their destruction orders, Speer failed to win them over. The Düsseldorf Party chief Florian read out to him an appeal to set the city ablaze, wallowing in the images of a burning sea of evacuated houses, into which the enemy would move as into a ghost town.[4]

By then Speer no longer even pretended to be obeying Hitler's instructions. Upon his urgings, Field Marshal Model declared himself willing, as far as possible, to keep military operations in the Ruhr away from industrial plants. Now Speer was also able to persuade Kesselring's headquarters east of Frankfurt to adopt a 'considerate interpretation' of the Nero order. The degree of confusion became clear when even the chief of staff of the commander-in-chief was unable to provide any information on the present line of the front – except that the Americans were advancing towards Frankfurt. When Speer was told that the Gauleiter of Baden, Wagner, had ordered the water and power installations in every town of his Gau to be blown up, he decided to drive to Heidelberg to countermand the orders and take leave of his parents. Keeping well clear of Frankfurt he found himself at one point in no-man's-land with depopulated villages lying in tense silence. Speer invalidated the demolition orders for Heidelberg by having them

Hitler in spring 1945. An observer of the final few months said of the atmosphere in the bunker below the Berlin Reich Chancellery: 'Nothing was genuine there except fear.'

countersigned, as prescribed, and then committing them to the mail which had long since ceased functioning. His next stop was Würzburg, where the Gauleiter had decided, among other things, to set fire to the Schweinfurt ball-bearings plant. Only by using the well-tried ruse that strong units had already been concentrated for a counterstroke did Speer succeed in preventing the plan. In the evening of 27 March he was back in Berlin.

There the process of stripping him of his power had continued. The day before, Hitler had put SS-Obergruppenführer Kammler, who was already responsible for the rocket weapons, in charge of all air armaments, also authorizing him to draw at will on any expert in the Speer ministry. To add insult to injury, Speer was required to confirm in writing Kammler's right to do so. In addition he found the implementation regulations to the destruction order of 19 March, worked out by the Führer's headquarters. In the field of communications, these stipulated that all telephone, telegraph or repeater stations, as well as the switching centres of long-distance cables, be made 'thoroughly unusable through explosives, fire or demolition' and that relocation and connection diagrams be destroyed, as well as all stores of spare parts, in order to prevent repair for the foreseeable future. Similarly, the implementation order for the transport system demanded the 'total destruction' of all rail tracks, operations and workshop facilities, as well as all rolling and floating stock. It continued: 'The objective is to create a transport desert ... shortage of explosives calls for inventive utilization of all possibilities of permanent destruction (use of all kinds of ammunition, including captured ammunition, firing equipment and the smashing of vital parts).'[5]

For a while Speer was uncertain how to react. After telephone calls to General Thomale, Guderian, the industrialist Röchling and others he again decided to proceed openly and walked over to the Reich Chancellery. As on previous occasions, he met with absent or frosty expressions in the corridors, and as soon as he approached a group of people they would casually drift apart, 'as if I were struck by a kind of leprosy'.[6] Everyone evidently knew about his insubordination and how matters stood with him. The day before Goebbels had noted: Speer 'keeps saying that he will not lend his hand to cutting the thread of life of the German people. That was to be left to our opponents.' The Führer intended to face Speer

with a very serious alternative. Either he conforms to the principles of the present conduct of the war, or the Führer will dispense with his services. He says bitterly that he would rather sit in emergency accommodation or crawl underground than have palaces built for him by a collaborator who fails at the critical phase. The Führer is getting extraordinarily tough towards Speer ... Above all, the Führer wants to put an end to Speer's talk which has a decidedly defeatist character.

Hitler, Goebbels added, was already talking 'of a possible replacement of Speer by Saur'.[7]

This time Hitler did not keep him waiting. No sooner had Speer's arrival been announced than an aide appeared, requesting that he follow him. The fifty steep steps which they descended in silence into the 'death vault' of the bunker seemed to him, he later recorded, like the precipitous slope on which he found himself. As he stepped into the office, Hitler was standing close to the door and for the first time Speer noticed the veins of anger on his forehead and temples. It struck him as all the more curious that Hitler again spoke in a low, almost toneless, voice and, without a word of greeting, immediately showered him with accusations. Bormann, he began, had informed him about Speer's conference with the Gauleiters of the Ruhr and told him that Speer had not only incited them openly to disregard Hitler's orders but had also described the war as finally lost. Speer knew what the penalty for that was, and were he not his architect he would apply to him the consequences necessary in such a case. Partly from exhaustion but partly also from a sense of being in the right, Speer remained entirely calm during the encounter: seeing Hitler's difficulty in keeping his emotions under control, Speer had, he wrote, for the first time even felt a sense of superiority over him. Then he replied tersely: 'Take the measures you think necessary and grant no consideration to me as an individual.'[8]

This almost blasé answer seemed to confuse Hitler, and a short pause ensued. Then he changed his tone and, as if he wanted to create an impression of solicitude, said that Speer had broken off his stay in Merano much too soon and was obviously overworked. He had therefore given instructions for him to take a 'belated holiday' and had already looked around for a deputy. Speer contradicted and, although Hitler did not relent, insisted that he was in good health and had no intention of taking any leave or allowing a deputy to take decisions in his name. If Hitler no longer wanted him as a minister, he would have to dismiss him. While they were getting more and more entangled in one of those absurd dialogues which had become typical of conversations with Hitler, Speer recalled that only a few hours earlier Guderian had told him that he had been sent on leave. Now, he thought, it seemed to be his turn, because Hitler wanted to do everything to ensure that his rule did not simply come to an end, but that the country and its people went down with him.

With growing impatience Hitler insisted that he was not, at this moment, in a position to dismiss one of his most important ministers: the effect at home and abroad would be devastating. But although he pulled out every emotional stop, Speer remained unmoved and obstinately repeated that he could not possibly take the leave Hitler wished him to take; so long as he was in office he would also run his ministry. 'I am not ill! If you think I am, then sack me!'

Until then they had stood facing each other in the little room. Awkwardly and as though looking for a new approach, Hitler sat down at the table and Speer, unasked, did likewise. If he were at least convinced, Hitler began again, that the war was not lost, then he could continue to run his ministry. Again Speer did not yield. Over the past few months he had declared the opposite too often to be able to retract, he rejoined; besides he did not wish to do so. Hitler then resorted to the long-windedness with which he had always talked away any contradiction, citing remote historical examples of seemingly hopeless situations, as well as personal experiences from the Time of the Struggle and even from the present war. But Speer remained unshaken. Not only his self-esteem, he argued, but even more so his respect for the Führer compelled him to stick to his view. Besides, he did not wish to be one of those who spoke of victory in Hitler's presence without believing in it.

There were several prolonged pauses during which they sat facing each other in silence. Then Hitler resumed the conversation and, often in a very roundabout way, returned to his initial demand. In the end he scaled down his demand step by step, to a purely formal concession. He would, he said, be satisfied with a statement by Speer that all hope was not lost. At that moment, Speer later recorded, he had suddenly realized the danger he was in. A further 'no' would have put an end not only to their conversation but quite possibly also to himself.[9] When therefore, instead of a reply, he stared dejectedly ahead of him, Hitler abruptly changed his tone, adopting the low menacing note on which he had begun the meeting. Perhaps, Speer later assumed, nothing had struck Hitler as forcefully as the realization that his persuasive powers no longer cut any ice even with Speer. Without getting up he indicated with a short impatient gesture that he did not wish to continue the conversation. But, he said, he must insist on an answer, giving him twenty-four hours to think it over: 'Tomorrow you will let me know whether you hope that the war can still be won.'

When Speer returned to his ministry he was welcomed by his staff as if he 'had returned from the dead', but he pointed out that the decision had only been postponed. Feeling a need to be alone, he went across to his emergency quarters and began searching for the one sentence that might satisfy Hitler. But his reflections kept running aground, as Hitler had already suggested the most non-committal formula and, by rejecting it Speer had more or less ruled it out. When he saw no way out he began writing a letter to Hitler, which eventually ran to twenty pages. In its combination of frankness and calculation, grandiloquence, lip-service and sentimentality it not only reflected a momentarily confused state of mind, it also presented, in all its paradoxes, an accurate self-portrait of its writer.

Speer began[10] by observing 'that I would be proud and happy if you would allow me to continue to work for Germany as your colleague. Any abandonment of my post – even if ordered by you – would seem to me, at this crucial time, like desertion.' He had been 'one of the few colleagues who had always been open and honest' with him, and he wished 'to go on doing so'. Then, for the first time, he approached Hitler's critical question whether he 'still had hopes of a successful continuation of the war', but he gave only a partial answer: 'My belief in a favourable turn of our destinies was unbroken until 18 March.' Instead of adding what had changed that day, Speer devoted several paragraphs to explaining that he was really an artist and 'as such had been confronted with a totally alien and difficult task'. He had, he continued, 'achieved a great deal for Germany. Without my work the war might perhaps have been lost in 1942/43.'

Then he spoke of his 'belief in his task', of 'inner decency' and of 'providence': 'I felt sick at heart in 1940 as I watched how we in the wider circles of our leadership lost our self-control during the days of victory. That was the time when we should have proved ourselves in the face of providence by decency and inner modesty. Victory would then have been ours.' Instead, everything had been gambled away and none of the warnings signalled by military reverses had been taken seriously. He had nevertheless managed to cling to his faith 'unshakeably until a few days ago'.

Only then did he come to the real point of conflict, quoting at length Hitler's remarks on the night of 18–19 March, to the effect that if the war were lost the German nation would be lost also and that no consideration should be given to its 'most rudimentary survival'." 'These words profoundly shocked me,' he went on. 'And when, a day later, I read the destruction order and soon afterwards the severe evacuation order, I saw these as the first steps towards the realization of those intentions. But I can no longer believe in the success of our good cause if, in these decisive months, we simultaneously and systematically destroy the basis of our nation's life.' The letter concluded with a string of repeated appeals to withdraw the orders issued: 'If you were able to do this in some form or other, I would have the faith and the courage again to continue working with the utmost energy. You will show understanding for what is going on within me ... It is our duty to make every effort to increase resistance to the utmost. I would not like to be missing from such an effort.' And: 'Destiny is no longer in our hands.' He concluded with the phrase: 'May God protect Germany.'

When Speer had finished the handwritten letter he asked one of Hitler's secretaries to type it out on the Führer's typewriter to make it more legible. But shortly afterwards she informed him that Hitler had forbidden her to accept the letter: 'I don't want a letter from him,' he had said. 'I want to see him and I want his answer by word of mouth.' While Speer was looking for a way out, an aide called on him and requested him to come to Hitler at once. Towards midnight he drove the few hundred metres to the Reich Chancellery. Once again he was led down the fifty steps to the bunker cave.

The time limit had expired and Speer had not succeeded in finding an answer 'which did not exist'. With the 'blind courage' that often drove his staff to despair, he relied on his presence of mind and on the power of empty phrases to which, as he said, they were all susceptible. When he found himself suddenly face to face with Hitler he therefore, after a moment's reflection, merely uttered the words: 'My Führer, I stand unreservedly behind you.' Hitler 'was moved', Speer recalled, his eyes filled with tears, and he himself had also been 'shaken for a moment'.[12] The scene was to repeat itself about four weeks later, more sombrely, more bombastically, and also more grotesquely.

Such was Speer's presence of mind that he immediately seized the opportunity to wrest a concession from Hitler. As he 'unreservedly' stood behind him, he said as soon as Hitler had regained control of himself, he must also be given back the responsibility for the destruction measures. Although Hitler probably suspected that he would continue to foil his instructions, he requested him to draw up an implementation order for the decree of 19 March, which he would sign there and then. When Speer returned with the document they agreed on the draft of a list which was to contain all installations definitely earmarked for destruction. Still relieved and touched at having found his friend again, Hitler remarked in their concluding talk that a 'scorched earth' policy was pointless anyway in a country like Germany and could only be effective in the vast spaces of Russia.[13] Speer never submitted that catalogue of factories and installations earmarked for destruction.

Towards two o'clock in the morning of 30 March he left the Reich Chancellery, not before informing his office from one of the secretariats that his full powers had been restored. Every available member of the staff, from the printers, drivers and teleprint operators to the top officials, was to be summoned immediately. In a short address he threatened: 'I shall punish every one of you who implements this ['scorched earth'] order and I shall protect everyone who refuses to implement this order.'[14]

By four o'clock the first cars and motorcycles were already leaving the ministry with the freshly printed implementation orders which nullified Hitler's demolition orders, as well as with directives for the maintenance of industrial and supply installations. As if he had regained his feverish activity, without which life was meaningless for him, and once more covered by Hitler's authority, he issued orders – here for the preservation of food enterprises, there for the distribution of clothing supplies to the population; he forbade the blowing up of bridges and locks, he travelled and telephoned. At Oldenburg he met the Reich Commissioner for the Netherlands, Arthur Seyss-Inquart, and agreed with him not to put into effect the large-scale inundations ordered by Hitler; similar instructions went out to offices in the east, in Bohemia-Moravia and in northern Italy. Speer stopped demolition measures which had already begun by claiming that his right to confirm them had been disregarded, and towards obstreperous Gauleiters he resorted again to the (by now absurd) assurance that the reconquest of certain territories had just been decided or was indeed under way. He justified the preservation of the rail track near Saalfeld by the manufactures of the Zeiss works in Jena, that of the bridges and tracks near Northeim by the transportation of the V-weapons, and so on.[15]

In all these cases Speer referred to Hitler's order, which, however, was only a blanket authority; Speer never sought to obtain the individual authorization which Hitler had promised him. He realized that Hitler's rule now only extended to some outposts with blindly devoted followers as well as to a zone which ended a few kilometres outside his bunker. Nevertheless, the machinery of the vast command apparatus appeared to continue undisturbed. Hitler issued his orders; Bormann or Keitel translated them into instructions, directives or circulars, and Goebbels furnished them with extravagant or apocalyptic incantations. But as each day passed, one more piece sunk into nothingness. Outside the bunker 'other laws' applied, as well as, increasingly, Speer's will. His long-time ambition of becoming 'the second man in the state' and Hitler's successor was now being fulfilled in a way, except that the state in question no longer existed.

The chains of information, which were the nervous system of the Führer regime, also began to break or to be deliberately interrupted. Even the reports reaching headquarters were increasingly subject to mood and opportunity. Since Guderian's departure the picture of the military situation had become increasingly distorted. The phantom armies which Hitler commanded, the confused operations for which he assembled non-existent formations for the 'decisive battle of the war' at the gates of Berlin, the armoured divisions and Luftwaffe formations which he nervously moved this way and that on his map were all the result not only of his flight from reality but, by then, also of the inadequate reports that were reaching him from the approaching fronts. Occasionally he invited Speer to see him. The old plans would be produced and together they would stare in silence at the architectural designs for Linz or Berlin. From the strange calm that seemed to fill Hitler, Speer concluded that the counter-measures he continued to pursue were kept from the Führer, partially at least. Indeed, Otto Ohlendorf, the head of the SS Security Service, later stated that during the final weeks he had been fully informed of Speer's activities, but had not passed this information on. At this time Speer received a radio signal from his former top officials in the Ruhr pocket: 'This is to say goodbye. Everything is proceeding according to plan. The Ruhr will always be grateful to you.'[16]

In March Speer had learned that Goebbels intended to call up the members of the Berlin Philharmonic Orchestra for the *Volkssturm*, the scraping of the barrel. To foil this plan he ordered the personnel records of the musicians at the Wehrmacht recruiting offices to be shredded. Speer informed the orchestra, as well as friends and acquaintances, that the irreversible end would have arrived, and that escape or hiding was advisable, as soon as Anton Bruckner's Fourth Symphony was on the programme. The concert took place on 12 April, and in addition to Bruckner's symphony, Beethoven's violin concerto and the final scene of Wagner's *Twilight of the Gods* were performed. When the audience, huddled in thick overcoats, left the unheated hall, uniformed boys from the Hitler Youth stood at the exits, handing out potassium cyanide capsules free of charge.[17]

Around that time Rudolf Wolters, who had meanwhile returned to his home in Westphalia, went back to the ministry in Pariser Platz again. When Speer questioned him about the mood of the country, Wolters replied that people could not understand why no one in the Führer's closer circle did not get him out of the way: 'Why don't they simply do him in?' Wolters added that 'surely no one' could do this 'better' than his interlocutor. Instead of a reply Speer produced the pistol which he had been carrying for some days and slid it across the table to Wolters in a gesture of resignation.

In spite of reinstating Speer's powers, Hitler kept returning almost compulsively to his destruction plans. When Speer submitted to him an order countermanding several bridge demolitions Hitler refused 'in the sharpest manner' to sign it. Undeterred, Speer then tried to have a similar text issued through Jodl as a Wehrmacht order, but the timid general passed the paper on to Hitler, who again rejected it and, as if to stress his resolve, had eight officers shot the same day for failing to obey a demolition order. As everything now indicated that the battle for Berlin was imminent, Hitler renewed his destruction order, especially for the bridges, and no one doubted that he was aiming at the certain ruin of the city. This time Speer did not attempt to change his mind. Instead he simply disregarded Hitler and turned to the commander-in-chief of the Oder front, Colonel-General Gotthardt Heinrici. Together they convinced the battle commander of the Reich capital to set the destruction orders aside sufficiently to prevent a catastrophe.[19] Almost on the same day, while still filled with outrage and despair over Hitler's lack of understanding, Speer encouraged his friend Karl Hanke, the commandant of the encircled fortress of Breslau, in a farewell letter: 'Your example, of which the magnitude is not yet recognised, will one day be of such inestimably great value for the nation as few heroes of German history ... You are not to be pitied. You are moving towards a fine and dignified conclusion of your life.'[20]

On 20 April, Hitler's fifty-sixth birthday, the leadership assembled at the Reich Chancellery for the last time. During the congratulatory ceremony Hitler moved from one group to another, trying to raise the dejected mood. 'He gave the impression of being galvanized,' Speer recalled.[21] But while he encouraged here, commended there, and even stepped out into the garden to decorate a few Hitler Youths, everybody was waiting with nervous impatience for the event to end, so they could get to their cars and drive off. Five days earlier the Red Army had opened its final offensive against Berlin with two and a half million men, more than 40,000 pieces of artillery and 6,000 tanks and, within a short period, it had almost closed the ring around the capital. Only narrow escape corridors were left to the south and to the north. The noose was tightening.

At the ensuing situation conference Hitler ordered that the Soviet formations, which had advanced right up to the city boundary in several places, be thrown back by a 'liberation blow' applied with full strength. As always when he got talking he lost himself in tactical details while his paladins, headed by the pale and sweating Reich Marshal, counted the passing minutes. At the end Hitler said that, contrary to his original intention, he had decided to remain in Berlin and, if necessary, seek death. No sooner had he declared the conference closed than the ministers and Party leaders pushed out of the conference room after a few hurried farewells and left the city, accompanied by endless columns of trucks. Speer initially wanted to stay in Berlin, especially as he had found no opportunity to say goodbye to Hitler. After nightfall, however, von Poser informed him that the Soviet formations had mounted their attack on the city and were rapidly advancing. Speer therefore decided to leave. A fortnight earlier he had sent his wife and six children to the estate of a friend in Schleswig-Holstein. He now set out to join them.

For a week he had carried with him the text of a broadcast address which he had drafted during a break on one of his trips to the Oder front. It replaced a similar manuscript written a few days earlier, which Speer had decided not to distribute after Hitler had asked to see it and mercilessly cut the draft. The new version quite simply prohibited the blowing up of factories, bridges, railway and communications installations, instructing the Wehrmacht to oppose 'the enemies of the people' bent on destruction 'with all means, if necessary with firearms'. It also demanded that 'prisoners of war' and 'political detainees, and therefore also Jews' be not only handed over to the opposing troops unharmed but also enabled to make their way to their homelands. Moreover, it banned the activity of the 'Werewolf' resistance organization formed by Ley and, finally, it gave the food industry top priority 'over all other enterprises'.[22]

In the afternoon of 21 April Speer and von Poser arrived in Hamburg. Together with Gauleiter Kaufmann, who had raised a number of armed squads made up chiefly of students, they succeeded in preventing the navy from proceeding with the demolition work at docks, port installations and the Elbe bridges which had already begun. Speer then showed his radio address to the Gauleiter, who agreed to have it broadcast. After some toing and froing they arranged for a gramophone record to be made, which Kaufmann was to take into safekeeping. Speer laid down significant conditions under which the Gauleiter was to broadcast the address immediately, without seeking further authority: in the event of Speer being assassinated or sentenced to death by Hitler, or after Hitler's death in the event of a successor deciding to continue the 'scorched earth' policy.

Even then he did not give up his 'struggle for the corpse of Germany'.[23] Immediately after leaving Kaufmann he drove to the headquarters of Army Group North-West in one of the suburbs of Hamburg where he met not only the commander-in-chief, Field Marshal Ernst Busch, but also Field Marshal von Manstein. But Speer did not get far with his plan to persuade the Army Group from halting all demolition measures. Busch was speechless when he heard Speer say that he had prevented the destruction of the port and of the Elbe bridges 'against the orders of the Führer'. Nothing, Busch said, gave Speer the authority to take such decisions together with the Gauleiter without the knowledge of the competent military commands.[24] Without having achieved anything Speer continued his journey.

From Hamburg he went to Lake Eutin, where two construction caravans containing his official papers and his personal belongings were shunted onto a dead track. They provided him with temporary accommodation. In the evening he met a colleague of his friend Dr Brandt at a nearby country estate. In the autumn of 1944 Brandt had been dismissed from his post as Hitler's escorting physician at Bormann's instigation and about a month before he had suddenly been arrested. Speer now learned that the charge against him was that he had moved his family 'in too good time' from Berlin to Thuringia, which was later occupied by American troops. The prosecution had turned this into 'treasonable activity' and a hastily convened court-martial, sitting in Goebbels' apartment, had sentenced him to death. Rumour had it that Hitler himself had insisted on the highest penalty, even though Brandt and his wife had called on Hitler a few days earlier to say goodbye. But, it was now said, Brandt had occupied a position of trust and even enjoyed 'the friendship of the Führer', making his 'treason' doubly despicable. Speer instantly realized that the same charge could be levelled against him, but he did not allow himself any time for such concerns. The news that Brandt was awaiting execution in a suburban villa in Berlin reignited his childhood love of playing cops and robbers, and for an instant he toyed with the idea of driving to Berlin and exploiting the reigning confusion to liberate his friend. In reply to a question about Dr Brandt two days earlier, he had already recklessly said to one of Hitler's secretaries: 'We shall free him illegally.'[25]

That was the first reason for wanting to return to the capital which was still not entirely cut off. Speer was also worried that his headlong departure on 20 April had given him no opportunity to say goodbye to the colleagues to whom he felt personally obliged, such as his friend Friedrich Lüschen. The next day Kaufmann informed him that the codeword 'Tusnelda' had been given out during the night, signifying that all leadership staffs were to leave Berlin. He also learned that the Gauleiters had received a teleprint from Bormann, which, along with various instructions, contained a special paragraph with the alarmingly

mysterious sentence: 'Where is Speer?' For a moment he was afraid that
Bormann, his power visibly growing, was about to strike at him. But
then his inclination not to evade a suspected danger but to make
straight for it got the better or him. His entourage was horrified and
tried to change his mind. But in the evening of 22 April he decided to
return to Berlin, despite all the uncertainties.

However, these and other motives discussed by Speer in detail were
only excuses. Although he did not admit to it at first, the real reason
behind his decision was Hitler. His failure to take leave properly seemed
to him like 'sneaking away'. Although by now he hated Hitler and his
'ash war' and awaited 'his death impatiently',[26] he also realized that he
owed him everything: the distinction of personal friendship, the great if
long-evaporated art dreams, his influence and his power – twelve years
in all. To vanish without bidding farewell would, it seemed to him, be
inappropriate. Besides, he felt that he must face Hitler. 'Surely I could
not act against his orders for months and then simply go away.' Some
time later he still wrote from his cell, 'in spite of all the "purification"
over the past few years [I would] act in much the same manner again.'
In a few lines he now informed his wife, who was staying nearby, of his
decision; but, to reassure her, he made it clear that he had no intention
of seeking death with Hitler in Berlin.

At first Speer tried to get through by car, but some hundred kilometres from the capital the journey along the crowded roads, jammed
with vehicles, refugees, livestock and aimlessly marching units, came to
an end. From a divisional headquarters Speer telephoned the villa
where Brandt was being detained, but learned that he had been taken
to Schwerin on Himmler's special orders. Speer was also unable to
contact any of his friends. Eventually he was put through to the Reich
Chancellery. He told one of the aides that he was coming to see Hitler,
before driving over to the nearby Luftwaffe trials field of Rechlin and
boarding a plane which had been provided for him. In the afternoon he
landed at the airfield of Gatow near Berlin, which was still open.
During the flight he had observed the brief flashes of rocket mortars
and artillery pieces, as well as the interplay of signal flares all around
the city. They marked the tight ring around the burning capital. From
Gatow he flew into the city centre in a Fieseler Storch.

With a sense of profound unease he set out for the Reich
Chancellery. On the way, he later reported with a hint of cynicism, he
asked himself whether he would be met by an execution squad, a tearful

scene or an indifferent Hitler.[27] But as soon as he was greeted in the corridors and antechambers with surprise and even warmth, his insecurity vanished. Bormann came up to him obsequiously, speaking of the 'overwhelming joy' he would be giving the Führer; never would this 'human and even historic gesture' be forgotten. Only when Speer made no response, did Bormann reveal the reason for the gushing reception. He asked Speer to use all his influence to persuade the Führer to leave, after all, for his 'Alpine redoubt' or at least help dispel the resignation to which Hitler had lately been subject.

Wherever Speer went, the bunker seemed to be still resounding with the storm that had broken the previous day when Hitler realized that none of the ordered relief operations outside the gates of Berlin had taken place. In an explosion such as none of those present had previously witnessed he had, after a brief stunned silence, railed against the world in general, the cowardice, corruption and disloyalty all around him, the treachery and failure everywhere. Roused by the shouting, the occupants of the bunker had congregated in corridors and on stairs, and anyone who caught a glimpse of the situation room through the pushing and shoving in front of the doors had seen Hitler raving, beating his fists against his temples as tears streamed down his cheeks. Everyone Speer spoke to had different details to report. His voice abruptly dropping to a whisper, Hitler had eventually said that this was the end. Anyone who wished to do so, could go to the south; he himself would stay in Berlin and die in action on the steps of the Reich Chancellery. He would not allow himself to be dragged any further, he should have ended everything in Rastenburg. As if intoxicated with the solemn and sacrilegious image of the 'steps of the Reich Chancellery', where he would seek his death, he had repeated this phrase several times and finally declared the conference closed.

As Speer entered, Hitler pretended to be deep in thought or busy with something more important. 'So you have come,' he said indifferently, as if he had not expected him any longer. Speer informed him about his trip, about Kaufmann and the demolitions in Hamburg. But Hitler impatiently signalled that he wanted to hear no more of this, as though it were not the right time for it. Instead he asked about Dönitz, who was 'also up there', and Speer spoke of the expert knowledge of the Grand Admiral, his patriotism and his loyalty. Biting his nails, Hitler sat there for a while, staring into nothingness. Aides entered and left, the daily routine proceeded normally, with all the signs of the breakdown of discipline that had appeared some time ago.

During one of the pauses Hitler suddenly asked Speer whether he should remain in Berlin or await death, for which he was destined anyway, at the Obersalzberg. Speer advised him to stay in the capital; the Führer could not end his life in his 'summer house'. There were more interruptions, and when they were alone again, Hitler kept opening his mouth to make some disjointed remarks. He had had great plans, he said at one point, for the Germans and for the world; a little later he added that no one had understood him, not even his oldest fellow fighters. Let no one think he had not seen through the hypocrisy and infamy on all sides. And, as if pulling himself together, he added that his day would come. There were more delays, so that the conversation dragged on for hours. Finally Hitler said that he was now giving in. He would not fight. The risk of falling into the hands of the Russians alive was too great. He had also given instructions that his body was to be burnt, as he was afraid of being 'dishonoured' even in death. And after one more interruption by an aide, he said that he found it easy to depart this life. Just that one moment, he said, uttering a contemptuous sound.

Hitler remained strangely relaxed throughout, Speer recalled, more strangely than ever before, and at one point Speer suspected that after the outburst of the previous day he had been given a sedative which may still have affected him. No matter how disjointed and jerky Hitler's speech now was, Speer had been involuntarily reminded of those monologues of long ago, of the dreams they had dreamed together, and how remote those dreams were from the desert of rubble through which he had passed on his way. This – rather than Hitler's words, which amounted to a tirade of dogmatism, self-pity and megalomania – had roused such a violent surge of 'emotion' that for a long time Speer could find no words. When he spoke again, his 'voice was hoarse'. After several attempts he had eventually been driven almost against his own will by a kind of 'compulsion to confess' and had started to speak of how, for several months, he had suspended the demolition orders and how he had persuaded generals, entrepreneurs, Gauleiters and others to 'spare the fatherland'. All in all, between January and April alone, there had been, he later calculated, some sixty contraventions of Hitler's orders, with hundreds of people in the know.[28]

Towards the end he even claimed to have shown Hitler three written notifications of 'local authorities', reporting the implementation of Speer's order to prevent any destruction measures.[29] Hitler, the account continues, had listened to him in a strangely absent-minded manner and as if he had long known everything. Now and again he had picked up one of the pencils on his desk and stabbed it into the desk till it broke. Although Speer was aware of the agitation he was causing and knew what an effort it was for Hitler to maintain his composure, he did not relent: 'somehow it was desperately important to me to get a glimmer of human contact with Hitler,' he later described his state of mind. After a further embarrassed pause Speer therefore added that, for all the disagreements of the past few months, his personal loyalty had never been impaired. At these words tears had again come into Hitler's eyes, more intensely than some three weeks before. But he said nothing, and even when in a gesture of sympathy Speer offered to stay with him in Berlin he made no reply. 'Perhaps he sensed that I did not mean it,' Speer wrote.[30]

The historical observer must at this point step out of his role as a dispassionate chronicler for a moment and admit his perplexity. For this is one of those scenes that could induce him to give up the rules of his craft. Ever since the autumn of the year before Speer, at first cautiously but soon with growing recklessness, had been working against the 'scorched earth' policy. Each of the countless conversations he had conducted, each of his instructions, was, according to the principles of the regime which he himself had helped to support, a crime punishable by death. His closest collaborators had thought him 'mad' because of his recklessness and he himself had described Hitler as a 'madman', by no means only to Dietrich Stahl; in a letter to Hitler he had accused him of equating his own life with that of the nation and called him 'a criminal'. Nothing in their conversation suggested that Hitler had moved away from his destruction mania of recent months. Yet, confronted by a tearful scene full of false notes, embarrassment and kitsch, Speer suspended his better judgement and spoke of the desperate importance which a human gesture by Hitler would have for him, as well as of his undiminished loyalty. Hitler may indeed have thought he detected a note of insincerity in Speer's assurance. What is more confusing is that Speer was speaking the truth.

As they sat in silence, the bursts of heavy gunfire could be heard and each time the room shook. It had been reported that morning that Russian troops had captured Pankow, Karlshorst and Frohnau and a few forward units had already appeared near the city centre. General Krebs, the newly appointed chief of the general staff, arrived for the situation report. But instead of the great entourage which would until recently have crowded into the room, instead of the rush of uniforms, he was accompanied only by a few middle-ranking liaison officers. Keitel, Jodl, Himmler and nearly all the others had left the city. Afterwards Speer called on Magda Goebbels, who was in bed, weary and waxy-faced, sick from the decision to take her children into death with her. For a few moments he stood in front of the woman whose friendly adviser he had once been, tried to say a few words but found none, especially as Goebbels stood by her side throughout with a severe expression, as if he feared Speer might again become privy to her anxieties and despair.

After standing there awkwardly for a while, Speer took his leave. As he stepped out into the corridor there was great excitement about a telegram just received from Göring, asking whether Hitler's decision to remain in Berlin had activated the law on the Führer's succession. Although Hitler had received the loyally phrased telegram calmly, Bormann had soon succeeded in presenting the inquiry as an attempted *coup d'état* by his old adversary and getting Hitler to strip Göring of all his offices and rights.

'Half amused and half depressed' by these absurd power-games which had long been overtaken by events, Speer turned away and went across to Eva Braun. In an almost carefree manner and with a degree of naive pride she told him that she had, for the first time, succeeded in getting her own way with Hitler, who until a few days earlier had tried to send her back to Bavaria. Then they reminisced together. Speer was startled when she suddenly asked where his wife and children were. But in all innocence she had immediately interrupted herself and expressed her pleasure at his having returned to the bunker. The Führer, she added, had already thought that Speer, too, had betrayed him. But she had always been certain that he would come back once more, and now everybody knew that she had been right. Then she spoke of the impending end and Speer noted, not without admiration, that she was the only person in Hitler's entourage who viewed their self-chosen death with calm.

Morning was approaching when he had himself announced to Hitler for the last time. And as he stood, close to tears, in front of 'the spent old man', searching for words, Hitler only glanced up briefly and casually held out his hand: 'So you're leaving. Good. *Auf Wiedersehen.*' Then he went back to what he had just been doing. Disappointed, Speer recorded that Hitler did not utter another word, no thanks, no regards, no wish.[31]

It was not the parting he had promised himself, even though Hitler's

At daybreak on 24 April 1945, on his last visit to an almost completely surrounded
Berlin, Speer walked once more through the Chancellery he had built. In the Mosaic
Room the glass ceiling had shattered and the floor was covered with shards and debris.
Ammunition boxes and field kitchens stood in the Court of Honour.

emotion and his hard-won equanimity revealed how much affection he was trying to hide from him. Before leaving the Reich Chancellery a few minutes later, Speer walked once more through the dark building to the mosaic hall: the dark red marble was blackened, there were traces of fire and missile craters everywhere, the glass ceiling had burst and crashed down. Next to it, in the rubble-covered 'Court of Honour', cases of ammunition and canned food had been stacked, a few field kitchens stood around. On his arrival in the afternoon he had already played through various solemn parting scenarios, each of them filled with gravity, a sense of drama, fate and certainly a degree of grandeur. Now he felt deflated. 'I would have even accepted a bad ending,' he recorded. It is indeed remarkable how often, during the preceding weeks, he had assured both his close collaborators and the hesitant generals that he was 'putting his head on the block' for his counter-orders, as though he were seeking death with a prospect of transfiguration. He had even quarrelled with Willy Stöhr, the Gauleiter of the so-called Saar Palatinate, about who would 'take the rap' for a refused Führer order.[32]

Speer maintained that he had not been 'suicidally inclined',[33] but he was certainly fatalistic and susceptible to the suicidal aura surrounding Hitler. More perhaps than he realized he had immersed himself in that fatal German ideology, revived by the philosophy of the regime, whereby anything exceptional could only be sealed by tragedy and death. Nothing seemed to him less in keeping with this picture than the limp hand Hitler had held out to him. Among the dramatic images of that parting that he had conjured up in his mind, there may have been a scenario of him being led at dawn across that paved Court of Honour, where he now stood among the ruins, his gaze directed at a wall of black uniforms lined up before him, waiting for the salvo of the squad, which would be the last sound he ever heard.

How little his closeness to Hitler had saved him from this end became clear to Speer three days later when SS-Obergruppenführer Hermann Fegelein, Himmler's liaison man at the Führer's headquarters, was executed. With the elegant opportunism of the gentleman rider he had been, Fegelein had worked his way into Hitler's court and, since his marriage to Eva Braun's sister, had become more or less a member of Hitler's family circle. Perhaps Speer envied Fegelein that dramatic 'thrust into nothingness' which Hitler had ordered for any act of insubordination to his commands. A note in his Spandau diary certainly suggests this. There Speer wrote that the determining motive of his last visit to the bunker had been of a 'romantic' nature, and that with his return to Berlin he had been seeking a kind of 'trial by ordeal': 'All I really wanted was to shuffle off the responsibility for my future life.' Since then, he continued, he sometimes 'despaired that Hitler, weary and in a forbearing mood as he was, responded to my confession of open disobedience with emotion instead of with an order to have me shot. That would have been a better end to my life.'[34]

Making his way through rubble and a wild chaos of fallen beams and cables, scorched lumps of walls and bomb craters, Speer reached the Brandenburg Gate shortly before four o'clock in the morning. What had it been like, Poser asked. Speer's reply reveals that he had not yet given up the idea of a kind of succession or at least of a major role, even though he pretended to be relieved: 'Thank God I won't have to do a Prince Max von Baden.'[35] From the East-West Axis they took off in their Fieseler Storch across the high tree stumps on both sides, past the Victory Column to Rechlin. Like the government quarter Speer had just left, the street was under the fire of the Soviet artillery. But the plane quickly gained height, and once more they saw the muzzle flashes, the trembling flares, and the conflagrations everywhere. Only the darkness in the north-west of the city indicated that a narrow gap was still open. They now flew into that darkness.

In Rechlin Speer learned that Heinrich Himmler was at nearby Hohenlychen. The multitude of British fighters in the sky meant that he had to wait until the evening before continuing his flight, and he was curious to see how the powerful Reichsführer SS had come to terms with the now certain defeat. Speer therefore flew to Hohenlychen in his Fieseler Storch. An hour later he was facing him in the very room where, about a year previously, he had lain as a patient. Gebhardt was there too, nervously running about, busying himself with dissolution matters. However, Speer's expectation of finding his arrogant rival unsure of himself or possibly even afraid was not fulfilled. Himmler informed Speer that he had long agreed with Göring, whom he continued to call 'the Führer's successor' despite his deposition by Hitler, that he would lead the new Reich government as 'prime minister' and that he was already busy forming his cabinet. Europe, he believed, could not do without him as police minister: 'one hour with Eisenhower and he will share my view.' Totally mistaking Speer's intention, he condescendingly rejected him once more. He had no use for him, Himmler said, and as if to make it clear to his visitor that his political role was over and he was demoted to being an architect again, he concluded the conversation with the remark that he was not, for the moment, planning any major buildings. Speer sarcastically offered him his plane for a farewell visit to Hitler in Berlin, from where he himself had just come. But Himmler declined; he had no time for that.[36]

In the afternoon Speer was back in Rechlin, and as dusk fell he and von Poser continued their flight. Now and again they got close to Soviet fighter planes, and the pilot pushed the plane down, almost touching the treetops. After a while Speer caught sight of the Mecklenburg lakes, which he had crossed by canoe on his honeymoon, and in the evening they landed in Hamburg. Kaufmann suggested that transmission of the broadcast address which Speer had left with him two days earlier be no longer delayed. Still dazed by his impressions from Berlin and the 'tragedy' which was just then unfolding in the bunker below the Reich Chancellery, Speer persuaded him, in a belated surge of sentimentality, to postpone the broadcast for another two or three days. When he arrived at his caravan at Eutin in the evening, he made contact with Dönitz, who had found accommodation for himself and his staff in some hutments in nearby Plön.

Dönitz asked Speer to come over and take up quarters with him. He was present therefore when, in the early evening of 30 April, a radio signal arrived from Bormann, appointing Dönitz as Hitler's successor. The attached cabinet list no longer contained Speer's name, but appointed Karl Otto Saur minister of armaments. The following day two more signals arrived from the Reich Chancellery, one of which announced that Hitler's will had come into force. Not until a telegram arrived in the early afternoon were those present informed that Hitler had 'passed away' nearly twenty-four hours earlier. That evening, when Speer moved into his room in one of the huts and opened his suitcase, he found right on top the leather cover with the dedicated photograph Hitler had given him on 19 March. The picture with the jerky writing, speaking of 'everlasting friendship', hit him like an unexpected blow. As he placed the frame on his bedside table he was suddenly seized by a weeping spasm which went on for a long time. It was some hours before he calmed himself with the thought that the death of the man in the photograph also meant the end of that dependency which had led him down strange roads, paths that he himself had often found mysterious. 'That was the end of my relationship to Hitler,' he recorded of that evening.[37] But in another way it was only just beginning.

SPEER

For years the struggle for Hitler's succession had smouldered, occasionally
flaring up openly. With the appointment of Dönitz it had come to an
unexpected end. All the pretenders who had fiercely jostled for the best
starting position had been eliminated in one fell swoop: Hitler's word was
still the supreme authority even in the eclipse. During the night of 28-29
April, shortly before signing his will, Hitler had followed Göring's dismissal with Himmler's after being shown a Reuter report stating that the
Reichsführer SS had made contact with the Allies through Sweden. In a
final outburst of fury he screamed that a traitor must never succeed him
as Führer: 'See to it that he does not.'³⁸ Goebbels and Bormann, who had
also counted themselves among the well-placed heirs to the throne, were
in encircled Berlin, and Speer had long been sidelined.

Speer had no intention of accepting this or of giving up all influence
even though he had been dismissed by Hitler and, as some believed,
even 'cast out'. He sought Dönitz's proximity not least in order to share
in the decisions of the new government now being formed, and possibly,
in the course of time, even becoming the real power at the side of the
politically inexperienced grand admiral. He assured the Luftwaffe
Colonel Werner Baumbach, with whom he had worked out the
Greenland plan, which had not been finally abandoned until then, that
he would see to it that Dönitz did not get up to 'any nonsense' and,
above all, that he lift the still valid demolition orders.³⁹

For a few days Speer performed rather subordinate tasks. He drafted
a number of signals and proclamations for the head of state, sticking to
the solemn and grandiloquent style of the late regime, including a statement 'To the German people', according to which 'the Führer … fighting against Bolshevism to his last breath' had 'been killed in action for
Germany'. And although he knew better from his visit to the bunker, he
kept silent about Hitler's suicide even to Dönitz, adding to one of the
proclamations the sentences: 'Today the Führer may still be a controversial figure. But one day his historical personality will be acknowledged by a just history.' The draft again concluded with the formula:
'May God protect Germany.'⁴⁰

Soon Speer made himself indispensable. On 3 May Dönitz established a kind of triumvirate with Speer and the finance minister Lutz
Schwerin von Krosigk. Speer took on the Ministry of Economic Affairs
and Production in the 'acting government' appointed by the group,
although amidst the fast disintegrating power structures the only serious
task of the new cabinet was to channel the stream of people fleeing in
panic and chaos from the advancing Red Army. After all those

By the end of April 1945 the Allies had largely occupied Germany. In the concentration camps, such as at Dachau on 30 April (pictured here), they were cheered as liberators.

exhausting and restless years Speer had still not abandoned his habit of sharing in decision-making. Nor had he rid himself of the self-delusion of nearly all the leading figures of the fallen Hitler regime. For he not only envisaged a role 'in the framework of an armistice commission' but was also ready to take on the task of setting production in motion again, as well as the enormous construction programme of the years to come.[41]

After the partial capitulation of the northern part of Germany, Dönitz moved with his cabinet to the naval college of Mürwik near Flensburg in the first days of May. Meanwhile Speer, again anxious to keep a distance, and Werner Baumbach accepted an invitation from the Duke of Mecklenburg-Holstein and found accommodation at Glücksburg Castle. Still concerned for Speer's safety, General Thomale provided him with an armoured platoon for his personal protection: this was not yet the end, he warned. One day, Himmler, still wanted by a warrant of arrest issued by the dead Führer, turned up among the many visitors to the castle. At last Speer found him restless and frightened. Himmler's illusions about a chancellorship and a reception by Eisenhower had evaporated. When Dönitz refused him a post in his acting government, Himmler demanded a plane from Speer, who suggested he address himself to Baumbach. Once more Himmler pulled out the old stop and replied menacingly: 'When one flies with your planes one never knows where one will end up.' Evidently he had heard of Speer's and Baumbach's plans to detain the leaders of the old regime and fly them to some remote location. His intelligence service, Speer concluded, was still functioning. But he no longer had any power and left angrily.[42]

While at Glücksburg, Speer learned, initially as a rumour, about the end at the Reich Chancellery, the execution of Fegelein, the disappearance without a trace of Bormann and the rest of the bunker residents, except for Hitler and Goebbels and their wives. He also heard that none other than his friend Karl Hanke had been appointed by Hitler to succeed Himmler as Reichsführer SS and Chief of Police and that Hanke, after a verbose appeal to defend Breslau to the end, had evidently escaped, as had the Gauleiter of Bremen, Paul Wegener, after a similarly radical appeal.

There was a veritable flood of reports and revelations exposing the old regime even in its demise. It was reported that at his temporary quarters in Blankenburg Saur had expected V weapons to be deployed even as American tanks were already driving into the yard of the building which served as his office. The Gauleiter of East Prussia and former General Commissioner for the Ukraine, Erich Koch, was said to have demanded a U-boat to escape to South America, and a little later Speer found himself once more facing Karl Gebhardt, who had suddenly turned himself into a 'Red Cross General'. One piece of news probably gave Speer particular satisfaction: SS-Obergruppenführer Hans Kammler, who had long regarded himself as his principal rival and had wrested various responsibilities from him, had unsuccessfully approached the Americans with an offer of handing over to them the complete technical data for the V weapons and the jet aircraft, together with the technical experts already concentrated in the Allgäu, in return for his escape. Later reports indicated that during a stop-over in (as yet unoccupied) Prague, Kammler had been 'executed' for this act of treason by his adjutant, who evidently took the SS slogan of loyalty and honour very literally. But there were many reports of that kind during those days and, as Speer soon discovered, they were often just attempts to muddy the trail.[43]

It was a strangely unreal, often quite absurd, situation. British units had now occupied the major part of northern Germany. Their troops were patrolling all roads, checking the identities of the milling crowds, maintaining prison camps and gradually tightening their grip on all executive power with orders and instructions – and right in their midst a German government was still in office. Every day it held cabinet meetings in the same building as the British Control Commission. Regardless of its vanishing authority, it argued about the appointment of a minister for the Churches, the proper form of address for the new head of state, and whether Hitler's pictures were to be removed from offices (Dönitz ruled that they should remain). On another occasion, according to reports, it discussed 'the steadily intensifying propaganda about conditions in German concentration camps' and issued a decree charging the Reich Labour Court with the 'investigation and punishment of incidents'. From time to time it granted interviews to the first reporters of Allied newspapers. Its performances gave rise to a brief moment of surprise and were immediately forgotten, as if neither its words nor even its existence merited any attention.

On 15 May an advance party of the American Strategic Bombing Survey turned up at Glücksburg and asked if Speer was willing to provide information on the air war and its effects. He agreed, and the director of the Survey, George Ball, arrived the very next day, as did shortly afterwards Paul Nitze and finally John Kenneth Galbraith, as well as several, mostly junior, members of the organization, many of whom were later to hold important positions. Still expecting a significant postwar career, Speer discussed with them the German 'armaments miracle' as well as the potential and the strategic miscalculations of modern bombing warfare. At lunchtime, when the American delegation drove up to the castle, Speer's guard regularly presented arms. It was just one more facet of the those bizarre days that Hitler's 'favourite minister' and members of the acting government of the Reich were exploring the seemingly inexplicable successes of German war production together with the enemy of yesterday, and strictly speaking, of the day.

After the first talks Speer's interrogators were already so impressed by his exact knowledge, his memory for figures, the frankness of his explanations, as well as his lack of subservience that their talks went on and on, and soon there was an atmosphere as among expert colleagues. Speer himself has spoken with some irony of 'our "university of bombing warfare"' and of the 'almost comradely tone' which quickly established itself.[44] Soon interested people came from all over: senior officers, economists and technicians from other countries involved in the war, as well as scholars who were anxious to collect information on the Hitler regime generally quite apart from the questions of the Bombing Survey. Many were also driven by curiosity to make the acquaintance of a man who had so suddenly emerged from the 'Caligula world'[45] of Hitler and was so very different from the accepted picture of the blinkered, energetic and brutal 'Nazi'.

As in the past, Speer was seen as an exception. He even encouraged this impression by beginning to distance himself, step by step, from the Dönitz government and by actually asking his interrogators to put an end to this 'bad drama'.[46] Success soon came. The military authorities silently tolerated his use of his own car in the evening, after his wearying interrogation, to visit his family, who were staying nearby; and later, at the various stations of his imprisonment, there were always British or

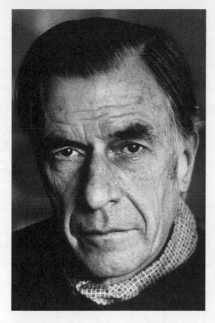

On 16 May 1945 the US Strategic Bombing Survey called on Speer at Glücksburg in Schleswig-Holstein, where he had taken refuge, to discuss with him the effect of the bombing war. The commission was headed by George W. Ball (left), Paul Henry Nitze (centre) and John Kenneth Galbraith (right), all of whom were later to occupy influential posts.

American officers who invited him on a day trip to Paris with a walk along the Seine or for an evening drive through the autumnal Taunus hills, although he was under arrest.

At Glücksburg only John Kenneth Galbraith disturbed the amicable agreement by asking sharp questions about the concentration camps and the slave labourers. But, as Galbraith has recorded, in his nonchalant manner Speer invariably succeeded in evading the answers and in changing the subject to the air war, its effect on production and on the population, or related matters. With the war against Japan still continuing, Speer benefited from the fact that his interrogators were particularly interested in these topics. Although Galbraith had strong reservations, he has conceded that apart from his cultured manner, his intelligence and technical knowledge, Speer had largely impressed those present by seeming totally unconcerned about his fate. 'He wanted us to know that he was aware of the danger he was in and did not care.' Even though Galbraith regarded this merely as a shrewd tactical move, he added: 'No one could doubt that he was a personality.'[47] In the moments of elation, which still came to him quite often, Speer already saw himself as the future 'minister of reconstruction' appointed by the Allies. His interrogators encouraged this illusion to make him more communicative.

On 23 May, just one week after the interrogations, the days at

Speer, Dönitz and Jodl immediately after their arrest on 23 May 1945.
The conversations between the representatives of the US Strategic Survey and Speer
had been suddenly terminated after a week. Together with the other members of the
Acting Reich Government he was arrested and taken by plane to an intermediate
camp at Mondorf in Luxemburg.

Glücksburg came to an abrupt end, chiefly under pressure from the
Soviet Union. In the early morning some tanks and guns drew up, surrounded the moated castle, and a detail of troops led by a sergeant
noisily came up the staircase with sub-machine-guns and hand
grenades. After some straying about, they burst into Speer's rooms,
arrested him, and heard him say: 'So now the end has come. That's
good. It was all only a kind of opera anyway.' Having told Speer to
pack his things, the sergeant unbuckled his belt and pistol and put them

on the table as he walked out. 'What did he mean by that?' Speer asked himself.[48]

Speer was taken by truck to Flensburg. There the commandos had already interrupted a cabinet meeting an hour before, shouting 'Hands up!' They had declared those present to be under arrest, and had followed up their command with another of 'Trousers down!' Shortly thereafter all officers, officials and secretaries were bundled into the same room and subjected to the same procedure, including a body search which left 'nothing unexplored'.[49] Then the soldiers pounced on the luggage of the detainees. That afternoon they were taken to the airport, guarded by a strong armoured detachment, and flown to Luxemburg. The Allies had set up a first collecting point for the prominent survivors of the late Reich at the Palace Hotel in Mondorf, and on arrival Speer discovered Göring, then Kesselring and a little later Karl Brandt, whom he had wanted to free from the grasp of the Gestapo a month ago. In order to quell the growing outrage over the luxurious accommodation of the leaders of the Hitler regime, the victors colloquially referred to the hotel as 'Ashcan'.

The contradictory behaviour of the Allied military authorities, who from one day to the next confronted the surviving leaders of the Reich as judges over a bunch of criminals, was probably not due only to the decision taken as early as 1942 to have them tried under international law. It may have reflected the disparate impressions that were crowding in on them. Speer's 'cultured' manner seemed particularly repellent as horror grew over the reports from concentration camps and the appalling conditions the conquerors had found there. All the observers who met him during his stay at Glücksburg and in the weeks that followed have commented, both at the time and in retrospect, on his astonishing grasp and penetrating intellect combined with his personal charisma – but also on their insuperable mistrust. The British sergeant who had led the arrest on the morning of 23 May had raced down the passages of Glücksburg Castle past the strange faces of the assembled occupants, asking: 'Who is Speer?'[50]

That indeed was the question.

Chapter Ten

JUDGEMENT AT NUREMBERG

Throughout the summer of 1945 Speer was in custody at Kransberg, a castle near Bad Nauheim, which he had himself reconstructed as Göring's headquarters and furnished with an extensive staff wing before the French campaign. From Mondorf he had first been taken to Chesnay, a small town not far from Paris, to a special camp mainly for technical staff. Kransberg, too, which the British labelled 'Dustbin', in imitation of the American 'Ashcan', served as an internment camp for technicians, entrepreneurs and senior civil servants, but not for the political hierarchy of the regime. There Speer met Hjalmar Schacht, for many years Hitler's minister of finance, Fritz Thyssen and the members of the IG Farben board, his own former departmental heads Hupfauer, Hettlage, Saur and Fränk, also Walter Dornberger, the director of the Peenemünde experimental institute, as well as Wernher von Braun, Ferdinand Porsche and many others.

Separating off the 'experts' probably encouraged the inmates in their assumption that they had nothing to do with the atrocities of the Hitler regime and would, if the victorious powers persisted in their idea of a trial of the principal war criminals, at most be called as witnesses. At any rate, after a short period of dejected silence the majority of the detainees had found their voices again and complained not only that their detention represented a breach of international usage, but soon also about the moral arrogance of their adversaries.

The hardening of opinions all round him may explain why Speer increasingly isolated himself from his surroundings and soon reacquired the reputation of unapproachability that had always surrounded him. While he regarded the idea of any guilt in the technical legal sense as 'absurd' as far as his case was concerned, he was by no means certain that he was being wronged. His doubts increased with every new revelation about the atrocities of the Hitler years. Compounded by the wasted days that dragged on endlessly, these reports threw him into a state of chronic depression.

A sympathetic American interrogation officer eventually drew him into prolonged conversations about 'politics and politicians in National Socialist Germany'. Much to the anger of some of his fellow detainees, Speer 'volunteered', as they disapprovingly believed, answers to these questions on record in sessions lasting several days, and in a number of written statements. He ignored the accusations of 'dishonourable' conduct. Only the prediction that he would above all harm himself by giving information, occasionally unsettled him. One day Schacht approached him, wagging his finger: 'You'll be getting yourself into the dock with your garrulousness!' In a written note Speer reminded himself: 'Could be wise enough, to say little. I should be capable of that.'[1]

In his statements he described the leading figures with whom he had been until four weeks ago, from Hitler, Göring and other top-level followers, to the Gauleiters, departmental heads and secretaries at Hitler's headquarters. In these thumbnail portraits of his own colleagues he stuck to the role of objective observer, abandoning it only in his judgements on Dorsch and Saur. In other memoranda he dealt with the political and economic reconstruction of the country and with technological and scientific developments of the near future. He supported a Western orientation of Germany, a general regionalization of power, and a continuation of the progressive, 'albeit not yet concluded projects' of German technicians in close co-operation 'exclusively with the United Nations'. Such a developmental organization, he wrote, would have to be led by 'a universally interested figure with a good all-round view and good organizational ability'.[2]

There is much to suggest that Speer was thinking primarily of himself for this position. The extent of his ambition also emerges from the fact that in Kransberg he began to 'schedule a kind of departmental head conference' and to 'gather the names and addresses of experts who were politically uncompromised'.[3] Speer was therefore 'thunderstruck' when early one morning one of his former colleagues woke him up with the news that, along with Hjalmar Schacht, he would be among the accused in the planned trial of the principal war criminals. For a few days he contemplated suicide, wondering for the first time why he had never been issued with one of the potassium cyanide capsules which Hitler and the 'SS distribution centre' had so generously handed out.[4]

When he had regained his composure he made a decision which not only reflected his inclination to go the whole hog, but was once again intended to create a clear distance between himself and the rest of the – as he now knew – twenty-two principal defendants. Speer asked none other than George Ball, then also in Kransberg, whether he would consider defending him in court, pointing out that young American attorneys often made their names by defending 'notorious characters'; where, he added with some sarcasm, would Ball find a client 'more notorious than me?' Ball thought the idea rather insensitive for such a civilized person and turned him down. One day, when Hupfauer asked Speer why he was keeping so conspicuously aloof, not taking part either in the keep-fit classes of the camp inmates or in the musical evenings and readings, Speer replied: 'I am preparing myself for twenty years.'[5]

John Kenneth Galbraith has supported the view that Speer had already begun to plan a survival strategy. First at Glücksburg, then at Mondorf and in the Dustbin camp, he had kept a carefully considered distance from his accomplices of yesterday, as if he had never been one of them. He had tried to establish a common cause with the representatives of the victorious powers. Together with his decision to hand over to them, of his own accord, all important documents kept in the safe-deposits of a Hamburg bank, the statements about his efforts to foil Hitler's destruction orders and other factors, these signs can be seen as part of a cunning attempt, staged with the composure of a born gambler, to save his own skin and to rise, so to speak, like a 'phoenix from the Ashcan'.[6]

Such reflections undoubtedly carry some weight. But they should not make us overlook other aspects of Speer's character which, for all his sobriety, was susceptible to the tug of emotion. If it is true that a person's behaviour is rarely determined by a single motive, then this applies even more to such a strangely complex figure as Speer, in whom, as this account has revealed, a mass of contradictory elements co-existed. Shrewdness and realism went hand in hand with curiously rapturous impulses. Speer combined an ability for far-sighted planning with a pronounced 'idealism' that was always on the look-out for the great cause worthy of his dedication. The seductive power of National Socialism lay in its ability to manipulate this widespread need, adding various components such as faith in the Führer, a sense of mission, 'redemption of the world' and other exhilarating fulfilments.

If Speer had indeed determined to use all possible means to pull his head out of the ever-tightening noose when he was still in Kransberg, he presumably realized then that he was more deeply involved than he had ever thought in a monstrous crime and that the time had therefore come to disclose both his role and his responsibility, or at least to take them more seriously than most of his fellow prisoners.

Towards the end of September an American jeep swept into the castle courtyard of Kransberg to collect Speer. After a short stop at the inter-rogation camp of Oberursel he was taken by lorry to Nuremberg the following day and, after driving through endless heaps of rubble in the devastated city, brought to the prison block of the court-house. After three weeks in solitary confinement, at one time furnished only with a palliasse and a few torn old blankets, the British major Airey Neave entered the room and handed him a folder with various papers. It con-tained the indictment, amounting to nearly thirty pages, a kind of con-stitution of the tribunal, and a compilation of treaties and international agreements which the Reich had violated during the Hitler years, as well as a list of forty German lawyers. Neave explained that every accused was naturally entitled to defend himself; but if he wished to have an attorney he had to choose one of those on the list. He would come again the following day to hear the accused's decision.

Until then Speer assumed that 'each of us would receive a separate indictment'. Now it turned out that all the accused were charged with 'all the monstrous crimes'[7] committed by the regime during its existence. Count I accused them of 'Joint Conspiracy' to rule over Germany and Europe, Count II of 'Crimes against Peace', Count III dealt with partic-ipation in numerous 'war crimes', and Count IV charged them with 'crimes against humanity'. Only a brief appendix explained to what extent the separate charges applied to the respective recipients of the document.

The reactions of the detainees were recorded in a brief statement which American forensic psychologist Gustav M. Gilbert made each of them write on the title page of the indictment. Göring wrote: 'The victor will always be the judge.' Ribbentrop, the former foreign minis-ter, suggested that the indictment was 'directed against the wrong people'. Fritz Sauckel declared: 'The abyss between the ideal of a social community which I imagined and advocated as a former seaman and worker, and the terrible happenings in the concentration camps, has shaken me deeply.' Field Marshal Keitel stated: 'For a soldier, orders are orders', while Dönitz saw the trial as 'typical American humour', and Julius Streicher, the boisterous anti-Semite and former Gauleiter of

Franconia, stated: 'This trial is a triumph of World Jewry.' Robert Ley, excitable and unstable as ever, gave a different answer by hanging himself in his cell shortly after receiving the indictment.[8]

Initially Speer was, as he himself reported, profoundly shocked and overcome by a sense of 'hopelessness'. But he soon recovered his composure and, as he did nothing by halves, he tackled his defence with the same energy he had once applied as an architect and later as armaments minister. J. K. Galbraith and others have accused Speer of pursuing a cunning policy of justification, which he had developed early on.[9] On closer inspection, however, one cannot help feeling that Speer regarded the trial as a kind of duel which he simply wished to survive. Despite the gravity of the situation, he may even have experienced a certain degree of gratification at finally having a task such as he 'always needed and wanted', and which now possibly meant more to him than his nonsensical expectation of a role as 'minister for reconstruction' acting for the Allies. He had no doubt of the fine thread by which his life hung and how easily it could break. But this realization merely made the task more attractive. At Gilbert's request he wrote on the title page of the indictment: 'The trial is necessary. There is a common responsibility for such horrible crimes even in a totalitarian state.'[10]

Speer's admission that everyone who occupied a leading position in the Hitler regime was responsible lay at the heart of a difference of opinion which arose a few days later when he made the acquaintance of his attorney, whose choice, significantly, he had left to the Court. Dr Hans Flächsner was a slight man with thick glasses and a modest manner, who had a small lawyer's office in Berlin. When, at the end of their conversation, he handed Speer a form, requesting him to give some thought to handing over power of attorney, Speer signed there and then. However, he made the condition that Flächsner would not mention anything in court that might impair the dignity of a former Reich minister or incriminate his former subordinates.[11]

Speer then explained to his lawyer how he intended to defend himself and that he wished to assume 'general responsibility' for the atrocities of the regime beyond his personal competence. Flächsner contradicted vigorously, calling Speer's intention nonsensical:

You will be sitting in the dock third from last. That amounts to being classified one way whereas Göring, Hess, Ribbentrop and Keitel are classified another way, at the top. If you go ahead and declare yourself responsible for everything that happened during those years, you

Speer sketching in his Nuremberg cell.

are making yourself out to be more important than you are, besides drawing an inappropriate degree of attention to yourself. That will not only make a dreadful impression but may also lead to a death sentence. Why do you yourself want to say that you are lost? Leave that to the court![12]

But Speer was not to be moved. He did not wish 'to get away with cheap excuses', he later stated, adding: 'I could not understand my fellow defendants who often even refused to take responsibility for events that had happened in their own areas. We had gambled, all of us, and lost: lost Germany, our country's good repute, and a considerable measure of our own personal integrity. Here was a chance to demonstrate a little dignity, a little manliness or courage, and to make plain that with everything else we were charged with, at least we were not also cowards.'[13]

In the end he agreed with Flächsner on a line of defence. This compromise proved so effective that some observers regarded it as a 'cunning' device.

During the trial Flächsner portrayed his client as an idealistic artist who had been thrust into high ministerial office by chance but who had always remained 'unpolitical' and, unlike the other defendants, had invariably discharged his functions as an 'expert minister' objectively. Flächsner pointed out that soon after assuming his ministerial duties Speer had, significantly, asked Hitler to give him a binding assurance that he would be allowed to return to architecture after the war. There was certainly nothing that linked him to the ideological darkness which had shaped the horrific image of the system. Against this background Speer's insistence on his own responsibility seemed all the more impressive. For he was accepting a charge of guilt which, according to Flächsner, applied less to him than to his fellow defendants. Speer's demeanour was all-important. Never subservient, he contradicted on points of detail while accepting responsibility in general, without any self-pity, thus clearly gaining respect not only among the judges but even among his prosecutors.

Five days before the opening session of the tribunal Speer made a move which, in the opinion of some observers, was not only a tactical master stroke, but also significantly improved his chances of survival. Sensing the inevitable conflict between the victorious powers, but driven above all by his increasing concern over current rumours that he was to be handed over to the Soviet Union after the trial, Speer approached the chief prosecutor of the United States, Robert H. Jackson, through an American intelligence officer. Speer pointed out that, during his interrogations at Glücksburg and later also under questioning by Western representatives, he had unreservedly and confidentially discussed his 'partially successful struggle' against the Allied air strategy. As these statements had been made 'out of conviction' and 'not in order to gain personal advantages in the future', he would feel 'wretched' if he were made to reveal his special knowledge openly in court. His letter could be understood as an invitation to Jackson not to question the witness Speer on any point where the answer might provide the Soviet Union with 'useful military and technical information'. In as much as Jackson agreed to this suggestion it could actually look like a secret agreement between Speer and one of the prosecutors.[14]

When the letter became known years later, it was indeed interpreted as an unspoken arrangement. But seen objectively, it is clear that Jackson did more than ignore Speer's request. In fact, on 31 July 1946, not long after the defendant had testified, Jackson and his deputy Thomas J. Dodd drafted a joint statement to the court summing up all the charges and the evidence against Speer and concluding: 'Justice demands that Speer should receive the maximum penalty for his crimes.' Moreover, a fortnight before sentence was passed Jackson explained in a 'guideline' for possible applications of clemency that not one of the defendants could claim 'mitigating circumstances' since none of them had rendered the slightest service to the prosecution.[15] On the other hand the American historian Bradley F. Smith, who knew the circumstances and those concerned well, stated that, over and above the condemnation of the Third Reich, Speer had shown an 'acceptance of the Anglo-American cause in ways that would make the most favorable impression on the majority of the prosecutors and judges'.[16]

The trial began on 20 November 1945 under the glare of the artificial light in the gloomy court of the Nuremberg Justice Building, where the windows were covered with long dark-green drapes. The English Lord Justice, Sir Geoffrey Lawrence, on whom the procedural authorities had conveyed permanent presidency, gave a brief opening address, and the indictment was read out. Then Robert H. Jackson stepped forward. In a passionate speech, reminiscent of the high tone of the American Founding Fathers, he described how first a people had been deprived of its rights, then how international agreements had been broken and countless atrocities committed by the system wherever it imposed its rule. After a comprehensive account of those atrocities, he declared: 'In the dock there are some twenty broken men who will have been deprived forever of the chance ever to cause misfortune again.' But one should, he went on, think of the power 'with which, as Nazi leaders, they once ruled a large part of the world and held nearly all the world in terror'. Their crimes had been so clever, so evil and so devastating that mankind 'would not survive a repetition of such horrors'. The fact that the victors were not taking vengeance but 'voluntarily handing over their captive enemies to the findings of the court [was] one of the most significant concessions ever made by power to reason', even though the proceedings, as Jackson frankly admitted, were not free from 'certain difficulties and shortcomings'.

Having illustrated some of these weaknesses, Jackson went on to say that the victors had no intention of 'indicting the whole German nation'. The existence of an extensive police apparatus as well as of the concentration camps proved that the broad masses had by no means willingly accepted the National Socialist programme. Indeed, 'no less than the outside world' the Germans also 'had accounts to settle with the defendants'. Towards the end he declared: 'The real complaining party at your bar is Civilization. In all our countries it is still a struggling and imperfect thing. It does not plead that the United States, or any other country, has been blameless... But it points to the dreadful

The American chief prosecutor, Justice Robert H. Jackson (in civilian clothes) and the Russian chief prosecutor, Colonel Pokrovsky.

sequence of aggressions and crimes I have recited, it points to the weariness of all flesh, the exhaustion of resources, and the destruction of all that was beautiful or useful in so much of the world.'[17]

Jackson's plea left a deep impression. Speer called it 'devastating' and Göring spoke of 'incredible' atrocities which had been 'kept secret from the rest of us'. But some of the defendants clung to Jackson's remarks about the 'difficulties and shortcomings' of the proceedings which they felt confirmed all their reservations.[18] The fundamental objections raised at the time soon became the subject of a protracted controversy which has not been resolved to this day. They were reinforced by the fact that the defence had a far worse starting position, not least because of the practicalities. As a matter of principle they had to obtain each document from the prosecution. Often the material came too late, or not at all, or the translation was inadequate. Application for any files had to be made in open court and be approved by the court. And if a counsel for the defence wished to submit evidence of infringements of rights by Germany's adversaries, especially the Soviet Union, the credibility or the relevance of these sources were challenged.

The situation was perhaps even more awkward for Speer than for the other defendants. Fully convinced of his innocence, he had, while still in Flensburg, voluntarily handed over his files to the British authorities, who were now making extensive use of them, whereas his counsel was largely prevented from having access to them. The resulting difficulties only came to an end when, one day, Speer's secretary Annemarie Kempf unexpectedly appeared on the scene; she was still being detained at Kransberg to sort out the mountains of Speer's papers. With a pass issued by the British, permitting her to visit her allegedly sick mother, she was soon commuting between Kransberg and Nuremberg. Thanks to her extensive familiarity with Speer's papers she provided Dr Flächsner with photocopies of all the documents he required. Claiming to be a 'reporter', she smuggled the papers through all the controls in her underwear.

Another problem was perhaps even more trying for Speer. The defendants soon divided into two groups. Almost automatically one of them was led by Göring and the other by Speer. Naturally the emergence of the two camps was connected with the old rivalry between the two men, which still persisted. Moreover, each believed the other to be in his debt. But now the main reasons for the rift lay in their sharply conflicting attitude to the former regime and to the present judicial proceedings. While Speer viewed the tribunal as an opportunity for 'accelerating our detachment from the past', Göring denied the victors' right to treat the defeat of the vanquished as a crime that could be prosecuted by law. Determined not to display the least trace of repentance, he saw the trial as an opportunity to create, as he hoped, a 'national legend' with himself as its hero and martyr. 'You don't get a chance to go down in history as a martyr every day,' he was heard to remark with cheerful irony. 'Fifty or sixty years from now, statues of Hermann Göring will be seen throughout Germany,' he asserted, adding with feigned modesty: 'Maybe little statues, but one in every home.'[19]

After the slimming and drug withdrawal treatment imposed on him by the American authorities, Göring had regained his sense of power and was in the mood for a fight. From the outset he made an all-out effort to lead the defendants into the 'final battle' as a united front. Stripped of all their power, Ribbentrop and Keitel, Sauckel and Rosenberg suddenly had the blank look of underlings imprinted on their faces. They duly followed Göring's instructions. During the trial they recited like a monotonous litany that they had only obeyed orders, leading observers to think that they could almost hear the distant voice of Göring. He continued to insist successfully on his superior rank of 'Reich Marshal'. Clearly the strongest personality in the dock, he got most of the defendants to do his bidding. Speer soon found himself increasingly isolated. Only Hans Fritzsche, the 'chief commentator' of the regime, on trial, as it were, in place of Joseph Goebbels, and, at times, the vacillating 'Reich Youth Leader' Baldur von Schirach, sided with him. All the others, more or less vociferously, accused him of having betrayed their common cause, both in the past and now in court.

About ten days after the indictment was read there was an intermezzo which spoiled the defendants' unshaken, part offended and part cynical, mood. Commander Donovan screened a documentary film made by American troops as they entered various concentration camps and which, in the introductory words of Thomas E. Dodd, would 'provide, in a short and unforgettable form, an explanation of what the word "camp" meant'.[20] Nearly all the defendants reacted with visible horror to the infernal scenario presented to them for more than an hour, to the bodies strewn over the ground or hanging on the barbed-wire fences, the tractors which cleared the compound of the dead, the smoking crematorium furnaces and the piles of bodies. Several of the defendants repeatedly shielded their eyes with their hands. G. M. Gilbert jotted down their reactions: 'Schacht objects to being made to look at film...Ribbentrop closes his eyes, looks away...Funk now in tears...Speer looks very sad, swallows hard...Schirach gasps...Göring looks sad...Dönitz has head bowed, no longer watching...Fritzsche pale, biting lips...Streicher shows signs of disturbance for first time' and, Gilbert relates, when Hess remarks at the end of the film that he does not believe it, 'Göring whispers to him to keep quiet.'[21]

Despite all his criticism of the Hitler regime, Speer had until then had a reasonably clear conscience, at least as far as his own person was concerned. The film shattered his self-righteousness. His admission of 'general responsibility', on which he had prided himself, had basically been little more than an idealistic phrase. Now, however, it turned out that he had manoeuvred himself into a trap. Flächsner did not fail to point this out to him, and urged him again not to keep wanting to stand out. But Speer persisted in his attitude. The 'delayed shock' of which he has spoken probably only hit him when he saw the film.[22] In various statements he described it as the 'definite turning point' in his judgement of the preceding years, of Hitler and the talk of 'annihilation' and 'extermination' which he had listened to for so long without contradict-ing. After the showing on 29 November 1945, he added, he had expect-ed the death sentence without even regarding it as unjust.[23]

From that day onwards, at least, Speer looks highly agitated in pho-tographs from the court room, he has an unsteady gaze and nervous twitches in his face, as if he needed to make an extreme effort to main-tain his composure. While most of his fellow accused usually pretended to be busy, studying documents, talking to their neighbours, or display-ing contemptuous boredom, he sat there calmly, introverted and as though warding off any interference. This time it was not just the social distance which he had instinctively kept, in whatever company he found himself. Now he seemed to have realized more clearly than all the others that this was a matter of life or death, and that any chance of survival, however slight, depended on him differentiating himself, not least in the eyes of the court, from the worthless figures with whom he shared the dock.

Thus, when his turn came a few months later, he defended himself earnestly and stubbornly. It may well be that he was concerned less with saving his own skin than with saving his reputation or what was left of it. The 'highlight' of his defence[24] was undoubtedly the theatrical skill with which he informed the court of his plan to kill Hitler, although it had been nipped in the bud and had probably not been taken entirely seriously even by himself. During their consultations Flächsner had advised him not to mention it at all, because Speer had not even got as far as making an attempt and as he could hardly call any witnesses, and an intended but then abandoned 'deed of glory' might only seem equiv-ocal or ridiculous. On Speer's insistence they eventually agreed that he would 'only mention the plan briefly' during the interrogation, 'more really in order to show how dangerous Hitler's destructive intentions had seemed to him'.[25]

However, Speer did not feel sufficiently sure of his lawyer's agree-ment. For that reason he made use of an absence of Flächsner on leave to ask Franz von Papen's attorney, Dr Egon Kubuschok, to inquire of the reputedly omniscient head of the SS Security Service, Otto Ohlendorf, during his questioning, whether he had ever heard of an assassination plan by Speer in mid February 1945. Of course Ohlendorf had to say no, but Speer had achieved his purpose: the plan had been brought to the knowledge of the court.

According to one of those present, this revelation came 'like a bomb-shell'. During the brief recess that followed shortly thereafter, Göring

The trial of the 22 'principal war criminals' began in the Nuremberg court building on 20 November 1945. Sitting in the front row (from the left): Hermann Göring, Rudolf Hess, Joachim von Ribbentrop and Wilhelm Keitel. In the row behind: Karl Dönitz, Erich Raeder, Baldur von Schirach and Fritz Sauckel. On the right, entering the room, is Speer who sat on the left-hand side of the dock, along with Hjalmar Schacht, Franz von Papen, Julius Streicher, Ernst Kaltenbrunner and others.

rushed through the dock over to Speer, planted himself in front of him, hands on hips, and 'demanded furiously how he had dared to make such a treasonable admission in open court and disrupt their whole united front'. After an excited exchange an indignant Speer told him 'to go to hell'. In the evening Göring still looked dejected. He spoke of that 'stupid fool Speer' and how he could stoop so low as 'to do such a rotten thing to save his lousy neck... – to put it bluntly – to piss in front and crap behind a little longer! *Herrgott, Donnerwetter!*' Next day, during the lunch break, he sent Schirach to call the 'traitor' Speer to order. Speer replied that Göring's fury did not affect him. 'Göring should have been furious when Hitler was leading the whole nation straight to destruction.' As 'the second man in the Reich,' Speer had told Göring in the course of the noisy quarrel in the passage outside the canteen, he 'had the responsibility of doing something about it, but then he was too much of a coward! Instead he doped himself up with morphine and looted art treasures from all over Europe.'[26]

It was one of Speer's rare outbursts and he remained agitated throughout the day. In the evening when Gilbert called on him in his cell to show him some pictures of the endless columns of German prisoners, of the ruins of German cities and of murdered internees, Speer suddenly struck his bunk with his fist and exclaimed: 'Some day I would just like to cut loose... I would just like to sit down and write one final blast about the whole damn Nazi mess and mention names and details and let the German people see once and for all what rotten corruption, hypocrisy and madness the whole system was based on! – I would spare nobody, including myself.'[27]

Moments later he had regained control and, as Gilbert has reported, declined his suggestion to write down a brief summary of the things he condemned. But he encouraged the psychologist in his intention of preventing Göring's presumptuous control over his fellow defendants. Soon afterwards the detainees were forbidden any contact outside the court room, except during meals. Even there the seating order was changed. Göring was allocated a room of his own, while the rest of the defendants took their meals in groups of four. From then onwards Speer found himself in the so-called 'Youth Lunchroom', along with Fritzsche, von Schirach and Funk.[28]

On 19 June 1946 Speer was called to the witness box. Shortly before, he had assured the prison psychologist that he would speak freely: 'I am not going to back down for the sake of getting off with life imprisonment and hate myself for the rest of my life.'[29] Under questioning he avoided any minimization of the misdeeds of the regime, defending himself with characteristic control and sobriety, albeit in full awareness of the special position he had always occupied and which he had no intention of abandoning simply because the accident of life had brought him before a tribunal. He offset the charge of arrogance by his winning demeanour, and stood out for refusing to plead that he had only obeyed orders. Speer also did not omit to point out his change of attitude. In the brief outline of his life, with which he began, he said: 'Through the predilection which Hitler had for architecture I had a close personal contact with him. I belonged to a circle which consisted of other artists and his personal staff. If Hitler had had any friends at all, I certainly would have been one of his close friends.'[30]

This remark, with which Speer, more than any other defendant, emphasized his closeness to Hitler, caused some astonished head-shaking on all sides. But Speer had clearly thought this through, and indeed his opening remarks represented a tactical move of the first order. The distance which he presently created between himself and Hitler and his regime, as well as his profession of 'general responsibility' a few sentences later, were bound to sound that much more convincing, coming as they did from one of Hitler's 'close friends'.

This war has brought an unconceivable catastrophe upon the German people, and indeed started a world catastrophe. Therefore it is my unquestionable duty to assume my share of responsibility for this disaster before the German people. This is all the more my obligation, all the more my responsibility, since the head of the government has avoided responsibility before the German people and before the world... Insofar as Hitler gave me orders, and I carried them out, I assume responsibility for them. I did not, of course, carry out all the orders he gave me.[31]

As he had hoped, this final remark in particular provided Flächsner with the opportunity of questioning Speer on his opposition to Hitler's 'scorched earth' policy, on the so-called 'protected enterprises', which not only saved many industrial plants in all parts of Europe from destruction, but also saved hundreds of thousands of workers from deportation, and about 20 July and how his name came to be on the conspirators' list of cabinet members. The exchanges about German armaments and the astonishing increase in production right up until the war was nearly over, and about Hitler's hopes of victory, revived time and again even in the face of defeat, lasted for several hours. When they were over Flächsner turned to the assassination plan. Referring to a written statement by Dietrich Stahl, which had meanwhile been confirmed by Speer's secretary, Flächsner asked Speer what had led him to that decision. Speer described the growing 'despair' which had seized him at the realization that Hitler was 'confusing his fate with that of the German people and that in his own end he also saw the end of the German people'.[32]

In his memoirs Speer protested that he had intended 'merely to mention' his assassination plan in court, and that he had by no means wanted to 'boast' about it.[33] In fact, under questioning, he did describe it on these lines, somewhat laconically at first. But he could be quite certain that the judges and the prosecutors would not heed this restraint, their curiosity and suspense being such that they were bound to ask for details. Speer's resolve to make the plan a keystone in his defence is borne out not only by the determination with which he had introduced it into the trial some six months previously, but also by the expansive manner in which, as if on cue, he now met the court's request for a detailed account of his intentions, and of the reasons for failure – not, however, without repeated assurances that he was describing all that 'very unwillingly, because such things always have something unpleasant about them'. Asked if the plan had called for special courage, he answered no. Speer commended Guderian and Jodl, he was critical of Göring, and concluded by saying that Hitler had 'knowingly betrayed' the people and tried to 'hurl it into the abyss for good'. The assassination plan, he said, like his actions against Hitler's demolition orders, had its justification in his 'loyal attitude' which he had always maintained towards the greater whole. For this reason also, he said in reply to a question from Flächsner, 'I considered it my duty to remain at my post after July 1944.'[34]

Speer's performance again caused considerable excitement, although this time opinion was divided. Göring left his seat in silence, Funk, 'half-blubbering', thought that one should hang one's head in shame, while Jodl found that Speer's behaviour was 'somehow not proper'. Papen, on the other hand, remarked, glancing smugly at Göring: 'That finishes that fat one!' Schirach, Fritzsche and Speer agreed that 'the Göring-Hitler legend' was now finished. Göring himself found his tongue again after a little while, mumbling 'dark threats and curses'. To some people standing around he said, half-turned towards Speer, that even if he came out of this trial alive, 'the Feme [Kangaroo] Court would assassinate [him] for treason'.[35]

In the evening Speer learned that, contrary to the original division of tasks, Justice Jackson would himself open his cross-examination. The news gave him particular satisfaction in view of his power struggle with Göring. For it represented a gain in prestige to be questioned by the Chief Prosecutor of the United States. Needless to say, this unexpected change fed suspicions of a 'secret arrangement'. In fact, Jacksons's motives were probably much simpler. A few weeks earlier he had suffered a bitter defeat in his cross-examination of Göring. Awkward and unfamiliar both with German and the totalitarian power-structures, Jackson had lost his way not only in the mass of titles, offices and responsibilities, but also in the voluminous material piled up in front of him. With his brazen intellect and quickness at repartee, Göring had snatched the opportunity to wrest the conduct of the questioning from Jackson. His defeat had been the more painful as Sir Geoffrey Lawrence had done nothing to check Göring's flow of words or his enjoyment of a rhetorical brawl. Indeed, the judge had looked on with a degree of indignant admiration. Jackson obviously hoped that his cross-examination of the more amenable Speer would make up for the rebuff from 'Defendant No. 1'.

However, Jackson did not do very well with Speer either. He got carried away by secondary matters, referred to questionable documents, tied himself up, and again showed how little he understood the curiously chaotic structure of the Führer state. After an exhaustive but meaningless discussion about titles and responsibilities he brought up the concentration camps and slave labour. Jackson asked about Himmler's armaments ambitions, and got Speer to admit that he had known both about anti-Semitism and the evacuation of Jews. But when Speer untruthfully denied having been a party 'to the implementation of these evacuation measures', Jackson dropped the subject after adding a few remarks and turned to the recruitment of foreign labour.

During the preceding hearing Speer had already stated 'of his own free will' that he did not wish to create the impression that he had not firmly demanded foreign workers from Sauckel.[36] Now he admitted that most of these workers had been brought to Germany against their will or been 'enrolled for service' in their home countries; however, he had inherited this practice from his predecessor. Next came questions about Hitler's plans for gas warfare, which Speer had foiled by stopping production, and about the various conspiracies he had initiated but then abandoned. Here Speer's answers were evasive. In the course of further questioning Jackson revealed himself as the last believer in Hitler's 'miracle weapons'. He referred to a 'newly invented destruction substance' which had been tested near Auschwitz, almost instantly annihilating 20,000 people 'in such a way that not the least trace was left of them'. Speer had no difficulty in rejecting Jackson's 'report' as an obvious invention.

Safer ground was reached in the second part of his examination, when Jackson produced some documents from the labour camps in the vicinity of the Krupp firm, testifying to inhuman conditions, under-nourishment and maltreatment. However, Speer disputed that the conditions described could be generalized: it had been in the interest of his office to have 'well fed and content' workers, and even Sauckel had fought against the 'wave of stupidity' which had existed at the time. The chief prosecutor did not ask any more detailed questions about the high mortality in the forced labour camps, or about the 'Dora' camp of which Speer had been reminded by blood-curdling images in the film about the liberation of the concentration camps – 'Dante's Inferno', as his head physician had said at the time.

A little later Jackson again found himself in some embarrassment. A 'steel box' which, according to the statements of several prisoners, had served as a specially constructed 'torture cell', 'so small that one could barely stand in it', was identified by Speer from a photograph as an ordinary clothes locker, although he did not dispute that it could have been used for torture by a brutal warder. A further piece of evidence about the scandalous accommodation and inadequate medical care in another camp turned out to be the situation after a heavy air-raid. Whenever Speer contradicted him, Jackson almost sheepishly agreed with him, stating on one occasion: 'That is the same inference that I drew from this document.'[37] As a result of his poor preparation the horror of the camps and the millions of slave workers deported by 'people-catchers' dissolved into a few, certainly deplorable, random images created by the SS, the arbitrariness of subordinate authorities, and, as Speer magnanimously conceded, the understandably exaggerated memories of former inmates, or indeed even by Allied bomber formations.

The British had waived their right to examine Speer. After a few questions by the defence attorneys, the court therefore called on the Soviet Deputy Chief Prosecutor, State Justice Counsellor General M. Y. Raginski. His very first sentences showed that he was not only far better prepared but much more focused than Jackson; besides, he naturally had no problems with the opacities of a totalitarian power apparatus. His short questions, put in a cutting voice, abruptly changed the conciliatory atmosphere of the preceding examination into a bitter duel. But Raginski was mistaken if he thought he could intimidate Speer. With the stubborn determination that was hidden under his outward courtesy, Speer contradicted Raginski's findings and conclusions. At times it seemed almost as if he wanted to show that he preferred an opponent like this to the confused Jackson stumbling through his documents. It helped that Speer was aware of the gradually emerging tensions between the great powers and that he could count on a certain degree of tacit agreement from the representatives of the West.

A question Raginski asked at the beginning typified the further course of the examination. He wanted to know whether as 'one of Hitler's friends', Speer had read *Mein Kampf* and whether he had been aware of the German dictator's anti-Soviet and other aims. Speer almost interrupted him, as if he had been waiting for this cue:

> I can say a few things on this. I was in close touch with Hitler and heard his personal views; and these personal views did not suggest that he had any plans of the kind set out in the documents here. I was particularly relieved in 1939, when the non-aggression pact with Russia was concluded; and after all, your diplomats must also have read *Mein Kampf*, yet even so they concluded the non-aggression pact. And they were certainly more intelligent than I, I mean in political matters.

At another point, when Speer again brought up Soviet conditions to illustrate an argument, Raginski irritably put him in his place with 'I am not asking you about our country.' Speer immediately retorted: 'I only wanted to contribute to your understanding.'[38]

The Soviet prosecutor's examination yielded no new insights of substance. Moreover, the questioning was interrupted by numerous disagreements about translation and by repeated conceptual problems which Speer, thanks to his superior knowledge of the facts, mostly decided in his favour. A few days later the examinations were concluded with the hearing of Neurath and Fritzsche, and a date was set for the opening of the final pleas.

On 23 July the court called Dr Flächsner. On the first two counts – participation in a 'conspiracy' and 'crimes against peace' – he only spoke briefly since, as he pointed out, they clearly did not apply to his client. He dealt all the more extensively with the really incriminating charges of 'war crimes' and 'crimes against humanity', and argued that they basically applied to the forcible provision of foreign labour and the illegal employment of prisoners of war in armaments production. In a chain of discerning and wide-ranging arguments Flächsner pointed out that this kind of employment had already been established under Todt and that Speer was therefore entitled to believe in its legality. Although

Speer's counsel at Nuremberg, Dr Hans Flächsner, during a hearing. On the left the
British deputy chief prosecutor, Sir David Maxwell Fyfe.

he had known since September 1942, at the latest, that the workers had
not come to Germany voluntarily, he had taken no part in deportations,
merely notifying his requirements and leaving everything else to
Sauckel, in line with the responsibilities laid down by Hitler. Nor had
Speer been responsible for the living conditions of foreign workers, even
less so for those of detainees, who were subject to the arbitrary powers
of the SS. On the whole he had always preferred German workers and
he had, furthermore, generally tried to achieve the required production
increases by better organization and rationalization. The documents,
Flächsner argued, also showed beyond any doubt that during Speer's
time in office the number of people employed in armaments production
had risen from four to less than five million, while output was increased
by a factor of five and a half or even seven.

It was this shrewd approach by Speer, Flächsner continued to argue,
that had led to a running battle with Sauckel. He then went on to the
dispute about the protected enterprises, which his client had set up with
the very intention of halting the wretched deportations, mainly from

Western Europe. In addition, Speer had done everything to put an end to shortcomings and to improve the living conditions of the workers, including the Soviet Russian ones, as shown by an order obtained from Hitler by Speer in March 1942 and now before the court, as well as by another order about a year later. Much the same applied to the prisoners of war, although one might have to consider how to define the term 'armaments industry' and whether the Hague Land War Convention, upon which the charge was based, was even applicable to modern war or whether it had long been outdated. Witnesses had testified to the marked improvement in living conditions of the camp inmates as soon as they were employed on armaments. Admittedly Speer had had no influence on the camps to which they returned after discharging their tasks.

Flächsner examined each count of the indictment relentlessly and with an almost painful degree of pedantry. In bringing together everything that supported the thesis of the unworldly artist who got involved with politics against his will, Flächsner created the 'legend' of Speer as the non-political expert minister. Towards the end he pointed out that, since June 1944, at the latest, his client had repeatedly informed Hitler of the critical situation in production and soon afterwards he had tried to make clear to him with increasing urgency the hopelessness of the war. Even Justice Jackson had to concede that among the top figures of the regime Speer had been 'the only man who unreservedly told Hitler the truth'.

Flächsner next dealt with Speer's disregard of orders. A wealth of documents and many witnesses, of whom he named seven (von Poser, Kempf, Schieber, Kehrl, Rohland, Seyss-Inquart and Hirschfeld), had testified that Speer had acted against Hitler's destruction orders at great personal risk, and that he had tried like no one else to save the basics of life not only in his own country but also in large parts of Europe. Flächsner only briefly mentioned Speer's various conspiracy plans, saying that he would have preferred not to mention them at all, but felt he had to touch on them because of the stir they had caused. He concluded with the words: 'Without consideration for his person and without consideration for his safety Speer acted as he considered it his duty to act towards his people. Speer had to betray Hitler in order to remain loyal to his people. One cannot but respect the tragedy which lies in this fate.'[39]

Speer only listened to his attorney's plea with half an ear. Almost throughout, he sat there drawing, as if his fate were sealed anyway and the plea scarcely worthy of attention. One of the sketches has survived. In scraggy lines it shows a fortified castle with sheer mountain faces rising behind, presumably symbolizing the situation in which he saw himself and his chance of survival. At the end of the sitting he gave it to Dr Flächsner, writing underneath: 'drawn during his plea on 23.7.1946. Nuremberg'.[40]

Maybe Speer was simply trying to force himself to stay calm by sketching. He himself has spoken of the 'extreme nervousness' with which he had awaited the court's verdict. A few days later when Lord Justice Lawrence suspended the sittings until the pronouncement of sentence, the thirty-two American journalists present opened a book on the penalties which the various accused would receive. For Speer, eleven of them predicted the death sentence, the others bet on a shorter or longer custodial sentence. Flächsner expected the death sentence, but was hoping for approximately fifteen years' imprisonment. Speer became increasingly discouraged and firmly expected to be sentenced to death.

For meanwhile, on 26 and 27 July, the prosecutors had delivered their final pleas. The performance of Sir Hartley Shawcross, the Chief Prosecutor for the United Kingdom, particularly depressed Speer. In a well-documented performance of cold and precise passion combined with a solid grasp of all the trial material, Shawcross pulled the statements of the defendants and their counsel to pieces, drawing on their own accounts to demonstrate how despicable the regime had been. The defendants, he argued, had themselves created the 'monster' Hitler and could not now complain if they were found to be guilty accomplices in the deeds of that monster. Despite all their efforts to defend themselves, they were nothing but 'perfectly ordinary murderers'. One of the highlights of his speech was the report of a German engineer who had been present at a mass shooting by SS units and Ukrainian militia of five thousand Jews in the Ukraine. His account drove home once again the horror of what had happened, after it had been exhaustively dwelt on to the point where it became submerged or reduced almost beyond recognition by all the excuses brought forward in the series of pleas for the defence. Shawcross also made the defendants aware of their responsibility.

The report of the German engineer stated:

The people descending from the trucks, men, women and children of every age, were made, on the order of an SS man with a horse-whip or dog-whip, to undress and put down their clothes in separate places,

Speer only half-followed his lawyer's summing-up. Convinced that his death sentence was more or less decided, he sat in his place most of the time sketching. This sketch, which Speer entitled 'Tyrolean Reminiscence' and dedicated to Dr Flächsner, has survived.

according to shoes, outer and undergarments. I saw a pile of shoes of approximately eight hundred to a thousand pairs, huge stacks of underwear and clothes. Without shouting or weeping these people undressed, standing together in family groups, kissing each other goodbye and awaiting the orders of another SS man...An old woman with snow-white hair was holding a child of twelve months in her arms, singing to it and tickling it. The child squealed with pleasure. The couple watched with tears in their eyes. The father was holding a boy of about ten by the hand, talking to him softly. The boy was fighting back his tears. His father pointed his finger at the sky, stroked his head and seemed to explain something to him. At that moment the SS man by the ditch called...I walked round the mound of earth and was facing an enormous grave. The people were lying in it pressed together so tightly that only their heads were visible. From nearly all the heads blood was running over the shoulders...[41]

Speer later stated that this report had made an equally ineradicable impression on him as the film shown at the beginning of the proceedings and that Sir Hartley Shawcross's plea had extinguished the last spark of hope. Over the next few days Speer tried to restore his composure by drafting the final address to the court that each defendant was entitled to. Then he wrote his Last Will and Testament and sent it to his 'devastated' friend Rudolf Wolters. Speer asked him to be the executor of his estate, to collect the data for a biography and, more particularly, to prepare the *Chronik* for publication, because he believed in his right to be presented to posterity 'as a different person from all the disgusting bourgeois revolutionaries who had risen with the Hitler movement'.[42] To distract himself he took out Dickens' *Tale of Two Cities*, with its description of a stay in prison, from the prison library. He also began to write his memoirs. During the weeks that followed he completed something over a hundred pages, mainly about his time as a minister.

On the last day of August the defendants made their final speeches. They were broadcast, just as the judgement was to be. All except Hess and, with a few justifications, Jodl condemned the crimes and terrible mass murders, but denied both their knowledge of them and their participation in them. Feeling that he had already said all there was to say, Speer did not deal with this matter. Instead he gave a kind of lecture on the devastating consequences of technology, which had radically transformed the state of the world and of the individual, starting with new means of psychologically enslaving entire populations and police surveillance methods, the possibility of keeping criminal deeds secret, right up to war with rockets, atom bombs and chemical weapons. These were his old reservations about the modern world, familiar from the days of his youth, to which he was now returning after so many detours and which almost concealed his personal failure. As 'the most important representative of a technocracy,' he explained in his final address, 'which had showed no compunction in applying all its know-how against humanity, I tried not only to confess but also to understand what had happened.' Earlier dictatorships, he said in court, had needed followers who thought and acted independently at all levels. A mechanized age, however, only required and produced the type of person who took orders uncritically. Speer concluded with the words:

The nightmare of many a man that one day nations could be dominated by technical means was all but realized in Hitler's totalitarian system. Today the danger of being terrorized by technocracy threatens every country in the world. In modern dictatorship this appears to me inevitable. Therefore, the more technical the world becomes, the more necessary is the promotion of individual freedom and the individual's awareness of himself as a counter-balance. Therefore this trial must contribute towards establishing rules whereby human beings can live together.[43]

A month later, on 30 September, the court again assembled. Taking turns, the eight judges took several hours to read the verdict. The following day the defendants entered the courtroom one by one to receive their sentences. Twelve of them, including Martin Bormann *in absentia*, were sentenced to death by hanging, three were acquitted, and the remaining seven were given sentences ranging from ten years to life imprisonment. Speer was sentenced to twenty years under counts III and IV, chiefly for his participation in the forced labour programme. In mitigation the court took into consideration 'that in the closing stages of the war he was one of the few men who had the courage to tell Hitler that the war was lost and to take steps to prevent the senseless destruction of production facilities, both in occupied territories and in Germany. He carried out his opposition to Hitler's scorched earth programme in some of the Western countries and in Germany by deliberately sabotaging it at considerable personal risk.'[44] Later it became known that the day of the pronouncement of judgement had been delayed largely because the Soviet judges and the American Francis Biddle had insisted on the death sentence for Speer in particular and had given in only after several days of embittered argument.[45]

In years to come, Speer was repeatedly accused of having gained the sympathy of the majority of the Nuremberg judges by questionable means, thus escaping the gallows. His efforts to offer his services to the Western interrogators, his letter to Justice Jackson, his arrogant behaviour towards the Soviet prosecutor and much else, from the very vague references to his conspiracy to the good manners which he was careful to maintain, were all regarded as calculated attempts to veil the truth and to fool the tribunal and even history. Speer's critics maintained that his assumption of 'general responsibility' had simply been a move in his survival strategy, that it had been a gesture, designed to impress the public and to secure for himself the customary leading role which he did not wish to give up even in court. It certainly had had no incriminating significance, they argued. Instead it had given him the opportunity to portray himself as a kind of abstract villain. But as soon as matters got specific, bloody and horrifying, he had invariably dissociated himself and, by denying any personal participation, he had also denied any criminal responsibility.[46]

Speer always accepted such objections with astonishment and equanimity. Only the accusation that he should not have defended himself at all, provoked an angry denial. What else did those people expect, he asked. Surely it was legitimate to defend oneself in court, provided this was not done at the expense of another party; like everyone else he had simply wanted to survive. He had certainly never denied his share in the injustice caused, neither in court nor when arguing with his attorney, and for weeks on end he had endured the accusation of treason from his fellow defendants. What more should he have done?

Of course he realized that this kind of response merely amounted to an admission of what his critics accused him of. But he had never had a problem as far as arrogance was concerned, he added ironically. After the verdict he had never really relished his success, if it could be described as such, indeed he had fallen into deeper depression than ever before. Dr Flächsner has suggested, by way of explanation, that perhaps 'the fact that he didn't get the death sentence diminished him in his own eyes'.[47]

There may have been another factor. At the time of his sentence Speer was forty-one. The idea of spending the most active years of his life mindlessly walking round a prison yard must have seemed a prospect worse than any other punishment for a man who could not live without a task and for whom restlessness had been the source of any satisfaction he could conceive of. When his wife visited him in the period following the pronouncement of judgement, a dull hammering was heard from the end of the prison tract, as the gallows were erected for those who were to be executed in a few days time. In the course of the vacuous conversation, broken by embarrassed pauses, Speer suddenly asked the 'desperate' question: 'What am I to do with all the many years ahead of me now? Do they not amount to a never-ending execution, starting anew each day?' Until then, he later explained, he had always had an answer to the emergencies he had found himself in, an answer consisting of plans, works and great objectives; now for the first time there was none.[48]

Chapter Eleven
SCHOOL FOR SURVIVAL

The first weeks were the hardest. The notes which Speer made at the time describe hours of 'dozing', periods of apathy and insomnia, as well as being haunted by the horrific images from the trial. In his daydreams he saw a recurrent 'movie in which a desperate man fights his way through the waters of a man-high Paris sewer to a distant exit'.[1] The books he ordered lay around untouched for days, now and again he tried to write something down, but soon gave up the effort.

Speer was also troubled by his relations with his fellow prisoners. One day, when Schirach questioned him on his 'general responsibility' and he contradicted him, all of them, as if by command, about-turned and left him standing on his own. He often calculated how many of the 'seven thousand three hundred days plus five intercalary days' had already passed, and came up with shattering figures. Towards the end of November 1946 the American prison commander, Colonel Andrus, arrived and informed the prisoners that they would shortly be moved to Berlin. But December passed without relocation, and so did the spring, because the victorious powers could not agree on the conditions of detention. Those were wearying weeks, filled with the fear, as Speer recorded, of 'drowning' in the void. Accustomed as he was to attributing all troubles to unsolved questions of organization, he decided to 'organize his life as a convict' and devise a 'technique of survival'.[2]

His first attempt aimed at prolonging his daily sleeping time from the usual six to twelve hours. He had calculated that this would reduce his sentence by another quarter, to about half the time. When this did not work, he forced himself to read regularly; he began to draw again, or he rehearsed imaginary dialogues, speaking both parts himself. Now and again he was summoned to meetings with lawyers involved in subsequent trials or for brief appearances in the witness box. Once he caught sight of Karl Brandt from the distance; he was accused of having performed medical experiments on human beings. On another occasion he saw Karl Otto Saur. It 'amused' Speer to observe how 'obsequiously' his former deputy was obeying the orders of a sergeant, recognizing in him the 'terrifying combination' of 'obedience and dynamism' to which 'the regime had owed so much'.[3] In between times he worked on his memoirs, started keeping a diary, and whenever something occurred to him about the years gone by, he made a note of it. He also corresponded with Wolters and his family, passing the letters to a prison chaplain for distribution.

In the summer of 1947 the complicated negotiations were brought to an end when the powers eventually agreed on the order of detention. On 18 July the prisoners were woken at dawn and flown to Berlin under heavy guard. After two years they were able to see the outside world for the first time. When they were over Berlin, Speer recognized the East-West Axis next to the new Reich Chancellery amidst the endless fields of rubble, with the Victory Column moved to the Grosse Stern. That, at any rate, was still there, he said to himself. Everything else he had designed and scheduled for completion that year would for ever remain 'architecture on the drawing board'.[4]

They drove in convoy from the Tempelhof airfield to the prison in Spandau in a bus with blacked-out windows, each prisoner handcuffed to a soldier. The prison, bathed in the brilliant glare of searchlights, had been renovated by the British. It was secured by an outer wall and an electrified barbed-wire fence. Immediately upon arrival the prisoners had to put on drill uniforms which came from the camps where Speer's slave workers had been kept. In the order in which they entered the room each one was allocated a number, which, from then on, served as his form of address: Speer received 'Number Five'. As he entered his cell, he discovered on the woollen blankets laid out for him the imprint GBI – short for Generalbauinspektion, where his career had begun.

The prisoners were treated with the 'utmost distance'. All conversation, even with the guards, was forbidden. For half an hour each day they were taken out, far apart from each other, to the overgrown garden behind the cell block. Visitors were not permitted, on principle. But every two months the prisoners could see a family member for fifteen minutes and they were allowed to receive or write a one-page letter every month. Although they were given paper for making notes or to write down thoughts, anything they had written was collected in the evening and – as the prisoners only learned twelve years later – put into the shredder. The methods of detention with which the prisoners had rightly been charged, were now being applied to them. As if to indicate that he had nothing to do with these conditions, the French chief warden observed after only ten days, under his breath but audibly: 'How can one treat them this way? It's shameful.'[5]

Speer had one advantage over his fellow prisoners in that he approved of his sentence, morally at least. This was confirmed when Raeder one day remarked to him with a touch of envy that he had evidently come to terms with his imprisonment more easily than the rest of them. A revealing note shows that Speer saw no difference between accepting his sentence and his continuous efforts to discipline himself, to read and to write. For him they all belonged to the organizational tasks he now had to deal with. How else, he noted, was he to survive twenty years of detention?[6]

As time went on, the strict regime was relaxed. In August the British prison director suggested to the prisoners that they might work in the garden for a few hours each day, and they all declared themselves willing. Again, for reasons of self-therapy Speer began to dream of a new 'life's work', his third as it were, resuming what he now regarded as his preordained career, where it was broken off when he met Hitler. He remembered his teacher Heinrich Tessenow, who, protesting against the architectural megalomania of the epoch, had stuck to the ideal of ascetic, craft-based construction. Speer now believed that, considering the general lack of funds, these teachings would unexpectedly assume a new importance. He would carry on Tessenow's work, he wrote, with a sense of at last having found a new task. 'I am ready to make a fresh start. I am not unhappy.'[7]

A few weeks later something occurred that had far greater consequences. About the middle of October one of the Dutch male nurses, a young man of twenty-three called Toni Proost, approached Speer with an offer to provide him with a secret, uncensored link with the outside world. Proost, it later emerged, was one of the millions of slave workers deported to Germany during the war and employed there in an armaments plant. Speer was taken aback when in an unguarded moment the Dutchman whispered to him that he had, on the whole, been lucky: he had fallen seriously ill, but had been cured at a specialist hospital; soon the chief surgeon had not only employed him as an operating-theatre assistant but he also taken him into his family 'like a son'.[8]

Speer admitted that this unexpected offer transformed his entire existence. The two men agreed on a sign language for whenever Speer needed paper or had something to 'drop'. A 'network' was already in existence, as Wolters had decided to help his friend and his family, particularly as he had himself got off scot-free. Together with the inde-fatigable Frau Kempf he organized a busy exchange of secret messages which soon comprised not only letters and documents. After some time books on the index, alcohol, and on special occasions even delicacies such as pâté de fois gras and champagne got into the heavily guarded prison. Eventually Wolters even succeeded in providing Speer with a small camera.[9] Despite the many hours spent by the prisoner at his table in his cell, which was under continual surveillance, and despite a number of slip-ups, the connection remained undiscovered throughout all Speer's years in prison. Everything Speer sent to Wolters was typed out by his assistant Marion Riesser. If one considers that, by the end of Speer's detention, the material amounted to some 20,000 pages, one gets an idea of the volume of traffic that had developed between Spandau and Coesfeld.

Outside the seemingly impenetrable walls of Spandau this unexpect-ed turn of events also led to new activity. Wolters opened an account under his own name, the so-called 'school fee account', designed to support Speer's large and needy family. Wolters pressed the minister's former colleagues in particular, many of whom by then held senior posi-tions, pointing out that, in a sense, Speer was 'inside' on behalf of them all. He also reminded the industrialists in the Düsseldorf and Dortmund area of the telegram at the end of the war, which had conveyed to Speer the enduring gratitude of the Ruhr region. The fund grew quickly and soon Speer's family, who had meanwhile returned to Heidelberg, received 200 marks a month. Later this account was used to support various other people. When Proost's son was gravely ill, Speer arranged for the cost of a blood transfusion to be remitted to him.

Speer's literary ambitions were also fired by the new opportunities. After various attempts to put his early meetings with Hitler into writing and describe his lasting power over other people, Speer decided at the beginning of 1948 to set himself a task once again. As if he could not do otherwise, he involuntarily conceived a 'book of major importance', as he recorded, and he could think of nothing more important than a biography of Hitler. He began to assemble his experiences and what-ever else occurred to him in connection with the man who had domi-nated his life in such an extraordinary way. But after several painful attempts the project got stuck, losing itself in trivialities and anecdotes. As his doubts grew, so the layers of recollections became inextricably mingled until he abandoned his intention without much ado. 'Listless-ness, scepticism, weariness', he recorded at first. After a few more false

SPEER

starts he admitted in August: 'For three months I have produced no notes.'[10]

Instead, unable as ever to do anything by halves, he devoted himself to the overgrown garden behind the cells, often to the point of exhaustion. Speer aimed to transform the approximately 6,000 square-metre plot of old nut trees, lilac and undergrowth into a park. In addition he prescribed for himself a daily stint of several hours' reading, he began to draw again, even designing building plans for some of the warders. In organizing his life he did not omit a period of 'leave', which he fitted in every six months and spent mostly sleeping with the help of sedatives. On one occasion the prison administration ordered the prisoners to make envelopes, but the order was soon rescinded for fear that it might give rise to a kind of trade in relics. Then again the American director conceived the idea of making the prisoners weave baskets, but they all protested so vehemently against this 'discriminatory' activity, which having obtained legal support they said was the preserve of penitentiaries and lunatic asylums, that the order was scrapped.

Apart from his ties with Toni Proost, which soon become cordial, the only other relationship Speer developed was with the French prison chaplain Georges Casalis. He had based his first service on the passage: 'In Israel the lepers were separated from the community of the people by a multitude of legal provisions; these were as insuperable as a prison wall.' Raeder, Dönitz and Schirach were outraged by his choice, claiming that Casalis had described them as 'lepers'. But Speer defended the chaplain and after that he sought his company and even his friendship. It was Casalis who helped him over the hardships of the first few years and it was a heavy blow to Speer when, in the summer of 1950, Casalis was recalled from Spandau. Until then, however, he helped him as his unrelenting spiritual adviser, even though the religious world remained closed to Speer all his life and, for all his attempts to understand it, he remained uncomprehending. But eager to learn as always, he followed the priest's recommendations and spent years struggling through the 9,000 pages of Karl Barth's *Kirchliche Dogmatik*. More than half-way through his studies he spurred himself on with the thought that even something one did not understand could have a calming effect.[11]

Relations with his fellow prisoners continued to be difficult. The warders of the four powers rotated monthly, and Speer on the whole got on well with them. But with his fellow inmates new tensions kept arising. They more or less openly accused him of 'opportunism' or even of 'masochism' and told him that he was 'defaming the whole German

One of his friends had procured a miniature camera for Speer, which was smuggled into the Spandau prison with the help of a warder. The prison regulations demanded that the prisoners were addressed not by their names but only by their numbers. Speer was 'No. 5.'

nation' with his craving for recognition. When, after some time, conversation among them was at least tolerated, he often saw them put their heads together; but, as a note in his diary records, whenever he approached 'they fall silent or turn away'. He was often tempted to give in: 'a few words' and they would take him back into their circle. Only his secret pride, which had always made him rise above everything, together with the feeling that he 'had never quite belonged fully anywhere', helped him over such moments of weakness.[12] But there was always a high degree of irritability among the others too. It was often sparked off by pointless disputes over their pecking order and whether Hess as Hitler's 'Deputy' or Dönitz as his successor should have precedence. Then they would move on to other equally long-standing conflicts, made redundant by time and surviving only in this spectral world. Often these arguments ended in aggressive self-pity. The prisoners were unanimous in rejecting the offer of the prison administration to let them take their meals together in future.

In 1949 Speer had his first visit from his wife; she had accumulated several two-month permits and was allowed to see him for a full hour. But it was 'torture', he recorded; watched by five watchers and one minuting clerk, separated by a double grille, 'we were unable to utter a single natural word'. When looking at the photographs of his children, whom he had not seen for four years, he repeatedly had trouble recognizing them. For the first time he sensed that he had 'lost them not just for the duration of [his] detention, but for ever'. Later when the children came themselves he usually sat stiffly facing them, forcing himself to smile, vainly searching for questions as if paralysed, and receiving polite answers which told him nothing. 'We exchanged monologues,' he remarked wearily, and for years afterwards he wondered 'whether it might not be better if I never came home again'.[13]

The prisoners only took in events in the outside world from afar, since newspapers were not at first allowed in and the staff had strict instructions not to pass any information on to the prisoners. Even so they learned about the Berlin blockade, about the foundation of the Federal Republic and, soon after, that of the German Democratic Republic, and about the war in Korea. They were particularly interested in reports about the increasing hardening of East-West relations, because these affected their own future. From hints and casual remarks they concluded that when the four-power administration collapsed, they would each be handed over to the power that had taken them prisoner. Shortly afterwards there was a rumour that the SS leader Otto Skorzeny, who had distinguished himself during the war in various commando actions, such as the liberation of Mussolini, was planning a helicopter attack on Spandau prison to free its inmates. Then there was another rumour that they were no longer in Spandau but had been taken to a 'villa with barred windows' near the Kurfürstendamm.[14]

In line with the public mood of the early fifties, aimed as it was at conciliation and forgetting, efforts were launched to achieve the release of the prisoners. Wolters persuaded the Düsseldorf lawyer and future minister in Northrhine-Westphalia, Werner Schütz, to intervene in Bonn, but Adenauer was never prepared to go beyond a few prevaricating statements, while any intercession whatsoever met with 'icy rejection' from the first Federal President, Theodor Heuss. The efforts of the lawyer Otto Kranzbühler, Dönitz's counsel in Nuremberg, to obtain a retrial at least for his client and for Speer, were similarly unsuccessful. As Dr Flächsner was busy warding off, or at least delaying, a de-Nazification court action against Speer, Wolters began to gather exonerating evidence. In addition to Heinrich Tessenow, the architect Paul Bonatz made statements in Speer's favour, as did many others whom he had helped against some Party authority or other. Further witnesses emerged, testifying to his fearless opposition to Hitler's 'scorched earth' orders. One of the greatest successes of these efforts was a letter which arrived one day from Paul Nitze, who had interrogated Speer at Glücksburg and had meanwhile become Director of Planning in the US State Department. He assured Speer of his sympathy and even spoke of the respect he felt for him.[15]

Even though the psychological organization of his period in prison involved avoiding any hope of premature release, the sudden efforts being made in all directions imperceptibly swept Speer along. They were lent additional weight by news of the rearmament of the Federal Republic. Dönitz for his part declared that raising a German army was impossible so long as senior officers like himself were detained in Spandau.[16] Another factor came into play in the spring of 1952 when Speer's second child Hilde gained a one-year school scholarship to the United States. There she had made contact with John J. McCloy, until recently the American High Commissioner in West Germany. Although he had by then withdrawn from politics to become president of a Boston bank, he was still well connected in Washington. He was impressed by Speer's daughter and not only sent a letter to Heidelberg, expressing his confidence that part of Speer's sentence would be remitted, but also arranged for Hilde to meet the American Secretary of State Dean Acheson.

The book project, which gradually took shape, was what kept Speer going during those months of waiting and misleading activity; 'Liberation by writing things down', was the maxim for survival which he had jotted down at the beginning of his detention.[17] He now realized, however, that the Hitler biography he had planned to write not only exceeded his possibilities, but that it also gave him less opportunity to achieve self-justification than the story of his own life, which, in any case, partly overlapped with the biography of the dictator. After several failed attempts he got down to work at the beginning of 1953, recording first of all the events of the final months of the war, Hitler's 'scorched earth' orders, the resulting disputes, and his last visit to the Reich Chancellery. But soon he hesitated, rejected what he had written, and started anew. This time he dispensed with an opening that would surround him with a kind of halo. Instead he began with his childhood and his parental home. Work progressed 'naturally', he stated with relief, and he was 'happy to have a task that will take years'.[18] In a letter accompanying the first delivery he asked Wolters not to judge what he had written too harshly and not to show it to any outsider. He himself was 'not satisfied with it', as he was constantly being disturbed by the guards and 'always had to keep one ear pricked up, which is distracting'.[19]

Speer's fear of his friend's judgement was by no means unfounded. But it had nothing to do with any literary shortcomings. Wolters had already observed Speer's performances at Nuremberg with astonished misgivings. Responding to a critical but cautiously phrased question, Speer had told him that in Nuremberg he had merely accepted responsibility, 'not the guilt'.[20] Although Wolters had never been a Party man, endeavouring over the years to keep an independent judgement, he regarded the vehemence with which Speer had moved away from the regime as an act of disloyalty to their past, to the great projects they had planned and to the potent visions of the future which they had conjured up and lost. Now that Wolters was complaining that Hitler was being referred to as a 'criminal' in the pages he had received, it dawned on Speer for the first time that he would 'lose a good many friends'. But, as he observed, 'there is no dodging that.'[21]

So as not to discourage the friend he still revered, Wolters kept silent in future. He even encouraged Speer, and the manuscript was indeed completed roughly a year later. For several months Speer was busy with corrections and additions, but on 29 December 1954 his *Diaries* reported that he had finished his memoirs 'as best he could'. The typescript ran to some 1,100 pages. In the depressive moods that came over him, particularly after Neurath and Raeder were released, he often clung to the idea of the unfinished book for support. 'It is becoming the sole task I can still see ahead,' he wrote.[22]

It may have been the thought of a new void that soon made his depression worse. Even while his work on the manuscript was drawing to a close he had been anxiously looking around for a new task that would absorb him. After some thought he hit on the the idea of covering the distance from Berlin to Heidelberg by walking around the garden – 626 kilometres, as he calculated. As he had no tape-measure, he marked out the path by shoe-lengths. It came to 870 units, which he multiplied by the thirty-one centimetres of a shoe, concluding that one circuit would equal roughly 270 metres. Then he fixed an approximate daily route and after four weeks recorded that he had covered 240 kilometres. Watching him do one round after another, Hess on one occasion called out to him jokingly whether he was training for a job as a rural postman.

As was his wont, Speer exerted himself even in a monotonous task such as this one and continually stepped up his daily stint. One day in November 1954, however, when he did more than twenty-four kilometres on his round, his body rebelled. His right leg swelled to nearly double its normal size, just as had happened eleven years earlier. He also developed bronchitis which caused a pulmonary infarction, as before, and confined him to an oxygen tent for three weeks. This time his illness obviously also had psychological causes, especially as it coincided with Neurath's release. When Speer was taken back to his cell shortly thereafter, prematurely as he believed, he suffered a nervous breakdown in the course of which he screamed at the assembled medical staff, shaking with rage. His overall condition was sufficiently alarming for the doctors to prescribe sedatives for some time, fearing that he might contemplate suicide. However, as soon as he recovered, he resumed his wanderings, first choosing Munich as his destination and continuing his journey from there. He read everything the Spandau municipal library could provide about his route, he ordered guidebooks, travelogues and cultural history books, in order to obtain as accurate a picture as possible of the regions through which he walked. Speer recorded his impressions in a kind of log book, combining what he had read or imagined about the route first across the Balkans, via Istanbul, and on through Afghanistan to India, or wherever his period of detention might take him.

So the years went by, each year the same as the next. Once again, confused hopes of early release alternated with phases of deep depression. In the night of 1 October 1956, ten years after the pronouncement of judgement, Dönitz left the prison. In the afternoon there had been a final excited argument with Speer in the prison garden, when all the irritations of the past decade erupted once more. The quarrels between those left behind also continued, as did the chicanery and humiliations inflicted by the guards. Speer observed how each of the prisoners developed his own way of dealing with them, either by flattery, servility or by trying to curry favour. They had, he believed, all had a double dose of an arbitrary regime – first at the top level and then at the bottom level, and he wondered which of the two had corrupted them more. From time to time important visitors came to view the once mighty as convicts, like the 'living inventory of a waxworks'.[23]

Speer spent much of his time inventing variants of his 'survival system'. Occasionally he would go to the theatre and in his imagination he would put on special clothes, compile cast lists, and walk about in a fantasy foyer until the curtain rose over an imagined scene and he began to declaim the play in an actor's voice. He rediscovered his pleasure in reading and tried to catch up on what he had missed for years through novels – Dostoevsky, Balzac and Hemingway, Tolstoy, Maupassant, Schnitzler, Swift or Dreiser, in any order – whereas, he noted, he could not relate to the 'moaning literature from Böll to Walser', adding that he doubted whether these writers presented 'a halfway reliable picture of present conditions', and whether 'that morass of greed, vice, conformism, Nazi mentality and mediocrity' which impinges itself on the reader actually existed in the outside world. Often he had the impression that this society 'only existed in idle talk'.[24]

One day, an American sergeant unexpectedly offered his services as a courier, so that Speer now had two lines to the outside. Initially he feared that two messengers, who were not meant to know about each other, would be too much for him, but then he agreed. It was a wise precaution, as Proost had to leave the service at the beginning of 1958, because of an incident with the Soviet occupying power. Around the same time, the seriously ill Funk was prematurely discharged. What Speer dreaded had come about. 'Now there are only three of us. I am really alone. Schirach and Hess do not count,' he wrote gloomily.[25]

Speer threw himself all the more tirelessly into gardening, often working to the point of exhaustion, planting fruit bushes and flowers, laying out rock gardens, creating mixed borders and lawns, and harvesting nuts together with the warders. He had to force himself to write: Speer had done with the past on completing his memoirs, and he still lacked the words to describe the monotony of prison life. Reading, which had helped him for a few years, was beginning to pall and he increasingly felt he was reading himself into fatigue. Calcutta had been the initial destination of the trek he had mapped out. In spite of all his doubts he had hoped to have been released by then, at the latest. Yet in October 1958 he crossed the Chinese frontier and, downhearted, proceeded to Peking and possibly to Vladivostok and maybe the American continent. He was getting increasingly worried that he had been forgotten by the world. Then one day the American ambassador David Bruce came to Spandau. The mere fact that he did not address him as 'Number Five', as the prison staff and all previous visitors did, but by his name, cheered Speer up. When he bade farewell, Bruce repeatedly

Behind the cell block of Spandau prison was an overgrown garden of 6,000 square metres. One of the tasks Speer set himself in order to cope with his time in prison was the conversion of the plot into a little park.

said, 'you are not forgotten!', as if he had guessed Speer's worries. All the hopes which had been buried, came back, at least for a time.

Meanwhile months went by and eventually the months became years. Speer passed Los Angeles and crossed the desert landscape into Mexico. 'Merciless sun on dusty roads,' he wrote; 'my soles burned on the hot ground...where kilometre stones mark my doleful passage.'[26] A Russian warder, with whom he got talking while gardening, told him of his disquieting experiences with officials of the German Democratic Republic. 'Germans under Hitler uncanny,' he said; 'and Germans under Ulbricht also. Everything always perfect. Everything always tidy.' Then, turning to me unexpectedly, 'You too with your garden.'[27]

Like all the fruitless endeavors of those years, the interventions on his behalf also continued. Herbert Wehner, Charles de Gaulle, George Ball, Martin Niemöller, Fabian von Schlabrendorff and many others called for his release. Eagerly he noted these reports, which mostly came from his daughter Hilde, but then nothing happened. Speer noticed that as time seemed to stand still he was becoming more and more of a 'hermit'. He almost felt as though he were lost to the world. He only glanced cursorily, if at all, at the newspapers which the prisoners had been permitted for some time, content that his circumstances spared him from participating in political life, in the struggles, pointless discussions and the self-importance of the politicians. He was back in the unpolitical world from which he had come, and yet he had once aspired to be the second man in a powerful Reich. 'How remote all that is!' he wrote. 'Another world!' The statics of a cupola, the façade of a Renaissance palace or the idea of the window in architecture, on the subject of which he began to write an essay, interested him more than the Hungarian Rising or the Cuban crisis. In those contemplative moods in which he liked to indulge he began to wonder whether, when it was all over, he would not miss the regular pace of prison life, his gardening, his books, his musings, and even the silly annoyances with the warders, so that, like the medieval hermit who was brought to Rome and installed as Pope, he would be tempted to ask for his desert back. 'The idea', he wrote, of spending the rest of my days here no longer frightens me.'[28]

What sustained him more than anything else were the academic achievements of his sons and daughters, above all the competitions won by his eldest son Albert, a budding architect, and the morally strict and caring attention of his daughter Hilde. Towards the end he abandoned the survival system kept up as if by reflex for so many years. The endurance strategies which he had thought up had supported him, but they had also exhausted him, he wrote.

> This idiotic organization of emptiness was more enervating than emptiness itself ever could have been. All I am left with in the end is nothing but the foolish satisfaction of having clung to a few resolutions ... Isn't that in itself an expression of the madness I was trying to escape? I always looked down on my fellow prisoners, who were unable to occupy themselves or to set themselves goals. But what goals did I really have? Isn't the sight of a man marching obstinately in a circle for decades far more absurd and weird?

In a mood of resignation he added, 'I cannot fool myself: I have been deformed.' Even his writing mania now seemed to him pathological and on several occasions he burned his notes. On the other hand he also wondered, 'Could I have survived this time if I had not been able to write a single line?'[29] As his last year began, he stood on a stool in order to watch, through the window high up in his cell, the pitiful firework display put on by the British soldiers outside.

The day before his release, 30 September 1966, passed like any other day. Twice Speer went out into the garden, he weeded the flower beds one more time and, walking round and round, covered ten kilometres of an imaginary desert track. In the afternoon a warder came and told him confidentially that the Mayor of Berlin, Willy Brandt, had sent his daughter Hilde a bunch of red roses to mark her father's release. In the evening Speer instructed his courier to send a telegram to Rudolf Wolters: 'Please collect me thirty-five kilometres south of Guadalajara (Mexico). Uncle Alex.'

One minute before midnight Speer and Baldur von Schirach, whose time was also up, were conducted to the prison exit by the four directors. When a clock began to strike somewhere, the blue double door opened and as Speer stepped across the threshold his wife ran up to him through an excited mêlée of British soldiers. A few steps away Dr Flächsner was waiting by a Mercedes. The forecourt and Wilhelmstrasse were crowded with people, a few drunks shouted 'Release Hess!' and a banner announced: 'The Persian people greet Speer and Schirach in freedom.'

Escorted by several police vehicles, the car pushed its way through the crowd in the blinding glare of numerous television spotlights and through fireworks of flashing cameras to Heerstrasse and towards the city centre to a secluded hotel in the Grunewald. There, too, an almost indescribable crowd of journalists and photographers, and countless curious onlookers, pushed and jostled in the lobby. When, standing at the foot of the stairs, Speer asked for understanding that this evening belonged above all to his wife and that he was therefore going to say only a few words, someone in the crowd shouted: 'You've nothing at all to say to us any longer, Herr Speer!' Speer hesitated for a moment and then decided not to reply. Asked how he saw his future, he pointed out that he was an architect and hoped that he would be getting commissions in the future.[30]

Early the following morning he and his wife succeeded in shaking off their pursuers and escaped by plane to Hanover. While still in Spandau Speer had, with Frau Kempf's help, made arrangements for a family reunion. He had rented a remote hunting lodge on the Kellersee in Schleswig-Holstein for a couple of weeks. Some fifteen people were awaiting him when he arrived at lunchtime, all happy to see him again and anxious to display the joy and the festive spirit of the occasion. Everyone seemed to have rehearsed their expressions, the uninhibited

Albert Speer with his wife at the Hotel Gerhus in Berlin immediately after his release
on the night of 1 October 1966. A little later he gave a short press conference for the
large number of journalists present, and then retired.

words and gestures which would overcome the inevitable inhibitions of
the moment.

The children were grown up by now and most of them had hardly
any memories of their father. They only knew the prisoner behind the
wire grille, while the sons- and daughters-in-law were meeting him for
the very first time, not without a certain amount of emotion. But the
sentences they had prepared in their minds, the slightly too familiar
tone with which they hoped to help themselves, and him, overcome the
awkward situation, the probing sympathy in every question and the
forced matter-of-factness they adopted made the conversation falter
time and again, until it broke off altogether. Speer himself kept going

back to Spandau, to the warders who had been sympathetic or hostile, the books he had read, the flowers he had planted, and the dragging time over which he had deceived himself. But most of this had long been familiar to those present and they merely listened with a patient air. Someone made a new start, but again those terrible pauses arose, someone else tried to bridge them with a casual remark which only made the embarrassment more audible and then the conversation petered out again.

Even in Spandau Speer had noticed, when his family visited, that he lacked the simple words and spontaneous warmth which are rooted in all sorts of trivialities, but at that time he had put these difficulties down to the circumstances. Now he realized that this estrangement went much deeper. During the years of his absence they had all created their own worlds. They had plans, friends, teachers or ideas which were alien to him. Everything they said was connected with experiences of which he had no part, and while they spoke about the future he was unable to get away from the past, which was all he had or ever would have. When he looked back on this family reunion he always spoke of a sense of bitter disappointment which had come over him; not even in Spandau had he ever felt so lonely. The fortnight seemed unending. Soon he was longing to be back in his cell, in his garden, with his books, his doggedly determined walks and the monastic life.[31]

The meeting with Rudolf Wolters, whom Speer visited after his family reunion, was also disenchanting. Showing no emotion, he entered the house with a deliberately casual 'How are you? Long time no see ...' There had already been some ill feeling between them a few days earlier because without saying anything to Wolters, Speer had invited the industrialist Ernst-Wolfgang Mommsen to Coesfeld for the evening. As armaments adviser Mommsen had been one of his 'young men' in the ministry. Speer felt all the more entitled to invite him as Mommsen had not only been one of the most generous contributors to the school fee account set up by Wolters but he had also provided the car which had picked Speer up at the Spandau prison gate. Wolters had wanted to spend the evening alone with his friend whom he had served as informer, courier, family adviser, administrator of funds and in various other capacities. Presumably he had also hoped to end their differences about the Hitler years, which still stood between them. But after a violent outburst of anger, he had decided to swallow his irritation for the time being, in order not to spoil their reunion.[32]

The very next day he gave Speer the numerous, carefully sorted stacks of papers which had accumulated at his home – the revised version of the *Chronik*, the secret messages from prison, the draft of *Inside the Third Reich* with all the supplements and addenda, the Spandau diaries, and numerous other notes including the log book of his globe-trotting, which eventually had amounted to nearly 32,000 kilometres. In most cases the material was made up of the (by then scarcely decipherable) original as well as the typed transcripts. The collection also comprised copies of his building plans, photographs of the completed buildings and of the models, and photographs from Spandau. Finally Frau Riesser handed over to him a cheque for 25,000 marks, representing the balance of the school fee account.[33] Together with the proceeds from the sale of his modest property in Berlin-Schlachtensee, made possible by Willy Brandt's suspension of Speer's de-Nazification proceedings, the sum provided his basic capital for the next few years. To end their meeting on a conciliatory note Wolters presented his friend with a Westphalian ham on the bone, first promised him ten years earlier while Speer was still in Spandau; it came from a pig born on 5 March 1953, the day Stalin died.

Speer drove on to Ratingen to see Walter Rohland. His thank-you letter to Coesfeld speaks of the 'wonderfully harmonious days' they had spent together. But Wolters was the more accurate observer. In his memoirs, *Lebensabschnitte*, he notes that at their first meeting he had known 'subliminally' that their friendship had 'reached its end'. 'As he stood before me again, in person, I suddenly saw him quite differently than at a distance in Spandau. I experienced something similar to what he did with Hitler when he met him again after a long illness.' Wolters no longer saw the endearing features of the other man, his generous and magnanimous qualities, but, as he wrote, 'only the "thick nose".'[34]

The estrangement almost reached breaking point when the news magazine *Der Spiegel* published an interview with Speer at the beginning of November. The mere fact that he had allowed himself be questioned by, of all papers, this magazine which was regarded as being an arrogant representative of the liberal left-wing spirit of the age, incurred Wolters' deepest displeasure. What possibly annoyed him even more was that his friend was again prepared to voice condemnations which, as he reproached him in an angry letter, had over the past twenty years set the tone for public opinion in all quarters, be it in schools or foreign affairs. Wolters accused him of blurring the historical picture by making these remarks and by demonizing Hitler. Asked, for instance, whether he thought responsibility for the war lay with Germany, Speer had replied: 'No, not with Germany, but with Hitler.' In fact, Wolters argued, at the time they had all equated Hitler with Germany and, in spite of their lack of enthusiasm for the war and the pervading gloom in the autumn of 1939, they had never lost sight of the provocation of the Poles and Britain's interest in widening the conflict. That was why it was wrong to turn Hitler into a devil. As for the originators of the war, they were 'all of us, Germans, Europeans, and eventually all ... nations'. In conclusion he asked Speer to show 'more interest and understanding' for these considerations in his future writings.[35]

Speer also gradually began to realize that the friendship with Wolters, which had lasted so long and survived so many upheavals, was breaking up. Not wishing to aggravate the breach or even make it irreparable, he did not answer the letter. Years ago he had appointed Wolters his literary executor, hinting that he would be relying on his help when it came to writing the final version of his memoirs. Touchy as he was, he presumably gave up this idea when their differences of opinion first emerged during his detention in Spandau and he quietly transferred full powers over his literary estate to his daughter Hilde. Now everything that had united them was disappearing step by step, particularly as the objections raised by Wolters were directed at the nub of the conclusions he had reached with regard to Hitler, the past and his own role.

Shortly after the beginning of his detention, the well-known American publishing firm of Alfred A. Knopf and a south German publisher had expressed interest in Speer's memoirs. At that time, however, the past was still too close and prison life still stretched too far into the future for Speer to wish to commit himself. In the autumn of 1963, however, Wolf Jobst Siedler, the director of the Ullstein and Propyläen publishing houses, had approached him and had met with a more positive response. Although Speer instructed his family 'to procrastinate politely' for the time being, he wrote in his diary: 'All the same, I am tempted by the thought of having my memoirs published under an imprint familiar to me since my days as a graduate student, when I read the Propyläen *History of Art*.'[36] When he met Siedler in person soon after his release he decided there and then to collaborate with him.

Collaboration was what the enterprise needed. Speer had a keen gift of observation, the ability to see things in a wider context, and an accurate memory. It soon turned out that he had no difficulty in using the piecemeal Spandau draft with all his own additions on hundreds of

Until the end of the sixties Speer's closest friend was Rudolf Wolters, whom he had known from their student days and later enlisted as a colleague. Soon after Speer's release from prison, the friendship broke up. This photograph shows Speer (third from left) and Wolters (sixth from left) at an architectural exhibition in Lisbon in 1942.

scraps of paper and the documents which he now had access to, to produce a book that was not only lively but also convincing. On the other hand, he was unable to judge what was essential and what was dispensable, he had no sense of dramatic tension and he failed to recognize when the reader's attention might flag. In the end the manuscript had grown to nearly 2,000 pages. At Speer's suggestion, Siedler therefore enlisted the help of an adviser to organize the material and help with the historical background. Together they cut the bloated manuscript down, made it more substantial and gave it shape.[37] They made no changes to the contents. After nearly three years the book, *Inside the Third Reich*, came out, in the autumn of 1969.

It caused more of a stir than any previous publication about the Third Reich. In common with most memoirs by senior officers, officials and others who were swept away by the maelstrom of those years, it struck an apologetic note. But Speer's integrity, which even strangers and enemies such as the participants of the July plot, the Oxford historian Hugh Trevor-Roper and Paul Nitze, as well as wide sectors of public opinion repeatedly acknowledged, lent unparalleled weight to his account. Besides, it presented an overall picture of the period, however subjective it may have been, and it gave the younger generation in particular an answer to the long-unanswered question of how a man of Speer's background and character could have subordinated himself to Hitler so unquestioningly. Speer's credibility and his closeness to Hitler made his verdict on the regime appear extraordinarily convincing. Even though the memoirs did not have the 'cathartic effect' with which they were credited,[38] their significance as a clarifying and liberating force was unmistakable. Robert M. W. Kempner, who had acted as prosecutor in the secondary Nuremberg trials, called it a 'true confession', Golo Mann included it among the 'pinnacles of the political memoir', and the *Wall Street Journal,* stunned by the existence of a penitent follower of Hitler, ranked them extravagantly with the *Confessions* of Saint Augustine and Jean-Jacques Rousseau. Those who were more critical pointed to Speer's controversial position in the power apparatus of a repulsive regime, to his lack of understanding of the dual role he had played, and to the conflict between belonging to Hitler's closest circle and claiming ignorance of the crimes; no protestations, they said, could cover up the prevaricating nature of the book.[39]

On the other side the response was equally uneven. Many of the older generation had followed the regime with blind enthusiasm and had remained stubbornly loyal to it to the end, and perhaps even beyond. For nearly twenty-five years they had been cheated of everything they had believed in and their dedication had sunk in a murky pool of accusations. The book not only led them to console themselves that it was possible to have believed in Hitler and yet remained a 'decent person', they drew from it deeper reassurance still. If Hitler's favourite minister, who had even been his chosen successor for a while, had known nothing about the mass crimes, then it was surely absurd to accuse the 'man in the street'. They often recognized themselves and their own attitudes in Speer's contradictions, in his blind ethos of dedication and in his repressions. Questionable as such equations might have been, especially as they overlooked Speer's late opposition to Hitler, he unexpectedly appeared to many people as the great exonerating figure. At the same time, however, he met with undisguised hostility from these quarters, and even close friends from the past turned away from him in outrage. Arno Breker, who owed him numerous commissions as well as a good part of his promotion to official sculptor of the Reich, told him in a letter that he now had to revise his view of the friend of days gone by, and a high-ranking officer from the Armaments Office spoke of a Speer 'as we did not know him then'. Others scornfully called him a 'Titan of penitence' and Wolters let his friend know that 'a more thrilling crime novel could not have been invented'.[40]

The censure from these quarters invariably centred on the accusation that he had played down his enthusiasm for Hitler, while exaggerating his reservations and later opposition, thereby betraying everything they had believed in, everything they had shared and that had once even been 'sacred' to them. Of course Speer was familiar with such accusations from his time in Nuremberg and later in Spandau. But the more people turned against him, the more his uncertainty grew. Although he had always foreseen the attacks against him, and accepted them, he was dismayed by their vehemence, and the pride and satisfaction of being an international success as an author were not always strong enough to counter this feeling.

The criticism from these circles was directed mainly against Speer's 'opportunism'. It was argued that he had once again conformed to the prevailing opinion, just as he had done during the Hitler period, and that by confessing he had prostrated himself before the current environment. Soon this objection was taken up well beyond the circle of his former friends or close colleagues. Many observers identified Speer's unprincipled flexibility, which only served his own advancement, as his most conspicuous trait. Offended, Wolters spoke of the 'artiste' Speer who mastered 'the double salto from a standing start'.[41] Such accusations were not entirely unjustified. But they did not take into account the many friendships which were now being broken and turned into hostile resentment. A whole world suddenly broke away from Speer, people whose expertise and devotion he had learnt to appreciate over the years. Their loss certainly meant as much to Speer as the goodwill of a fickle spirit of the age, and it is remarkable that he stuck to his judgement on the Hitler years despite all these pressures.

In the letter he sent Wolters along with his memoirs, Speer said, 'I am a little nervous about your reaction.' Not long afterwards, in November 1969, when he announced that he would be visiting Coesfeld, Wolters wrote a tortuous letter, advising against meeting. He quite understood if Speer were to abandon the idea of the trip in view of his many pressing engagements. At the same time he sent him a lengthy comment which, while praising the structure of the book, went on to voice the old accusations. Returning once again to their familiar ironic tone, he ended by writing, 'When one has read your book one is inclined to conclude that the author would now walk through life in a hair shirt, distributing his fortune among the victims of National Socialism, forswear all the vanities and pleasures of life and live on locusts and wild honey.'[42]

Nevertheless Speer went to Coesfeld. As soon as he entered the house, he adopted the ironical tone that had been customary between them since their student days. He was trying to save their friendship or what was left of it, before it was too late. As they sat down to lunch, Speer asked jocularly: 'Where are the locusts?'[43] But the attempt to circumvent the contentious points between them had little effect.

At the beginning of 1971 Speer agreed to give a detailed interview, conducted over ten days, to Eric Norden of the American edition of *Playboy*. He did not dodge any of the persistent questions put to him by Norden. Again Speer spoke of the criminal character of the Hitler regime and admitted his mistake in not having taken the hateful threats against the Jews seriously. His guilt, he said, consisted in having 'condoned' the mass murders, albeit without any detailed knowledge, as a follower and leading collaborator of Hitler, and in having sought a form of excuse by thinking that this kind of thing did not concern him 'so long as I did not personally participate'. He once again admitted: 'If I didn't see it, then it was because I didn't want to see it.'[44]

When the interview was published, the deep anger which Wolters and his followers had for years borne against Speer burst into the open. 'What on earth has got into you,' he reproved Speer in a letter of 24 May 1971, 'to make you go on and on presenting yourself more and more radically as a criminal even after the confessions of guilt in your memoirs?' Wolters said he was just as pained by the discrepancy between public appearances where his friend seemed burdened and his light-hearted manner in private, as he was by Speer's accusations against the minor accomplices and his inclination to 'land old friends ... in the soup'. Speer was not only incriminating himself, but also his country 'most seriously', while being careful not to 'adopt an equally clear attitude to today's wars in East Asia or the Middle East'. Finally he suggested that they should put their friendship on hold and not resume contact until Speer had got over 'this phase'.

Speer replied ten days later. He criticized certain arbitrary changes made by Norden, who, he claimed, had rewritten or dramatized whole passages. 'However by and large,' he continued, 'the interview corresponds with my views, and I imagine that this is what counts for you. What I ... have written on the issue of my guilt already angered you during my time in Spandau. But it still applies. It does not bother me if many people regard it as opportunism.' He rejected the accusation that his private life was not in keeping with the burden that was allegedly weighing on him, adding: 'Besides, about a year ago, I already made a contractual agreement with the Propyläen publishing house that large parts of my revenue would be channelled to charitable purposes. After tax I shall be left with about twelve per cent net of the original fees for the book.' In conclusion he wrote stiffly: 'I would be very pleased if one day you were to lift the barrier you have erected. You will understand that I for my part cannot approach you again.'[45]

The friendship had been vital for both of them. It never recovered from this dispute and eventually foundered, not only because of the issues that came between Speer and Wolters but also because of major differences in their characters, which had been hidden by circumstances for so long. Not until Speer's seventieth birthday four years later, did Wolters, who was by then gravely ill, attempt a rapprochement in the form of some doggerel verses which somewhat laboriously adopted their former amicable tone and concluded with the ironical lines: 'Let us continue then in silence/we're both so used to it by now!' But then the differences of opinion were compounded by misunderstanding. A few days later Speer thanked him emotionally for 'the best birthday present he had received,' adding that he would come running to him, at the slightest hint. He failed to see that Wolters' letter was the very hint he was hoping for. Two months later he tried to explain their differences of opinion in a long letter, urging his friend to practise mutual forbearance in view of the 'imprisonment' in which they were both living. 'For', he concluded, 'despite all inherent contradictions, I am very attached to you.' But the gap could no longer be bridged. The two men never met again.

After his breach with Wolters, Speer felt even more lonely than before. Hardly any of his former colleagues kept in touch with him. The readiness with which he invited interviewers, correspondents, reviewers and indeed anyone who called on him into his house was presumably largely due to his growing sense of estrangement from so many sides. He had always determined the distance which people had to keep from him. Now they had the upper hand and for the first time he began to suffer from these distances. Theodor Hupfauer, who continued to stand by Speer, tried to draw him out of his isolation. He suggested holding regular meetings with former friends and followers at the house of a Munich industrialist. But like the family reunion, these 'conventions' also ended in embarrassment. As if under some compulsion, Speer later recalled, at these gatherings he had talked endlessly about the past which they all wanted to forget, and whenever he listened to them speak of their successes, production increases and new markets, he had felt as if he was being confronted by numerous time-displaced copies of the man he once was. After two or three meetings the project came to an end. 'I was only in the way,' Speer admitted.[46]

Autumn 1975 saw the publication of *Spandau: The Secret Diaries*, put together from nearly twenty thousand scraps of paper with reflections, self-observations and fragments of recollections from his time in prison. If the selection, which Speer made from the almost unmanageable mountain of paper, put more emphasis on the depression of those years than was perhaps warranted by the original notes, then this reflected not least the melancholia which had seized him since his release from Spandau and which refused to let go of him. Many observers certainly found it difficult to recognize in the shy, strangely inhibited man of these years the dynamic economic dictator described in the history books. Some also had the impression that the 'school of survival' was still continuing.

For a while Speer thought of going back to architecture. Friends were shown designs for a brewery and for a packing plant. But he was soon persuaded to give up the idea, because all the plans he drew up subconsciously evoked the backdrop of the world capital 'Germania', against which the façades of brewing plants and storehouses seemed oddly inappropriate. Finally his various attempts to return to architecture led to a book which presented his life's work, built and unbuilt. 'Faced once more with this architectural legacy of a mere decade,' Speer wrote in the introduction, gave him a 'sense of satisfaction', even though he had left these plans far behind him: 'The seventy-year-old looks with astonished and alarmed pride at the misdirected élan of the thirty-year-old ... I feel like criticizing it, but I cannot distance myself from it.'[47]

These were hectic years, and anyone who asked Speer what was driving him would conclude from his answer that he was above all concerned with restoring his reputation. He travelled extensively and purchased a small property in the Allgäu, to which he frequently withdrew. The argument with Erich Goldhagen affected him deeply and may have been partly responsible for the embolism which troubled him again. From time to time he longed for the solitude of his Spandau cell. In retrospect his life there seemed to him more bearable than the troublesome present, with the same accusations and the same litany of attempts at justification. On several occasions he went to the Benedictine Abbey of Maria Laach for spiritual exercises: he knew all about escapes, he remarked with a sad smile. Again he found a religious adviser who looked after him and tried just as unsuccessfully as his predecessor in Spandau to arouse in Speer a capacity for spiritual insight.[48] But after the five days which he regularly spent there his restlessness returned, driving him once more to the telephone, to journeys and to the television appearances from which he could not escape.

In order to have a task again, Speer started another book project, this time at his own instigation. He called it *The Slave State*. For several months he drove to the Federal Archive in Koblenz, mainly to study the documents of the SS. The result was a bitter, rather untidy work, filled with disappointment and accusations about the machinations by which Himmler had created, and progressively developed, the SS para-state. The subtitle of the German edition, 'My disputes with the SS', implied that he had initiated the antagonism, when in fact Himmler had done so. Meanwhile Speer continued to answer the countless letters he received, checked the translations of his books, and received visitors from all over the world, no matter how irritating and trivial they often were. He was still a figure from the waxworks, he would observe, sometimes adding that this was where he really belonged.

In the spring of 1977 the Chairman of the Board of Deputies of South African Jews wrote to him, asking for his support in a legal action against a racist organization which had recently published a pamphlet, *Did Six Million Die?*, disputing the systematic murder of the European Jews. They would, the letter said, be obliged to Speer for an affidavit to the effect that there had indeed been a plan for the extermination of the Jews, that he had known about it, and it had also been implemented, and how he knew that it had been. Drawing mainly on the documents and testimonies of those directly involved before the Nuremberg tribunal, Speer answered the questions as the writer wished in a three-page letter, so that distribution of the pamphlet was shortly afterwards banned by a court decision. He concluded his account with the statement that not only the Nuremberg trial but also his own sentence had been 'largely correct'. He continued: 'But beyond this I still consider it essential today to take upon myself the responsibility, *and thus the blame* in general, for all crimes which were committed after I became a member of Hitler's government on 8 February 1942...That is why I for my person accepted overall responsibility at the Nuremberg trial and reaffirm this now. To this day I still consider my main guilt to be my tacit acceptance of the persecution and the murder of millions of Jews.'[49]

The letter had a postlude. Early the following year Gitta Sereny came to interview Speer in Heidelberg. At the end of the conversations she conducted with him she, too, asked the question he had been asked a hundred times and which he always expected with a mixture of seriousness, exhaustion and nervousness. Gitta Sereny wanted him to clarify what he had known about the murderous actions against the Jews. When Speer admitted that he had 'sensed' that 'dreadful things were happening with the Jews,' she immediately insisted: 'But if you "sensed" … then you knew.' One could not simply sense or suspect in a void. However, looking back, Speer repeatedly emphasized the difference between 'knowing', which was based on evidence, and 'suspecting', which, while not coming from nowhere, did not mean certainty. Instead it consisted of hints, rumours, and of signals picked up here and there, which only coalesced into a picture through the mistrust which had been alien to him then. It was this 'sensing', he argued, which also described the point beyond which the majority of his contemporaries had not gone, possibly culpably, whenever the subject of the fate of the Jews had come up during the Hitler years.

According to Gitta Sereny's account Speer did not raise these philological objections during their conversation. Instead he had handed her his letter to the Board of Deputies and told her to use it as she saw fit. But when she quoted the text in a profile published in German by the weekly *Die Zeit*, Speer requested the editor to insert a footnote on the concept of 'tacit acceptance' (*Billigung*). By using that word he had indeed implicitly admitted that he had not only been aware of the persecution of the Jews but had accepted its murderous consequences. Gitta Sereny therefore also concluded that he would undoubtedly have been hanged in Nuremberg for such a thoroughgoing admission. The footnote with which he now withdrew that remark ran: 'Tacit acceptance by looking away, not by knowledge or execution of an order. The first is as grave as the second.' He had returned to subtleties and to his old line of defence.[50]

Over the following years Speer became increasingly reclusive. Even the few people who were close to him rarely heard from him, and at times the family also seemed remote, although he showed his pride in the achievements of his eldest son, who was collecting architectural prizes all over the world. Those who did meet him could gain the impression that the past was gradually releasing him from its grip. With satisfaction he remarked one day that he had met Georges Casalis again, whose instructions had helped him through the despair of the early years of imprisonment. His new friendship with the former rabbi Robert Raphael Geis, who had written him an emotional letter after the publication of *Inside the Third Reich*, probably meant even more to him. In his letter Geis had assured him of his respect 'even when I don't understand you' and he had spoken of 'forgiveness'.[51] It seemed as if the struggles and defensive efforts, in which he had been engaged for so long, were coming to an end after all. Somewhere he had read of the 'happiness of forgetting'. Although this could not apply to him, he said with a penitent gesture, which seemed studied, he was at least enjoying the 'happiness of being forgotten'.

Then, almost belatedly, the whole confessional edifice built of genuine fear, self-criticism, caution and routine suddenly began to totter after all. Towards the end of 1979 Matthias Schmidt, a young research student of the Friedrich Meinecke Institute, called on him. As was his wont, Speer readily provided the young man with the information he required, and referred him to his knowledgeable former colleague Rudolf Wolters, who would be sure to help with some unanswered questions. Wolters had repeatedly hinted that one day he would reveal not only the original *Chronik* but also the truth about its location, and the angry undertone of these threats could hardly have been missed. Trusting that the loyalty of his friend had not wavered despite all their disputes, Speer had dismissed these threats with sovereign unconcern. But as on several occasions in the past, Wolters found this 'superior manner' of Speer's, even where friendship and loyalty were concerned, extremely hurtful. He had been ill for a long time, and the more obvious it became that his life was drawing to an end the stronger was his wish to pay his former friend back for the many disappointments he had inflicted on him.

When Schmidt came to Coesfeld in the spring of 1980 Wolters took an instant liking to him. He allowed him to see the original *Chronik* with the visibly deleted passages about the evacuation of the Jews from Berlin, which he had not shown to any outsider until then. Moreover Wolters told him about the plot which he had hatched with Speer. Schmidt realized that he was on to a sensational scoop and immediately went back to Heidelberg. Speer was so appalled by his friend's disclosures that he not only denied ever having heard of the original *Chronik*,

Speer after his release from Spandau in the garden of his parents' house in Heidelberg.

but also denied the existence of the correspondence he had conducted with Wolters in order to deceive the Federal Archive. Still confused, he raised no objections when Schmidt announced that he would use the excised passages. To be on the safe side, Schmidt enquired whether

335

Speer would try to take legal steps to stop their publication. Speer assured him that he would not, referring to the long friendship between Wolters and himself.

But as soon as Schmidt had left him, Speer changed his mind and with each passing day he became angrier. Now it was he who spoke of 'betrayal'. Schmidt, whom Speer increasingly saw as a tool of Wolters' revenge, was certainly in a position to bring down everything Speer was or seemed to be: his credibility, his renunciations and the whole image he had constructed for himself. About a month after Schmidt's second visit Speer therefore handed the dispute over to his lawyer. Wolters for his part also sought legal advice. Very soon both parties were engaged in an irritable correspondence concerning not only the author's rights regarding the original *Chronik*, including copies, but also the power of attorney which Speer had given his friend while in Spandau and silently revoked a few years later. To be quite sure, he had a notice published in the September 1980 issue of the *Börsenblatt für den deutschen Buchhandel*, the journal of the German book trade, headed 'Aufhebung der Vollmacht' (revocation of the power of attorney). This rescinded all rights ever given by him for access to his private or official papers and claimed his own exclusive and personal copyright for them.[52] The dispute fluctuated for months and was far from concluded when something happened that put a sudden and unexpected end to it.

Among the letters that Speer received around the time of his break with Wolters there was also one from a young woman. Years ago, she wrote, she had married and brought up two children in England. Being German by birth she still experienced some difficulties. She carefully hinted how lonely she often felt in her noticeably reserved environment. But all her temporary dejection had suddenly vanished not long ago when she had read Speer's *Spandau Diaries*. The notes of his period of detention, she assured him, were the most moving book she knew. It had made her cry and she wanted him to know that.

The simple tone of the letter evidently so touched Speer that he invited her to Heidelberg, as he did with a number of other correspondents, the next time she found herself in Germany. No one knows when they first met or how the mutual attraction and late love developed. At first it was kept secret. One of the few people to whom Speer confided in this matter was Wolf Jobst Siedler. After a conversation about publishing matters Speer had apparently begun to speak 'in the rapturous manner of a schoolboy' of a young 'Englishwoman' and of how he was still overcome by the fact that well into his seventies he was having his first passionate experience with a woman. Never in the many years they had known one another, Siedler reported, had Speer seemed to him so 'liberated'. All his obsessions with the past, his brooding over Hitler, guilt and repentance, seemed to have disappeared. Towards the end of their conversation Speer had produced a photograph showing him, happy and carefree, with a young woman on the terrace of a house in the south of France.[53]

On the last day of August 1981 Speer travelled to London at the invitation of the BBC. He spent the evening with television officials and with the historian Norman Stone, who was to interview him on a programme the following day. Speer was obviously in a cheerful mood and, as Stone later reported, 'in very good shape', so that their meeting dragged on into the night. Immediately after the recording session on the following morning Stone suggested a farewell lunch, but Speer declined the invitation, saying that he had an appointment with a woman friend and asking to be driven to the Park Court Hotel in Bayswater.

Three hours later the hotel management announced that Speer had been admitted to St Mary's Hospital with a stroke. A little later news came from there that he was in a deep coma. An attractive young woman, it was said, was at his bedside, evidently a relation or friend. As the patient's condition became increasingly critical she went to the nearest telephone and asked to be put through to Frau Speer. Some time later the agencies reported that Albert Speer had died in the evening of 1 September 1981.

It has occasionally been suggested that Speer's death was largely due to the blow which Wolters had dealt him. The threat of disclosure certainly darkened the final months of his life and perhaps his late 'schoolboy happiness' had been the last of those escapes which, as he put it, he 'knew a lot about'. If one insists on bringing in psychological factors, then his death probably had more to do with loneliness. He had accepted the loss or open defection of his erstwhile friends. But he realized that his new friends, or those who pretended to be that, were no compensation. In the features even of those who were closest to him he could see doubts lurking with the question whether, leaving aside all the words he uttered, he could be trusted. He himself saw the hopelessness of this situation and once hinted at the dilemma of those years. There were those, he more or less said, who accused him of having believed in Hitler for too long and of having yielded to him to the point of slavishness, while others accused him of having betrayed him. There had been no middle ground between them.

Only rarely did he betray the nervousness with which he awaited the attacks from both sides. On various occasions he remarked that, in spite of everything, fate had been kind to him. In this light his unexpected death at St Mary's Hospital perhaps suggests that fate had once more been on his side. Schmidt's book, which spoke of the 'end of a myth', came out in the spring of 1982, six months after Speer's death. It attracted little attention. Speer's credibility, his errors and the weaknesses which drew him to Hitler, were no longer an issue of public interest. His days as a media figure who allowed himself to be put on display and enabled everyone to enjoy a sense of moral superiority were over. Now the questions should have begun. Instead they came to an end.

Conclusion
THE RULE AND
THE EXCEPTION

The pattern is not unusual. At first glance Albert Speer's life seems like a parable of promotion, brief glory, entanglement and fall, of which there are countless examples in history. On closer inspection, however, the life curve suddenly breaks off, loses its thread, and starts afresh. Speer himself observed that he had, in a way, led four lives, each self-contained, yet inconceivable without the preceding life: the beginning when everything was possible, then the decade as an architect and Hitler's favourite minister, followed by more than twenty years of prison. And finally what he once called his 'posthumous' life[1] – his success as an author and witness to an era.

Any biographical portrait of Speer has to start from the centre of gravity represented by Hitler. Without him this life would not have been what it was. All observers have noticed the strange captivation by the dictator, for which Speer used such helpless terms as 'enthralment' or 'magic'. They have, in the first instance, attributed it to admiration for the 'great man' who personified the expectations of the epoch. 'We were all fascinated by towering historical personalities,' Speer wrote; 'and even if a man … only acted the part with a modicum of skill, we prostrated ourselves.'[2] The dazzling possibilities with which Hitler fired his ambition when he laid 'a world at his feet', his easy manner, his successes at home and abroad, the overwhelming cheers which greeted him everywhere and the personal friendship he showed him – all this is not difficult to understand.

This relationship has rarely been viewed from Hitler's point of view, even though he played the more puzzling part in this strange friendship. All that has become known of Hitler's personal ties shows a person diminished by egomania, who was never moved by an unselfish emotion and who even allowed his most private feelings to be ruled by political considerations. But a transformation, perceptible to everyone, appeared to have taken place in him ever since the day, shortly after the beginning of his chancellorship, when he met the young architect, not yet thirty, on the building site of the Reich Chancellery. He drew Speer to him like no one else, he singled him out and made him great. Hitler only ever used pompous expressions of esteem and in this vein he called first the architect, then the organizer and finally the armaments minister a 'genius' on various occasions. Over and above pride in the chosen disciple these and other admiring remarks, which kept recurring for a time, contain an unmistakably erotic motif. Conversely, the intermittent tensions which inevitably arose after Speer's appointment as minister were never merely factual differences of opinion, such as Hitler had with Göring, Milch or the generals. This study has revealed to what extent hurt feelings, jealousy, defiance and disappointment were involved as well as a lack of inhibition. Who else would have dared to interrupt the flow of Hitler's speech by taking some sheets of paper from his briefcase and dealing with some other matter? And a photograph such as the one which shows Hitler and Speer, in conspicuous ill humour, sitting at opposite ends of a bench on the Obersalzberg, is inconceivable with any other of the paladins.[3]

Speer almost always emerged from these disputes as the stronger of the two. In his memoirs he described how, on one of the afternoons in the tea house, Hitler had fixed his gaze on him for a seemingly interminable period. Speer recounts how he accepted the challenge and summoning up all his strength held out until Hitler gave in and lowered his eyes.[4] This trivial episode reflected the pattern which their disputes invariably followed. Irritated by some arbitrary action of Speer's, Hitler would take an 'irreversible' decision. Speer would contradict with a memorandum or show his annoyance by staying away from the Führer's headquarters or withdrawing altogether, on one occasion even threatening to resign. As soon as he gave an indication of yielding, mostly by a purely formal concession, Hitler impatiently accepted the gesture, regardless of whom he compromised, not even sparing himself. It always seemed to be understood between them that Hitler could merely take certain powers away from Speer, whereas Speer could withdraw his affection.

Speer's most unusual triumph came towards the end of the war. The emotional scene on the night of 27/28 March 1945, when Hitler surrendered to Speer's empty declaration of loyalty with tears in his eyes, was the prelude. In his joy over the reconciliation that Speer held out to him, Hitler withdrew, at least in practice, his 'scorched earth' orders whose implementation he had so relentlessly demanded and reinforced with numerous death sentences. He would 'shed no tears' over the German nation if it proved inferior to its enemies, Hitler had declared on 27 November 1941,[5] already hinting at the punitive measures which he implemented during the weeks of the collapse. But, in a sense, he shed tears over Speer, who remained Hitler's 'favourite minister' in every respect. All his acts of more or less open rebellion never met with more than the dictator's disfavour, weakened by sentiment and quickly softened. Hitler's leniency towards Speer and his hundreds of acts of disobedience, which had undoubtedly been reported to him, lasted to that final encounter on 24 April 1945 when Speer confessed his counter-manding of the destruction orders. Hitler's reaction can only be explained by his emotional dependence. There was certainly no one else in Hitler's immediate or less immediate proximity from whom he would have tolerated similarly brusque contraventions of his orders – as Brandt, Fegelein, Göring, Himmler and nameless others discovered in the final phase of the war. Even at the beginning of April 1945, when the relationship had more or less broken down, Saur heard Hitler say that Speer was still 'the best of them all'.[6]

On the other hand Speer did not regard him only with the cold equanimity of the careerist. Undoubtedly he was attached to Hitler by more than just admiration for his 'antique hero' or the pharaonic euphoria which overcame them at their drawing boards. The fact that Speer could not detach himself even when these mutual excitements had long passed and when 'the profoundly criminal aspects of Hitler's face' had emerged,[7] reveals the emotions which moved him to the very end and which did not abate with the 'crying spasm' that overcame him in Flensburg. Their relationship could not be reduced to factual moti-vations, Speer stated with his characteristic shyness in emotional matters. The paradoxical nature of all personal relationships for which there is no rational explanation was also a factor.[8]

Had he been the ruthless opportunist whom many have seen in Speer, he would surely have stuck to his intention to resign in Merano and he would not have returned at the end to an encircled Berlin for a funereal farewell. Apart from that 'icy coldness' which has repeatedly been attributed to him, there was also a youthful emotionalism, a touch of puerile never-quite-grown-up 'idealism'. This dichotomy underlies the many contradictions which were always part of his life. His 'mind-less' devotion to Hitler had something to do with it, but so had the

From the first, Hitler and Speer were united by an emotional relationship. In 1935, in a rare distinction, Hitler asked Speer to move to the Obersalzberg; after that he soon became Hitler's 'favourite companion' on his daily walks.

firmness with which he eventually opposed him 'for the sake of the whole'.

The emotional foundation of the relationship made Speer an exception. His life therefore is only representative in some respects. Most of them concern the apparently non-political beginnings which almost inevitably drove him, like so many others, into Hitler's camp. Added to this was the conviction that all the early excesses of the regime, the persecutions and the broken treaties, represented, inasmuch as anyone objected to them at all, nothing more than an evil imposed on Germany by fate. Increasing numbers of people believed that there was no other way to achieve order and the country's re-emergence, and wherever possible people tried to keep out of it all.

Another feature which Speer shared with probably the overwhelming majority of Germans was his lack of interest in ideology. Except for a vague and over-wrought sense of patriotism which wanted Germany to be great, united and feared, and a few demands for social fraternization, the programme of the regime meant nothing to him at all. He really did not have a 'crippled psyche' and like most people he viewed National Socialism not so much as a matter of conviction as of uplifting emotions. Significantly Speer admitted that he would also have placed himself at the disposal of a ruler of a completely different ideological orientation, if he had offered him similar opportunities.[9] His blind belief in the 'ethics of efficiency', which spared him any questions about where his actions were leading, has to be seen in this context. Finally, the exhilaration he felt – as did the country as a whole – after Hitler's rise to power, was typical. Speer's meteoric career seemed almost a symbol of the rise of the whole nation.

Everything else receded into the background. The sinister, often even distinctly shabby features of the regime, the mixture of arbitrariness, corruption and infamy under the cover of emotive dedication, never worried him; it was just 'politics'. Like many others, he used that phrase to deceive himself or to justify his indifference. On the contrary, it was his 'idealism and devotion' which, as he believed, distinguished him from the 'repulsive bourgeois revolutionaries' in Hitler's entourage[10] that forced him into extreme positions again and again. He was radical – as one of the spokesmen of the 'war party' in 1939, in the mass recruitment of compulsory labour, in his championship of 'total war', and finally, against his better judgement, as the disseminator of false victory slogans.

But then, unexpectedly, the chain broke and Speer abandoned all that had made him representative and indeed a kind of role model in the typology of the rulers. When it came to Hitler's destruction orders he freed himself from his 'bondage', albeit with difficulty and with relapses. He had never been servile. One of the aspects of the final phase of the war that is still difficult to fathom was the obedience, and often indeed the enthusiasm, with which a large part of the population obeyed the regime's order of self-annihilation. Gauleiter Florian, who revelled in images of burning Düsseldorf and pictured the enemy entering a deserted city, devastated by a self-inflicted firestorm, was by no means an exception. This account has shown how Kesselring refused even to discuss Hitler's 'scorched earth' orders with Speer, how Field Marshal Model left him standing when he sensed the disgrace into which the minister had fallen, and how Field Marshals von Manstein and Busch were 'dumbfounded' when after his return from the Berlin bunker, Speer informed them on 24 April 1945 that 'against the Führer's orders' he was determined to prevent the Elbe bridges in Hamburg being blown up. 'Against the Führer's orders', they repeated as if thunderstruck.[11]

But it was not only the top ranks of the Party and the army who followed the annihilation orders obediently, as if sucked into a general frenzy of destruction. Reports from the final weeks of the war reveal that this mood engulfed all sections of society, right down to the lowest level, including many who had not been particular adherents of the regime. Of course one cannot dismiss the ever-present terror of the security system that was stepped up once more at the end, the effect of propaganda and the fears of the vengeance of the victors, which were imaginatively encouraged. Even so, basic survival instincts seemed to have been curiously suspended, as can be seen from the countless suicides, often by entire families, but also from the spying on and denunciation of neighbours which revived to an almost unprecedented degree, as if there were no end and no one to answer to.

At that time, if not before, Speer can no longer be seen as being representative. Unlike the rest of the Führer's paladins all round him, his will to survive had remained intact and certainly uncorrupted by belonging to the court, but he was probably also driven by a higher sense of responsibility, possibly even by a long-buried memory of his origin which, like all bourgeois concepts of existence, aimed at preservation. Amidst the staged destruction Goebbels complained at the end of March 1945 that Speer was not after all a revolutionary like the real National Socialists, but had remained 'half a bourgeois'.[12] Combined with his characteristic determination, this in itself proved enough for him first to minimize, then to delay and finally to sabotage Hitler's last intention. His behaviour in no way fits the image which Speer had presented in virtually all the previous phases of his life.

Not only his architectural projects, which often surpassed even Hitler's wild fantasies, but also his running of the armaments ministry show that one of the features of Speer's 'genius' was his talent for adaptation. In spite of his many abilities it seems as if he lived long stretches of his life second hand. Critical assessments have therefore often emphasized his sleekness and credited him with an almost clairvoyant ability to foresee impending mood swings. In Nuremberg Göring had already declared: 'We should never have trusted him.' The line continued with Gustav M. Gilbert, Airey Neave, J. K. Galbraith and a large number of observers of the trial, via Wolters and other erstwhile friends on to a good many reviewers of Speer's books of reminiscences.[13] Speer himself gave them all a kind of confirmation of their view. In one of his soul-searching sessions while in prison he asked himself 'whether there is not some inexplicable instinct within me that always makes me follow the spirit of the times, whether I want it or not; as if the prevailing

His friendship with Speer may have been the only emotional relationship in Hitler's life. A scene like this, showing an obviously sulky Hitler and Speer on a bench on the Obersalzberg, is unthinkable with any other of the leadership figures. The photograph was presumably taken in the summer of 1939.

current always carried me here and there. My feeling of guilt at Nuremberg was certainly completely sincere, but I wish I could have felt it in 1942.'[14]

The final eight or nine months before the collapse, on the other hand, were different. During that period Speer's actions were not dictated by the promptings that he had followed for so long, as if he wanted to face up to a realization, once at least, whatever the risk. When passing judgement it is impossible to disregard the fact that in his decision to stop the Wagnerian spectacle of self-destruction as best he could, he exposed himself to extreme danger, and if it was the 'spirit of the times' to which he had all too often given way, then it should be remembered that its power was never greater or its threat more frightening than during Hitler's final months, when Speer opposed him.

He stuck to this obstinate line in spite of all the accusations of betrayal levied against him after the trial and during his detention by his fellow prisoners. His Spandau notes are also a diary of growing isolation, and the dilemma did not end when he had served his sentence. Those who were part of the old camaraderie, such as Hitler's pilot Hans

Baur, concluded that 'Speer must have taken leave of his senses.' Others often accused him of adapting to the changed circumstances, even though it was these people who believed that the society of the Federal Republic had scarcely altered. Both sides united in charging Speer with being all too readily at one with the spirit of the times, just as he had been before. However, if words mean anything at all, then after Nuremberg he was more dismayed and stunned than any of his fellow accused about what they had all done during the years they had been in power.

Perhaps his horror was less than he claimed, because the weight of evidence about the extent of his knowledge of the crimes is indeed crushing. But it was only then that he got an idea of the reality behind the phrases which he had believed and the columns of figures which had served to block his view. He was not one to remain indifferent to this reality, and it is surely too simple to claim that during the trial he had only paid lip-service, and, truth or not, he had known and pursued only one goal with great strategic circumspection – 'the salvation of Albert Speer'.[15]

In fact many reflections converge on the question of whether the Nuremberg trial actually was the drama of revelation for Speer that shook him and never let go of him again. The more emphatically he insisted on it, the more irritable the reactions became. He constantly spoke of the atrocities committed by the regime, of the responsibility and soon also about the guilt which he had saddled himself with. However, despite divergences on individual points, critical opinion agreed that his words seemed to come from a long way off, as if he himself were scarcely affected by them. Some attributed this 'detachment' to his self-control, others to his 'coldness'. An interviewer who spent several days at his house found it disturbing that Speer spoke in the same tone of the horrors of the past one minute as he did a moment later when he offered him a piece of apple flan. Some theologians, on the other hand, were under the impression that Speer was genuinely repentant about his part in the fate of those who were persecuted, killed, or otherwise destroyed. John Kenneth Galbraith called Speer a 'very intelligent escapist from the truth' and one of the Nuremberg prosecutors remarked in retrospect: 'He was cold. But he thawed in Spandau.'[16]

The broad range of such unequivocal judgements was based on increasingly accurately perceived nuances. Some observers came to the conclusion that Speer's confessions stemmed not so much from regret over the victims as from a sense of disappointment about the shattered dreams and the disgrace that Hitler had inflicted on him. His contention that his only theme was the past, met with the response that endlessly digging up what had been was merely an expression of his narcissistic need for recognition and that he readily accepted even the most unforgivable sins so long as they recalled the days when he was powerful. But had he not spoken out, he would also have been reproached. Some criticized him for having made his views and confessions public at all; genuine lament, they said, did not display itself but was served out in seclusion.[17]

It is true that Speer's admissions soon began to look curiously dutiful. The answers he gave to countless questioners seemed drained of all emotion and the words sounded as if he had memorized them. Speer himself stated that 'no one could go on asserting his own guilt for so many years and seem sincere.'[18] Eventually repeating the same thing over and over again was nothing but a burden to him, which he bore patiently. Everyone, he once remarked, wanted to hear him say what he had already said innumerable times. In reality, he added, 'confessions of guilt' meant 'nothing', they were 'at most a beginning'. The questions, he said, which he now asked himself began somewhere beyond that point: what personal or perhaps even social circumstances had made him what he had become; how had he freed himself from them against some inner and outer resistance, and why were others finding it so difficult; and why did the person he once was sometimes seem to him like a 'stranger' he would pass in the street without a second glance. But he thought no one wanted to know about any of that; they were just after his guilt. Perhaps, he wondered, all they wanted was to feel better than he did. He would also like to find out sometime whether Heinrich Mann and many others had ever been asked how much guilt they felt in retrospect, having not only condoned Stalin's murders but actually defended them with powerful eloquence.[19]

The irritation reflected in such rare semi-asides during his final years probably had its deepest root in the fact that, by his very nature, he was incapable of comprehending guilt. It was like a blind spot. He worked hard on the humble gestures which belonged to his role as a sinner and he gravely repeated the formulas which the indulgence imposed on him. But at times it seemed as if he was like a puppet on a string and that, indeed, he was not without pride in the historic significance confirmed by the raised voices of his accusers. He only had a superficial understanding of the fundamental norms against which he had offended, why he had incurred guilt and how he could have emerged from those years differently and unblemished. As if aware of this inability, he once quoted Oscar Wilde in his Spandau diaries: 'There is no error more common than that of thinking that those who are the causes of occasions of great tragedies share in the feelings suitable to the tragic mood.'[120]

This shortcoming was ultimately due to the fact that the whole spiritual dimension of life was alien to him. Speer certainly was not morally deaf, and there are several instances when he stood by people in trouble or at least covered up for colleagues in the ministry. His reputation for integrity was also not unfounded. It arose because he was trustworthy, incorruptible and reliable. But all these characteristics were due more to his self-esteem and, leaving aside such personal motives, he would have been unable to say why he should obey any moral commandments or regard them as a universal law. In that respect he really was an 'incomplete person' who, with all his outstanding gifts, lacked the one element which makes a human being a person.[21] On the recommendation of the prison chaplain, he had read several thousand pages of moral theological writings in Spandau, devoting special attention to the chapters on sin, repentance and atonement, but, as he admitted with embarrassment, he had not retained a single sentence or thought in his memory.

The notes Speer wrote when he felt that he was not, as it were, being watched, also reveal how all those years of reflection on guilt had passed without result. With reference to Hitler he mentions a sentence in his *Diaries* which Leonardo da Vinci had made a note of after the flight of his powerful patron Lodovico of Milan: 'The Duke lost the State and his property and freedom and brought none of his works to completion.' The natural way in which he equated his own patron with the Duke of Milan shows how little he understood the new phenomenon, without any historical precedent, that had burst onto the European world with Hitler. Similarly, when asked whether he would have behaved differently after all that he had since learned about Hitler and the system created by him, he replied, after an astonished pause: 'I don't think so.'[122]

Speer felt that his moral indifference was justified by the prevailing image of the artist. The idea of the artist as standing outside society, not subject to any norm and moral law, had become accepted ever since the Romantic movement. As a young, admiring art student Hitler himself had already created this image for himself from what he had heard of the unbridled thinking and lifestyle of the Viennese and

Munich *bohème*, while Richard Wagner had added political direction, gravity and preceptorial dignity. Although Hitler developed his programme after entering politics to fit the circumstances, he took the moral authority for disregarding any human rights to justice, freedom or happiness and for establishing a 'new world order' from that image of the artist. By calling Speer a 'genius' he, in a way, elevated him to the altars of art and released him from the 'bourgeois' values which he might have clung to because of his background.

Speer did indeed feel freed of all moral ties as soon as art was involved. Everything he said about the 'intoxication' and the 'high spirits' of those years of planning, and the ruthlessness with which he drove his building projects right through the old districts of Berlin, indicates that where art was concerned he believed in a higher right outside any legal or bourgeois rules. The clearance of thousands of Berlin apartments also seemed morally justified to him from the moment when he initiated the programme towards the end of the thirties, if not before. Therefore it is not far-fetched to suspect that Speer deliberately made no secret of his part in the illegal resettlement programme even before it became public knowledge. Instead, he viewed this, like the 'untenanting measures' and the 'boxing-in', as no more than a consequence of that 'eternal right of the artist', which was granted to him, the more so as the evacuations served the *Gesamtkunstwerk* 'Germania'.[23]

Speer's appointment as armaments minister did nothing to alter this sense of privilege. It merely moved it to another plane. Nor did people at the time believe that technology was subject to any moral standards, and the 'technical genius' was regarded as a kind of half-brother of the artist, who had simply exchanged the studio for the workshop or laboratory. In Nuremberg Speer recognized that he had made himself guilty by his mere proximity to politics. That was why both he and particularly his lawyer had insisted that, as an artist and technician, he had belonged to another, innocent world, and that he had basically never left it. In a wider context this defence originates from the century's ideology of the special privilege of the intellectual and his supposed right not only to impose laws on reality, but also to punish it for any deviation from the ideal. This notion contributed hugely to the atrocities of the age. The circumstances keep changing, but the champions of this belief continue to claim for themselves the mission that exempts them from any human rule.

All this was part of the perceptual block that cocooned Speer from any moral misgivings. It explains the amnesia regarding the burned-out building on Fasanenstrasse in Berlin, his heartless and awkward silence during Hitler's anti-Semitic outbursts, as well as the suppression of his knowledge of the crimes. Even the controversial issue of whether he had been present at Himmler's Posen speech or whether he had left the meeting in the early afternoon is of little more than academic interest. Certainly nothing penetrated the system of bolts which he had erected for himself. Then it collapsed. The force of the shock is illustrated by the desperate efforts with which Speer persistently placed his ideology of the artist and the technocrat before the abysses opening up all around him. Only then did he understand that a regime like Hitler's did not admit any value-free collaboration and that the Führer was a 'King Midas in reverse' who turned anything he touched 'not into gold but into corpses'.[24]

Two motifs kept recurring among the accusations which were permanently levied against Speer – criticism of his lack of compassion, and of his 'method of planned repression'.[25] To reach a balanced judgement it is necessary to point out the logical error of bracketing the two. If Speer was still incapable of any human emotion after the fall and after his imprisonment, then there was nothing for him to repress. Another point should be made. In the spectral gallery of totalitarian leaders he has, to this day, remained the only high-ranking figure to admit his responsibility and guilt. Thousands of so-called dignitaries were driven from their command posts after the fall of both Hitler's and Stalin's tyranny. They endeavoured to exculpate their rule of terror, or at least the idea from which it sprang, they complained about unfavourable circumstances or of treachery on so many sides. All these excuses showed how difficult it is to recant. Even those who fell silent have resorted to resentment against mankind, against history and the way of the world to counterbalance their discredited visions.

Perhaps not enough attention has been paid to the fact that Speer never indulged in this way of thinking and never showed any bitterness or self-pity despite increasing doubts about the justice of his sentence. For all the covert attempts at justification which he undertook, the gaps in his memory and his self-delusions, he never actually tried to absolve the regime from blame. The way in which he exposed the regime, to the outrage of many of his former colleagues, his accounts of the degree to which everyone was out for his own advantage and of the incompetence in the leading circles, have possibly proved the most effective way of preventing any mythologizing, such as Hitler, Göring, Goebbels and others had hoped for even at the very end. That, too, should be taken into account when reviewing his life.

'Your husband will construct for me buildings such as have not been created for four thousand years,' Hitler had told Margarete Speer in 1934. Looking back, Speer himself remarked that of all his grandiose plans only a few dozen street lamps had survived in Berlin.

On the debit side Speer always recorded his unrealized architectural projects, yellowing in his office cupboards. Hitler had once indicated that Speer would 'erect buildings such as have not been created for the past four thousand years'. Now an insignificant house in Heidelberg, which he had designed for his in-laws when he was still a student, the shattered foundations of his Nuremberg complex and a few dozen street lamps along the East-West Axis in Berlin, represent his entire architectural legacy. Even the 'small spark of hope' that at least some of his designs would not go down in architectural history merely 'as monstrosities'[26] has remained unfulfilled. They were forgotten, gawped at as the bizarre products of a bygone age, like mammoths or mastodons, or deliberately alienated from their intended purpose. The new Reich Chancellery was the quarry for a Soviet memorial in Berlin, the Nuremberg 'place of pilgrimage' served as a rubbish dump for a while, and Speer's official residence in Pariser Platz was used by the East German secret police as a prison for so-called 'fugitives from the republic'.

Those with a predilection for historical lessons have regarded these new uses as the appropriate end of Speer's architectural endeavour. But the effects of certain plans did survive. His strongest influence can be found in the concepts developed by his former colleagues, which determined the reconstruction programme after the war, making the old urban centres misprized relics of a bygone age.[*] No matter how much he hated admitting it, Speer's real legacy was not a particular building, but the disregard Hitler and he had for buildings of the past. One could perhaps also mention his architectural lighting, which Wieland Wagner developed into a spectacular theatrical style in the first Bayreuth productions after the war. Ironically it purported to break with the very past it was continuing in other ways.

Doubts about Speer's rank as an architect go much deeper, to the question whether his domes of light and massed flags, his liturgical settings and, finally, his architectural designs ever made him more than the 'designer general' of the regime, his role model secretly being not so much Schinkel as Barnum & Bailey. Looking back at the dictatorial position he had achieved and how it had satisfied his ambition, he observed that he would have given up 'all the power in the world without regrets if a single perfect building had been granted to me'. But perhaps he lacked the passion and the ability to aspire to grand form to be a great architect. In one of his Spandau reflections he asked himself why, in all those years of endlessly searching for something to do, it had never occurred to him to undertake an ambitious architectural design, so that, given that nothing he built had survived, he could at least obtain a place in the history of art 'with high-minded plans'. He left the question unanswered.[28]

Perhaps the dilemma of his life lay in the multitude of his gifts. They were, in a sense, on call for anyone who laid claim to them, enabling Speer to perform the most diverse services, be they artistic, organizational, technical or administrative. This may also explain his unusual ability to live in paradoxes, which has often been noted. Without resolving them he simply switched from one track to another. What enabled him to change roles perpetually was his growing self-assurance, his determination and his charisma. Presumably he would have made a career just as easily as a diplomat, big businessman or strategic planner on a general staff, or indeed as a Reich Commissioner or plenipotentiary in one of the occupied territories.

There was only one weakness in this balance sheet – during the years of public activity he was not an independent personality. Speer invariably needed a catalyst to realize his many possibilities, an impulse from an external force. He was a man of many abilities, but of no qualities. Perhaps he really was right when he suspected in Spandau that Hitler alone had made him productive. Speer kept going back to the question how his life would have turned out without that chance encounter towards the end of 1933, when he was drawn from an aimless past to a life of the most extreme tension. The traditional picture of human nature assumes that everyone has an innate wish to live an independent life, with responsibility to themselves. But there is also a need for an existence with an allotted role, and many find greater contentment in discharging a duty than in a self-determined life. In renouncing this self-determination Speer found the highest satisfaction.

In the spring of 1944 Sebastian Haffner published a profile of the armaments minister in the London *Observer* under the title 'Albert Speer – Dictator of Nazi Industry'. This combined a stunningly accurate knowledge of his life, abilities and character with a pessimistic outlook for the future. Speer, Haffner wrote, was a 'rather cocksure' young man, certainly 'not one of the flamboyant and picturesque Nazis', but 'very much the successful average man, well-dressed, civil, non-corrupt'. In a certain sense he was 'more important for Germany today than Hitler, Himmler, Göring, Goebbels, or the generals. They all have, in a way, become the mere auxiliaries of this man ... In him is the very epitome of the "managerial revolution".'

[He] rather symbolizes a type which is becoming increasingly important in all belligerent countries: the pure technician, the classless bright young man without background, with no other original aim than to make his way in the world...It is the lack of psychological and spiritual ballast, and the ease with which he handles the terrifying technical and organizational machinery of our age which makes this slight type go extremely far nowadays...This is their age. The Hitlers and Himmlers we can rid ourselves of, but the Speers, whatever happens to this particular specimen, will long be with us.[29]

He did in fact personify the man of the future – pragmatic, ambitious, without convictions. The sense of not belonging that he always felt amidst the leadership of the regime largely stemmed from this. If the thesis of the double face of the Third Reich is correct, then

Speer represented its modern side. Significantly he saw nothing but 'humbug' in the archaic, strangely contorted aspects of the ruling ideology which spoke of 'racial contamination', of 'Germanic walls of blood' and of 'redeeming the world'. But the contempt he felt for this never interfered with his hunger for advancement and his desire to co-operate. On the contrary, he effectively covered up the insane roots of the regime and credited it with a will to the future, which was its main attraction.

About three years after Haffner's profile, Hugh Trevor-Roper's study of *The Last Days of Hitler* was published, in the summer of 1947. Drawing on extensive interrogations of surviving members of the regime he painted an accurate picture of the end of the Reich. Along with many other sketches he also portrayed Albert Speer, who had obviously impressed him. Trevor-Roper characterized him as the only man in Hitler's entourage 'whose judgement was not corrupted by attendance on that dreadful master', and thought it a 'mystery that he should have survived, a single, solitary, disapproving figure, in that ambuscade of vigilant and vindictive conspirators'. 'As an administrator he was undoubtedly a genius,' Trevor-Roper continued, 'his ambitions were peaceful and constructive: he wished to rebuild Berlin and Nuremberg.' Then came the unexpected, brusque turn with which Trevor-Roper narrowed down Haffner's broad perspective to German peculiarities: 'Nevertheless, in a political sense, Speer is the real criminal of Nazi Germany, for he, more than any other, represented that fatal philosophy which has made havoc of Germany and nearly shipwrecked the world,' he wrote. 'His keen intelligence diagnosed the nature and observed the mutations of Nazi government and policy... he heard their outrageous orders and understood their fantastic ambitions; but he did nothing.'[30]

This accusation not only questioned Speer's attempts to justify himself, but those of non-political Germany as a whole after the end of the Hitler regime. In the eyes of the British historian, Speer was nothing less than its representative figure. No one personified more authentically the type of the stubbornly loyal, unthinking subject, dedicated to his personal ambition. By keeping aloof from politics and insisting on having done only what they saw as their 'duty', Speer and the likes of him had made possible the establishment of the regime and all the horrors it engendered. People like Sauckel, Ley and Streicher, Trevor-Roper observed, explained nothing: social desperados of their kind existed in any society. They had only formed Hitler's core troop and had been exchangeable at any moment; not so the Speers and countless dutiful and unselfish citizens.

As the years went by, Speer admitted more and more frequently that it may have been so. But he found that the world was full of 'technocrats' or of people who put personal matters before the public interest. What, he asked, gave them the certainty with which they judged him and his actions? Had not his accusers, often young people, who were now speaking out everywhere and pointing their fingers at him, always been part of that tradition, or had it suddenly come to an end? Would they have been more discerning, or shown greater moral strength and greater firmness in a similar situation? Would they have been less afraid of social exclusion, of professional discrimination and even of violence?

There was no end to the questions, and at times he could barely cope with all the views and unresolved answers. He realized, he pointed out, that much that was being said about him seemed irrefutable, but he did not recognize in it anything of himself or his life.[31] It was all too remote and speculative. Anyway, mere ideas had never meant much to him. In Spandau he had first come across a question which kept catching up with him now. But he never got beyond the conclusion he had reached then. Faced with the choice of

leading a quiet and respected life as city architect of Augsburg or Göttingen, with a house in the suburbs, two or three decent buildings a year, and family holidays in Hahnenklee or Norderney – if I had been given all that or everything else all over again, the fame and the guilt, the world capital and Spandau, and the feeling of a life misspent – which would I choose? Would I be prepared to pay the price all over again? My head reels when I pose this question. I scarcely dare to ask it. I cannot answer it.

And, remembering that passage, he sometimes added, not without *double entendre*: 'How comforting that now everybody I have any dealings with is sure of his own answer.'[32]

His irony was directed against the same deceptive certainty to which he had himself succumbed years ago, when he told himself that, unlike the students around him, he would never join the Hitler crowd. This self-deception is one of the reasons why his life deserves attention, over and above his personal circumstances. How could he, in his own words, fall for Hitler so 'unreservedly and unthinkingly' soon afterwards?[33] The very fact that he was so full of self-assurance, so civilized, and so open to rational argument, makes the question disconcerting.

It has been said that the European world suffered a culture shock as a result of the totalitarian experience before the middle of the twentieth century. But Hitler and the other dictators of the period only provided the impulse. The deeper effects of the shock go back to the realization how easily, given appropriate conditions, people will allow themselves to be mobilized into violence, abandoning the humanitarian traditions they have built up over centuries to protect themselves from themselves.

Hitler, as it were, came from nowhere – the returning primal being, as the historian Otto Hintze has remarked. The likes of him will always crop up again. Speer, on the other hand, was, by origin and upbringing, the product of a long process of civilization. He came from a respected home with strict values and had futhermore received his training from a teacher who endeavoured to communicate to his students not only professional knowledge but also standards that would withstand all the temptations of the age. Speer far more than Hitler makes us realize how fragile these precautions were and how the ground on which we all stand is always threatened.

This led to the breach which is the true legacy of those years. It has killed the fundamental belief held since the Enlightenment that despite many checks and setbacks, the world was moving steadily towards more humane conditions. The destructive will came from Hitler. But he would not have achieved any of his objectives without the helpers, of which Speer is but one example.

A postscript should be added. Speer once remarked that he had always expected everything to be easier after the years of imprisonment. After all, he had admitted responsibility, confessed his guilt and served his sentence. But he had been wrong. Perhaps he had never been as wrong as on this question. For the burden had not become any lighter, and at times it seemed to him that everything he had so arduously strived for was completely futile. Maybe it all amounted to a pointless effort, like so much in his life. That too, he added, was one of the questions for which he had no answer.

NOTES

Introduction: Questions, Contradictions and More Questions (pp. 1–10)

1 Matthias Schmidt, *Albert Speer: The End of a Myth*, London 1985; Gitta Sereny, *Albert Speer: His Battle with Truth*, London 1995; and Dan van der Vat, *The Good Nazi: The Life and Lies of Albert Speer*, London 1997.

2 Esther Vilar, *Speer*, Berlin 1998; David Edgar, *Albert Speer*, London 2000.

3 Golo Mann, 'Noch ein Versuch über Geschichtsschreibung' in *Zwölf Versuche*, Frankfurt/Main 1973, p. 8.

4 In fact Hitler did not know for a long time that Speer had already joined the NSDAP at the beginning 1931; he had never asked him about it. In January 1939, Hitler awarded the 'Golden Party Badge' to his architect to mark the completion of the new Reich Chancellery; cf. Chapter 4.

5 Both Sereny and van der Vat discuss this question at great length.

6 Albert Speer, *Spandau: The Secret Diaries*, London 1976, p. 244.

7 Cf. Chapter 10. There are however indications that Speer's remark, made at the very beginning of his testimony, was intended as tactical move in the trial.

8 Author's note.

9 Speer, *Diaries*, pp. 141f.

10 Schmidt, *Speer*, p. 204.

11 Airey Neave, *Nuremberg*, London 1978, pp. 138ff. and 144ff.

12 Sereny, *Speer*, p. 553 (report by Paul Nitze).

Chapter One: Awakening (pp. 11–38)

1 See, for instance, Alice Miller, *Am Anfang war Erziehung*, Frankfurt/Main 1980, passim, with the statement 'Hitler would scarcely have met with so much support if his own upbringing pattern and the damage resulting from it had not been so widespread.' This essay and the sentence quoted are typical of a multitude of psychological attempts at interpretation, especially of Hitler's middle-class followers.

2 Thus van der Vat, *Speer*, despite many a critical reservation about oversimplified connections between parental home and later character features; in the same sense also Sereny, *Speer*, passim.

3 Albert Speer, *Inside the Third Reich*, London 1975, p. 4.

4 Speer, *Diaries*, p. 390.

5 Speer, *Third Reich*, p. 133. The quoted remark about Hitler is from Otto Hintze and is recorded by Friedrich Meinecke, *Die deutsche Katastrophe*, Wiesbaden 1959, p. 89.

6 For the vast literature on the bourgeoisie in the Weimar Republic cf. the exceedingly informative résumé by Horst Möller, 'Bürgertum und bürgerlich-liberale Bewegung nach 1918' in *Historische Zeitschrift*, special issue 17, Munich 1997, pp. 293ff. This also contains numerous assessments with appropriate references to the literature. Other than on the role of the bourgeoisie in the nineteenth century we still lack a comprehensive study of its agony during the twenties, despite several, often quite important, specialist studies. On the economic and social weight of the bourgeoisie in imperial Germany see also David Blackbourn and Geoff Eley, *The Peculiarities of German History: Bourgeois Politics in Nineteenth-Century Germany*, Oxford 1984. With their central thesis that the German bourgeois revolution had not foundered, but had merely taken different forms from England or France, the authors triggered the controversy about the German 'special road'.

7 Benito Mussolini, 'La dottrina del fascismo', quoted from Ernst Nolte, *Theorien über den Faschismus*, Cologne/Berlin 1967, p. 216.

8 Cf. van der Vat, *Speer*, p. 41.

9 This evidently widespread phrase is quoted also in Theodor Eschenburg, *Deutsches Geistesleben und Nationalsozialismus. Eine Vortragsreihe der Universität Tübingen*, Tübingen 1965, p. 40.

10 Author's note.

11 Quoted from Ulrich Herbert, *Best. Biographische Studien über Radikalismus, Weltanschauung und Vernunft, 1903–1989*, Bonn 1996, pp. 43ff.

12 Author's note.

13 Speer, *Third Reich*, p. 10.

14 Paul de Lagarde, *Ausgewählte Schriften*, ed. Paul Fischer, Munich 1934, p. 34.

15 Speer, *Diaries*, pp. 109 and 286.

16 Rudolf Wolters, *Lebensabschnitte*, BA NL 1318/51, pp. 106 and 222f. The real friendship between Speer and Wolters did not begin until they met again in Berlin.

17 S. Gerda Wangerin and Gerhard Weiss, *Heinrich Tessenow. Ein Baumeister, 1876–1950*, Essen 1976, passim; also Speer, *Third Reich*, p. 10.

18 Cf. Helmut Heiber (ed.), *Das Tagebuch von Joseph Goebbels 1925/1926*, Stuttgart, n.d., p. 118.

19 Letter by Speer from Spandau to his children, quoted from Sereny, *Speer*, p. 72.

20 Cf. Schmidt, *Speer*, p. 29.

21 Speer, *Diaries*, p. 141. It is revealing that Rudolf Wolters on one occasion calls his teacher, 'rather like Oswald Spengler, Ernst Jünger and Gottfried Benn', an 'intellectual trail-blazer of the Third Reich', even though he meant

by it something totally different from what later became reality. Cf. Wolters, *Lebensabschnitte*, p. 191.

22 Speer, ibid., p. 82.

23 Speer, *Third Reich*, p. 18.

24 Author's note.

25 *Die Tagebücher von Joseph Goebbels. Sämtliche Fragmente*, ed. Elke Fröhlich, Munich 1987, vol. 2, pp. 388ff.

26 Cf. Max Domarus, *Hitler's Speeches and Proclamations 1932–1945*, London 1990, vol. 1, pp. 311ff., esp. p. 316.

27 Speer, *Third Reich*, p. 27.

28 Speer, ibid., p. 31.

29 Speer, *Diaries*, p. 370.

30 Speer, *Third Reich*, p. 9.

31 Cf. Lothar Gall, *Bürgertum in Deutschland*, Berlin 1989, pp. 466ff.

32 Speer, *Third Reich*, p. 33.

Chapter Two: Within the Inner Circle (pp. 39–65)

1 Cf. Joachim Fest, *Hitler*, London 1987, p. 523; also Alexander Mitscherlich, 'Hitler blieb ihm ein Ratsel – Die Selbstblendung Albert Speers', in Adelbert Reif, *Albert Speer. Kontroversen um ein deutsches Phänomen*, Munich 1978, pp. 466f.

2 Otto Dietrich, *12 Jahre mit Hitler*, Munich 1955, p. 235.

3 Herbert Lüthy, 'Der Führer persönlich', in *Nach dem Untergang des Abendlandes. Zeitkritische Essays*, Cologne/Berlin 1964, p. 128. Lüthy was evidently the first to bring out this point in a brilliant analysis of Hitler's personality, published as early as 1953.

4 Speer, *Third Reich*, p. 31. On Speer's lack of success in the contest for the 'Reich Leader School of the NSDAP' in Munich-Grünwald cf. Karl Arndt, 'Architektur und Politik', in Albert Speer, *Architektur. Arbeiten 1933–1942*, Berlin 1978, p. 117.

5 Adolf Hitler, 'Die Reichskanzlei', in Völkischer Beobachter, 16.7.1939; also Speer, *Third Reich*, p. 80 and Christa Schroeder, *Er war mein Chef. Aus dem Nachlass der Sekretärin von Adolf Hitler*, 2nd edn, Munich 1985, p. 132.

6 The future Field Marshal Erhard Milch, who became Speer's friend during the latter's time as a minister and remained close to him even after the war, called him 'ambitious, indeed greedy for power', cf. Schmidt, *Speer*, p. 113. Rudolf Wolters, admittedly only after his break with Speer, stated that 'money and status' had been the motives which had driven his friend all his life, cf. BA Koblenz, NL/1318/44. Walther Funk probably meant much the same when he accused Speer in Spandau of having acted 'like a Parsifal' while having been 'more cunning' than all the rest of them; cf. Speer, *Diaries*, p. 235.

7 Speer, *Diaries*, p. 405; also id., *Third Reich*, p. 80.

8 Speer, *Diaries*, p. 406.

9 Ibid., p. 30.

10 Ibid., p. 353.

11 Speer, *Third Reich*, pp. 46f. and 125.

12 Ibid., pp. 46 and 90.

13 Günther Weisenborn, *Memorial*, Munich 1948, pp. 212f. Speer quotes this passage in slightly abridged form in *Diaries*, p. 139.

14 Speer, *Diaries*, p. 399.

15 Speer, *Third Reich*, p. 49. Contrary to Speer's assertion in *Third Reich*, he is thought never to have visited Troost's studio with Hitler, but to have met the architect at a building site in Hitler's company; cf. the note by Rudolf Wolters about a conversation with Frau Gerdy Troost in Salzburg on 9.1.1978, BA NL 1318/46.

16 Speer actually believed that Hitler, as he put it with some embarrassment, had had an 'affair' with Winifred Wagner. 'On the strength of countless small but revealing indications' he had then been 'entirely sure'. Hitler had always seemed 'strangely elated' on his return, 'with a certain gleam in his eyes – simply enraptured'. Speer dismissed the objection that this could have been due to Bayreuth itself, nor did he accept that Winifred Wagner's relationship with Tietjen would have stood in the way. Nearly all those travelling with Hitler had come to more or less the same conclusion as Speer. Sometimes, when Hitler had been in a bad mood for days on end, they would remark 'jokingly' that the Führer was probably in need of another 'Bayreuth treatment'. Nevertheless, the assertion seems highly implausible and is probably more of an 'officers' mess speculation'.

17 Speer, *Diaries*, p. 23.

18 David Schoenbaum, *Die braune Revolution. Eine Sozialgeschichte des Dritten Reiches*, Cologne/Berlin 1968, p. 150.

19 Cf. *Der Parteitag der Arbeit vom 6. bis 13. September 1937. Offizieller Bericht.* Although at this later date, to which the report refers, the production was more perfectly staged, it did not essentially differ from earlier occasions.

20 Albert Speer, Interview with *Spiegel*, No. 46/1966, p. 52; also id., *Third Reich*, p. 59.

21 Konrad Heiden, *Die Geburt des Dritten Reiches. Die Geschichte des Nationalsozialismus bis Herbst 1933*, Zurich 1934, p. 266.

22 Robert Coulondre, *Von Moskau nach Berlin 1936–1939*, Bonn 1950, p. 473. See also André François-Poncet, *The Fateful Years: Memoirs of a French Ambassador 1931–1938*, New York 1972, p. 209, who remarks on the subject of the Party Rallies that many were 'seduced and won over' on the journey home; also Speer, *Third Reich*, p. 59.

23 Speer, *Diaries*, p. 81; also id., *Third Reich*, p. 49.

24 Speer, *Third Reich*, p. 79.

25 Cf. Domarus, *Hitler's Speeches*, vol. 1, p. 529.

26 Ernst Nolte, *Der Faschismus in seiner Epoche*, Munich 1963, p. 358; also Speer, *Diaries*, p. 103; also id., *Third Reich*, p. 35.

27 Speer, *Third Reich*, p. 58. On the remark mentioned before, cf. Domarus, *Hitler's Speeches*, vol. 1, p. 545: it was made in conversation with Jean Goy, the

chairman of the French Front Fighters' Union.

28 Speer, *Diaries*, p. 406.

29 *Chronik 1941*, vol. 1, p. 31; also Speer, *Third Reich*, pp. 36f.

30 Arndt in A. Speer, *Architektur*, p. 119; also Speer, *Third Reich*, p. 55.

31 Jost Dülffer, Jochen Thies, Josef Henke, *Hitlers Städte. Baupolitik im Dritten Reich*, Cologne 1978, pp. 211f. Not until after the war was it possible to establish the actual figures, at least with approximate accuracy. In the late sixties Speer himself estimated the total building costs at about three billion marks.

32 Hans Frank, *Im Angesicht des Galgens*, Neuhaus 1955, p. 312. On the Nuremberg constructions see Joachim Petsch, *Baukunst und Stadtplanung im Dritten Reich*, Munich/Vienna 1976, esp. pp. 91ff. There is also a multitude of further bibliographical references.

33 Petsch, *Baukunst*, p. 92.

34 Speer, *Third Reich*, p. 64.

35 Cf. Schmidt, *Speer*, p. 218, note 46; also Gregor Janssen, *Das Ministerium Speer. Deutschlands Rüstung im Krieg*, Berlin/Frankfurt 1968, p. 36; also Speer, *Third Reich*, p. 63. Interesting in this context is a comparison with the official residence Goebbels acquired not long afterwards (1938/39) and had furnished. The costs of this were at least 3.2 million marks; cf. Ralf Georg Reuth, *Goebbels*, Munich 1990, pp. 414ff.

36 Speer, *Third Reich*, p. 73.

37 Ibid., p. 75.

38 Cf. Jochen Thies, *Architekt der Weltherrschaft. Die Endziele Hitlers*, Düsseldorf 1976, p. 8.

39 Ibid., p. 85.

40 Speer, *Third Reich*, p. 74.

41 Ibid., p. 76.

42 Speer in a note to the author.

43 Interview with *Spiegel*, No. 46/1966, p. 48. Rudolf Wolters has expressed criticism of Speer's ability as an architect. 'Speer's talent', he recorded in his memoirs, 'was not on the artistic side of his profession. Nevertheless he aimed at the "artist" and – as he himself occasionally stated – wished to become a second Schinkel. His critics, however, miss the point when they simply describe Speer the architect as an unartistic manager. No doubt the Muse kissed him, too, but she did so with, as it were, chaste restraint, never with full or fervent passion.' Cf. Wolters, *Lebensabschnitte*, p. 224.

Chapter Three: Germania: the Capital of the World (pp. 66–93)

1 A. Speer, 'De Bauten des Führers', in *Bilder aus dem Leben des Führers* (Reemtsma-Bilderdienst), Altona 1936, p. 72.

2 BA R43 II/1187a, fol. 137ff.

3 *Libres propos sur la guerre et la paix*, ed. François Genoud, Paris 1952, p. 46 (27/28.9.1941).

4 Cf. Ernst Hanfstaengl, *Zwischen Weissem und Braunem Haus*, Munich 1976,

p. 80; Heinrich Hoffmann, *Hitler, wie ich ihn sah*, Munich/Berlin 1974, p. 146.

5 Genoud, *Libres propos*, p. 46.

6 Speer, *Third Reich*, p. 74. The letter-card which Speer received from Hitler was in his possession until the early seventies. After the publication of *Third Reich* an exhibition was staged in New York, where it was to be shown. The card was 'lost' in transport, along with a few other original sketches by Hitler. It has not reappeared since. The so-called sketchbook is owned by Speer's heirs.

7 Goebbels, *Fragmente*, vol. 1, p. 197 (25.7.1926).

8 Adolf Hitler, *Reden, Schriften, Anordnungen*, Munich/New Providence/London/Paris 1994, vol. 3, p. 192: speech at the NSDAP meeting in Munich on 9.4.1929. The frequently marked omissions are based on the written record which reproduces the extempore speech with all its repetitions and redundancies. The text is 28 pages long. Hitler's remarks were predominantly directed against the 'decadent' art world in Munich.

9 Cf. Fest, *Hitler*, p. 369.

10 Speer, *Third Reich*, p. 74.

11 Cf. Paul Ortwin Rave, *Schinkel, Lebenswerk*, Berlin 1948, pp. 29ff.; also Martin Mächler, *Denkschrift über Gross-Berlin*, Berlin 1920, with further historical information on this issue.

12 Cf. Wolters, *Lebensabschnitte*, pp. 202ff.

13 On the whole subject here discussed cf. Speer, *Third Reich*, pp. 77ff. and 132f.; also Thies, *Weltherrschaft*, pp. 70ff.; J. Petsch, *Baukunst*, pp. 98ff.; Lars Olaf Larsson, *Albert Speer. Le plan de Berlin 1937–1943*, Brussels 1983, passim. All the works here listed contain further bibliographical references.

14 Genoud, *Libres propos*, p. 81.

15 Speer, *Third Reich*, p, 160. On the preceding cf. Adolf Hitler, *Mein Kampf*; also Thies, *Weltherrschaft*, pp. 88 and 81.

16 Speer claimed occasionally to have laughed at Hitler's 'mania for records'. But now and then it was Hitler who probably expressed his astonishment at Speer's megalomania. As Wolters has reported (*Lebensabschnitte*, p. 257), Hitler, viewing the model of the Triumphal Arch, observed ironically: 'a neat little victory archlet'. At another inspection Willi Schelkes recorded the following dialogue: 'The Führer then asks: "How high is the hall?" Speer: "Over three hundred metres. It's a point of honour not to have it lower." Führer: "So that would be the height of the Obersalzberg above Berchtesgaden"...' This incident is also in Wolters, *Lebensabschnitte*, p. 225. The pedantic manner in which Speer tried to follow Hitler's suggestions emerges from a remark made by Speer to the author. According to Speer he had Hitler's sketch of the domed hall photographically enlarged to a multiple of its size and arranged for the people drawn in as dots to be carefully measured. He then determined the size of the building by setting one set of figures in proportion to the other. Hitler, the report continues, had been 'alarmed' and had voiced technical misgivings. Only when Speer had dispelled these had he 'enthusiastically'

approved of the building on the scale worked out. On the above-mentioned feeling of 'drunkenness' cf. Speer, *Diaries*, p. 23; there also on p. 406 is the remark that, unlike Hitler and many of his followers, he had had no 'crippled psyche'.

17 Speer, *Third Reich*, p. 155. The palace in Lenin's honour was most probably the above-mentioned design of B. M. Iofan, which received a prize in 1932, to which was joined a quarter with gigantic representational buildings grouped, as in Berlin, around a Grand Avenue. Cf. Wolfgang Pehnt, *Das Ende der Zuversicht. Architektur in diesem Jahrhundert*, Berlin 1983, p. 61, ill. p. 189. On the whole subject see also Thies, *Weltherrschaft*, p. 79.

18 Cf. Pehnt, *Zuversicht*, pp. 37ff. Wolters has ascribed the successful series of rooms in the new Reich Chancellery to Tessenow's teachings. But when Wolters sent him an illustrated book on *New German Architecture*, his former teacher replied: 'I certainly do not love the icy cold which dominates here, nor the frowning strength which is no strength any more, not these...massive façades which are not "great", and not this inhuman seriousness without a smile. As you know, my dear Wolters, I believe in a different world.' Quoted from Wolters, *Lebensabschnitte*, p. 269.

19 Author's note.

20 Henry Picker, *Hitler's Table Talk*, London 1953, p. 104. On Hitler's lack of understanding for the classical style cf. also Speer, *Third Reich*, p. 159 as well as id., *Diaries*, p. 112.

21 Speer himself later made the comparison with Cecil B. de Mille, cf. *Third Reich*, p. 159. Wolters, likewise, did not think the buildings too large, particularly when compared for example to the buildings and avenues of Washington. The dimensions, he argued, could not be managed with the traditional classical elements. It had therefore been more the architect's 'lack of artistic competence' that led to the failure of the plans for Berlin. Cf. Wolters, *Lebensabschnitte*, p. 226.

22 Cf. Wangerin and G. Weiss, *Tessenow*, pp. 19f. and 56ff.; also *Chronik*, May 1943, p. 61, where it is reported that Speer invited his teacher to an evening party with architects.

23 Speer, *Diaries*, p. 140. Speer's quoted observations of his architectural impressions during his trips are found both in *Third Reich* and in *Diaries*.

24 Author's note.

25 Joseph Goebbels, *Die Tagebücher*, ed. Elke Fröhlich, Munich, various years, vol. 5, p. 519 (17.9.42); also BA NL 1318/7, p. 11.

26 Cf. Domarus, vol. 1, pp. 530 (5.9.1934) and 378 (15.10.1933).

27 Thies, *Weltherrschaft*, p. 99; also J. Dülffer, J. Thies, J. Henke, *Hitlers Städte*, passim.

28 BA R3/1582.

29 Cf. Schmidt, *Speer*, p. 53.

30 Cf. Hermann Giesler, *Ein anderer Hitler. Bericht seines Architekten Hermann Giesler*, Leoni 1982, pp. 341ff., esp. p. 346; also *Chronik*, January 1941, vol. 1, p. 5.

31 Giesler, *Hitler*, p. 213; cf. also Speer, *Third Reich*, p. 99.

32 Author's note.

33 Giesler, *Hitler*, p. 213; also Speer, *Third Reich*, pp. 181 and 534, where the letter by which Speer laid down his Party offices is printed in excerpt. Cf. also *Chronik*, January 1941, pp. 5f., 6f., as well as BA R3/1573.

34 The document was signed by altogether seventeen artist friends of Speer's, including Breker, Thorak, Kreis, Kasper, Tamms, Hentrich, Pinnau; cf. also Giesler, *Hitler*, p. 352.

35 *Chronik*, February 1941, vol, 1, p. 10.

36 Speer's letter to Lippert of 1.6.1940. BA NS 19/2046. The entire correspondence with Lippert, quoted from here on, as well as Speer's correspondence with the *Reichssicherheitshauptamt* is filed under this reference.

37 Goebbels, *Fragmente*, p. 255 (27.7.1940); also pp. 265 and 291.

38 BA NS 19/2046, pp. 20ff.

39 Speer, *Third Reich*, p. 173.

40 Speer, *Diaries*, p. 114; also id., *Third Reich*, p. 155.

41 Speer, *Diaries*, p. 391.

42 Cf. the photograph on page 92.

43 Domarus, *Hitler's Speeches*, vol. 1, German text p. 527. This speech is not contained in the English translation. Among the notes of the author there is a remark by Speer about Hitler's unexpected reaction to the drawing of the ruins.

44 Cf. Speer, *Technik und Macht*, ed. Adelbert Reif, Esslingen 1979, pp. 49f.; also id., *Third Reich*, p. 56.

45 Speer, *Diaries*, p. 169.

46 Speer, *Third Reich*, p. 133. This was the visit during which Speer's father had the meeting with Hitler described in Chapter 1.

Chapter Four: Entanglements (pp. 94–126)

1 Speer, *Third Reich*, p. 84.

2 BA NL 1318/11; report of 17.12.1953, p. 18.

3 BA NL 1318/11; report of 15.11.1953, pp. 21f.; also Speer, *Third Reich*, pp. 46f. and 93.

4 Speer, *Diaries*, p. 144.

5 Speer, *Technik und Macht*, pp. 186ff.; also id., *Third Reich*, p. 112, according to which 'anti-Semitic slogans...provided the topic of the tea parties'.

6 It is said that after a report delivered at table by his press rival Goebbels, Hanfstaengl had made a derogatory remark about the fighting spirit of the German troops engaged in the Spanish Civil War. Those present thereupon decided to teach him a lesson. A few days later he received a sealed order from Hitler with a covering letter instructing him not to open it until after an aircraft that had been provided for him had taken off. The plane was scarcely airborne when a flabbergasted Hanfstaengl read that he was en route to Spain, where he would be set down behind the Red lines in order to work as an agent for Franco. In despair he begged the pilot to turn back, saying that there must be

some misunderstanding, but the pilot, who had been taken into the plotters' confidence, referred to an order by the Führer and refused. While Hanfstaengl was sweating blood, the pilot circled above the clouds for several hours, with false reports of his position, until eventually he informed him that he had to make an emergency landing because of engine trouble. When he climbed out of the aircraft Hanfstaengl discovered that he was in Leipzig and that he had been the victim of a prank. Thereupon he drove home, packed his most essential belongings and left Germany. Efforts to persuade him to return failed. Cf. E. Hanfstaengl, *Erinnerungen*, pp. 362ff.

7 Author's note. On the routine of the days on the Obersalzberg generally, cf. Speer, *Third Reich*, pp. 98ff.

8 Cf. Schroeder, *Chef*, pp. 189f., author's note, as well as Speer, *Alles, was ich weiss. Aus unbekannten Geheimdienstprotokollen vom Sommer 1945*, ed. Ulrich Schlie, Munich 1999, p. 27.

9 BA NL 1318/11, report of 17.12.1953, p. 19; also Speer, *Third Reich*, pp. 86f.

10 Speer, *Diaries*, p. 131.

11 Author's note.

12 Speer, *Diaries*, p. 101.

13 Wolters, *Lebensabschnitte*, S. 232. When Wolters himself asked him if he should join the Party, Speer replied: 'If you absolutely want to collect on Sundays, yes!' Ibid., p. 234.

14 Speer, *Third Reich*, p. 70.

15 Ibid., p. 102; cf. also Speer, *Geheimdienstprotokolle*, p. 177.

16 Speer, *Architektur*, p. 126.

17 Speer, *Third Reich*, p. 114.

18 Cf. *Die Neue Reichskanzlei*, Munich, n.d. (1939), p. 7.

19 Cf. Saul Friedländer, *Das Dritte Reich und die Juden. Die Jahre der Verfolgung 1933–1939*, Munich 1998, pp. 294ff.; also Goebbels, *Fragmente*, vol. 3, p. 533 (13.11.1938).

20 The advisers whom Speer had enlisted were the publisher Wolf Jobst Siedler and the present author. The result of their interventions can be found in *Inside the Third Reich*, pp. 111.

21 Speer, *Third Reich*, p. 112.

22 Sereny, *Speer*, p. 165.

23 Speer, *Diaries*, p. 8.

24 Cf. Speer, *Diaries*, p. 139. Hettlage's remark was probably also meant as a warning. For when Speer, with naive astonishment, asked him how he was to understand that, Hettlage replied: 'It applies both in a good and a bad sense. Reflect on this.' Beyond that nothing was to be got out of him, Speer said, according to an author's note.

25 Wolters, *Lebensabschnitte*, p. 229.

26 Speer, *Third Reich*, p. 115.

27 During those months Hitler repeatedly spoke of his fear that he would not have enough time. Cf. Fest, *Hitler*, p, 536; also Speer, *Third Reich*, pp. 103ff.

28 Wolters, *Lebensabschnitte*, p. 256.

29 Speer, *Third Reich*, pp. 162f.

30 Ibid., p. 168.

31 Ibid., p. 133.

32 This is how Speer himself put it in the caption to the picture showing Hitler in front of the Eiffel Tower. In it he mentions Breker, but not Giesler walking on his right. Besides, the event is controversial. Understandably, Speer did not mention it, but Giesler too, who was a friend of Breker's to the end, fails to mention his subsequent invitation. In conversation Speer remarked that Giesler had been distinguished 'beyond merit' by Hitler's invitation. Asked if he had been jealous of his rival, he replied: 'How should I have been jealous of him? Giesler was a frightful petit-bourgeois! How could he supplant me in Hitler's favour?' But cf. also William Hamsher, *Albert Speer, Victim of Nuremberg?*, London 1970, pp. 103ff. How unremitting Speer's feelings were for Giesler emerges also from the fact that he almost consistently misspells his name, with what seems like pointed indifference.

33 Speer, *Third Reich*, p. 171; cf. also A. Breker, *Im Strahlungsfeld der Ereignisse*, Preussisch Oldendorf 1972, pp. 154ff.

34 H. Giesler, *Hitler*, p. 391.

35 A. Speer, *Third Reich*, p. 172; also Breker, *Strahlungsfeld*, p. 166. In this context Speer also points to Hitler's earlier intention to destroy Paris. At the same time he saw the city as the greatest model for all architects and town planners.

36 Speer, *Third Reich*, pp. 172 and 177.

37 Author's note. On Hitler's remark about a possible '*Finis Germaniae*' cf. Speer, *Diaries*, p. 199.

38 Goebbels, *Fragmente*, vol. 4, p. 48 (11.2.1940).

39 Schmidt, *Speer*, pp. 184f.; also Goebbels, *Fragmente*, vol. 4, p. 547 (22.3.1941). No detailed information is available about Dietrich Clahes. Although his name appears in Wolters' 'Organigramm' (hierarchical plan of the ministry), and once also in Speer's *Slave State*, the organization chart of Speer's ministry, admittedly from 1.1.1944, does not include his name. Nor is he mentioned in the literature about the persecution of the Berlin Jews.

40 *Chronik*, 1941, vol. 1, p. 21.

41 *Chronik*, 1941, pp. 65ff.; further entries p. 87. ('At the end of November the third large-scale drive for the de-tenanting of Jewish flats was started' and 'a further 3,000 Jewish flats made available' for the accommodation of possible bomb victims.) In all, 23,765 Jewish flats in Berlin were 'covered'.

42 Report by Dr Martha Mosse, in *Archives of the Wiener Library, London: Testaments to the Holocaust, Section Two: Eyewitness Accounts*, Reading 1998, Roll 50, Index No. PIII, c, No. 962.

43 Monika Richarz (ed.), *Bürger auf Widerruf Lebenszeugnisse deutscher Juden 1780–1945*, Munich 1989, p. 543 (report by Camilla Neumann). There are many eyewitness reports of those events. Cf. e.g. Hildegard Henschel,

'Gemeindearbeit und Evakuierung von Berlin', in *Zeitschrift für die Geschichte der Juden*, 1972, issue 1–2, pp. 33ff. For the wider context cf. also Wolfgang Scheffler, *Judenverfolgung im Dritten Reich*, Berlin 1964, Christopher Browning, 'Zur Genesis der Endlösung', in *VJHfZ* 29/1981, Gerald Fleming, *Hitler und die Endlösung*, Wiesbaden/Munich 1982, as well as recently the above-mentioned (n. 19) work by Friedländer with further bibliographical references. The background of the transition from resettlement to deportation is described in Christian Gerlach, 'Die Wannseekonferenz', in *Werkstattgeschichte*, 1997, issue 18, pp. 7ff.

44 *Chronik*, 1942, p. 108.

45 Report by H. Henschel, *Gemeindearbeit*, p. 40.

46 Cf. the illust. on p. 166 of *Von Berlin nach Germania. Eine Ausstellung des Landesarchivs Berlin, 7.11.1984 to 30.4.1985*, p. 77.

47 Speer, *The Slave State: Heinrich Himmler's Masterplan for SS Supremacy*, London 1981, p. 255. Incidentally, Speer made a mistake about the name of the railway station. According to available reports the transports left from Grunewald and Wannsee stations. There is no mention anywhere of Nikolassee station.

48 Speer, *Diaries*, p. 23f.; cf. also ibid., p. 52.

49 Wolters, *Lebensabschnitte*, p. 236.

50 Ibid., pp. 502ff. There also is the explanation of the deletions made by Wolters and of his correspondence with Speer. It is interesting in this connection that Speer's above-named advisers asked him after the completion of *Inside the Third Reich* whether he had forgotten or kept silent about any incidents, especially those of an incriminating nature: it would surely be better for his reputation and credibility if he mentioned it himself rather than having to justify himself later. He reflected for a long time and eventually stated that he had re-examined everything and found nothing; there were 'no secrets'.

51 The letter, written on 22.1.1970, seemed to Speer unsuitable for forwarding to the Federal Archive, because of its informal tone. He therefore asked Wolters for a more formal version, BA NL 1318/40. Under the same archive reference there is also an 'Official Record' by Wolters, dated 8.2.1945. It is marked 'Secret' and records the location of the remaining copies of the *Chronik* in view of the approaching end of the war.

52 For the further development of the dispute see below, in Chapter 11. Schmidt's merit remains beyond argument, even though he evidently accepted some of the prejudices of his source. This is shown, *inter alia*, by the fact that he repeatedly refers to a '*Schuldgeldkonto*' – a 'guilt money account' – into which Wolters, during Speer's detention, paid sums of money collected from former collaborators. These were intended to support Speer's family, living in Heidelberg without any means. These funds were in fact kept under the name '*Schulgeldkonto*' – 'school fee account'. Incidentally, Speer tried, albeit unsuccessfully, to prevent publication of Schmidt's book. He was not able to comment on its published form because it did not appear until early 1982, six months after Speer's death in September 1981.

53 Das *Kriegstagebuch des Oberkommandos der Wehrmacht*, ed. Percy Ernst Schramm, Frankfurt 1961, vol. 1, p. 258.

54 Speer, *Third Reich*, pp. 180 and 187.

55 *Chronik* of 29.11.1941, p. 91. By March 1941 Speer's and Wolters's friend Willi Schelkes recorded a remark by Hitler, regretting 'that all these magnificent building ideas could not yet be executed because Churchill was robbing him of a third of his time'. Cf. Wolters, *Lebensabschnitte*, p. 269.

Chapter Five: Minister and Economic Dictator (pp. 127–159)

1 Speer, *Third Reich*, p. 193; on Todt's 'Roman head' see Wolters, *Lebensabschnitte*, p. 242.

2 Ibid., p. 193.

3 Janssen, *Ministerium*, pp. 33f. (though with a wrong date). According to Janssen, Hitler had three further conversations with Todt after 7.2.1942, but no details about these are known. It is of some interest that Speer read this work, written as a doctoral thesis, in Spandau and sent the author some comments. Wolters subsidized a special edition, contributing DM 500 towards printing costs. The work is still the most thorough examination of the war economy and represents a valuable supplement to Speer's *Inside the Third Reich*. Cf. also David Irving, *Hitler's War, 1939–1942*, London 1983, pp. 338f. Irving was able to look at Walter Rohland's 'memo book'. Further details in Walter Rohland, *Bewegte Zeiten*, Stuttgart 1978, pp. 77ff.

4 Cf. Speer, *Third Reich*, p. 197. (The English edition does not include this detail; the notes for Chapter 14 are only half as long as in the German original.) Rohland, who, like Speer, was also to have accompanied Todt, remarked after the crash: 'There must have been something fishy about it.' Later, however, he changed his view, cf. *Zeiten*, p. 81.

5 Speer, *Third Reich*, p. 197.

6 Ibid., p. 196; also Picker, *Table Talk*, p. 304. Speer does not mention Himmler's presence at lunchtime or in the evening in *Third Reich*.

7 At least according to Speer, *Third Reich*, p. 197. There has also been a good deal of suspicion that General Dietl, the mountain troops general operating in Finland, who was killed in a plane crash in June 1944, had been the victim of a plot shortly after a violent argument with Hitler. Cf. Alexander Stahlberg, *Bounden Duty. The Memoirs of a German Officer 1932–45*, Brasseys UK, 1990, pp. 356f. Stahlberg gives as his source General Fellgiebel, who, as Chief of Intelligence, had good background information.

8 *Chronik*, 1944, p. 83 as well as an author's note. In this context Speer also speaks of the 'coldblooded infamy' which he would not even think Hitler capable of. Yet one of Todt's daughters, asked years later by Wolters about Speer's implication in her father's death, answered: 'I would not put anything beyond him', cf. BA NL 1318/46 (notes of Wolters about a conversation with Frau Todt on 7.1.1978). But this points more to resentment against Speer in the Todt household.

9 Nicolaus von Below, *Als Hitlers Adjutant 1937–45*, Mainz 1980, pp. 305f. In the following years the Speers were close family friends of the Belows.

10 Author's note; also Alan Milward, *The German Economy at War*, London 1965, p. 55. Milward believes that Speer was not astonished by Hitler's decision to appoint him as Todt's successor; cf. also ibid., p. 73.

11 Thus Speer in *Third Reich*, p. 198. On Hitler's dilettantism see ibid. as well as Speer, *Diaries*, p. 347; on Speer's move into politics cf. *Third Reich*, pp. 257f.

12 Speer, *Diaries*, p. 406.

13 Thus Golo Mann, 'Der Teufelsarchitect', in Reif, *Speer*, p. 318; also Speer, *Third Reich*, p. 197.

14 Hans Kehrl, *Krisenmanager im Dritten Reich. 6 Jahre Frieden – 6 Jahre Krieg. Erinnerungen*, Düsseldorf 1973, p. 245. On Speer's introductory address see also the photograph on page 135.

15 Speer, *Third Reich*, p. 201.

16 Cf. David Irving, *The Rise and Fall of the Luftwaffe: The Life of Erhard Milch*, London 1973.

17 *Chronik*, 1942, pp. 26f. This is a controversial point. According to Janssen, *Ministerium*, pp. 65 and 357, Speer claimed that the order had never been applied. This contradicts his statement at a press conference on 19 February 1942 that he had already had two plant managers sent to a concentration camp because they had employed armaments manpower in their private households. Subsequently Speer stated that this remark had been one of the 'fictitious shock reports' customary at the time, designed to demonstrate that he was entirely serious in these matters. In fact there is no evidence in the records that any penalty had ensued on the strength of the order. M. Schmidt, on the other hand, *Speer*, pp. 120f., mentions three cases; one of these had been stopped, while the outcome of the other two was not known. Cf. also Speer, *Slave State*, pp. 144ff. In view of these figures one can probably accept Speer's assertion that in practice the order ensured the protection of his staff, despite its draconian text.

18 Kehrl, *Krisenmanager*, p. 244; for the incorporation of the Baustab Speer into the Organisation Todt, cf. *Chronik*, 1942, vols. 3–4, pp. 14f.

19 Speer, *Third Reich*, pp. 267f.

20 Ibid., p. 205.

21 *Chronik* of 11 February 1942; also Wolters, *Lebensabschnitte*, p. 246.

22 On the agreements in detail cf. Speer, *Third Reich*, pp. 206. Incidentally, Speer relied on Göring's 'sluggishness', which certainly meant the conflict which had been coupled with a threat of resignation was unfounded.

23 Thus Speer in 1979 in a conversation with Alan Bullock; cf. *Die Zeit* of 2.11.1979.

24 Viscount Haldane of Cloan, *Before the War*, London 1920, p. 71.

25 Kehrl, *Krisenmanager*, p. 256, also pp. 202ff.

26 Speer, *Third Reich*, p, 204; on the general context cf. Ludolf Herbst, *Der totale Krieg und die Ordnung der Wirtschaft. Die Kriegswirtschaft im Spannungsfeld von*

Politik, Ideologie und Propaganda 1939–1945, Stuttgart 1982.

27 Milward, *German Economy*, pp. 7of. On the preceding cf. Speer, *Third Reich*, p. 204.

28 Kehrl, *Krisenmanager*, p. 244.

29 Janssen, *Ministerium*, p. 49.

30 Ibid., p. 57.

31 Speer, *Third Reich*, p. 204; concerning 'signs of favour' cf. Milward, *German Economy*, pp. 84f.; on the number of posts in Speer's ministry, Willi A. Boelcke, *Deutschlands Rüstung im Zweiten Weltkrieg. Hitlers Konferenzen mit Albert Speer 1942–1945*, Frankfurt 1969, p. 21.

32 Author's TV interview with Speer on NDR 1970 (precise date unknown); cf. also Speer, *Third Reich*, pp, 211 and 255. According to this, Speer also considered introducing self-assessment of tax since, given the billions swallowed by the war, the loss of a few millions through dishonesty would be insignificant.

33 Boelcke, *Rüstung*, pp. 27f.

34 *Chronik*, 1942, pp. 33f.

35 Author's note. Speer's speech to the Gauleiters is in BA R3/1547.

36 Speer, *Third Reich*, pp. 220 and 540. According to van der Vat, *Speer*, p. 178, Germany was lagging behind Britain in aircraft production until 1944.

37 Kehrl, *Krisenmanager*, p. 342. Sauckel's appointment by Hitler (not by Göring) gave him a special position of which he repeatedly reminded Speer; cf. Speer, *Geheimdienstprotokolle*, p. 121.

38 Speer, *Third Reich*, p. 219.

39 Sauckel's speech on 6.1.1943, *IMT*, vol. XLI, p. 225, when he said that 'the voluntary principle is failing everywhere'. Cf. also *IMT*, vol. V, pp. 480ff. On the different groups of slave workers and their internal hierarchy, which determined their treatment, cf. Ulrich Herbert, 'Das Millionenheer des modernen Sklavenstaats' in *Frankfurter Allgemeine Zeitung* of 16.3.1999; also id., *Fremdarbeiter, Politik und Praxis des 'Ausländereinsatzes' in der Kriegswirtschaft des Dritten Reiches*, Berlin/Bonn 1985.

40 The exact total was 3,638,056; cf. Janssen, *Ministerium*, p. 85.

41 Irving, *Rise and Fall*, pp. 168ff., esp. p. 169.

42 Speer, *Third Reich*, pp. 255 and 543; there Speer conceded that he was for the moment quite pleased with the idea of not having prevailed with his demands.

43 'Secret Order for the Preparation of Total War', dated 13.1.1943, in Wolfgang Michalka, *Das Dritte Reich. Dokumente zur Innen- und Aussenpolitik*, Munich 1985, vol. 2, pp. 294f. Goebbels' remark about the 'socialistically waged' war goes back to the autumn of 1941. Cf. Goebbels, *Tagebücher*, vol. 2, p. 226 (13.8.1941); also ibid., vol. 7, p. 283 (8.2.1943), as well as numerous entries until well into 1943, when Goebbels almost imploringly records that Hitler was 'vigorously taking the position of total war' (thus vol. 8, p. 348), though in reality this was not the case, at least as far as the interests of his own public and the Gauleiters was concerned.

44 Speer, *Third Reich*, p. 258.

45 Ibid.; in his diaries Goebbels also records his 'desperation' over Hitler's indecision at that time.

46 Goebbels, *Tagebücher*, vol. 7, p. 576 (18.3.43); cf. also Schmidt, *Speer*, p. 47.

47 Speer, *Third Reich*, p. 263; Goebbels, *Tagebücher*, vol. 7, pp. 516f. (10.3.1943).

48 Goebbels, *Tagebücher*, vol. 7, p. 561 (16.3.1943), as well as, on the *Sportpalast* speech, ibid., pp. 375ff. (19.2.1943). There is also the remark about the 'silent coup d'état' he had staged with his speech.

49 Cf. Günter Moltmann, 'Goebbels' Rede zum totalen Krieg', in *VJHFZ* 1961/1, pp. 13ff. On this also Kehrl, *Krisenmanager*, pp. 294f. For Goebbels' remark about the Gauleiters cf. *Tagebücher*, vol. 7, p, 577 (18.3.1943).

50 Both Speer's and Goebbels' speeches are published in *Ursachen und Folgen. Vom deutschen Zusammenbruch 1918 und 1945 bis zur staatlichen Neuordnung Deutschlands in der Gegenwart*, Berlin n.d., vol. xix, pp. 127ff. and 136ff. For the remarkable lead-up cf. Speer, *Third Reich*, p. 268. Originally Speer was to appear together with Göring, but Göring backed down at the last moment because, as Goebbels noted, 'he no longer has any real confidence in his effectiveness with the people'. Cf. *Tagebücher*, vol. 8, p. 393 (30.5. 1943).

51 Goebbels, *Tagebücher*, vol. 8, p. 157 (24.4.1943). On the generally untroubled collaboration between Speer and Sauckel cf. also *Chronik*, after 1942, passim. That any differences of opinion between the two had nothing to do with moral considerations on Speer's part emerges also from the fact that even before his appointment as minister, Speer had, on a visit to Prague in December 1941, arranged with Heydrich that 'the Protectorate would make available each year 50,000 Czechs of younger age groups for the Berlin tasks after the war'; cf. *Chronik*, 1941, vol. 1, p. 94.

52 Manifesto of the General Plenipotentiary for Manpower Employment of 20.4.1943, in *Ursachen und Folgen*, vol. xix, pp. 117ff.

53 Janssen, *Ministerium*, p. 121. Cf. also Goebbels, *Tagebücher*, vol. 8, pp, 136f. (20.4.1943). The discrepancy in the numbers is partly due to the fact that any labourer changing his place of work was statistically recorded as a new enrolment without his departure from his earlier job being recorded.

54 Cf. Speer, *Third Reich*, p. 271.

55 Thus Funk himself, with helpless humour; cf. Kehrl, *Krisenmanager*, pp. 310ff. However, Speer had obtained Funk's consent to his impending loss of responsibilities in preliminary talks.

56 Janssen, *Ministerium*, p. 137. On this Goebbels, *Tagebücher*, vol. 9, p. 447 (8.9.1943): 'In these measures the Four-Year Plan was largely excluded.'

57 Janssen, *Ministerium*, p. 135.

58 Hugh Trevor-Roper, 'Porträt des wirklichen Nazi-Verbrechers', in Adelbert Reif ed., *Albert Speer, Kontroversen um eine deutsches Phänomen*, Munich 1978, p. 236.

Chapter Six: Stations of Ambition (pp. 160–192)

1 Goebbels, *Tagebücher*, vol. 4, p. 343 (23.5.1942), vol. 7, p. 267 (5.2.1943), and p. 513 (9.3.1943).

2 Ibid., vol. 6, p. 48 (2.10.1942).

3 Speer, *Third Reich*, pp. 302f.

4 Goebbels, *Tagebücher*, vol. 7, p. 213 (28.1.1943), pp. 458f. (2.3.1943). On what follows cf. vol. 5, p. 347 (20.8.1942), p. 603 (30.9.1942), as well as vol. 6, p. 131 (16,10.1942); also vol. 8, p. 43 (3.4.1943) and vol. 6, p. 33 (1.10.1942).

5 Cf. Picker, *Table Talk*, passim. An instructive instance of mutual ideological heat in conversation with Hitler is found in Goebbels, *Tagebücher*, vol. 8, pp. 286ff. (13.5.1943).

6 Goebbels, *Tagebücher*, vol. 8, p. 126 (18.4.1943); also A. Speer, *Slave State*, pp. 252ff., as well as Reuth, *Goebbels*, pp. 524f. Cf. also the numerous references in Goebbels' diaries, e.g. vol. 4, p. 351 (24.5.1942), ibid., p. 405 (30.5.1942), vol. 7, p. 515 (9.3.1943), vol. 8, p. 126 (18.4.1943). On 2 March 1943 he recorded angrily that 'the better circles, especially the intellectuals', had 'betrayed the action, so that a whole lot of Jews slipped through our fingers'. Cf. vol. 7, p. 449 (2.3.1943).

7 Speer, *Slave State*, p. 252. The remark about the 'pincer movement' by which Goebbels had compelled him to give in is to be found in a letter to Wolters from the end of January 1970, when he called Goebbels the 'swine Joseph'. BA NL 1318/40.

8 Cf. Janssen, *Ministerium*, p. 348. Speer declined an honorary SS rank not only because he was unable to relate to Himmler's 'order' and its scurrilous rituals, but also because he feared that the SS would thereby – as Himmler no doubt intended – gain influence on him and his work. Cf. Speer, *Slave State*, pp. 178, as well as id., *Third Reich*, pp. 369.

9 Goebbels, *Tagebücher*, vol. 9, p. 229 (6.8.1943).

10 Janssen, *Ministerium*, p. 251; also *Kriegstagebuch des OKW*, vol. iii, 2nd half-volume, p. 1127.

11 Milward, *German Economy*, p. 119.

12 Author's note.

13 Speer, *Third Reich*, pp. 285 and the notes referring to it, esp. on pp. 546f. In point of fact, the 'Economic Warfare Division' had already recommended in December 1942 causing 'a high degree of destruction in a few really war-deciding industries rather than a slight degree of destruction in many industries'. However, the suggestion was brushed aside. On Operation Schweinfurt cf. Friedhelm Golücke, *Schweinfurt und der strategische Luftkrieg*, Paderborn 1980.

14 Speer, *Third Reich*, p. 287. This success was in part due to the fact that some ball-bearings had meanwhile been replaced by so-called sliding bearings; ibid., p. 286.

15 On the so-called 'SO' (Selbstopfer = self-sacrifice) men, cf. Werner Baumbach, *Zu spät? Aufstieg und Untergang der deutschen Luftwaffe*, Munich 1949, pp. 268ff. There also is the claim that it was Hitler himself who rejected 'total engagement'.

16 On this and some further data cf. mainly Milward, *German Economy*, p. 136,

as well as Janssen, *Ministerium*, pp. 178ff. The chaos in air armaments was due also to the fact that they were still 'independent' and thus unable to count on Speer's support. Milward calls the production of aircraft one of the 'great overall failures of the German war economy'.

17 Cf. Irving, *Rise and Fall*, p. 178.

18 Thus one of the constructors of the machine at a meeting in June 1943; cf. Janssen, *Ministerium*, p. 180; also Speer, *Third Reich*, p. 362; likewise Milward, *German Economy*, pp. 102f.

19 Speer, *Diaries*, p. 340.

20 Speer, *Third Reich*, pp. 234 and 542; on this also Kehrl, *Krisenmanager*, pp. 331f.; Janssen, *Ministerium*, pp. 231f., as well as Speer, *Slave State*, p. 179. Very clear and detailed, though not without critical objection in certain cases, the statistics on armaments production 1941–45 in Boelcke, *Rüstung*, pp. 13ff. and the table on pp. 20ff.

21 Speer knew how to place his production reports in the most favourable light by using confusing methods of calculation and careful selection. Even though he did not distort the figures, he did at times convey an inaccurate impression. His data are moreover modified by his own statement that, when he assumed the ministry, there had been no armaments strategy in the proper sense. Goebbels at times notes in his diaries that, whenever Speer produced brilliant figures, the staffs at the front were asking what had happened to those thousands of aircraft, armoured fighting vehicles or artillery pieces. Cf. e.g. Goebbels, *Tagebücher*, vol. 13, p. 136 (23.7.1944). In mid-November 1944 Speer admitted: 'I have not yet found a single person outside our building who would believe our armaments figures if they were simply put before him. Everywhere we encounter disbelief, everyone claims it is a lie. We are fibbing.' Cf. Boelcke, *Rüstung*, p. 8.

22 Speer, *Third Reich*, p. 276.

23 Speer, *Slave State*, p. 239.

24 Cf. e.g. the remark in *Adolf Hitler. Monologe im Führerhauptquartier 1941–1944. Die Aufzeichnungen Heinrich Heims*, Hamburg 1980, p. 234 (25/26.2.1942).

25 Schmidt, *Speer*, p. 82. Cf. also Speer, *Geheimdienstprotokolle*, p. 32.

26 Kehrl, *Krisenmanager*, p. 335.

27 Thus Speer in a chapter heading of *Third Reich*, p. 267.

28 Giesler, *Hitler*, p. 434, as well as Speer, *Slave State*, p. 223.

29 Goebbels, *Tagebücher*, vol. 10, p. 137 (20.10.1943); cf. also Speer, *Third Reich*, p. 268.

30 Speer, *Third Reich*, p. 268.

31 Ibid., pp. 289f.; cf. also *IMT*, vol. xvi, pp. 584f.

32 Thus Speer at a meeting of Central Planning and subsequently to Hitler; cf. Irving, *Rise and Fall*, p. 229. On Speer's work during Hitler's lengthy tirades cf. Stahlberg, *Duty*, p. 316, where Speer claims that he sometimes began to draw and instantly aroused Hitler's attention. In that way, he said, he gained control of the conversation again.

33 Kehrl, *Krisenmanager*, p. 335.

34 Speer, *Third Reich*, pp. 365f. On the whole context cf. the informative presentation of Karl-Heinz Ludwig, 'Die wohlreflektierten "Erinnerungen" des Albert Speer', in Reif, *Speer*, pp. 411ff.; a detailed account of the controversy in the armaments area, esp. with regard to the V weapons, in Janssen, *Ministerium*, pp. 189ff.

35 Speer, *Slave State*, p. 207.

36 A compilation of Speer's sceptical remarks about the 'miracle weapons' in Janssen, *Ministerium*, pp. 204ff.

37 Speer, *Slave State*, p. 208.

38 Ibid., pp. 137f., 140 and 147.

39 Ibid., p. 213; also Joachim Fest, 'Die andere Utopie. Eine Studie über Heinrich Himmler', in *Fremdheit und Nähe*, Stuttgart 1996, pp. 138ff. Also Milward, *German Economy*, pp. 155f. On Himmler's undermining work see ibid., pp. 88f. and 113ff.

40 Irving, *Rise and Fall*, p. 208.

41 BA NS 317 (letter of 17.12.1943).

42 Author's note, as well as Speer, *Third Reich*, p. 373 and id., *Slave State*, pp. 217ff. It was typical of Kammler that in the course of a conference he boasted that he had 'simply taken 50,000 people into protective custody' in order to get manpower for the SS factories.

43 Speer, *Slave State*, p. 211; also Peter Kuhlbrodt, *Mittelbau-Dora bei Nordhausen 1943–1945. Ein Überblick*, Nordhausen 1991.

44 Cf. *Chronik*, 10,12,1943. In 1968 Speer gave evidence as a witness in the trial of supervisors of the Dora camp, but did not remember the planned execution and his successful intervention which had been mentioned, before him, by the Kapo of the camp crematorium; cf. IfZ Ge 0108/1.

45 Speer, *Slave State*, p. 211. On the visit to the Mauthausen concentration camp cf. *IMT*, vol. xvi, p. 445.

46 *Chronik*, 1943, p. 246 and 1944, pp. 8ff. Details in Angela Fiedermann *et al.*, *Das Konzentrationslager Mittelbau Dora: Ein historischer Abriss*, Berlin/Bonn 1993; also Speer, *Third Reich*, pp. 371. Ley objected because he believed that as representative of the workers he was also responsible for their medical care. In point of fact, Sauckel on 7 September 1942 had given the German Labour Front and thereby Ley 'the sole and exclusive task of looking after all foreign labour employed on Reich territory'. To this end the two some time later set up a Central Inspectorate, whose rights, however, were meaningless in view of the real power which Himmler wielded over the concentration camps.

47 Speer, *Slave State*, pp. 230ff. In the preface of that book Speer states that it was only in the seventies, while examining the sources in the Federal Archive in Koblenz, that he realized to his 'surprise' the comprehensively planned strategy with which Himmler sought to deprive him of power – another proof of his political naiveté. Cf. also in this context Enno Georg, *Die wirtschaftlichen Unternehmungen der SS*, Stuttgart 1963.

48 Kehrl, *Krisenmanager*, p. 297; on his assessment of the war situation towards Rohland cf. *IMT*, vol. xli, p. 493; also Janssen, *Ministerium*, p. 157. Wolters, too, even for the following year, records Speer's 'spectral optimism', cf. *Lebensabschnitte*, p. 342.

49 Goebbels, *Tagebücher*, vol. 10, p. 69 (7.10.1943); also the Goebbels quotations which follow.

50 BA R3/1548. In *Chronik* of October 1943 Speer criticizes countless further 'luxury articles' which, in the face of all war necessities, are still being produced, e.g. riding boots for officers or cube sugar, for the packaging of which a single factory uses eighty tonnes of paper; cf. BA NL/1318/4, pp. 190ff.

51 Speer, *Third Reich*, p. 313.

52 Wolters, *Lebensabschnitte*, p. 341.

53 Cf. e.g. Goebbels, *Tagebücher*, vol. 7, p. 454 (3.3.1943), as well as Andreas Hillgruber (ed.), *Staatsmänner und Diplomaten bei Hitler. Vertrauliche Aufzeichnungen über Unterredungen mit Vertretern des Auslands*, Frankfurt 1967/70, vol. ii, p. 377; also Speer, *Third Reich*, p. 293.

54 Himmler's appointment book, Moscow Special Archive 1372–5-23, fo. 334. Cf. also Chr. Gerlach, *Die Wannsee-Konferenz*, p. 22. On the general problem cf. Martin Broszat, 'Hitler und die Genesis der "Endlösung"', in *VfZ* 25/1977, pp. 739ff. Further extensive bibliographical references in Klaus Hildebrand, *Das Dritte Reich*, Munich 1995, 5th edn, pp. 281ff.

55 The text of the speech is published in Bradley F. Smith and Agnes F. Peterson, *Heinrich Himmler. Geheimreden 1933-1945*, Frankfurt/Berlin/Vienna 1974, pp. 162ff. On the speech made by Himmler two days earlier see *IMT* 1919-PS, vol. xxix, pp. 110ff.

56 Baldur von Schirach, *Ich glaubte an Hitler*, Hamburg 1967, pp. 269f. Schirach, however, makes Bormann invite the company 'to lunch' and gives the date of the event as 29 May 1944. That could possibly be Himmler's speech to generals on 5 May 1944 or on 24 May in Sonthofen; cf. *Geheimreden*, pp. 202ff. But as his quotations come from Himmler's speech on 6 October 1943 there is evidently a mistake.

57 Erich Goldhagen, 'Albert Speer, Himmler and the Secrecy of the Final Solution', in *Midstream*, 1971, pp. 43ff. Cf. also Reif, *Speer*, pp. 383ff., who presents Goldhagen's text in German translation.

58 Author's note. Speer made a mistake in *Inside the Third Reich*. There he states that on the evening of that 6 October 1943 he had travelled by the Gauleiters' special train to the Führer's headquarters. Later he corrected this by saying that this had been the case after his second performance in Posen on 3 August 1944. To that extent Goldhagen's attack is to be understood, but not the following remark by Himmler, which he has invented.

59 Affidavit by Rohland of 6 July 1973, quoted in Speer, 'Ein Nachtrag (zu Erich Goldhagen)', in Reif, *Speer*, p. 405; there also Siegmund's affidavit and Milch's confirmation. Cf. also Rohland, *Zeiten*, pp. 87f., where the course of the evening and the conversation with Hitler are described. Doubts concerning

Speer's premature departure from Posen, as well as Rohland's and Siegmund's affidavits, are expressed in Sereny, *Speer*, pp. 394ff. Siegmund, she states, had told her that he had been 'bombarded' by Speer about the affidavit 'with I don't know how many telephone calls, so in the end I gave him what he wanted.' But Siegmund told the author that this assertion was invented by Gitta Sereny and that Speer had only written to him once. Since he remembered that the Minister of Armaments was not present he did not hesitate to provide the affidavit he had asked for. On Rohland's affidavit Sereny remarks that 'the most probable explanation' was that 'Rohland was a good friend', which evidently was intended to mean that, no matter what had really happened, he wanted to help Speer. The evidence she produced does not, however, prove her view.

60 Goldhagen, *Final Solution*, p. 47; also van der Vat, *Speer*, p. 349.

61 Speer, *Diaries*, pp. 28.

62 Speer, *Third Reich*, p. 313.

63 Ibid., p. 376.

64 Author's note following a conversation with Annemarie Kempf, Speer's secretary for many years. Speer himself confirmed Frau Kempf's account.

65 Speer, *Diaries*, p. 101; also author's note.

66 Speer, *Third Reich*, p. 375. Cf. also Goebbels, *Tagebücher*, vol. 7, p. 267 (5.2.1943): 'Speer works like a beast.'

67 Speer, *Technik und Macht*, p. 123; the quotation comes from Arthur Koestler.

68 Author's note.

Chapter Seven: Crises and Intrigues (pp. 193–219)

1 In *Third Reich*, p. 317, Speer rather vaguely gives the date from which Hitler received the monthly armaments production figures not from him but from Saur as the autumn of 1943. In conversation with the author, however, he explained the change as the direct consequence of the Posen conference of Gauleiters and Hitler's resultant loss of trust in him.

2 Speer, *Third Reich*, p. 316.

3 Erich Kästner, *Notabene 45. Ein Tagebuch*, Berlin 1961, p. 55; also Speer, *Third Reich*, pp. 314f. On the decree for reconstruction planning cf. Boelcke, *Rüstung*, p. 243, as well as Werner Durth and Niels Gutschow, *Träume in Trümmern. Planungen zum Wiederaufbau zerstörter Städte in Westen Deutschlands 1940–1950*, Braunschweig/Wiesbaden 1988, pp. 55ff.

4 Giesler, *Hitler*, p. 334, has denied that Hitler had chosen the tower of the Linz Party House for his burial place. But Speer stuck to his recollection, pointing out with some plausibility that this dramatic idea was far more in line with Hitler's character. He also used the opportunity to emphasize Giesler's lesser standing with Hitler: Hitler, he thought, was 'evidently embarrassed' to confide in Giesler 'who, after all, was much more of a stranger to him that I was'. Cf. also Speer, *Diaries*, p. 172. Besides, a mausoleum for Hitler's parents was to be established in the lower part of the Linz bell tower: cf. Karl Brandt,

'Frauen um Hitler', in Speer, *Geheimdienstprotokolle*, p. 241.

5 Speer, *Third Reich*, p. 140.

6 Cf. Peter Hüttenberger, *Die Gauleiter. Studie zum Wandel des Machtgefüges in der NSDAP*, Stuttgart 1969, pp. 184f. Also Speer, *Third Reich*, p. 317.

7 Author's note.

8 Speer, *Slave State*, p. 224.

9 Thus e.g. Mitscherlich, *Selbstblendung*; cf. Reif, *Speer*, pp. 469f.; also Speer's secretary Annemarie Kempf in Sereny, *Speer*, p. 412, or Sereny herself, pp. 418f., who admittedly uses a more complex argument, quoting Speer's remark: 'I think, finally, I did want to die'.

10 NA R3/1515.

11 Erhard Milch, *Notebook of Generalfeldmarschall Erhard Milch*, IfZ ED 100/137. Göring's donation amounted to 100,625 RM and emerges from a letter of the *Accounts Office of the Prussian State Ministry* of 20.1.1944, which had made the amount available and now requested reimbursement. Speer intended to build a grand house on the property after the war and had prepared a number of designs for it; on the letter cf. Special Archive Moscow 700-01-45.

12 BA R3/1515 and NL 1318/46; on Ley see Speer, *Third Reich*, p. 336.

13 Speer, *Third Reich*, p. 328.

14 Speer's letter to Bormann, undated, BA R3/1612.

15 Speer, *Third Reich*, pp. 329f.; BA R3/1630.

16 Speer's letter to Dorsch of 27.1.1944, BA R3/1515 and BA R3/1630.

17 A different account e.g. in Schmidt, *Speer*, pp. 87ff. Schmidt, in his general endeavour to prove Speer's insincerity, asserts that Speer himself had instructed none other than Professor Gebhardt to call in Professor Koch, as might be seen from the medical record prepared by Gebhardt. It evidently never occurred to him that Gebhardt may have been untruthful. Schmidt similarly disputes Speer's suspicion of Gebhardt. But this is attested by witnesses such as Speer's secretary and close confidante Annemarie Kempf, by Speer's wife, by Professor Friedrich Koch and others.

18 Sereny, *Speer*, p. 414. According to Koch's statement Gebhardt had approached him with the remark: 'Now we must blow up Speer's lung'. When Koch resolutely refused, Gebhardt had retreated, declaring that he had 'only wanted to test' his colleague; cf. Speer, *Slave State*, p. 224.

19 Cf. Speer, *Third Reich*, pp. 331f., as well as Janssen, *Ministerium*, p. 158, and Sereny, *Speer*, pp. 414ff. A different version again in Schmidt, *Speer*, p. 89, who speaks of the 'spectre of a medical assassination', arguing, against Speer, that after the war Professor Koch made no mention of the 'life-threatening intervention' Gebhardt allegedly demanded of him. Significantly the obvious explanation that Koch's discretion might have something to do with professional usages does not occur to him. Cf. Koch's revealing statement on oath before the Nuremberg Tribunal on 12.3.1947, the relevant passage of which is reproduced in Speer, *Third Reich*, p. 552.

20 Quoted in Schmidt, *Speer*, p. 90. Incidently, at the same time that Speer was

at Hohenlychen, Himmler also detained the SS and Police General Kurt Daluege there against his will; cf. Speer, *Slave State*, p. 228.

21 Speer, *Slave State*, p. 223. After his release from Spandau Speer got three reputable medical men to examine Gebhardt's records. Their unanimous opinion was that such mistakes could 'not even be forgiven an orthopaedic surgeon'; cf. ibid., p. 225.

22 Sereny, *Speer*, p. 415.

23 van der Vat, *Speer*, pp. 188 and 192. The fact that Professor Koch shared Speer's distrust of Gebhardt emerges also from an episode which is reported in Koch's affidavit. He says there: 'When in February 1945 I collided with a lorry in Upper Silesia and suffered slight injuries, Gebhardt immediately got on a special aircraft to bring me to his clinic. My personal assistant, Karl Cliever, foiled this intention without giving me any reasons, although – as he then said to me – there had been reasons.' A point of interest in this connection is also that Jean Bichelonne, Speer's French minister friend, had come to Hohenlychen in January 1945, moreover at Speer's recommendation, for a knee operation and had, as nearly happened to Speer, died of a lung embolism.

24 Thus the surmise of Speer's secretary Annemarie Kempf, who also pointed out that 'it's impossible to understand the games they played'; cf. Sereny, *Speer*, p. 425. Gebhardt's letter to Himmler, informing him of Speer's invitation to accompany him to Merano, did not become known until after Speer's death. He could not therefore be asked about his motives.

25 Author's note. The quotations in the following passage also refer to notes made during the conversation or to Speer's account of the meeting and its consequences in *Third Reich*, pp. 333f.

26 Boelcke, *Rüstung*, pp. 349ff.

27 BA R3/1516; cf. also Speer, *Third Reich*, p. 338.

28 Speer, *Third Reich*, p. 338; also M. Bormann to Speer on 1.3.1944, BA R3/1573.

29 Speer, *Erinnerungen*, p. 567; not in *Third Reich*.

30 Rohland, *Zeiten*, p. 99.

31 Milch, *Notebook*.

32 In his account of Milch's visit Speer has both fudged the text of Hitler's message ('Almost like a declaration of love') and toned down his own rude response ('No, I'm sick of it...'). Cf. *Third Reich*, p. 339.

33 In *Third Reich*, p. 342, Speer only used the term 'content'. According to the author's notes, however, he had been 'relieved and even happy'.

34 Cf. Janssen, *Ministerium*, p. 236; also Milward, *German Economy*, p. 163. On the effect of Operation Big Week see also Irving, *Rise and Fall*, p. 274, as well as, on the impending end of the German fighter bombers, Baumbach, *Aufstieg*, p. 230.

35 Speer, *Third Reich*, p. 346.

36 Cf. the reproduced text in Janssen, *Ministerium*, pp. 238ff.; also Speer, *Third Reich*, p. 554, with further figures about fuel production.

37 Irving, *Rise and Fall*, p. 234.

38 BA R3/1560.

39 Hüttenberger, *Gauleiter*, p. 186; Milward, *German Economy*, p. 153. In his book *The Slave State* Speer had described in great detail the machinations of Bormann and above all Himmler and the SS against the armaments ministry and himself.

40 Speer, *Third Reich*, p. 345; also author's note.

41 von Below, *Adjutant*, p. 368.

42 Speer, *Technik und Macht*, pp. 182f. There Speer also noted the 'declining trend' of these Führer conferences. In the first year of his work as a minister they discussed 938 agenda points, in 1943 over 700, in 1944 over 530 and in the first five months of 1945 merely 53.

43 Milch, *Notebook*; cf. also Speer, *Third Reich*, pp. 351 and 407f.

44 Irving, *Rise and Fall*, p. 284.

Chapter Eight: Scorched Earth (pp. 220–251)

1 Goebbels, *Tagebücher*, vol. 12, p. 464 (14.6.1944). A few days later Goebbels noted that the rockets had, at his suggestion, been called V weapons, 'V' standing for *Vergeltung* (retaliation); cf. also ibid., p. 525 (22.6.1944). On Milch's remark see Irving, *Rise and Fall*, p. 356.

2 Cf. Speer, *Third Reich*, p. 356.

3 BA R3/1587 (address to commanding generals on 13.1.1945).

4 Speer, *Third Reich*, p. 358.

5 Speer, *Slave State*, p. 110.

6 Speer, *Third Reich*, pp. 382ff. There also, unless otherwise indicated, the subsequent quotations.

7 BA R3/1627.

8 Wilfried von Oven, *Verrat und Widerstand im Dritten Reich*, Coburg 1978, p. 57; von Oven, the personal press officer of the propaganda minister, adds the observation that Speer would have had to be 'a very cunning actor if he had really been in the conspiracy'.

9 BA NL 1318/14; Speer, *Die Tätigkeit als Minister*, p. 32.

10 Cf. also Schmidt, *Speer*, p. 104, who also reports an attempt by Carl Goerdeler to make contact with Speer despite being critical of his activity. On the ministerial list see Peter Hoffmann, *Widerstand, Staatsstreich, Attentat*, Munich 1979, p. 454.

11 *Chronik*, 1944, p. 22; also Speer, *Third Reich*, p. 392. In fact, Speer was mistaken. According to *Chronik*, vol. 2, for example, he also concluded his address on taking over the ministry with 'Sieg Heil!'

12 Cf. *Spiegelbild einer Verschwörung. Die Kaltenbrunner-Berichte an Bormann und Hitler über das Attentat vom 20. Juli 1944*, Stuttgart 1961, p. 445; also Speer, *Third Reich*, p. 392.

13 Goebbels, *Tagebücher*, vol. 13, p. 259 (18.8.1944): also p. 239 (10.8.1944).

14 Thus Speer in a remark to Sereny, *Speer*, p. 450. On the people for whom

Speer intervened and on his letter of 29.12.1944, protesting against Kaltenbrunner's suspicions and defending one of his departmental heads, see Janssen, *Ministerium*, p. 270 with list of sources. On Hitler's refusal to let him testify in favour of Colonel-General Fromm, cf. Speer, *Third Reich*, pp. 445f.

15 Goebbels, *Tagebücher*, vol. 12, p. 518 (22.6.1944).

16 Speer memorandum of 20.7.1944, BA NL 1318/13.

17 Speer, *Slave State*, pp. 54ff., 66ff. and 173ff.; also Janssen, *Ministerium*, pp. 283f.

18 Goebbels, *Tagebücher*, vol. 12, p. 521 (22.6.1944).

19 Ibid., vol. 13, p. 180 (27.7.1944).

20 Quoted according to Helmut Heiber (ed.), *Goebbels-Reden 1939–1945*, Düsseldorf 1972, vol. 2, pp. 342ff.

21 See Bormann's letters of 14.8.1944 and 24.8.1944 in BA R55/665 and BA R55/666a.

22 Speer, *Third Reich*, p. 397.

23 Goebbels, *Tagebücher*, vol. 13, pp. 526f. (20.9.1944); also Speer, *Third Reich*, p. 399, as well as *Chronik* of beginning of October 1944.

24 Cf. Speer's memorandum of 20.9.1944, published in *Ursachen und Folgen*, vol. xxi, pp. 607ff., as well as Speer, *Third Reich*, p. 397.

25 Irving, *Rise and Fall*, p. 281.

26 Goebbels, *Tagebücher*, vol. 13, p. 203 (3.8.1944).

27 Irving, *Rise and Fall*, p. 281; on Hitler's clash with Speer and Galland see Speer, *Third Reich*, p. 408.

28 Speer, *Third Reich*, p. 415. On the meetings with Dorpmüller and others cf. Lutz Graf Schwerin von Krosigk, *Es geschah in Deutschland. Menschenbilder unseres Jahrhunderts*, Stuttgart/Tübingen 1951, p. 302. On Saur see Walter Lüdde-Neurath, *Regierung Dönitz. Die letzten Tage des Dritten Reiches*, 3rd edn, Göttingen 1964, p. 18.

29 *IMT*, vol. xvi, p. 491.

30 Speer, *Third Reich*, p. 401.

31 Hermann Rauschning, *Hitler Speaks*, London 1939, pp. 119ff. Rauschning's book has for some time been regarded with considerable scepticism, but in this case it is possible also to refer to Hitler's *Mein Kampf*, to his so-called *Secret Book*, and to *Hitler's Lagebesprechungen. Die Protokollfragmente seiner militärischen Konferenzen 1942–1945*, pp. 713 and 739. Besides, the remark again occurs, almost verbatim, after the failure of the Ardennes offensive, cf. below, n. 44.

32 Joachim Fest, 'Albert Speer und die technizistische Unmoral', in *The Face of the Third Reich*, New York 1970, p. 205.

33 Trevor-Roper, *Last Days*, pp. 87f.

34 Thus Theodor Hupfauer, cf. Sereny, *Speer*, p. 388, as well as Wolters, *Lebensabschnitte*, p. 342.

35 Author's note. Cf. Rohland, *Zeiten*, p. 103.

36 *IMT*, vol. xli, pp. 515f.

37 Speer, *Third Reich*, pp. 404f.

NOTES

38 Author's note. Sereny received a monthly schedule from von Poser, but this only started in mid-February, though it came to much the same total; Sereny, *Speer*, p. 482.

39 Author's note.

40 Speer, interview with *Spiegel*, No. 44/1966, p. 59.

41 Cf. *IMT*, vol. xli, pp. 527 and 529; also ibid., vol. xvi, p. 502; also Reimer Hansen, 'Albert Speers Konflikt mit Hitler', in *Geschichte in Wissenschaft und Unterricht*, 1966, pp. 596ff., Sereny, *Speer*, p. 471, as well as Speer, *Third Reich*, pp. 457 and 496. On the dispute with Göring, cf. also id., *Diaries*, pp. 192 and 195. The Luftwaffe colonel whom Speer claims to have told of this plan was the much decorated fighter pilot Werner Baumbach. In his memoirs Baumbach deals at length with his connection with Speer, mentioning some of their jointly considered intentions such as the Greenland enterprise mentioned below, but he does not mention the plan here reported. Perhaps in retrospect it seemed to him too adventurous. Certainly Stahl, as he informed the American intelligence service after the war, was privy to the plan; cf. van der Vat, *Speer*, pp. 223f.

42 Speer, *Diaries*, pp. 200f.

43 von Below, *Adjutant*, p. 391; on the Ardennes offensive as an expression of Hitler's retaliation plans against his own nation, cf. also Sebastian Haffner, *The Meaning of Hitler*, London 1978, pp. 154ff.

44 von Below, *Adjutant*, p. 398. For the ratio of shot-down aircraft between the Luftwaffe and the Allied formations cf. Lüdde-Neurath, *Dönitz*, p. 20; on Speer's consternation over Hitler's decision to continue the war despite the failure of the Ardennes offensive cf. Gustav M. Gilbert, *Nuremberg Diary*, London 1948, p. 135.

45 Cf. Franz Kurowski, *Der Luftkrieg über Deutschland*, Düsseldorf/Vienna 1977, pp. 328ff.

46 Speer, *Third Reich*, pp. 419f.

47 Ibid., p. 423.

48 Cf. BA NL 1318/7, as well as the materials in *Ursachen und Folgen*, vol. xxii, pp. 365ff. An instructive example of the arguments between Hitler and Guderian, along with a lengthy, quite absurd dialogue, can be found in Heinz Guderian, *Panzer Leader*, London 1952, pp. 393ff.

49 BA NL 1318/7.

50 Speer, *Third Reich*, p. 425.

51 Hitler, *Mein Kampf*.

52 BA NL 1318/7; also Speer, *Third Reich*, pp. 429ff.

53 Stahl's evidence before the Nuremberg Tribunal, see *IMT*, vol. xli, p. 517.

54 Thus Giesler in a letter of 22.12.1970 to Propyläen Verlag, cf. BL NL 1318/44.

55 Speer, *Third Reich*, pp. 465f. and 495f.; also Baumbach, *Aufstieg*, pp. 230ff. For a while there was also a plan to detain Hitler and the leaders of the regime, and to hand them over to Britain; thus at any rate Hamsher, *Victim*, p. 172, who quotes talks with Baumbach and Galland as his source.

56 Goebbels, *Tagebücher*, vol. 15, p. 500 (14.3.1945).

57 Ibid., vol. 15, p. 511 (15.3.1945).

58 The memorandum submitted in the evening of 18.3.1945 is dated 15.3.1945. Presumably Speer held it back for a few days, submitting it only on the eve of his fortieth birthday in the expectation that Hitler might be in a more conciliatory mood that day. On the text cf. *Ursachen und Folgen*, vol. xxii, pp. 531ff., as well as Speer, *Third Reich*, pp. 436ff.

59 Thus the previously mentioned Secretary, Annemarie Kempf; cf. Sereny, *Speer*, p. 484. In her testimony at Nuremberg, Frau Kempf stated: 'We feared more than once that his reports to the Führer or his statements in a wider circle were bound to lead to his arrest. He himself was not bothered about it, he considered it his duty.' Cf. Karl Anders, *Im Nürnberger Irrgarten*, Regensburg 1948, p. 121.

60 BA NL 1318/10.

61 Speer, *Third Reich*, p. 440.

62 *IMT*, vol. xli, p. 430f.

63 Sereny, *Speer*, p. 486.

Chapter Nine: End Without End (pp. 252–281)

1 Report from Spandau to Wolters, BA NL 1318/7. On the Kolberg film see Goebbels, *Tagebücher*, vol. 15, p. 542 (19.3.1945). In fact, the Wehrmacht communiqué only reported the fall of the city two days later; cf. ibid., p. 552.

2 Irving, *Rise and Fall*, p. 281; also Speer, *Third Reich*, p. 455.

3 Cf. Janssen, *Ministerium*, p. 313. The relevant note names the participants of the circle which included General Guderian, along with Paul Pleiger of the Reich Association Coal and Otto Steinbrink of *Vereinigte Stahlwerke*; cf. ibid., p. 412.

4 BA NL 1318/7, as well as Speer, *Third Reich*, p. 447. On the various meetings with the Ruhr entrepreneurs and the issue of submachine-guns cf. also Rohland, *Zeiten*, pp. 100ff.

5 Published in *Ursachen und Folgen*, vol. xxii, pp. 518f.

6 Author's note. Whenever no references are given for the subsequent arguments between Hitler and Speer, the quotations are based on Speer's *Inside the Third Reich*, amplified by details from the author's notes.

7 Goebbels, *Tagebücher*, vol. 15, pp. 619f. (28.3.1945).

8 Speer, *Third Reich*, p. 451. With regard to the account of the two last conversations between Hitler and Speer it should, of course, be remembered that all our knowledge of them goes back to Speer alone. The conversation on that day, however, is confirmed in its decisive passage by a letter which Speer addressed to Hitler immediately on his return from the Führer's bunker. Cf. also the quotation in Chapter 8, n. 61.

9 Cf. *Spiegel*, No. 46/1966, p. 60.

10 The letter, mostly quoted only in excerpt, is reproduced in full in *IMT*, vol. xli, pp. 426ff., as well as in *Ursachen und Folgen*, vol. xxii, pp. 534ff.

11 See Chapter 8, n. 61.

12 Speer, *Third Reich*, p. 455.

13 Ibid., p. 457.

14 Testimony of Speer's collaborator Dr Mauterer; cf. *Spiegel*, No. 40/1966, p. 60.

15 These and further instances with appropriate sources in Janssen, *Ministerium*, pp. 317ff.

16 BA NL 1318/7.

17 Author's note of a conversation with Speer who described this information as 'a rumour then circulating in Berlin', which he could not confirm. However, he had heard it the same evening after the concert and had immediately remembered the Hitler Youth boys who had, unusually, stood at the exits.

18 Wolters, *Lebensabschnitte*, p. 347.

19 *IMT*, vol. xvi, p. 497, as well as Janssen, *Ministerium*, pp. 309f. On the Berlin bridges cf. Speer, *Third Reich*, pp. 467f.

20 BA R3/1625 (Speer's letter to Karl Hanke of 14.4.1945).

21 Author's note.

22 *IMT*, vol. xli, pp. 438ff. Speer's address was eventually broadcast by Hamburg radio on 3.5.1945 in a slightly abridged and updated form; cf. BA R62/11a.

23 Trevor-Roper in Reif, *Speer*, p. 238.

24 Cf. Stahlberg, *Duty*, p. 396.

25 Cf. Schroeder, *Chef*, p. 202; also Speer, *Third Reich*, pp. 476f., as well as Speer, *Geheimdienstprotokolle*, p. 224. In Berlin Speer learned that Himmler had moved Dr Brandt 'to northern Germany' and that he was therefore too late. He saw Brandt again in Luxemburg and later in Nuremberg. In the Nuremberg doctors' trial Brandt was sentenced to death and executed because of his part in experiments on human beings, as was the SS doctor Gebhardt.

26 Speer, *Third Reich*, pp. 476f.; there also a reference to his short letter to his wife, mentioned below, according to which he had no intention of dying with Hitler. In his first Spandau draft of *Inside the Third Reich* Speer set out his motives for going to Berlin in greater detail than in the version published later. The remark that 'in spite of all purification' he had not changed his view is in his report to Wolters, BA NL 1318/7.

27 This remark, as well as the general account of the scene, goes back to several reports made by Speer to the author in connection with his account in *Inside the Third Reich*, pp. 478ff. The published version is less detailed and contains only a few of Hitler's remarks. Speer revised the text several times and, to the author's knowledge, progressively shortened it – for whatever reasons. He once observed to Wolters that he did not like describing that visit, because the account had earned him 'black marks' in various quarters. (Letter of 6.7.1975, BA NL 1318/40.)

It is worth noting in this context that, in an earlier letter to Wolters at the beginning of the 1950s Speer maintained that, after their exchange about

Dönitz and the question of whether he should remain in Berlin or go to Berchtesgaden, hardly any other words had been exchanged between Hitler and himself; the conversation had 'not mentioned our personal relationship with a single word' (BA NL 1318/7). There could be even less question of any 'confession' of his actions against the 'scorched earth' commands. That is precisely what Speer explained in *Inside the Third Reich* (p. 480) and his *Spandau: The Secret Diaries* (pp. 210f.), as well as in several conversations with Siedler and the present author. However, it cannot be ruled out that Speer invented this in retrospect. This is the view of Sereny, *Speer*, pp. 529ff. She maintains that the idea of a 'confession' had only come to Speer after a dramatized report in the French periodical *Carrefour* in 1952. On the other hand it may be the case that Speer concealed the incident to Wolters in order to represent Hitler once again as the impersonal 'monster' in whom his friend did not want to believe. He also intended, as he wrote to Wolters, 'to de-heroize' the whole affair. Significantly his account of the meeting in his letter to Wolters concludes with the words: 'This final period – I regret (!) to say this to you – is apt to expunge the positive aspects of earlier days.' The question therefore is whether Speer was trying to deceive Wolters or the public. Both are possible. It certainly remains inexplicable why Gitta Sereny credits the account of Speer's last meeting with Hitler in the version of the Spandau draft of Speer's memoirs as having 'the unmistakable ring of truth' (p. 530).

The strongest argument against Gitta Sereny's thesis – that Speer had simply appropriated the inventions of the sensationalist reportage in *Carrefour* – comes from another source. The article appeared in the periodical on 3.9.1952. Yet as early as the summer of 1945 Speer had assured Hugh Trevor-Roper that he had flown into encircled Berlin on 23 April in order, according to the notes of the British historian, 'to see Hitler and explain to him the decision which he had made "in his conflict between his personal loyalty and his duty towards the people".' Surely this suggests a confession, and Trevor-Roper gained the definite impression from his conversation that Speer had spoken out openly to Hitler. These remarks by Speer came more than seven years before the publication of the *Carrefour* report. Certainly, as emerges from Trevor-Roper's notes, Speer had been well aware of the risk of his undertaking and had expected 'to be arrested or even shot'. But his friendship with Hitler proved its worth one last time, because 'Hitler, Speer says, was deeply moved by his candour'. Thus Trevor-Roper in a letter to the author.

It remains to be said that the confession episode, as reported by Speer, fits perfectly into the picture of his character. In the half dream-like and half melancholy mood he was in during those weeks in particular, he could really have believed that the great friendship with Hitler, that was then drawing to a close, needed a grand finale and should be appropriately ended by an act of complete openness. If one may use an extravagantly romantic image, but one which belonged to his way of thinking, it was as if he wished once more to build a 'cathedral of light' with himself as the last hero in the apse.

28 Cf. Milward, *German Economy*, p. 188.

29 This, at any rate, was reported by Gauleiter Kaufmann, referring to Speer's report after his return to Berlin. Trevor-Roper found this reference in his notes of summer 1945 and communicated it to the author. Naturally, there are legitimate doubts about Kaufmann's statement as well as about Speer's report.

30 Speer, *Third Reich*, p. 480.

31 Ibid., p. 481.

32 Ibid., pp. 435f. and 442.

33 Ibid., p. 459.

34 Speer, *Diaries*, pp. 200f.; Hitler's last mention of the 'thrust into nothingness' was at the situation conference of 27.4.1945. Cf. *Spiegel*, No. 3/1966 (first publication).

35 At the beginning of October 1918 Prince Max von Baden was appointed head of government as a kind of transition chancellor to negotiate the armistice offer of Germany's adversaries. On 9 November at 12 noon he handed the chancellorship over to Friedrich Ebert, and two hours later Scheidemann proclaimed the German Republic.

36 BA NL 1318/7, as well as, slightly different, Speer, *Third Reich*, p. 487.

37 Speer, *Third Reich*, p. 488.

38 Fest, *Hitler*, p. 744.

39 Baumbach's testimony, *IMT*, vol. xli, p. 540; also Lüdde-Neurath, *Dönitz*, p. 52.

40 BA R62/2, fol. 18f.

41 BA R3/1624 (Speer's letters to Schwerin von Krosigk of 5.5.1945 and of 15.5.1945); also Lüdde-Neurath, *Dönitz*, p. 84.

42 BA NL 1318/7.

43 Speer, *Slave State*, p. 244, also Janssen, *Ministerium*, p. 284, as well as Speer, *Third Reich*, pp. 495f. The end of SS-Obergruppenführer Kammler has apparently never been cleared up. At the end a corps general (special duties) and general commanding a division, he was, according to some sources, killed in action in the battle for Berlin; according to others he was executed by Soviet troops near Prague in May 1945. Cf. *Lagebesprechungen*, p. 914, as well as Peter-Ferdinand Koch (ed.), *Himmlers graue Eminenz. Oswald Pohl und das Wirtschafts-Verwaltungshauptamt der SS*, Hamburg 1988, p. 218. Speer's note would therefore be a third version.

44 Speer, *Third Reich*, p. 507.

45 John Kenneth Galbraith, *A Contemporary Guide to Economics, Peace and Laughter*, 1971, p. 292.

46 Ibid., p. 284.

47 Ibid., p. 287.

48 BA NL 1318/10.

49 Lüdde-Neurath, *Dönitz*, p. 182; BA NL 1318/7. Lüdde-Neurath, pp. 116f., also mentions that Colonel-General Jodl, who was one of those arrested, described the luggage examination and body search as 'organized looting'.

50 Author's note.

Chapter Ten: Judgement at Nuremberg (pp. 282–307)

1 The American officer who encouraged Speer to make his extensive observations at Kransberg was Captain Hoeffding, who had succeeded in establishing with Speer a relationship of trust based on mutual respect. The record of these conversations was, as previously mentioned, recently published by Ulrich Schlie, see Speer, *Geheimdienstprotokolle*.

2 Cf. *IfZ* ed. 99/19 and *Report on 'Technical Development and Scientific Research in Germany'* of 19.6.1945.

3 Kehrl, *Krisenmanager*, p. 435. In the first version of *Inside the Third Reich*, written in Spandau, Speer denied having expected to be employed in a leading position by the Western Allies for the reconstruction of the country. The idea, he said, had not come from him, but more than one of his interrogators had said to him: 'If only we could appoint you!' Cf. BA NL 1318/7. This, however, conflicts with what Speer told Wolters on 8.2.1945, when he voiced the expectation that after the end of the war the Allies would 'most probably...employ him in the reconstruction'. BA NL 1318/51.

4 Speer, *Diaries*, p. 36. Speer often asked himself this question in retrospect because the answer might reveal something of Hitler's true feelings for him. He told the present author that he did not believe Hitler had 'simply fogotten' it.

5 Galbraith, *Peace and Laughter*, p. 285; also Sereny, *Speer*, pp. 548 and 556.

6 Thus Hannah Arendt in a conversation about Speer with the present author.

7 Speer, *Third Reich*, p. 510.

8 On the comments which Gilbert made the individual accused give him in writing, cf. Gilbert, *Nuremberg*, pp. 4ff.

9 Thus especially Schmidt, *Speer*, pp. 157ff.

10 Gilbert, *Nuremberg*, p. 11.

11 Thus Schmidt, *Speer*, pp. 159f. on the basis of personal information from Dr Flächsner.

12 Speer, *Diaries*, p. 37.

13 Ibid., p. 14.

14 Cf. Bradley F. Smith, *Reaching Judgement at Nuremberg*, New York 1977, p. 221. The suspicion of a secret arrangement between Jackson and Speer was publicly voiced by the author Werner Maser in a book entitled *Nürnberg, Tribunal der Sieger*, Düsseldorf/Vienna 1977, especially p. 386. It should be pointed out that Speer did not approach Jackson directly, but that he gave his written statement to the intelligence officer Major John J. Monigan who, while accepting it, remarked that Speer could address it 'to Mr Justice Jackson'. The text of the letter is published in Reif, *Speer*, pp. 224f.

15 The first of Jackson's two statements mentioned is titled 'Closing Brief Against Albert Speer', BA Koblenz, Bestand Alliierte Prozesse: AllProz 1 Rep. 501, XXXVII YE 12. The final sentence of the Closing Brief, declaring Speer guilty also on the Point of 'Conspiracy against Peace' and holding that Speer could not be judged according to the technical limits of his responsibilities but

NOTES

with an eye to his exalted position as a man enjoying Hitler's trust, stated: 'Justice demands that Speer should receive the maximum penalty for his crimes.' On the second letter, addressed to the US War Department, cf. Reif, *Speer*, p. 230. On the strength of the first document, however, Werner Maser concludes that there was a 'Speer-Jackson arrangement'. A letter by which Jackson wished to cover up his deal with Speer 'would have to look like the one he signed (together with Dodd) on 31 July 1946'; Maser in *Welt am Sonntag* of 14.11.1976.

16 Smith, *Judgement*, p. 222.

17 *IMT*, vol. ii, p. 155.

18 Speer, *Third Reich*, p. 513; Gilbert, *Nuremberg*, p. 39. On the problems of the Nuremberg trials cf. also Joe Heydecker and Johannes Leeb, *Der Nürnberger Prozess*, Cologne 1979; Gerhard E. Gründler and Arnim von Manikowsky, *Das Gericht der Sieger*, Oldenburg/Hamburg 1967; Telford Taylor, *Kriegsverbrechen und Völkerrecht. Die Nürnberger Prozesse*, Zurich 1951; also David Irving, *Nuremberg: The Last Battle*, London 1996.

19 Douglas M. Kelly, *22 Männer um Hitler*, Olten/Bern 1947, p. 86. Göring's remarks about his martyr's glory are found in Gilbert, *Nuremberg*, p. 85 and passim. Cf. also Speer, *Diaries*, p. 61.

20 *IMT*, vol. iii, p. 401.

21 Gilbert, *Nuremberg*, pp. 45f.

22 Speer, *Diaries*, p. 29.

23 Author's note.

24 Schmidt, *Speer*, pp. 161ff.

25 Speer, *Third Reich*, p. 517.

26 Gilbert, *Nuremberg*, pp. 102ff. Göring also accused Speer of failing to inform him that Ohlendorf would be questioned about an alleged plan to assassinate the Führer.

27 Ibid., p. 143. In May 1946 Speer again told Gilbert that he would not deviate from his line: 'I'm not wavering like Frank or von Schirach. I'll go through with it all right, but I hope that I don't choke up and fail to make myself clear. I had to fight with my attorney to make him accept my line, and he has warned me that a confession will justify any kind of a sentence.'

28 Ibid., pp. 152ff.

29 Ibid., p. 329.

30 *IMT*, vol. xvi, p. 430.

31 Ibid., p. 497.

32 Ibid., p. 205.

33 Speer, *Third Reich*, p. 517.

34 *IMT*, vol. xvi, pp. 497f.

35 Gilbert, *Nuremberg*, pp. 398 and 402.

36 The text of the cross-examination is in *IMT*, vol. xvi, pp. 475ff., continued on pp. 557ff.

37 Ibid., p. 546.

SPEER

38 For the record of the examination by M. Y. Raginski see ibid., pp. 563ff.

39 Ibid., vol. xix, p. 216. The plea from which the quotations are taken begins on p. 173.

40 Cf. illustration on page 304.

41 The account of the engineer Hermann Friedrich Gräbe, quoted here in excerpt, is published in *IMT* vol. xxxi, pp. 433ff. Gräbe was an engineer and senior employee of the construction firm Josef Jung in Solingen, working for his firm in the occupied territories. Shocked by the persecution of the Jews, he employed Jewish labourers whenever possible in order to save them from the execution commandos, and helped numerous other Jews to escape. According to witnesses he saved 'approximately 300 persons in all'. Cf. Horst Sassin, *Hermann Friedrich Gräbe. Ein Solinger 'Schindler'*, Solingen 1997. On Sir Hartley Shawcross's plea see *IMT*, vol. xix, pp. 433ff. It was also Sir Hartley Shawcross who in his speech quoted two lengthy observations by Goethe, which caused a great stir at the time. Later it turned out that they came not from Goethe, but from Thomas Mann's *Lotte in Weimar*.

42 Speer's letter to Wolters of 10.8.1946 in BA NL 1318/42.

43 Speer, *Third Reich*, p. 520; also *IMT*, vol. xxii, p. 406.

44 *IMT*, vol. xxii, p. 579. On further considerations leading to a more lenient penalty for Speer, cf. above all the statement of the American court counsellor Adrian Fisher, in Reif, *Speer*, pp. 228f.

45 Smith, *Judgement*, pp. 222f.

46 Thus, for instance, van der Vat, *Speer*, pp. 343ff.; also Schmidt, *Speer*, pp. 159ff.

47 Quoted in Sereny, *Speer*, p. 596.

48 Author's note. Speer later corrected his impression: the hammering at the far end of the building could not have been the erection of the gallows, since these, as he learned after his wife's visit, were erected only a few hours before execution; cf. Speer, *Diaries*, pp. 10f.

Chapter Eleven: School for Survival (pp. 308–338)

1 Speer, *Diaries*, p. 19.

2 Ibid., p. 26.

3 Ibid., p. 38.

4 Ibid., p. 65.

5 Ibid., p. 68. It was only in the autumn of 1958 that the prisoners learned that everything they wrote was collected and fed into the shredder; cf. p. 327.

6 Ibid., pp. 54 and 64.

7 Ibid., p. 70.

8 Ibid., p. 75. In *Spandau: The Secret Diaries* Toni Proost figures throughout under the cover name Anton Vlaer.

9 Wolters, *Lebensabschnitte*, p. 487.

10 Speer, *Diaries*, pp. 98 and 107; on the Hitler biography ibid., p. 75.

11 Sereny, *Speer*, ascribed a crucial significance to Speer's encounter with

Casalis. But no one who ever discussed religious issues with Speer, who was rarely lost for words in debate, could fail to observe his, as it were, spiritual incompetence. Even Speer's remarks quoted by Sereny refute the very points they are meant to prove. Cf. also Speer, *Diaries*, pp. 74, 76, 79 and 337.

12 Speer, *Diaries*, pp. 244 and 260.

13 Ibid., pp. 138, 281, 285 and *passim*.

14 Ibid., pp. 219f.

15 Ibid., p. 176. On Theodor Heuss' 'icy rejection' cf. Wolters' account in *Lebensabschnitte*, p. 496.

16 Ibid., pp. 184 and 186.

17 Ibid, p. 86.

18 Ibid., p. 224.

19 BA NL 1318/7, p. 1.

20 Wolters, *Lebensabschnitte*, p. 470.

21 Speer, *Diaries*, p. 228.

22 Ibid., p. 286.

23 Ibid., p. 287.

24 Ibid., pp. 418f. and 398.

25 Ibid., p. 310. The Soviet intelligence service had tried to recruit Toni Proost. But Proost revealed this to the Western powers and followed their advice to leave Berlin. Cf. pp. 320ff.

26 Ibid., p. 429.

27 Ibid., p. 371f.

28 Ibid., p. 348.

29 Ibid., pp. 429f. and 442.

30 *Frankfurter Allgemeine Zeitung* of 3.10.1966.

31 Author's note. Compare also the dream sequence with which *The Diaries* concludes, p. 451.

32 Wolters, *Lebensabschnitte*, p. 467. Cf. also Kempf's account in Sereny, *Speer*, p. 667. When she discovered that Wolters was seriously annoyed about Speer inviting Mommsen without asking, Frau Kempf had called on Wolters to ensure that the reunion went off peacefully.

33 Altogether DM 154,138.34 was paid into the school fee account. The main contributors were his former colleagues Hettlage, Rohland, Fränk, Schlieker, Bücher, Sohl and Mommsen, as well as the architects Schelkes, Hentrich, Pinnau and Tamms. When, some time before Speer's release, Wolters asked the contributors to top up the rather low balance of the account in order to provide Speer with a kind of starting help, they all readily contributed a further amount; cf. BA NL 1318/31ff.

34 Wolters, *Lebensabschnitte*, p. 499.

35 BA NL 1318/40.

36 Speer, *Diaries*, p. 397.

37 The adviser was the present author. Apart from editorial work, his task consisted chiefly in drawing the author's attention to omissions or to matters

dealt with too skimpily on the one hand and at excessive length on the other. One of the omissions which has raised a certain amount of attention in the literature on the subject was Speer's account of his reaction to the so-called *Reichskristallnacht*, cf. pp. 107–8 above; others concerned his attitude to the war, etc. According to van der Vat, *Speer*, p. 336, Wolters is said to have claimed that the present author had put Speer through his paces like an 'animal trainer'. In fact, Speer was not directly influenced in his judgement on Hitler or the regime either by the present author or by Siedler. This is apparent from Speer's statements before the Nuremberg tribunal and by the first version of *Inside the Third Reich*, which considerably predate their collaboration.

38 van der Vat, *Speer*, p. 275.

39 Robert M. W. Kempner, 'Albert Speer verfälscht das Bild der dunklen Jahre in Deutschland nicht', in Reif, *Speer*, p. 289. There also other reviews, e.g. by Golo Mann. The most emphatic critics of Speer included Geoffrey Barraclough, Rebecca West, Elias Canetti, Hans Mommsen and others.

40 Wolters, *Lebensabschnitte*, p. 479; cf. also Giesler, *Hitler*, p. 318.

41 Wolters, *Lebensabschnitte*, p. 476. Cf. also Schmidt, *Speer, passim*; also van der Vat, *Speer*, esp. p. 367. Author's note from the time when *Inside the Third Reich* appeared, reads: 'Speer exhibits a naive pleasure at the success of the book and asks nearly every day about sales figures. He has obviously found a new, unexpected subject for his old intoxication with figures. But today he also spoke of the increasing talk behind his back, which was continually being drawn to his attention. Sometimes he wondered whether he had not gone too far in his condemnation of the regime, thereby impairing the instructive effect of his book. He said that he was also pained by the loss of some friends and former close colleagues and hoped that time would put some things right again. Certainly these problems worried him more than he had imagined.'

42 Wolters, *Lebensabschnitte*, pp. 479ff.; also Speer's letter of September 1969, BA NL 1318/40.

43 Ibid., p. 481.

44 Interview with Eric Norden, *Playboy* (American edition) of June 1971.

45 Speer's letter of 5.6.1971, BA NL 1318/44, where the subsequent exchange of letters, mentioned below, is also kept, especially Wolters' letter on Speer's seventieth birthday and his reply of 6.7.1975, in which he tried once more to explain their differences of opinion. Sereny, *Speer*, p. 686, calculated in some detail the sums Speer had directed to be remitted to charitable organizations, including several Jewish institutions, although he was always careful to keep his anonymity. He also supported Frau Kempf, who was by then working in a school for handicapped children.

46 Author's note.

47 Speer, *Architektur*, p. 8. While still in Spandau Speer had been invited by two architects to join their practices. However, one of them, Karl Piepenburg, died in January 1966, and the other, Otto Apel, two months later. Cf. Speer, *Diaries*, pp. 414f., 438 and 441.

48 The Benedictine monk who became Speer's friend, Father Athanasius, came up frequently in Speer's private conversations and letters of that time.

49 Author's italics. The letter is published in full in Speer, *Technik und Macht*, pp. 132ff.

50 Cf. also Sereny, *Speer*, pp. 707f. Speer was greatly upset by Sereny's denial of a distinction between 'knowing' and 'sensing', and sought confirmation for his dissenting view in numerous conversations (also with the present author). In fact one has to agree with him, and his observation that one of the tragedies of those years was that the majority of his contemporaries had not gone beyond 'sensing', carefully trying not to advance to 'knowing', is certainly plausible. He was even more worried about the conclusions being drawn from his use of the concept of 'tacit acceptance' (*Billigung*). 'It was thoughtless,' he said on several occasions. 'I have to take so much into account whenever I speak and I am inclined to be rash.' As Hitler's minister he had broken this habit, the same applied in Spandau, 'but after my release I returned to it.' Yet he was well aware, he added entirely without self-pity and rather ironically, that 'they are all after me, just as they were then. It's not all that different.' Subsequently serious ill-feeling arose between Sereny and Speer because of the profile she wrote long before her biography, mainly because of the conclusions she drew from the concept of 'tacit acceptance'. Sereny thinks that if he had made such an admission in Nuremberg, Speer would undoubtedly have been hanged; cf. ibid., p. 708.

51 Quoted from Sereny, *Speer*, p. 692.

52 Cf. the detailed account in van der Vat, *Speer*, pp. 360ff., as well as Chapter 4 above, note 43. The account which Wolters has given of their quarrel still betrays his fairly understandable outrage at Speer's behaviour. Speer, it is stated there, had let him know through his lawyer that the executor's powers he had given him shortly before the passing of sentence at Nuremberg on 10.8.1946 had been annulled on 6.3.1963 'by transfer to his daughter Hilde...and that he, Herr Speer, [had] the sole right of publication and utilization'. 'But what was the last straw for me,' Wolters continued, was Speer's remark that the 'tasks' he had given him in Nuremberg at the time were to be regarded as 'an unpaid act of friendship'. 'Considering my total commitment to Speer and his family throughout the twenty years of his imprisonment in Spandau I could no longer answer this shameless remark directly. I too had to get a lawyer to deal with this as quickly as possible. This led to the abrupt end of our friendship of nearly fifty years.' Cf. BA NL 1318/64, p. 506.

53 Report by Siedler. The conversation between Speer and Siedler was about the manuscript of *The Slave State* which Speer had offered to the publisher some time previously. But Siedler thought that Speer had overreached himself. It was his first attempt at a thematic monograph, unlike his two previous books which had been structured by his personal experiences and chronology. Siedler declined to do the book, which was subsequently published by Deutsche Verlags-Anstalt, Stuttgart. Sereny believes that it was a failure chiefly because it

was written at the time of Speer's late love and that too many distractions had prevented him from giving it the same care as his previous work. She even goes further by asserting that the young woman was bound in the long run, to destroy, though involuntarily, 'that very "best"' in Speer for which, paradoxically, she loved him; cf. *Speer*, pp. 712 and 714.

Conclusion: The Rule and the Exception (pp. 339–356)

1 Speer, *Technik und Macht*, p. 220.

2 Speer, *Diaries*, p. 33.

3 See the photograph on page 345. Speer could not reliably recall the cause of the quarrel, but he thought it must have been one of the many arguments about Bormann and his destructive interference with the landscape of the Obersalzberg, when, as Speer had done only once or twice in all, he had dared to question Bormann's actions as well as his person generally.

4 Speer, *Third Reich*, p. 100.

5 Cf. Andreas Hillgruber (ed.), *Staatsmänner und Diplomaten bei Hitler. Vertrauliche Aufzeichnungen über Unterredungen mit Vertretern des Auslands 1939–1941*, Frankfurt 1967, p. 661.

6 Uwe Bahnsen and James P. O'Donnell, *The Bunker: The History of the Reich Chancellery Group*, Boston 1978.

7 Speer, *Diaries*, p. 14.

8 Author's note.

9 *Spiegel* interview 1966, No. 46, p. 53; also Speer, *Diaries*, p. 406. The question of the availability of artists and technicians has given rise to a vast literature which cannot be referred to here. A particularly striking example is Edward Teller. When, during the development of the hydrogen bomb, he became involved in a permanent dispute with his rivals, he is said to have threatened to leave the project, remarking: 'If I can't work with the peacemakers, then I'll work with the fascists.' This remark was transmitted by Robert Oppenheimer, who, it has to be said, was one of Teller's most bitter opponents. Whatever the facts, the episode is instructive in that it shows the unscrupulousness with which scientists are prepared to achieve their own plans. Cf. Richard Rhodes, *The Making of the Atomic Bomb*, New York 1986, as well as the memoirs of Ken Alibek, one of the leading Soviet scientists in the development of so-called biological weapons (smallpox, bubonic plague, ebola and anthrax), who said: 'I had no moral reservations whatever.' Ken Alibek, *Biohazard: The Chilling True Story of the Largest Covert Biological Weapons Program in the World, Told from the Inside by the Man who Ran It*, New York 1999.

10 Speer's letter to Wolters of 10.8.1946 from Nuremberg. BA NL 1318/42; cf. Chapter 4, note 29.

11 Author's note.

12 Goebbels, *Tagebücher*, vol. 15, p. 120 (28.3.1945).

13 An informative, albeit short, survey of assessments of Speer can be found in Reif, *Speer*, pp. 233ff. On Göring's remark, cf. Gilbert, *Nuremberg*, p. 367.

14 Speer, *Diaries*, p. 134.

15 van der Vat, *Speer*, pp. 276f.

16 Thus Henry T. King, one of the US prosecutors, in a BBC television programme in 1997, which is also the source of Galbraith's remark ('Speer was a very intelligent escapist from the truth'). The reporter mentioned was Eric Norden, who made his observation in the brief profile with which he prefaced his *Playboy* interview of 1971. The theologians in question were Helmuth Gollwitzer, Georges Casalis and Markus Barth, the son of Karl Barth, cf. BA NL 1318/44.

17 Thus Jean Amery, *Offener Brief*, quoted in Reif, *Speer*, p. 455.

18 Speer, *Diaries*, p. 421.

19 Author's note. Cf. also the similar entry, relating to a Cocteau quotation, in Speer, *Diaries*, p. 322.

20 Speer, *Diaries*, p. 426.

21 Thus Father Athanasius, mentioned in Chapter 11, quoted from Sereny, *Speer*, p. 699.

22 Speer gave a similar answer to Hugh Trevor-Roper. When asked whether, as a member of the 'war party', which he was in 1939, he would later also have looked on Hitler merely as an 'architectural patron', whose conquests enabled him to build palaces and triumphal arches all over the European continent, Speer, 'as always', had thought for a moment and then answered 'Yes!' Thus Trevor-Roper (Lord Dacre) in a letter to the author. Speer's answer, Trevor-Roper said, had so shaken him that he revised his whole view of him. On the Leonardo quotation, cf. Speer, *Diaries*, p. 284.

23 It is significant that Speer initially also told Schmidt that he would not oppose the publication of the *Chronik* texts deleted by Wolters, as related in Chapter 11. At that time he evidently still thought he was morally covered by the traditional ideology of the artist. Only later did he change his mind, presumably under the influence of the lawyers he had employed. This is another example of the extent to which, despite all his admissions of guilt, he had misread the character of the regime when faced with unexpected questions. On the 'artistic and technocratic immorality' cf. also Fest, *The Face of the Third Reich*, 1970, pp. 202f.

24 Speer, *Diaries*, pp. 369f.

25 Schmidt, *Speer*, pp. 181f.

26 Speer, *Technik und Macht*, pp. 62f.

27 Cf. Werner Durth, 'Architektur und Stadtplanung im Dritten Reich', in Michael Prinz and Reiner Zitelmann (eds.), *Nationalsozialismus und Modernisierung*, Darmstadt 1991, p. 170.

28 Speer, *Diaries*, p. 406.

29 *Observer*, 9.4.1944. In conversation with the author, Haffner stated that he had received his information 'from Berlin', mainly from the circles of the Technical University. He had forgotten the details. When the article appeared, Speer was at Goyen Castle near Merano; as soon as he learned of the

publication he immediately had several copies made, which he sent to Hitler and to other acquaintances at the Führer's headquarters. Haffner told the author that Speer had 'evidently taken from this article the crucial ideas for his defence strategy in Nuremberg'. The 'thesis of the pure technocrat without ideological ballast' had 'clearly appealed to him' and he had reached out for it 'as for a saving anchor'. It should, however, be pointed out that this line of defence was fairly obvious and that Speer scarcely needed Haffner's article to think of it. When questioned, Haffner conceded this.

30 Trevor-Roper, *Last Days*, pp. 84 and 265. In a profile written in 1949 Trevor-Roper repeated this view, albeit in a slightly weakened form. His concluding sentence then ran: 'Because his philosophy is the philosophy of so many Germans who, unconsciously, made National Socialism possible, *future historians may well* [author's italics] view Albert Speer as the real criminal of Nazi Germany.' Cf. Reif, *Speer*, p. 239.

31 Author's note.

32 Speer, *Diaries*, pp. 405f.

33 Speer, *Third Reich*, p. 49.

BIBLIOGRAPHY

All the books and essays referred to in the Notes are listed, as well as a few additional titles.

Alibek, Ken, *Biohazard: The Chilling True Story of the Largest Covert Biological Weapons Program in the World, Told from the Inside by the Man who Ran It*, New York 1999

Allen, William Sheridan, *The Nazi Seizure of Power: The Experience of a Single German Town, 1922–45*, Harmondsworth 1989

Amery, Jean, 'Kontroverse um Albert Speer', in Adelbert Reif, *Albert Speer*

Anders, Karl, *Im Nürnberger Irrgarten*, Regensburg 1948

Arndt, Karl, 'Architektur und Politik', in Albert Speer, *Architektur*

Bahnsen, Uwe and James P. O'Donnell, *The Bunker: The History of the Reich Chancellery Group*, Boston 1978

Baumbach, Werner, *Zu spät? Aufstieg und Untergang der deutschen Luftwaffe*, Munich 1949

von Below, Nicolaus, *Als Hitlers Adjutant 1937–1945*, Mainz 1980

Blackbourn, David (with Geoff Eley), *Mythen deutscher Geschichtsschreibung. Die gescheiterte bürgerliche Revolution von 1848*, Frankfurt/Berlin/Vienna 1980

Boelcke, Willi A., *Deutschlands Rüstung im Zweiten Weltkrieg. Hitlers Konferenzen mit Albert Speer 1942–1945*, Frankfurt 1969

Bracher, Karl Dietrich, *Die deutsche Diktatur. Entstehung, Struktur, Folgen des Nationalsozialismus*, Cologne/Berlin 1969

Brandt, Karl, 'Frauen um Hitler', in Albert Speer, *Alles, was ich weiss. Aus unbekannten Geheimdienstprotokollen vom Sommer 1945*, Munich 1999

Breker, Arno, *Im Strahlungsfeld der Ereignisse*, Preussisch Oldendorf 1972

Brenner, Hildegard, *Die Kunstpolitik des Nationalsozialismus*, Reinbek 1963

Browning, Christopher, 'Zur Genesis der, Endlösung', in *VJHfZ* 29/1981

Coulondre, Robert, *Von Moskau nach Berlin, 1936–1939*, Bonn 1950

Dietrich, Otto, *Zwölf Jahre mit Hitler*, Munich 1955

Domarus, Max, *Hitler's Speeches and Proclamations: The Chronicle of a Dictatorship*, London 1990

Dülffer, Jost, 'Die Machtergreifung und die Rolle der alten Eliten im Dritten Reich', in Wolfgang Michalka, *Die nationalsozialistische Machtergreifung*,

Paderborn/Munich 1984

Dülffer, Jost (with J. Henke and J. Thies), *Hitlers Städte. Baupolitik im Dritten Reich*, Cologne/Vienna 1978

Durth, Werner (with Niels Gutschow), *Träume in Trümmern. Planungen zum Wiederaufbau zerstörter Städte im Westen Deutschlands 1940–1950*, Braunschweig/Wiesbaden 1988.

Eley, Geoff and D. Blackbourn, *The Peculiarities of German History: Bourgeois Society and Politics in Nineteenth-Century Germany*, New York 1984

Fest, Joachim, *The Face of the Third Reich*, London 1970

Fest, Joachim, *Hitler, a Biography*, London 1987

Fest, Joachim, 'Die andere Utopie. Eine Studie über Heinrich Himmler', in *Fremdheit und Nähe. Von der Gegenwart des Gewesenen*, Stuttgart 1996

Fiedermann, Angela, *Das Konzentrationslager Mittelbau Dora: ein historischer Abriss*, Berlin/Bonn 1993

Fleming, Gerald, *Hitler and the Final Solution*, London 1985

François-Poncet, André, *The Fateful Years. Memoirs of a French Ambassador in Berlin 1931–1938*, London 1949

Frank, Hans, *Im Angesicht des Galgens. Deutung Hitlers und seiner Zeit auf Grund eigener Erlebnisse und Erkenntnisse*, 2nd edn, Neuhaus 1955

Friedländer, Saul, *Nazi Germany and the Jews. Vol. 1; The Years of Persecution*, London 1939

Galbraith, John Kenneth, *A Contemporary Guide to Economics, Peace and Laughter*, Boston 1971

Gall, Lothar, *Bürgertum in Deutschland*, Berlin 1989

Genoud, François (ed.), *Libres propos sur la Guerre et la Paix*, Paris 1952

Georg, Enno, *Die wirtschaftlichen Unternehmungen der SS*, Stuttgart 1963

Giesler, Hermann, *Ein anderer Hitler. Bericht seines Architekten Hermann Giesler. Erlebnisse, Gespräche, Reflexionen*, 5th edn, Leoni 1982

Gilbert, Gustav M., *Nuremberg Diary*, New York 1995

Goebbels, Joseph, *Die Tagebücher. Sämtliche Fragmente*, ed. Elke Fröhlich, 4 vols, Munich 1987

Goebbels, Joseph, *Die Tagebücher*, ed. Elke Fröhlich, 15 vols, Munich, various years

Goebbels, Joseph, *Reden 1932–1945*, ed. Helmut Heiber, 2 vols, Düsseldorf 1971/72

Goldhagen, Erich, 'Albert Speer, Himmler and the Secrecy of the Final Solution', in *Midstream* 1971

Golücke, Friedhelm, *Schweinfurt und der strategische Luftkrieg*, Paderborn 1980

Gründler, Gerhard E. (with Arnim von Manikowski), *Das Gericht der Sieger*, Oldenburg/Hamburg 1967

Gutschow Niels (with W. Durth), *Träume in Trümmern. Planungen zum Wiederaufbau zerstörter Städte im Westen Deutschlands 1940–1950*, Braunschweig/Wiesbaden 1988

Haffner, Sebastian, *The Meaning of Hitler*, London 1979

Hamsher, William, *Albert Speer. Victim of Nuremberg?*, London 1970

Heiden, Konrad, *Die Geburt des Dritten Reiches. Die Geschichte des Nationalsozialismus bis Herbst 1933*, 2nd edn, Zurich 1934

Henke, Josef (with J. Dülffer and J. Thies), *Hitlers Städte. Baupolitik im Dritten Reich*, Cologne/Vienna 1978

Henschel, Hildegard, 'Gemeindearbeit und Evakuierung von Berlin', in *Zeitschrift für die Geschichte der Juden*, 1/2, 1972

Herbert, Ulrich, *Fremdarbeiter. Politik und Praxis des 'Ausländereinsatzes' in der Kriegswirtschaft des Dritten Reiches*, Berlin/Bonn 1985

Herbert, Ulrich, *Best. Biographische Studien über Radikalismus, Weltanschauung und Vernunft 1903–1989*, 3rd edn, Bonn 1996

Herbst, Ludolf, *Der totale Krieg und die Ordnung der Wirtschaft. Die Kriegswirtschaft im Spannungsfeld von Politik, Ideologie und Propaganda 1939–1945*, Stuttgart 1982

Heydecker, Joe, J. (with J. Leeb), *Der Nürnberger Prozess. Bilanz der Tausend Jahre*, Cologne/Berlin 1958

Hildebrand, Klaus, *Das Dritte Reich*, 5th edn, Munich 1995

Hillgruber, Andreas (ed.), *Staatsmänner und Diplomaten bei Hitler. Vertrauliche Aufzeichnungen über Unterredungen mit Vertretern des Auslands*, 2 vols, Frankfurt 1967/70

Hitler, Adolf, *Mein Kampf*, London 1940

Hitler, Adolf, *Hitler's Table Talk*, Oxford 1988

Hitler, Adolf, *Monologe im Führerhauptquartier 1941–1944. Die Aufzeichnungen Heinrich Heims*, ed. Werner Jochmann, Hamburg 1980

Hitler, Adolf, *Lagebesprechungen. Die Protokollfragmente seiner militärischen Konferenzen 1942–1945*, ed. Helmut Heiber, Stuttgart 1962

Hitler, Adolf, *Reden, Schriften, Anordnungen. Februar 1925 bis Januar 1933*, ed. and commentary by Klaus A. Lankheit, Munich/New Providence/London/Paris, various years.

Hoffmann, Peter, *Widerstand, Staatsstreich, Attentat. Der Kampf der Opposition gegen Hitler*, 3rd edn, Munich 1979

Hüttenberger, Peter, *Die Gauleiter. Studie zum Wandel des Machtgefüges in der NSDAP*, Stuttgart 1969

IMT, *The trial of German Major War Criminals. Proceedings of the International Military Tribunal sitting at Nuremberg*, 23 pts., London 1946–51

Irving, David, *Hitler's War, 1939–1942*, London 1983

Irving, David, *The Rise and Fall of the Luftwaffe: The Life of Luftwaffe Marshal Erhard Milch*, London 1976

Irving, David, *Nuremberg, The Last Battle*, London 1996

Janssen, Gregor, *Das Ministerium Speer. Deutschlands Rüstung im Krieg*, Berlin/Frankfurt/Vienna 1968

Kästner, Erich, *Notabene 45. Ein Tagebuch*, Berlin 1961

Kehrl, Hans, *Krisenmanager im Dritten Reich, 6 Jahre Frieden – 6 Jahre Krieg. Erinnerungen*, Düsseldorf 1973

Kelley, Douglas M., *22 Männer um Hitler*, Olten/Bern 1947

Kempner, Robert M. W., 'Albert Speer verfälscht das Bild der dunklen Jahre in Deutschland nicht', in A. Reif, *Albert Speer*

Koch, Peter-Ferdinand (ed.), *Himmlers graue Eminenz. Oswald Pohl und das Wirtschafts-Verwaltungshauptamt der SS*, Hamburg 1988

Kuhlbrodt, Peter, *Mittelbau-Dora bei Nordhausen 1943–1945. Ein Überblick*, Nordhausen 1991

Kurowski, Franz, *Der Luftkrieg über Deutschland*, Düsseldorf/Vienna 1977

Larsson, Lars Oloff, *Albert Speer. Le plan de Berlin 1937–1943*, Brussels 1983

Leeb, Johannes (with Joe J. Heydecker), *Der Nürnberger Prozess. Bilanz der Tausend Jahre*, Cologne/Berlin 1958

Ludwig, Karl-Heinz, 'Die wohlreflektierten "Erinnerungen" des Albert Speer – Einige kritische Bemerkungen zur Funktion des Architekten, des Ingenieurs und der Technik im Dritten Reich', in A. Reif, *Albert Speer*

Lüdde-Neurath, Walter, *Regierung Dönitz. Die letzten Tage des Dritten Reiches*, 3rd edn, Göttingen 1964

Lüthy, Herbert, 'Der Führer persönlich', in *Nach dem Untergang des Abendlandes. Zeitkritische Essays*, Cologne/Berlin 1964

Mächler, Martin, *Denkschrift über Gross-Berlin*, Berlin 1920

von Manikowski, Arnim (with G. E. Gründler), *Das Gericht der Sieger*, Oldenburg/ Hamburg 1967

Mann, Golo, 'Des Teufels Architekt', in A. Reif, *Albert Speer*

Mann, Golo, *Zwölf Versuche*, Frankfurt 1973

Meinecke, Friedrich, *Die deutsche Katastrophe. Betrachtungen und Erinnerungen*, Wiesbaden 1946

Michaelis, Herbert and E. Schraepler (eds), *Ursachen und Folgen. Vom deutschen Zusammenbruch 1918 und 1945 bis zur staatlichen Neuordnung Deutschlands in der Gegenwart*, 26 vols, Berlin, various years

Michalka, Wolfgang (ed.), *Das Dritte Reich. Dokumente zur Innen- und Aussen-politik*, 2 vols, Munich 1985

Milch, Erhard, *Notebook*, Institut für Zeitgeschichte

Milward, Alan S., *The German Economy at War*, London 1965

Mitscherlich, Alexander, 'Hitler blieb ihm ein Rätsel – Die Selbstblendung Albert Speers', in A. Reif, *Albert Speer*

Möller, Horst, 'Bürgertum und bürgerlich-liberale Bewegung nach 1918', in *Historische Zeitschrift*, special edition 17, Munich 1997

Moltmann, Günter, 'Goebbels' Rede zum totalen Krieg', in *VJHfZ* 1/1961

Mosse, Martha, 'Eyewitness Account', in *Archives of the Wiener Library London*, Reading 1998

Neave, Airey, *Nuremberg*, London 1978

Nolte, Ernst, *Der Faschismus in seiner Epoche. Die Action Française. Der italienische Faschismus. Der Nationalsozialismus*, Munich 1963

Nolte, Ernst, *Theorien über den Faschismus*, Cologne/Berlin 1967 von Oven, Wilfried, *Verrat und Widerstand im Dritten Reich*, Coburg 1978

Pehnt, Wolfgang, *Das Ende der Zuversicht. Architektur in diesem Jahrhundert*, Berlin 1983

Petsch, Joachim, *Baukunst und Stadtplanung im Dritten Reich*, Munich/Vienna 1976

Prinz, Michael and R. Zitelmann (eds), *Nationalsozialismus und Modernisierung*, Darmstadt 1991

Rave, Paul Ortwin, *Schinkel. Lebenswerk*, Berlin 1948

Reichel, Peter, *Der schöne Schein des Dritten Reiches. Faszination und Gewalt des Faschismus*, Munich/Vienna 1991

Reif, Adelbert, *Albert Speer. Kontroversen um ein deutsches Phänomen*, Munich 1978

Reuth, Ralf Georg, *Goebbels*, Munich 1990

Rhodes, Richard, *The Making of the Atomic Bomb*, New York 1988

Richarz, Monika (ed.), *Bürger auf Widerruf. Lebenszeugnisse deutscher Juden 1780–1945*, Munich 1989

Rohland, Walter, *Bewegte Zeiten. Erinnerungen eines Eisenhüttenmannes*, Stuttgart 1978

Scheffler, Wolfgang, *Judenverfolgung im Dritten Reich 1933–1945*, Berlin 1960

Schieder, Theodor, *Hermann Rauschnings 'Gespräche mit Hitler' als Geschichtsquelle*, Opladen 1972

von Schirach, Baldur, *Ich glaubte an Hitler*, Hamburg 1967

Schmidt, Matthias, *Albert Speer: The End of a Myth*, London 1985

Schoenbaum, David, *Die braune Revolution. Eine Sozialgeschichte des Dritten Reiches*, Cologne/Berlin 1968

Schraepler, Ernst and H. Michaelis (eds), *Ursachen und Folgen. Vom deutschen Zusammenbruch 1918 und 1945 bis zur staatlichen Neuordnung Deutschlands in der Gegenwart*, 26 vols, Berlin, various years

Schramm, Percy Ernst (ed.), *Das Kriegstagebuch des Oberkommandos der Wehrmacht*, 7 vols, Frankfurt, 1961ff.

Schroeder, Christa, *Er war mein Chef. Aus dem Nachlass der Sekretärin von Adolf Hitler*, 2nd edn, Munich 1985

Schwerin von Krosigk, Lutz Graf, *Es geschah in Deutschland. Menschenbilder unseres Jahrhunderts*, Tübingen/Stuttgart 1951

Sereny, Gitta, *Albert Speer: His Battle with Truth*, London 1996

Smith, Bradley F., *Reaching Judgement at Nuremberg*, London 1977

Smith, Bradley F. (ed.), *Heinrich Himmler. Geheimreden 1933 bis 1945 und andere Ansprachen*, Frankfurt/Berlin/Vienna 1974

Speer, Albert, *Inside the Third Reich*, London 1978

Speer, Albert, *Spandau: The Secret Diaries*, London 1977

Speer, Albert, *The Slave State: Heinrich Himmler's Masterplan for SS Supremacy*, London 1987

Speer, Albert, *Technik und Macht*, ed. Adelbert Reif, Esslingen 1979

Speer, Albert, *Architektur. Arbeiten 1933–1942*, Frankfurt/Berlin/Vienna 1978

Speer, Albert, *Alles, was ich weiss. Aus unbekannten Geheimdienstprotokollen vom Sommer 1945*, ed. Ulrich Schlie, Munich 1999

Speer, Albert, 'Die Bauten des Führers' in *Adolf Hitler. Bilder aus dem Leben des Führers*, pub. by Cigaretten/Bilderdienst, Hamburg/Bahrenfeld 1936

Spiegelbild einer Verschwörung. Die Kaltenbrunner-Berichte an Bormann und Hitler über das Attentat vom 20. Juli 1944. Geheime Dokumente aus dem ehemaligen Reichssicherheitshauptamt, pub. by Archiv Peter, Stuttgart 1961

Stahlberg, Alexander, *Bounden Duty: The Memoirs of a German Officer 1932–1945*

Taylor, Telford, *The Anatomy of the Nuremberg Trials: A Personal Memoir*, Boston 1992

Taylor, Telford, *The Anatomy of the Nuremberg Trials. A Personal Memoir*, London 1993

Teut, Anna, *Architektur im Dritten Reich 1939–1945*, Frankfurt/Vienna 1967

Thies, Jochen (with J. Dülffer and J. Henke), *Hitlers Städte. Baupolitik im Dritten Reich*, Cologne/Vienna 1978

Trevor-Roper, Hugh (Lord Dacre), *The Last Days of Hitler*, London 1995

Trevor-Roper, Hugh (Lord Dacre), 'Poträt des wirklichen Nazi-Verbrechers', in A. Reif, *Albert Speer*

van der Vat, Dan, *The Good Nazi: The Life and Lies of Albert Speer*, London 1997

Vilar, Esther, *Speer*, Berlin 1998

Wangerin, Gerda and Gerhard Weiss, *Heinrich Tessenow. Ein Baumeister. 1876–1950*, Essen 1976

Weisenborn, Günther, *Memorial*, Munich 1948

Wolters, Rudolf, 'Lebensabschnitte'. 'Die Erinnerungen des langjährigen Freundes von Albert Speer sind im ganzen vorerst nicht zugänglich. Lediglich die Abschnitte über die gegenseitige Entfremdung und den späten Bruch mit Speer liegen als Privatdruck vor, vgl. BA Koblenz, Br I 2178. Der Privatdruck enthält die Seiten 467–517.'

Zitelmann, Rainer and M. Prinz (eds), *Nationalsozialismus und Modernisierung*, Darmstadt 1991

INDEX

Soldatenhalle (Berlin), 71, 82, 83, 93

Sonthofen (National Socialist elite school), 84

Sorpe dam, 165

Soviet Union, 78, 79, 124–6, 128–9, 138, 149, 150, 151, 162, 167, 172, 290

Spaatz, General Carl, 213

Spandau prison, 36, 309–21, 346

Speer, Albert, *20, 23, 96, 100, 114, 135, 139, 145, 158, 163, 169, 173, 182, 197, 208, 280, 287, 335, 342, 345;* contradictions of, 1, 7–8, 9–10, 341–2, 353–6; description of, 1, 9; memoirs, 1, 120, 185, 188, 191, 297, 305, 315–16, 325–30, 331, 344, 348; position of, 2; studies on, 2–3; detachment from politics, 3–4, 5–6, 19–20, 25, 26, 27, 89, 107–9; public/private world, 3–4; response to injustices, 4; as armaments minister, 6, 134–59, 174–7, 179–80, 212–16, 349; arrogance of, 6, 174; lack of power base, 6, 172; relationship with Hitler, 6–7, 39–40, 42–5, 47–8, 51–2, 160–1, 210, 339–41; comment on the 'world–view', 7; criticisms and accusations against, 8–9, 347, 350, 354–5; self-examination, 8; birth and childhood, 11–12; relationship with family, 11, 14–15; education, 13; health of, 14, 82, 196, 198, 199, 200–4, 317, 331; interest in lower class/impecunious people, 15–16; marriage, 15–16, 25; at university, 19, 21, 23, 24; effect of Versailles treaty on, 19; love of nature, 21, 23, 25, 30, 196; rejection of reality, 21; similarities with youth movement, 21–4; character of, 23–4, 25, 37, 284–5, 342–8, 353–4; friendship with Wolters, 23–4, 323–5, 330; made assistant to Tessenow, 24–5, 94; first encounter with Hitler, 27–9; joins National Socialist Party, 29, 31; returns to Heidelberg, 29; important early commissions, 30–4; comes to attention of Hitler, 33–5; self-deception, 35, 43–4, 231, 342–3, 355–6; dislike of middle-class world, 36–7, 108; in Spandau, 36, 309–21; appointed head of Building Department, 45; special position in inner circle, 45, 94–101; takes over 'Beauty of Work' office, 45–6; as chief architect, 47, 55–6; as chief designer of Party Rallies, 49–51; use of theatrical light devices, 50–1, 53, 352; plans for Nuremberg, 56–61; as freelance architect, 61–2; appointed Inspector–General of Building for the Reich capital, 64–5; ambitions of, 66–7, 85, 86, 88–9, 133–4, 136–8, 157, 171–2, 283; plans for Berlin, 66, 69, 71–9, 81, 90–3; makes tactical political allies, 67; grandiloquent schemes, 72–3, 76, 77–8, 362n; European travels, 82–3; quarrel with Geisler, 84–8; weakness of architectural concepts, 90–1, 92; admiration for, 101; plans for Reich Chancellery, 101–4, 106; countermands Hitler's orders, 111–12, 247, 253–4, 259–60, 261–2, 263–4, 268, 298, 302, 343; supports war, 111; sets up transport units, 115; and evacuation of Jews, 116–24,

PHOENIX
PRESS

GENERAL EDITORS:
SIMON SCHAMA AND ANTONIA FRASER

Phoenix Press publishes and re-publishes hundreds of the very best new and out of print books about the past. For a free colour catalogue listing more than 500 titles please

telephone: +44 (0)1903 828 503
fax: +44 (0)1903 828 802
e-mail: mailorder@lbsltd.co.uk
or visit our website at www.phoenixpress.co.uk

The following books might be of particular interest to you:

Spandau
The Secret Diaries
ALBERT SPEER

The only defendant to plead guilty at Nuremberg, Hitler's former architect and master of the German war machine Albert Speer wrote these diaries during his 20-year imprisonment. 'A deeply moving human document…so fascinatingly written that I could not put it down before I finished it' Erich Fromm.

Paperback
UK: £14.99   480pp + 32pp b/w   1 84212 051 4

War Diaries 1939–1945
FIELD MARSHAL LORD ALANBROOKE
EDITED BY ALEX DANCHEV & DANIEL TODMAN

Field Marshal Lord Alanbrooke's own day-by-day account of the Second World War is one of the most important documents of the period. 'It is not merely the record of events that makes it so distinguished, but the study in leadership and greatness, relevant for all time, that it comprises' Simon Heffer, *Country Life* 'Superb' Michael Howard, *The Spectator* 'Marvellous' *Irish Times*.

Paperback
UK: £9.99   816pp + 8pp b/w   1 84212 526 5

Hitler and the Holocaust
ROBERT WISTRICH

By exploring the origins of anti-Semitism in Europe, and especially in Germany, Wistrich explains how millions of Jews came to be systematically killed by the Third Reich. He then considers the legacy of Nazi crimes since 1945: the Nuremberg trials, the impact of the Holocaust and the rise of neo-Nazism and Holocaust-denial.

Paperback
UK: £6.99   336pp   1 84212 486 2

The Hitler of History
Hitler's Biographers on Trial
JOHN LUKACS

In this brilliant and original book the historian John Lukacs delves to the core of Adolf Hitler's life and mind, by examining him through the lenses of his surprisingly diverse biographers, whom he puts on trial. 'No contemporary historian should be without a copy' M.R.D. Foot, *TLS*. 'nobly produced and nobly written...the book is full of gems of serious historical thought' *TLS*

Paperback
UK: £12.99   320pp   1 84212 524 9

The Duel
Hitler vs. Churchill 10 May–31 July 1940
JOHN LUKACS

The 80-day struggle between Hitler, convinced of victory and Churchill, on the verge of defeat. 'An unforgettable portrait of the mortal duel between two men and the titanic personalities involved' Book of the Month Editorial Review Board.

Paperback
UK: £12.99   288pp   1 84212 161 8

The Klemperer Diaries
Volumes I & II: 1933–1945
VICTOR KLEMPERER

A single paperback edition of the two volumes *I Shall Bear Witness* and *To the Bitter End* of Victor Klemperer's diaries of his experiences as a Jew in Nazi Germany. 'Klemperer's diary deserves to rank alongside that of Anne Frank' *Sunday Times*. 'Few English readers will fail to be moved as I was – ultimately to the point of tears' Niall Ferguson *Sunday Telegraph*.

Paperback
UK: £16.99   1070pp   1 84212 022 0

Hitler's Table Talk 1941–1944
INTRODUCED AND WITH A NEW PREFACE BY HUGH TREVOR-ROPER

On Martin Bormann's instructions the secret conversations at Hitler's headquarters were all recorded. This extraordinary document is the result. A compelling and frequently repellent read.

Paperback
UK: £16.99   800pp   1 84212 028 X

The Meaning of Hitler
SEBASTIAN HAFFNER

The celebrated psychological study of the enigma of Adolf Hitler and his impact on the 20th century.

Paperback
UK: £9.99   176pp   1 84212 194 4

The Brutal Friendship
Mussolini, Hitler and the Fall of Italian Fascism
F.W. DEAKIN

A narrative history that reads like a psychological thriller describing the 'brutal friendship' of two notorious despots and its fatal consequences.

Paperback
UK: £16.99   912pp   1 84212 049 2

Second World War
MARTIN GILBERT

A new edition of the first total, global history of the Second World War, by the foremost historian of the twentieth century. 'Gilbert's epic is a remarkable achievement' *Daily Express*.

Paperback
UK: £18.99   864pp + 130 b/w photos & 102 maps   1 84212 262 2

The Secret Front
The Inside Story of Nazi Political Espionage
WILHELM HOETTL

This was the first full account of Hitler's political spy network to be published after the war. Written by one of Himmler's key men in Italy and the Balkans during the war, it is a unique document showing the mechanics of tyranny at work.

Paperback
UK: £10.99   336pp + 4pp b/w   1 84212 218 5

Gocring
RICHARD OVERY

Richard Overy's major biography of one of the most powerful, fascinating and complex members of Hitler's inner circle from his hey-days as Hitler's deputy to his trial and suicide.

Paperback
UK: £12.99   320pp + 16pp b/w   1 84212 048 4

Ciano's Diary 1937–1943
COUNT GALEAZZO CIANO

Newly edited and translated and made available in a single volume, this is one of the most important and influential diaries to come out of World War II. Count Galeazzo Ciano was both Mussolini's Foreign Minister and his son in law.

His unexpurgated and revealing diaries cover events from 1937 until 1943 and finish days before Ciano's execution by firing squad on his father in law's orders. 'Of all the documents to come out of the 1939–45 War... Ciano's Diary is the most interesting and will probably prove the most useful to historians' Malcolm Muggeridge.

Paperback
UK: £16.99   656pp   1 84212 476 5

Commandant of Auschwitz

RUDOLF HOESS

INTRODUCTION BY PRIMO LEVI

The notorious Commandant of Auschwitz, Rudolf Hoess, was ordered to write this autobiography in the weeks between his trial and his execution. The royalties go to Auschwitz survivors. 'The book is filled with evil ... reading it is an agony ... and yet it is one of the most instructive books ever published' Primo Levi.

Paperback
UK: £9.99   256pp + 8pp b/w   1 84212 024 7

Mussolini Memoirs 1942–1943

BENITO MUSSOLINI

EDITED AND INTRODUCED BY RAYMOND KLIBANSKY

Mussolini's own story written while incarcerated by his own troops from July–September 1943. Includes the Cardinal of Milan's final conversation with Il Duce three days before his execution by Italian partisans.

Paperback
UK: £12.99   352pp   1 84212 025 5

Hitler's Generals

EDITED BY CORRELLI BARNETT

Outstanding historians write about the characters and careers of twenty-six Nazi generals. 'That this book ... both in its parts and as a whole, is successful ... says a great deal about the excellence of the essayists; it says even more about the discretion and skill of Corelli Barnett' *Economist*.

Paperback
UK: £14.99   512pp + 21pp b/w & maps   1 84212 517 6

Hitler's Diplomat

Joachim von Ribbentrop

JOHN WEITZ

INTRODUCTION BY TOM WOLFE

A social and political biography of Hitler's Ambassador to Great Britain and, later, Foreign Minister.

Paperback
UK: £12.99   352pp + 16pp b/w   0 75380 003 9